Finance and Financial Markets

Finance and Financial Markets

Edited by
Leo Morris

MURPHY & MOORE
www.murphy-moorepublishing.com

Published by Murphy & Moore Publishing,
1 Rockefeller Plaza,
New York City, NY 10020, USA

ISBN: 978-1-63987-224-4

Cataloging-in-Publication Data

Finance and financial markets / edited by Leo Morris.
p. cm.
Includes bibliographical references and index.
ISBN 978-1-63987-224-4
1. Finance. 2. Capital market. 3. Money market. 4. Financial institutions. I. Morris, Leo.
HG173 .F56 2022
332--dc23

For information on all Murphy & Moore Publications
visit our website at www.murphy-moorepublishing.com

MURPHY & MOORE

Contents

Preface

This book has been an outcome of determined endeavour from a group of educationists in the field. The primary objective was to involve a broad spectrum of professionals from diverse cultural background involved in the field for developing new researches. The book not only targets students but also scholars pursuing higher research for further enhancement of the theoretical and practical applications of the subject.

Finance can be understood as the management of money by undertaking activities such as investing, borrowing, lending, budgeting and saving. The three broad branches of business finance are corporate finance, investments, and financial markets and institutions. Financial markets allow the flow of money in the form of investments and financial instruments. Capital, commodity, money, derivative and foreign exchange markets are some of the important types of financial markets. They help in enhancing income, capital formation, price determination, and promoting savings and investment, leading to balanced economic growth. These markets are facilitated by financial services and investment management which are termed as money management for individuals and asset management for institutions. This book provides significant information of this discipline to help develop a good understanding of financial markets and related fields. It will also provide interesting topics for research which interested readers can take up. This book will help the readers in keeping pace with the rapid changes in this field.

It was an honour to edit such a profound book and also a challenging task to compile and examine all the relevant data for accuracy and originality. I wish to acknowledge the efforts of the contributors for submitting such brilliant and diverse chapters in the field and for endlessly working for the completion of the book. Last, but not the least; I thank my family for being a constant source of support in all my research endeavours.

Editor

1

Using Grey Incidence Analysis Approach in Portfolio Selection

Tihana Škrinjarić * **and Boško Šego**

Faculty of Economics and Business, University of Zagreb, 10000 Zagreb, Croatia; bsego@efzg.hr

* Correspondence: tskrinjar@net.efzg.hr

Abstract: Due to the development of financial markets, products, financial and mathematical models, portfolio selection today represents a comprehensive set of activities. Investors take into consideration many different factors, such as the market factors, return distribution characteristics and financial statements information. This research applies a Grey Relational Analysis (GRA) approach to evaluate the performance on a sample of stocks by taking those different factors into consideration. The results based upon a sample of 55 stocks for the trading year 2017 on the Croatian capital market show that using GRA approach in portfolio selection provides useful guidance for investors when making investment decisions, and better portfolio results in terms of risk and return are reachable compared to an equally weighted portfolio benchmark.

Keywords: portfolio selection; Grey Relational Analysis; stock market; financial ratios; market data; performance measurement

JEL Classification: C61; G11

1. Introduction

Portfolio selection today represents a very difficult task in portfolio management due to many investment possibilities on the financial markets, many factors influencing the investors' decisions and constant dynamic changes on the markets as well. Investors have to make daily decisions based upon different information. Thus, a quality decision making process should be supported with quantitative modelling which can ease this process and achieve investment goals. Utility function theory has been developed regarding an investor's utility being based upon first m moments of return distributions (see Jurczenko and Maillet 2005) explaining that investors make their decisions based upon those distribution moments. Moreover, many studies have shown that financial ratios data are useful in portfolio management as well (Chen and Thomas 1981; Singh and Schmidgall 2002). In that way, many different methodologies in mathematics and econometrics have been developed in order to provide some of the answers to investor's questions regarding stock performance and portfolio selection. Some of the most popular approaches to deal with large amounts of information include Data Envelopment Analysis (see Chen 2008 or Dia 2007), Multicriteria Decision Analysis (Steuer et al. 2008 or Edirisinghe and Zhang 2007) and Multivariate analysis (clustering, principal components analysis and similar approaches, see Korzeniewski 2018). However, a relatively unknown and new approach is the Grey Relational Analysis (GRA) approach. This methodology, i.e., the wider term Grey Systems, was firstly developed in the field of modelling uncertain systems and it was applied over different areas such as decision making processes, ecological, hydrological, geological and similar systems (see Liu et al. 2016 for the history development and different areas of applications). The novelty and contribution of this research is applying the GRA approach in the decision making process in portfolio selection, since this approach is found to be extremely rare in financial applications, especially when making decisions on the structure of the stock portfolio. The results from GRA approach ranking of stocks is used for the simulation of portfolio investing, an approach which is also rarely found in applications. Moreover, the contribution of this study compared to existing ones is in providing the rationale of why we include chosen variables, i.e., factors in the modelling procedure, based upon financial theory and empirical findings over decades. This is in the majority cases ignored in the empirical applications.

Thus, the main goal of this study is to empirically evaluate market and financial statement data on a sample of stocks by using the GRA approach in order to obtain information on whether this approach could be applicable to portfolio selection. This will be achieved by comparing the portfolios which are a result from taking into consideration the best stocks from the GRA ranking system in sample and by comparing the out of sample performances of simulated portfolios in the empirical analysis. The GRA approach of evaluating performance has several advantages compared to other approaches such as Data Envelopment Analysis, Analytic Hierarchy Process and other approaches: it is not sensitive to data transformations, easier estimations are available, and straightforward interpretations can be made, etc. (Wei 2011). Thus, two main research questions are as follows. First, can the Grey Relational Analysis provide a useful guidance for investors when making investment decisions? This question asks if results given with one number from the GRA provides useful information on how to form stock portfolios. The second question is whether portfolios formed based upon the GRA approach can provide better results in terms of risk and return compared to a simple benchmark (equally weighted portfolio).

The rest of the paper is structured as follows. The second section deals with previous related research. The third section describes the methodology used in the study. Results and discussion are given in the fourth, fifth and sixth sections. The final section concludes the paper.

2. Previous Research

By analyzing previous existing research which applies the GRA approach in finance, it can be seen that there is a great scarcity of research in this area. The majority of the applications were made in different fields (see Liu and Lin 2010).

Huang et al. (2008) combined weight clustering model with the *K*-means Clustering approach and the Grey Systems Theory with the Rough Set theory in order to create automated stock market forecasting with portfolio selection on the Taiwanese market for the period 1Q2003—4Q2016. Authors thus apply a dynamic analysis in which in every quarter they collect financial data on selected stocks and cluster them by using *K*-means clustering. Finally, the GRA approach is used to rank the stocks and include the portfolios. The results indicate that such formed portfolios obtain significant returns over the observed period. It can be seen in this research that authors observe those investors who only aim at the greatest returns possible. Several financial ratios were chosen in the research and rationale is based upon investment principles advocated by W. Buffett, as authors' state. Huang and Jane (2008) extended this research by combining Fuzzy C-means theories with Variable Precision Rough Set theory when comparing stocks with the Average Autoregressive Exogenous prediction model of the future stock market movements. The GRA analysis was also used to specify the weighting of the selected stocks, with the same approach as in the previous paper, to achieve maximum rate of return. Again, a dynamic analysis was performed for the period 2004 until 2006 based upon quarterly data and financial ratios. Here, the authors do not state why they used the financial data which was included in the empirical research. However, the authors conclude based upon the results that such combination of the aforementioned approaches leads to achieving great portfolio rate of returns.

Li et al. (2010) combine the AHP (Analytic Hierarchy Process) methods for the stock selection on 8 listed companies within the steel industry on the Chinese stock market. There is no time span stated in the research, and authors use the following factors to rank stocks: profitability (profit margins and net profit margins), profit and sales growth rates, earnings per share, price to earnings ratio, solvency ratios and operating ability ratios. The approach in this study is to obtain weights via AHP for the second step of GRA and conclude that the results are promising. However, no investment decisions were applied in order to compare portfolio results. Jane and Huang (2013) focus again on the automatic stock selection mechanism, this time by combining Artificial Neural Network with the GRA modelling. All companies listed on the Taiwanese market in the period from November 2008 until April 2013 were used for comparison purposes. The results were very promising with obtaining extraordinary results as in Huang and Jane (2008). Salardini (2013) combines the AHP and GRA approaches on the sample of 16 stocks on Tehran Stock Exchange in year 2010. Both approaches were used in order to obtain optimal weights in the ranking system. Stocks were ranked based upon several factor, but no explanation is given for the usage of chosen variables. Mohammadi Pour et al. (2016) is one of the last to apply GRA analysis on the stock selection process. Authors compared 14 stocks from the Tehran Stock Exchange for the period 2009–2014. In total 4 financial ratios were used in the study (with no explanations on why those) and rankings were made and compared to the Johnson forecasting ranking. Results indicated similar ranking results for both methods.

As can be seen from the literature overview, not many studies exist within this field. Moreover, portfolio selection as in terms of risk diversification was not observed as well. Finally, not many papers include explanations and rationale from the financial theory standpoint which factors should be included in the analysis. This is why this research is trying to fill that gap.

3. Methodology

For describing the methodology used in this study, we follow Liu and Lin (2006, 2010). This methodology was firstly developed in Deng (1982) and since then it was applied in different areas of research (for overview, please see Deng 1989; Liu et al. 2016). This approach of modelling is used to build a ranking system of alternatives in order to choose the best one. Denote with $(x_i(1), x_i(2), ..., x_i(n))$ the behavioural sequence of the k-th factor, $k \in \{1, 2, \ldots, n\}$ for observed alternatives $i \in \{1, 2, \ldots, m\}$. All of the data can be formatted into the matrix X:

$$X = \begin{bmatrix} x_1(1) & x_1(2) & \cdots & x_1(n) \\ x_2(1) & x_2(2) & & x_2(n) \\ \vdots & \vdots & \ddots & \vdots \\ x_m(1) & x_m(2) & \cdots & x_m(n) \end{bmatrix} \quad (1)$$

The data is normalized so a comparability sequence can be obtained: $(y_i(1), y_i(2), \ldots, y_i(n))$, with normalization accordingly to rules of data being the greater (larger) the better:

$$y_i(k) = \frac{x_i(k) - \min\limits_i x_i(k)}{\max\limits_i x_i(k) - \min\limits_i x_i(k)}, \quad (2)$$

the smaller the better:

$$y_i(k) = \frac{\max\limits_i x_i(k) - x_i(k)}{\max\limits_i x_i(k) - \min\limits_i x_i(k)}, \quad (3)$$

or the closer to the desired value $x^*(k)$ the better:

$$y_i(k) = \frac{|x_i(k) - x^*(k)|}{\max\limits_i x_i(k) - x^*(k)}. \quad (4)$$

Normalization could be made by dividing each value for factor k by the first value $x_1(k)$ as well. When using expressions (2) and (3) to normalize data, every new value will be within the interval [0, 1]; and the greater the normalized value is, the closer is the original value to the minimum or maximum, depending on the criteria. In order to calculate the Grey Incidence Index, absolute differences are calculated compared to the referent value $y^*(k)$:

$$\Delta y_i(k) = |y^*(k) - y_i(k)|. \quad (5)$$

Kuo et al. (2008) define the reference sequence as all values $y^*(k)$ being equal to one. The Grey Relational Coefficient is calculated as:

$$G_i(k) = \frac{\Delta_{\min} + p\Delta_{\max}}{\Delta y_i(k) + p\Delta_{\min}}, \tag{6}$$

where p is the distinguishing coefficient, $0 \leq p \leq 1$; $\Delta_{\min} = \min\{\Delta y_1(k), \ldots, \Delta y_m(k)\}\ \forall k$; $\Delta_{\max} = \max\{\Delta y_1(k), \ldots, \Delta y_m(k)\}\ \forall k$. Finally, the Grey Relational Degree (Relational Grade) for each alternative is a weighted average of relational coefficients for different factors:

$$r_i = \sum_{i=1}^{n} w_i G_i(k), \quad \forall i, \tag{7}$$

where weights w_i satisfy the condition: $\sum\limits_{i=1}^{n} w_i = 1$. The Grey Relational Grade in (7) for each alternative is interpreted as the degree of similarity between the reference sequence of $y^*(k)$-s and the alternatives being compared to it. In some literature it is interpreted as the correlation coefficient. Thus, the greater the value of r_i for an observed alternative, the better the performance it is considered to have compared to others. As it can be seen, this approach is relatively simple, straightforward and directly interpretable. More details can be seen in Liu et al. (2016).

4. Empirical Results

4.1. Data Description and Rationale for Used Factors

For the purpose of the empirical analysis, daily price data on most liquid[1] stocks on the Croatian stock market, Zagreb Stock Exchange (ZSE 2018) was collected for the year 2017. Most liquid stocks are observed in order to have as much as data possible. In that way, the sample consists of 55 stocks in total. Moreover, additional data on return series was collected in the first half of 2018 for the out of sample calculations and comparisons (see Section 5). Moreover, several financial ratios for each stock have been obtained from financial statements of 2017 as well. In that way, the analysis can be undertaken based upon the newest data possible. Thus, the analysis will include ranking of the stocks based upon the return distribution characteristics, as well as on financial statements of each company. Based upon the daily prices, daily continuous returns were calculated and average return for the 2017 was calculated for each stock. Next, standard deviations as a risk measure and coefficients of asymmetry and kurtosis were calculated as well for each stock. It is assumed that investors base their decisions on investing based upon the first m moments of return distribution. As Arditti (1967) discussed: investors prefer positive skewness of returns as a result of decreasing absolute risk aversion; and the famous theorem of Müller and Machina (1987, p. 351) which states that investors with von Neumann–Morgenstern utility functions rank probability distributions on the basis of their first m absolute moments. Based upon the investor's utility function theory, in the analysis we assume that investors prefer higher odd moments of return distribution (first and third moments: average return and skewness), whilst they prefer smaller event moments (second and fourth moments: standard deviation and kurtosis). For more details on investor's utility functions discussion and preferences towards the m moments of return distribution please see Arditti and Levy (1975), Athayde and Flôres (1997), Hwang and Satchell (1999), Briec et al. (2006), Jurczenko and Maillet (2005), Jondeau and Rockinger (2006) or Gardijan and Škrinjarić (2015).

Two liquidity measures used in the study, trading volume and number of transactions, are referred to as market measures. Previous literature finds negative relationship between the liquidity premium and stock returns (Datar et al. 1998; Pástor and Stambaugh 2003; Liu 2006; Hur et al. 2018; Hur and

[1] Liquid in terms of number of transactions. Although research exists on how (il)liquidity affects stock returns, here we include more liquid stocks due to having more data to make calculations with. In 2017, in total 93 stocks were traded on ZSE. Problems with liquidity are not something new for ZSE. Namely, as Škrinjarić (2018a) states: in the period from September 2014 until May 2018, there were only 9 stocks which were traded at least 90% of the time, 17 with 75%, 25 with 60% and 37 with 30% of the whole period. The usual approach is to pick the liquid stocks which have been traded most frequently in a period. More details can be seen in Škrinjarić (2018b) or Vidović (2013).

Chung 2018). Thus, the approach in this research is that investors aim for lower liquidity in order to obtain illiquidity premiums. Inclusion of financial statements data is based upon previous research which finds that there exist differences in stock returns depending upon financial ratios. Basu (1977) was one of the first studies to find that firms with a small price to earnings (PE) ratio had higher returns compared to other firms on the US market in the long term. Shiller (2005) showed that long-term investors should focus on lower PE ratios, whilst in short term it is possible to obtain excess returns with higher PE ratios. Since we observe a short-term in this study, we focus on greater PE ratios. Book to market ratio (BM) was extensively studied over the last couple of decades. Banz (1981) and Reinganum (1981) were some of the first studies to conclude that smaller stocks have greater returns compared to bigger ones. This stimulated Fama and Fama and French (1992, 1993, 1995, 1996) to include this ratio into their famous 3-factor model and found a strong positive effect of BM ratio on cross-sectional stock returns. That is why we are aiming for a greater value of this ratio in the analysis. Furthermore, Wu (2000) conducted a survey of institutional and individual investors and found that earnings per share (EPS), return on assets (ROA) and liquidity ratios are some of the most used financial ratios when investors make their investment decisions in practice. This was confirmed in Muhammad and Scrimgeour (2014), who add return on equity (ROE) to this list as well and conclude that these ratios give information to investors on effective and efficient usage of the firm's assets and equity in order to generate profits. Moreover, investors should aim towards greater value of mentioned ratios due to them being a proxy for performance measurement of firms and efficiency of their management. That is why investors should aim greater values of EPS, ROA and ROE (evidence was found as well as in Dimitropoulos and Asteriou (2009) and Palepu and Healy (2010)). Finally, the positive relationship between the Dividend per Share (DPS) ratio and expected returns has been found very early in the literature in work of Fama and Schwert (1977) and Campbell (1987); and has been continuously confirmed over the years as well in Fama and French (1988), Campbell and Shiller (1988), Kothari and Shanken (1997) or Lewellen (2004).

Table A1 in Appendix A depicts the used factors in the study, with their abbreviations in brackets and the preferred values of each factor. If investor should prefer higher value, a plus sign is added; and opposite is true for those factors which should be lower. Table 1 shows the average, minimum and maximum value of each factor in the analysis. It can be seen that the values vary significantly. However, due to the many factors upon which to base investment decisions, the GRA approach seems appropriate.

Table 1. Average, minimum and maximum values of factors for the whole sample.

Factor	Average	Min	Max
SD	0.020	0.003	0.073
CS	23.570	3.194	127.755
TV	637,612.691	800.000	7,892,835.000
NT	2914.218	260.000	16,276.000
ER	0.000	−0.003	0.003
CA	0.722	−6.847	9.195
BM	2.923	0.001	78.930
PE	5.121	−30.875	79.841
ROA	0.428	−2.230	26.362
ROE	−0.343	−50.453	68.125
EPS	1584.294	0.028	45,894.157
TBR	1.047	0.201	2.673
ATR	7.926	0.007	208.657
DPS	41.831	0.000	1649.937

SD—standard deviation; CS—coefficient of skewness; TV—trading volume; NT—number of transactions; ER—expected return; CA—coefficient of asymmetry; BM—book to market ratio; PE—price to earnings ratio; ROA—return on assets; ROE—return on equity; EPS—earnings per share; TBR—total business efficiency ratio; ATR—asset to earnings ratio and DPS—dividend per share. Source: authors.

4.2. Results in Sample

Firstly, based upon the signs in Table A1 (in Appendix A), each factor was normalized by using Formulas (2) and (3). The distinguishing coefficient was chosen ranging from 0.1 to 0.9 and the results of the degrees of grey incidence for each stock. Since the ranking does not change with respect to the distinguishing coefficient (see Figure 1), Table 2 is showing Grey relational grades for the value of the coefficient being 0.5. This could be interpreted as the correlation between the performances of each stock with respect to all factors to the optimal value of 1 for each factor. Moreover, here we have chosen equal weights for all of the factors in the analysis as a starting point. This means that it is assumed that investors are regarding all of the information (factors) on stocks in an equal manner. It can be seen that the best stocks in terms of performance in Table 2 are TUHO, MDKA, ATLN, LKRI and LPLH, due to them having the greatest values of degree of incidence. The worst performance had LEDO, OPTE, DDJH, DLKV and INGR. This conclusion is robust when changing the distinguishing coefficient, as it can be seen on Figure 1. Thus, from an initial larger sample of stocks available, investor can use this information to narrow his set of interesting stocks to evaluate further or to invest in the best performing stocks.

Table 2. Grey relational grade for each stock, distinguishing coefficient value is 0.5.

Stock	$p = 0.5$	Stock	$p = 0.5$
ADPL	0.5303	KRAS	0.5418
ADRS	0.5401	LEDO	0.4358
ADRS2	0.5213	LHRC	0.5535
ARNT	0.5276	LKPC	0.569
ATGR	0.5364	LKRI	0.5771
ATLN	0.5886	LPLH	0.5746
ATPL	0.518	LRH	0.5652
AUHR	0.5224	MAIS	0.5454
BD62	0.5205	MDKA	0.5889
BLJE	0.4855	OPTE	0.4592
CKML	0.5406	PLAG	0.5526
DDJH	0.461	PODR	0.5417
DLKV	0.4702	PTKM	0.4829
ERNT	0.5224	RIVP	0.511
HDEL	0.5152	RIZO	0.5229
HHLD	0.5104	SAPN	0.533
HMST	0.5458	SLRS	0.5356
HT	0.4984	THNK	0.4873
HUPZ	0.4959	TPNG	0.5398
IGH	0.4874	TUHO	0.6111
INA	0.5435	ULPL	0.5248
INGR	0.4778	ULJN	0.514
IPKK	0.5242	VART	0.5281
JDGT	0.5255	VIRO	0.521
JDPL	0.5139	VLEN	0.5076
JMNC	0.5269	ZB	0.5198
JNAF	0.5537	ZVZD	0.5389
KOEI	0.5477		

Source: authors.

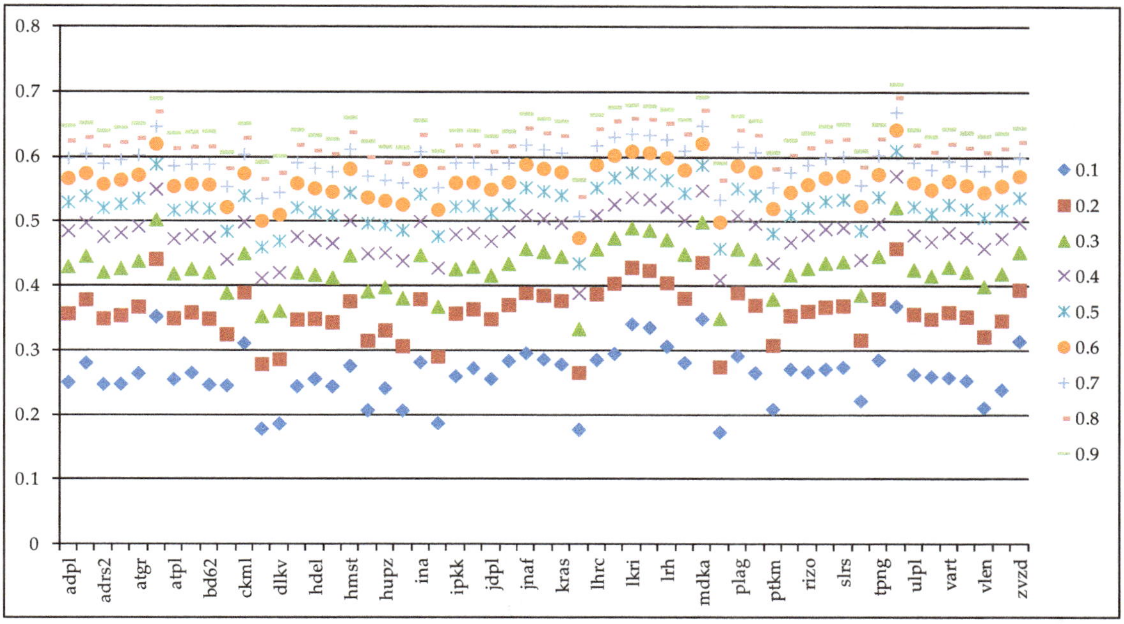

Figure 1. Grey relational grades for the analyzed stocks, different values of distinguishing coefficients.

In order to obtain more information on the usefulness of using the GRA approach, an additional ranking was made based upon several other criteria. In the first scenario it is assumed that an investor regards only the first two moments of return distribution equally and gives them equal weight. Moreover, the investor ignores all other factors. This scenario is denoted "2 moments". Other scenarios include: investor equally weights only the first three moments ("3 moments"); first four moments ("4 moments"); only the financial ratios data ("only financial"); major weight is given to the risk (50%, whilst other 50% is equally distributed to all other factors; "risk"); major weight is given to the return (50%, whilst other 50% is equally distributed to all other factors; "return") and final scenario in which 70% of the weight is given to return distribution moments, whilst other 30% to other factors (named "0.7 moments; 0.3 other"). Thus, the whole procedure of calculation was performed again and the Grey incidence indices are compared on Figure 2. Although it seems that for many cases the ranking remained the same, some major differences arise when investors change their preferences. The detailed ranking is shown in the Appendix A, in Table A3. Some major differences occur for, e.g., stock ZVZD, which was ranked the best according to the scenarios "3 moments" and "return", but is almost the worst (53 rank out of 55) when taking into account scenario "risk". Thus, the ranking will depend upon investor's preferences and subjective goals.

We wanted to obtain information whether this ranking system can provide a successful portfolio selection in terms of risk and return, by constructing efficient frontiers in terms of the Markowitz portfolio (Markowitz 1952, 1959). Firstly, an original efficient frontier was constructed based upon the whole sample in order to compare how closely the investor can approach this frontier with the analysis of GRA approach. This is depicted on Figure 3 and denoted with "efficient frontier". This original frontier was constructed based upon varying the risk in the Markowitz (1959) model from the minimum variance portfolio until the portfolio with the maximum return.

Next, based upon the rankings on Figure 2, several frontiers were constructed as a second step of the whole analysis. Notation is the same as on Figure 2. However, these frontiers are not efficient in terms of the Markowitz model, due to them being constructed based upon several points: the first point was constructed such that weights to individual stocks were constructed based upon the grey incidence indices. Every weight is equal to the value of the individual index divided by the total sum. In that way, all of the stocks entered the portfolio. The second point was constructed by giving equal weights to the first 3 best stocks based upon the grey indices. The third point was constructed by giving equal weights to the first 5 best stocks based upon the same indices. In that way, we wanted to observe how the point changes from the starting value when all of the stocks are included in the portfolio. By undertaking this analysis, we can obtain information if the portfolio goes closer to the Markowitz efficient frontier or away from it.[2] As can be seen on Figure 3, interesting results arise, depending upon what investor takes into consideration. The best approach in this analyzed sample was for all of those scenarios which included portfolio moments, due to these frontiers expanding towards the original efficient frontier. The worst performance was obtained for only financial data. This means that in this observed period, if investors based their analysis mostly on the return distributions, they could have formed such portfolios to obtain good results in terms of portfolio risk and return. On the other hand, the inclusion of financial data did not result in desiredoutcomes. However, it can be seen as well that when the portfolios are compared to the equally weighted portfolio (denoted with "equally w portfolio"), investor can achieve better results (greater return and/or smaller risk) with respect to this benchmark.

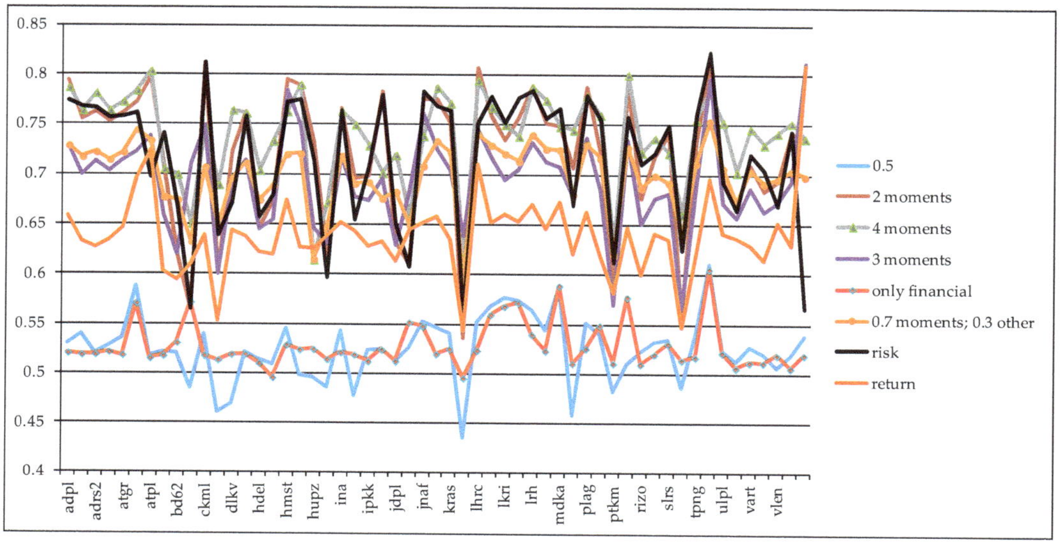

Figure 2. Grey relational grades for the analyzed stocks, different criteria.

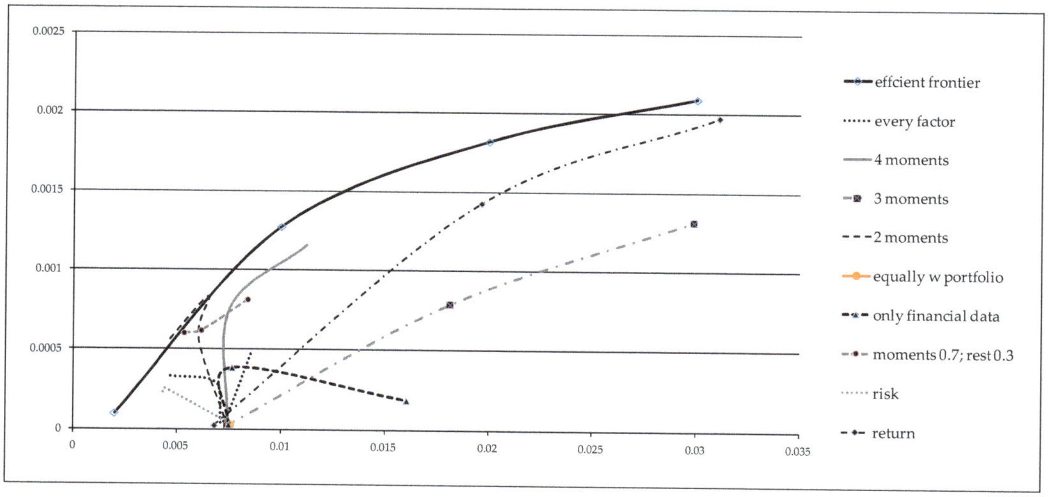

Figure 3. Comparison of efficient frontier with other frontiers, fixed weights of stocks in portfolios.

2 Moreover, we do not choose to invest only in the best stock, due to diversification possibilities within Modern Portfolio Theory.

Finally, we wanted to construct efficient frontiers for the best performing scenarios from Figure 3 in the Markowitz spirit. Thus, additional models were optimized in which stock weights were obtained for the best performing 3, 5 and 10 stocks by the ranking in Table A2. Now, all of the frontiers are efficient in terms of Markowitz portfolio optimization, where we change the risk of the portfolio ranging from the minimum variance portfolio until the maximum return. The efficient frontiers are shown on Figure 4. It can be seen that "2 moments" and "4 moments" efficient frontiers are very close to the original frontier; meaning that ranking stocks based upon return distribution moments gives insights for investing into more efficient portfolios, especially compared to the equally weighted portfolio (denoted with "equal weights"), at least in sample.

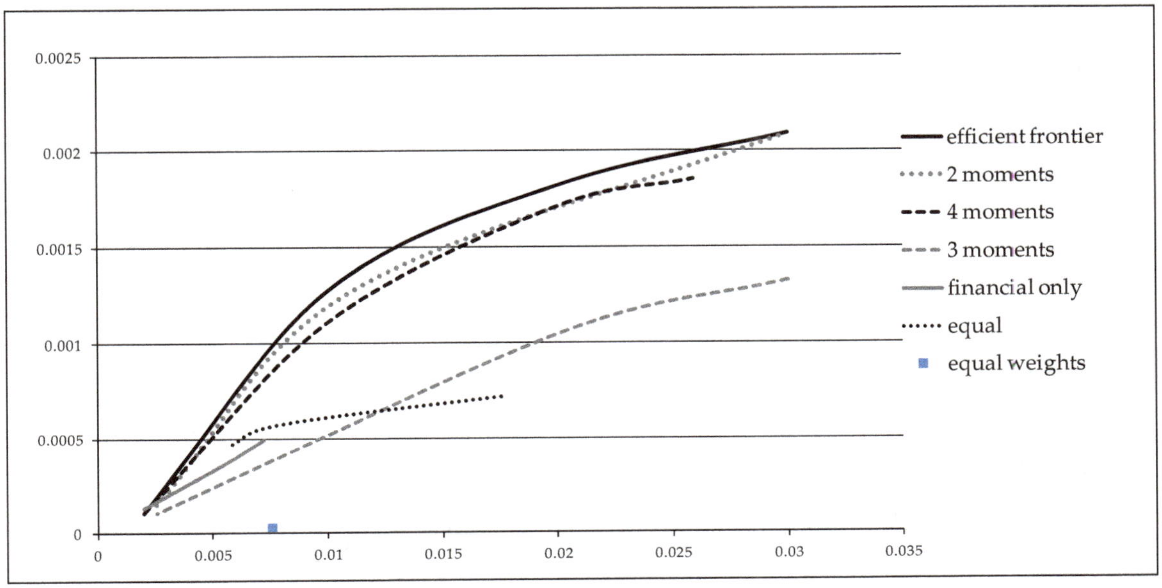

Figure 4. Comparison of efficient frontiers, optimization resulted weights.

5. Backtesting Portfolio Results

Now we focus on the out of sample results by performing backtesting of the portfolios constituting the efficient frontiers on Figure 4 in order to evaluate the performance based upon ranking from the GRA approach. The performance measures are calculated based upon the Knight and Satchell (2002) performance measurement book. It is assumed that an investor uses the GRA ranking system results from Table A2 in order to construct portfolios at the beginning of 2018 and holds those portfolios until mid 2018. For every efficient frontier from Figure 4, we extracted 4 portfolios: minimum variance, maximum return and two in between to represent different risk aversions in the analysis. Thus, in total we observe 24 different portfolios and the equally weighted one as well. The characteristics of those portfolios are given in Table 3. It can be seen that regarding the realized return, the best portfolio in total was the one where equal weights were given to all of the criteria in the GRA ranking system with the return maximization approach. In general, the "2 moments" portfolios obtained the best results regarding the realized returns, due to having positive returns on for all of the selected portfolios. In terms of risk, the overall best performing were the "Financial only" criteria portfolios. However, investors observe these measures in combination and not separately. That is why firstly we compare Sharpe ratios for every portfolio in order to obtain reward to risk ratios. It can be seen that in general, the "2 moments" portfolios achieve greatest (positive) values of the Sharpe ratio, especially when investors aim to maximize the portfolio returns. The "3 moments" portfolios obtained the worst performance regarding this ratio out of sample. This is somewhat in line with Figure 4 where the "3 moments" frontier was the farthest from the original efficient frontier, while the "2 moments" frontier was the closest.

Table 3. Comparison of performances of simulated portfolios in 2018.

Portfolio		Realized Return (%)	Standard Deviation (%)	Sharpe Ratio	Certainty Equivalent (CE)			
					1	2	3 mom	4 mom
Efficient frontier	Min risk	0.827	**0.462**	**1.399**	0.008	0.008	0.347	**1.777**
	Portfolio 1	0.827	0.462	1.788	0.008	0.008	0.347	1.777
	Portfolio 2	−3.567	3.455	−1.032	−0.036	−0.037	−0.679	−0.880
	Max return	−5.152	4.520	−1.140	−0.053	−0.054	−0.766	−1.038
2 moments	Min risk	**0.941**	0.797	1.181	0.009	0.009	**0.442**	1.724
	Portfolio 1	1.382	0.713	1.937	0.014	0.014	−0.084	1.194
	Portfolio 2	2.024	0.755	**2.681**	**0.020**	**0.020**	0.143	1.695
	Max return	5.917	**1.388**	**4.262 ***	**0.059**	**0.059**	−0.194	−1.081
3 moments	Min risk	0.197	0.591	0.333	−0.044	−0.044	0.025	0.594
	Portfolio 1	−2.660	1.067	−2.493	−0.018	−0.018	**0.714**	**1.778**
	Portfolio 2	−1.792	0.746	−2.403	−0.027	−0.027	**0.747 ***	**1.845 ***
	Max return	−4.367	1.817	−2.403	−0.002	−0.002	**0.721**	**1.819**
4 moments	Min risk	−0.223	0.952	−0.235	−0.002	−0.002	0.304	−0.178
	Portfolio 1	**2.790**	0.951	**2.935**	0.028	0.028	−0.927	−1.336
	Portfolio 2	−0.563	2.597	−0.217	−0.006	−0.006	−0.590	−0.850
	Max return	−6.778	5.960	−1.137	−0.070	−0.071	−0.784	−1.057
Financial only	Min risk	0.311	0.615	0.506	−0.044	−0.044	−0.850	−1.353
	Portfolio 1	0.196	**0.383**	0.512	0.002	0.002	−0.851	−1.352
	Portfolio 2	0.161	**0.319 ***	0.505	0.002	0.002	−0.848	−1.343
	Max return	−4.367	1.817	−2.403	0.003	0.003	0.721	**1.819**
Equal	Min risk	−1.677	0.812	−2.065	−0.017	−0.017	−1.395	−2.722
	Portfolio 1	1.371	1.017	1.349	0.014	0.014	−1.456	−2.713
	Portfolio 2	**3.888**	1.684	2.309	**0.039**	**0.039**	−0.751	−1.010
	Max return	**7.977 ***	3.065	2.602	**0.079 ***	**0.079 ***	0.262	0.793
Equal weights	-	0.470	0.593	0.793	0.005	0.005	−0.441	0.135

Note: greatest return, minimal risk, greatest Sharpe ratio[3] and greatest Certainty Equivalent for each category of 4 portfolios is in bold and the values with asterisks are denoted as being best in respective rows. Numbers 1 and 2 denote the coefficient of absolute risk aversion for calculation of Certainty Equivalent with respect to the quadratic utility function[4]. 3 mom and 4 mom columns denote the Certainty Equivalent with respect to 3 and 4 moments based utility functions as in Jurczenko and Maillet (2005), where equal weights were added to all portfolio moments. Source: authors.

Finally, we calculated Certainty Equivalent (CE) values for every portfolio in the sample, by comparing in first two columns rankings based upon only the first two moments of each portfolio and in the last two columns by adding the skewness and kurtosis preferences into account as well. In that way, the rankings of the portfolios are based upon all of the portfolio moments, since we assumed that investor's preferences depend upon first 4 moments. Although the "2 moments" portfolios had in general greater values of CEs for the first two moments, the last two columns indicate that the "3 moments" portfolios could be preferred over other ones. Although these portfolios had negative realized returns, in these scenarios the skewness and kurtosis had such preferable values that in the overall ranking of the portfolios, the rankings change. This is affected by investor's preferences and aversions towards each portfolio moment (in these two last scenarios it is assumed that every moment is equally weighted in the utility function). Since the "3 moments" portfolios were not attractive based upon the return, risk and Sharpe ratio criteria, it could be said that these portfolios could be recommended to those investors who are more focused on higher moments of the portfolio rather than

---

3 Sharpe ratio was calculated based upon the 91 day Treasury bill interest rate of the Ministry of Finance (2018) in Croatia which was equal to 0.36% in the observed period.

4 Values of 1 and 2 were chosen based upon Guidolin and Guidolin and Timmermann (2008) who used 2, 5 and 10; Ang and Bekaert (2002) where authors used 5 and 10. Guidolin and Timmermann (2007) showed that the results of ranking are robust if the coefficient is in the interval (0, 20]. Additionally, we calculated Certainty Equivalent for values 5 and 10 and the rankings remained the same. Quadratic utility function was chosen for the calculation of Certainty Equivalent due to results in Pulley (1981), Kroll et al. (1984) and Cremers et al. (2003) who compared the rankings of the quadratic utility function to other functional forms of investor's utility and the results showed that the differences were nonsignificant.

risks and returns (especially returns since they were negative for the majority of cases). By excluding the "3 moments" portfolios, again it can be seen that the "2 moments" portfolios exhibit the greatest CEs in majority cases.

Finally, the simulated values of each portfolio from the maximization[5] scheme in Table 3 were depicted on Figure 5 in order to see which scenario could have been beneficial for the investor. The "equally weighted" and "2 moments" portfolios could have achieved greatest returns for the investor if he had structured his portfolio based upon the GRA analysis in 2017. There exists the potential to form the portfolio based upon the GRA ranking, since several portfolios achieved greater values compared to the value of the original efficient frontier portfolio.

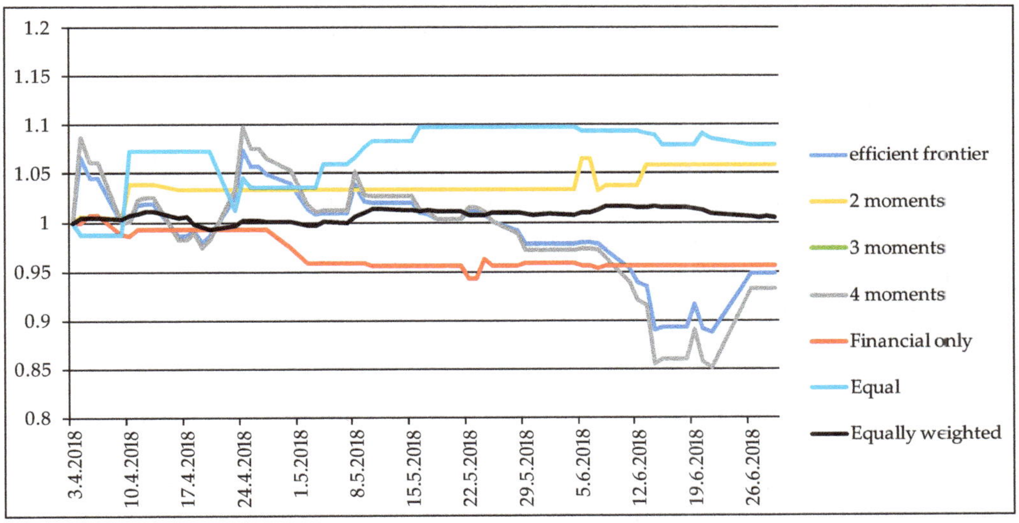

Figure 5. Simulated portfolio values for the case of maximizing the return portfolio.

6. Discussion

Based upon the results from the empirical analysis, several key points can be concluded. Firstly, both of the hypotheses can be confirmed. The first research question asked if GRA approach results can indicate a good portfolio structure. This was observed on Figures 3 and 4 and how the GRA portfolios moved towards the original efficient frontier. The resulting portfolios moved closer to the efficient frontier in cases where return distribution moments were taken into consideration. This is in line with previous empirical and theoretical research on the importance of distribution moments when investors make their decisions. The second question asked if portfolios resulting from GRA approach are better in terms of risk and return compared to the benchmark of the equally weighted portfolio. This was confirmed when both figures were commented, where it can be seen that all of the GRA portfolios had greater returns for the same value of risk and had lower risk with the same level or portfolio return. Moreover, these two questions were further explored in the out of sample analysis where, based upon the results in 2017, we simulated 25 portfolio scenarios in order to obtain risks, returns and other measures (in Table 3). Next, the potential of this analysis can be seen in many different scenarios which can be simulated before making investment decisions. Here, we observed only about a dozen of different scenarios in which investors can observe how the characteristics of portfolios change by changing the structure of the portfolio based upon the GRA approach. Thus, future work can be extended upon developing reliable criteria and scenarios. Future work will extend this research as well by including partial moments of return distributions to see whether concepts from Post Modern

5 Maximization of portfolio return problems were chosen since these portfolios could have enabled an investor to achieve the best results in terms of return series. Other 3 scenarios from Table 3 are omitted, but are available upon request; the portfolio values have similar relations one to another.

Portfolio theory could result in better portfolio characteristics. Moreover, a dynamic analysis will be observed to see how factor changes over time influence portfolio selection and restructuring. Finally, different risk aversions will be included in the analysis as well, in order to obtain more insights into investor's decision making based upon their risk aversion as well.

7. Conclusions

With many data available today on financial markets, many factors influence the decision making process when making investment decisions. Quantitative methods and models are constantly being developed in order to facilitate the portfolio and risk management process. The goal of this study was to investigate how results from GRA affect portfolio construction. The results were compared to the original efficient frontier constructed based upon Markowitz portfolio optimization.

Some of the pitfalls of the study were as follows. We observed only the full moments of return distributions and not partial moments (such as lower partial risk measures, etc.). Moreover, a static analysis was conducted due to observing the entire year 2017 characteristics of return distributions. In that way, it was possible to carry out the out of sample analysis only for the first half of 2018. However, a dynamic analysis could be provided only on a quarterly basis as well if all of the firms provide quarterly financial statements. The monthly or a weekly basis of the analysis could be possible only with market data. Some subjectivity is always present when making decisions based upon several criteria. This was the case in this study as well, when investor has to choose the weights on the factors in the GRA analysis, as well as when ranking the portfolios based upon their risk aversion, skewness preference and/or kurtosis aversion. We cannot discuss the usefulness of specific moments or financial ratios when ranking stocks, due to this being an empirical problem. This means that some factors used in the analysis can change over time and affect the ranking. In that way, dynamic analysis should be provided when applying this in practice. In this specific example, it is not advised to use financial ratios in the analysis, due to the efficient frontier being lower compared to other ones and being very short (i.e., small, providing less investment possibilities compared to other approaches).

Finally, since the results showed the potential of this methodology, there is hope that further applications will extend to achieving even better results in portfolio selection. However, the contribution of this research can be found in initial analysis of the GRA approach when making investment decisions.

Author Contributions: All authors contributed equally.

Funding: This research received no external funding. The APC was funded by institutions through the Knowledge Unlatched initiative and partially funded by MDPI.

Acknowledgments: The authors would like to thank three anonymous referees for their valuable comments and suggestions which contributed to the quality of the paper.

Conflicts of Interest: The authors declare no conflict of interest.

Appendix A

Table A1. Factors used in the analysis with corresponding desirable values.

Return Distribution:	Market:	Financial Ratios:
Expected return (ER) + Standard deviation (SD) − Coefficient of asymmetry (CA) + Coefficient of skewness (CS) −	Trading volume (TV) − Number of transactions (NT) −	Book to market ratio (BM) + Price to earnings ratio (PE) + Return on assets (ROA) + Return on equity (ROE) + Earnings per share (EPS) + Total business efficiency ratio (TBR) + Asset turnover ratio (ATR) + Dividends per share (DPS) +

Source: authors.

Table A2. Stocks included in the analysis.

ADPL[h]	ADRS[p]	ADRS2[p]	ARNT[l]	ATGR[j]	ATLN[o]	ATPL[k]	AUHR[j]
BD62[b]	BLJE[a]	CKML[b]	DDJH[p]	DLKV[i]	ERNT[f]	HDEL[i]	HHLD[l]
HMST[l]	HT[m]	HUPZ[l]	IGH[q]	INA[d]	INGR[p]	IPKK[b]	JDGT[k]
JDPL[k]	JMNC[b]	JNAF[k]	KOEI[g]	KRAS[b]	LEDO[b]	LHRC[l]	LKPC[k]
LKRI[k]	LPLH[k]	LRH[l]	MAIS[l]	MDKA[j]	OPTE[m]	PLAG[l]	PODR[b]
PTKM[e]	RIVP[l]	RIZO[f]	SAPN[e]	SLRS[l]	THNK[i]	TPNG[k]	TUHO[l]
ULPL[k]	ULJN[h]	VART[c]	VIRO[b]	VLEN[h]	ZB[n]	ZVZD[b]	-

Source: ZSE (2018). Note: sector classification of the stocks is as follows: [a]—agriculture, forestry and fishery; [b]—food and tobacco production; [c]—production of textiles, clothing, leather and related products; [d]—manufacture of coke and refined petroleum products; [e]—manufacture of chemicals and chemical products; [f]—manufacture of computers and electronic and optical products; [g]—manufacture of electrical equipment; [h]—manufacture of transport equipment; [i]—construction; [j]—wholesale and retail trade; repair of motor vehicles and motorcycles; [k]—transport and storage; [l]—activities of providing accommodation and preparation and serving of food; [m]—telecommunications; [n]—financial and insurance activities; [o]—real estate business; [p]—legal, accounting, management, architectural and engineering engineering and technical testing and analysis; [q]—scientific research and development. Thus, in total 17 out of 23 sectors are included in the analysis.

Table A3. Ranking of stocks in the analysis.

Stock.	$p = 0.5$	2 mom	4 mom	3 mom	Only Financial	0.7 mom; 0.3 other	Risk	Return
ADPL	24	6	7	12	26	9	10	12
ADRS	18	21	17	26	35	20	13	34
ADRS2	34	17	10	19	34	14	14	38
ARNT	26	22	18	25	24	22	24	32
ATGR	21	18	13	17	36	15	20	19
ATLN	3	14	9	14	6	2	18	5
ATPL	38	4	1	8	40	6	37	2
AUHR	33	35	43	43	38	43	30	49
BD62	36	49	47	52	14	46	43	51
BLJE	49	53	52	21	5	52	54	48
CKML	17	2	29	5	37	27	2	26
DDJH	53	51	48	53	43	49	48	53
DLKV	52	32	16	29	32	34	40	23
ERNT	32	16	21	18	31	25	21	28
HDEL	39	46	44	48	50	45	45	41
HHLD	43	44	37	45	55	39	39	43
HMST	12	5	20	3	15	18	11	6
HT	45	8	4	6	20	17	9	39
HUPZ	46	31	55	47	18	54	33	40
IGH	47	48	49	50	42	50	52	27
INA	14	15	19	15	25	19	17	16
INGR	51	39	27	37	33	38	46	22
IPKK	30	38	39	39	45	36	35	37
JDGT	28	11	46	27	19	44	6	33
JDPL	41	47	42	51	44	41	47	47
JMNC	27	50	51	34	9	48	51	21
JNAF	8	12	33	4	11	26	4	17
KOEI	11	13	6	13	28	5	12	11
KRAS	15	23	14	24	17	13	16	30
LEDO	55	55	54	49	54	55	55	55
LHRC	9	3	3	7	21	3	26	3
LKPC	6	19	15	16	8	8	7	14
LKRI	4	29	26	28	7	16	27	10
LPLH	5	20	34	23	4	23	8	13
LRH	7	9	5	11	12	4	3	8
MAIS	13	24	12	20	22	11	23	20
MDKA	2	25	28	22	2	12	15	7
OPTE	54	37	31	36	49	42	42	42
PLAG	10	10	11	9	16	7	5	9
PODR	16	33	22	33	10	21	25	44
PTKM	50	52	53	54	48	53	50	52

Table A3. *Cont.*

Stock.	$p = 0.5$	2 mom	4 mom	3 mom	Only Financial	0.7 mom; 0.3 other	Risk	Return
RIVP	42	7	2	10	3	10	22	18
RIZO	31	43	40	46	51	40	34	50
SAPN	23	34	36	38	27	31	31	24
SLRS	22	27	41	35	13	35	28	31
THNK	48	54	50	55	41	51	49	54
TPNG	19	30	23	31	39	24	19	45
TUHO	1	1	8	2	1	1	1	4
ULPL	29	41	24	41	23	28	38	25
ULJN	40	45	45	44	52	47	44	29
VART	25	36	30	32	46	30	32	35
VIRO	35	42	38	42	47	37	36	46
VLEN	44	40	32	40	30	33	41	15
ZB	37	26	25	30	53	29	29	36
ZVZD	20	28	35	1	29	32	53	1

Source: authors.

References

Ang, Andrew, and Geert Bekaert. 2002. International Asset allocation With Regime Shifts. *Review of Financial Studies* 15: 1137–87. [CrossRef]

Arditti, Fred, and Haim Levy. 1975. Portfolio efficiency analysis in three moments: The multiperiod case. *The Journal of Finance* 303: 797–809. [CrossRef]

Arditti, Fred. 1967. Risk and the Required Return on Equity. *The Journal of Finance* 22: 19–36. [CrossRef]

Athayde, Gustavo, and Renato Galvão Flôres. 1997. *A CAPM with Higher Moments: Theory and Econometrics*. Discussion Paper EPGE-FGV. Rio de Janeiro: EPGE/FGV.

Banz, Rolf. 1981. The relationship between return and market value of common stocks. *Journal of Financial Economics* 9: 3–18. [CrossRef]

Basu, Sanjoy. 1977. The Investment Performance of Common Stocks in Relation to their Price to Earnings Ratio: A Test of the Efficient Markets Hypothesis. *The Journal of Finance* 32: 663–82. [CrossRef]

Briec, Walter, Kristiaan Kerstens, and Octave Jokung. 2006. Mean-variance-skewness portfolio performance gauging: A general shortage function and dual approach. *Management Science* 531: 135–49. [CrossRef]

Campbell, John, and Robert Shiller. 1988. The dividend-price ratio and expectations of future dividends and discount factors. *Review of Financial Studies* 1: 195–228. [CrossRef]

Campbell, John. 1987. Stock returns and the term structure. *Journal of Financial Economics* 18: 373–99. [CrossRef]

Cremers, Jan-Hein, Mark Kritzman, and Sebastian Page. 2003. Portfolio Formation with Higher Moments and Plausible Utility. In *Revere Street Working Paper Series in Financial Economics 272-12*. Cambridge: State Street Associates.

Chen, Hsing-Hung. 2008. Stock selection using data envelopment analysis. *Industrial Management & Data Systems* 108: 1255–68. [CrossRef]

Chen, Kung, and Shimerda Thomas. 1981. An Empirical Analysis of Useful Financial Ratios. *Financial Management* 10: 51–60. [CrossRef]

Datar, Vinay, Narayan Naik, and Robert Radcliffe. 1998. Liquidity and stock returns: An alternative test. *Journal of Financial Markets* 12: 203–19. [CrossRef]

Deng, Ju-Long. 1982. Control problems of Grey Systems. *Systems and Control Letters* 5: 288–94. [CrossRef]

Deng, Ju-Long. 1989. Introduction to Grey System Theory. *The Journal of Grey Systems* 1: 1–24.

Dia, Mohamm. 2007. A Portfolio Selection Methodology Based on Data Envelopment Analysis. *INFOR: Information Systems and Operational Research* 47: 71–79. [CrossRef]

Dimitropoulos, Panagiotis, and Dimitrios Asteriou. 2009. The Relationship between Earnings and Stock Returns: Empirical Evidence from the Greek Capital Market. *International Journal of Economics and Finance* 11: 40–50. [CrossRef]

Edirisinghe, Nalin Chanaka, and Xin Zhang. 2007. Generalized DEA model of fundamental analysis and its application to portfolio optimization. *Journal of Banking & Finance* 31: 3311–35. [CrossRef]

Fama, Eugene F., and Kenneth R. French. 1988. Dividend yields and expected stock returns. *Journal of Financial Economics* 22: 3–25. [CrossRef]

Fama, Eugene F., and Kenneth R. French. 1992. The Cross-Section of Expected Stock Returns. *The Journal of Finance* 47: 427–65. [CrossRef]

Fama, Eugene F., and Kenneth R. French. 1993. Common risk factors in the returns on stocks and bonds. *Journal of Financial Economics* 33: 3–56. [CrossRef]

Fama, Eugene F., and Kenneth R. French. 1995. Size and Book-to-Market Factors in Earnings and Returns. *The Journal of Finance* 50: 131–55. [CrossRef]

Fama, Eugene F., and Kenneth R. French. 1996. Multifactor Explanations of Asset Pricing Anomalies. *The Journal of Finance* 51: 55–84. [CrossRef]

Fama, Eugene F., and William Schwert. 1977. Asset returns and inflation. *Journal of Financial Economics* 5: 115–46. [CrossRef]

Gardijan, Margareta, and Tihana Škrinjarić. 2015. Estimating investor preferences towards portfolio return distribution in investment funds. *Croatian Operational Research Review* 62: 1–16. [CrossRef]

Guidolin, Massimo, and Allan Timmermann. 2007. Asset allocation under multivariate regime switching. *Journal of Economic Dynamics and Control* 31: 3503–44. [CrossRef]

Guidolin, Massimo, and Allan Timmermann. 2008. International Asset allocation under Regime Switching, Skew, and Kurtosis Preferences. *The Review of Financial Studies* 21: 889–935. [CrossRef]

Huang, Kuang Yu, and Chuen-Jiuan Jane. 2008. An Automatic Stock Market Forecasting and Portfolio Selection Mechanism Based on VPRS, ARX and Grey System. Paper presented at IEEE Asia-Pacific Services Computing Conference, Yilan, Taiwan, December 9–12.

Huang, Kuang Yu, Chuen-Jiuan Jane, and Ting-Cheng Chang. 2008. A RS Model for Stock Market Forecasting and Portfolio Selection Allied with Weight Clustering and Grey System Theories. Paper presented at IEEE Congress on Evolutionary Computation, CEC 2008, Hong Kong, China, June 1–6, pp. 1240–46. [CrossRef]

Hur, Seok-Kyun, Chune Young Chung, and Chang Liu. 2018. Is Liquidity Risk Priced? Theory and Evidence. *Sustainability* 10: 1809. [CrossRef]

Hur, Seok-Kyun, and Chune Young Chung. 2018. A novel measure of liquidity premium: Application to the Korean stock market. *Applied Economics Letters* 25: 211–15. [CrossRef]

Hwang, Soosung, and Stephen Satchell. 1999. Modeling emerging market risk premia using higher moments. *International Journal of Finance and Economics* 44: 271–96. [CrossRef]

Jane, Chuen-Jiuan, and Yu Kuang Huang. 2013. A Fusion Model for Stock selection Based on Decision Tree, Artificial Neural Network and Grey Relational Analysis. *International Journal of Kansei Information* 4: 115–22.

Jondeau, Eric, and Michael Rockinger. 2006. Optimal portfolio allocation under higher moments. *European Financial Management* 121: 29–55. [CrossRef]

Jurczenko, Emmanuel, and Bertrand Maillet. 2005. The Four-moment Capital Asset Pricing Model: Between Asset Pricing and Asset Allocation. In *Multi-Moment Asset Allocation and Pricing Models*. New York: John Wiley and Sons.

Knight, John, and Stephen Satchell. 2002. *Performance Measurement in Finance*. Oxford: Elsevier Science Ltd.

Korzeniewski, Jerzy. 2018. Efficient Stock Portfolio Construction by Means of Clustering. *Folia Oeconomica* 1: 85–92. [CrossRef]

Kothari, Smitu P., and Jay Shanken. 1997. Book-to-market, dividend yield, and expected market returns: A time series analysis. *Journal of Financial Economics* 44: 169–203. [CrossRef]

Kroll, Yoram, Haim Levy, and Harry Markowitz. 1984. Mean-Variance Versus Direct Utility Maximization. *The Journal of Finance* 39: 47–61. [CrossRef]

Kuo, Yiyo, Taho Yang, and Guan-Wei Huang. 2008. The use of a grey-based Taguchi method for optimizing multi-response simulation problems. *Engineering Optimization* 40: 517–28. [CrossRef]

Lewellen, Jonathan. 2004. Predicting returns with financial ratios. *Journal of Financial Economics* 742: 209–35. [CrossRef]

Li, Hong-Yi, Chu Zhang, and Di Zhao. 2010. Stock Investment Value Analysis Model Based on AHP and Grey Relational Degree. *Management Science and Engineering* 4: 1–6.

Liu, Sifeng, and Yi Lin. 2006. *Grey Information Theory and Practical Applications*. New York: Springer.

Liu, Sifeng, and Yi Lin. 2010. *Grey Systems, Theory and Applications*. Berlin/Heidelberg: Springer.

Liu, Sifeng, Yingjie Yang, and Jeffery Forrest. 2016. *Grey Data Analysis: Methods, Models and Applications*. Singapore: Springer Science + Business Media.

Liu, Weimin. 2006. A liquidity-augmented capital asset pricing model. *Journal of Financial Economics* 823: 631–71. [CrossRef]

Markowitz, Harry. 1952. Portfolio Selection. *The Journal of Finance* 7: 77–91. [CrossRef]

Markowitz, Harry. 1959. *Portfolio Selection: Efficient Diversification of Investments*. New York: Wiley.

Ministry of Finance. 2018. Available online: https://www.mfin.hr (accessed on 13 December 2018).

Mohammadi Pour, Rahmatollah, Zhaleh Alavimoghadam, and Adel Fatemi. 2016. Comparison of Selected Performance of Portfolio Investment Companies by Using of Grey Forecasting and Johnson's Index in Tehran Stock Exchange Market. *Advances in Mathematical Finance & Applications* 1: 15–28.

Muhammad, Noor, and Frank Scrimgeour. 2014. Stock Returns and Fundamentals in the Australian Market. *Asian Journal of Finance & Accounting* 6: 271–90. [CrossRef]

Müller, Sigrid, and Mark Machina. 1987. Moment preferences and polynomial utility. *Economics Letters* 23: 349–53. [CrossRef]

Palepu, Krishna, and Paul Healy. 2010. *Business Analysis & Valuation: Using Financial Statements*, 4th ed. Nashville: South-Western College Pub.

Pástor, L'uboš, and Robert Stambaugh. 2003. Liquidity risk and expected stock returns. *Journal of Political Economy* 1113: 642–85. [CrossRef]

Pulley, Lawrence. 1981. A General Mean-Variance Approximation to Expected Utility for Short Holding Periods. *Journal of Financial and Quantitative Analysis* 16: 361–73. [CrossRef]

Reinganum, Marc. 1981. Misspecification of asset pricing: Empirical anomalies based on earnings yields and market values. *Journal of Financial Economics* 9: 19–46. [CrossRef]

Salardini, Firoozeh. 2013. An AHP-GRA method for asset allocation: A case study of investment firms on Tehran Stock Exchange. *Decision Science Letters* 2: 275–80. [CrossRef]

Shiller, Robert. 2005. *Irrational Exuberance*, 2nd ed. Princeton: Princeton University Press.

Singh, Arjun, and Raymond Schmidgall. 2002. Analysis of financial ratios commonly used by US lodging financial executives. *Journal of Retail & Leisure Property* 2: 201–13. [CrossRef]

Steuer, Ralph, Yue Qi, and Markus Hirschberger. 2008. Portfolio Selection in the Presence of Multiple Criteria. In *Handbook of Financial Engineering*. New York: Springer Science, pp. 3–24.

Škrinjarić, Tihana. 2018a. Revisiting Herding Investment Behavior on the Zagreb Stock Exchange: A Quantile Regression Approach. *Econometric Research in Finance* 3: 119–62.

Škrinjarić, Tihana. 2018b. Testing for Seasonal Affective Disorder on Selected CEE and SEE Stock Markets. *Risks* 6: 140. [CrossRef]

Vidović, Jelena. 2013. Investigation of Stock Illiquidity on Central and South East European markets in Naive Portfolio Framework. *Economic Thought and Practice* 22: 537–50.

Wei, Guiwu. 2011. Grey Relational Analysis Model for Dynamic Hybrid Multiple Attribute Decision Making. *Knowledge-Based Systems* 24: 672–79. [CrossRef]

Wu, Liansheng. 2000. A Survey and An Analysis of Investor's Demands for Listed Companies' Accounting Information. *Economic Research Journal* 4: 41–48.

ZSE. 2018. Available online: https://www.zse.hr (accessed on 1 November 2018).

2

Stock Market Analysis: A Review and Taxonomy of Prediction Techniques

Dev Shah, Haruna Isah * and Farhana Zulkernine

School of Computing, Queen's University, Kingston, ON K7L 2N8, Canada; dshah@cs.queensu.ca (D.S.); farhana@cs.queensu.ca (F.Z.)

* Correspondence: isah@cs.queensu.ca

Abstract: Stock market prediction has always caught the attention of many analysts and researchers. Popular theories suggest that stock markets are essentially a random walk and it is a fool's game to try and predict them. Predicting stock prices is a challenging problem in itself because of the number of variables which are involved. In the short term, the market behaves like a voting machine but in the longer term, it acts like a weighing machine and hence there is scope for predicting the market movements for a longer timeframe. Application of machine learning techniques and other algorithms for stock price analysis and forecasting is an area that shows great promise. In this paper, we first provide a concise review of stock markets and taxonomy of stock market prediction methods. We then focus on some of the research achievements in stock analysis and prediction. We discuss technical, fundamental, short- and long-term approaches used for stock analysis. Finally, we present some challenges and research opportunities in this field.

Keywords: stock exchanges; stock markets; analysis; prediction; statistics; machine learning; pattern recognition; sentiment analysis

JEL Classification: G10; G15; G17; D53

1. Introduction

Financial markets are one of the most fascinating inventions of our time. They have had a significant impact on many areas like business, education, jobs, technology and thus on the economy (Hiransha et al. 2018). Over the years, investors and researchers have been interested in developing and testing models of stock price behaviour (Fama 1995). However, analysing stock market movements and price behaviours is extremely challenging because of the markets dynamic, nonlinear, nonstationary, nonparametric, noisy, and chaotic nature (Abu-Mostafa and Atiya 1996). According to Zhong and Enke (2017), stock markets are affected by many highly interrelated factors that include economic, political, psychological, and company-specific variables. Technical and fundamental analysis are the two main approaches to analyse the financial markets (Park and Irwin 2007; Nguyen et al. 2015). To invest in stocks and achieve high profits with low risks, investors have used these two major approaches to make decisions in financial markets (Arévalo et al. 2017).

According to Hu et al. (2015), fundamental analysis is mainly based on three essential aspects (i) macroeconomic analysis such as Gross Domestic Product (GDP) and Consumer Price Index (CPI) which analyses the effect of the macroeconomic environment on the future profit of a company, (ii) industry analysis which estimates the value of the company based on industry status and prospect, and (iii) company analysis which analyses the current operation and financial status of a company to evaluate its internal value. Different valuation approaches exist for fundamental analysis. The average growth approximation technique compares Stock-A with other stocks in the same category to better understand valuations, i.e., assuming two companies have the same growth rate, the one with the lower Price-to-Earnings (P/E) ratio is considered to be better. Hence the fair price is the earnings times target P/E. The P/E method is the most commonly used valuation method in the stock brokerage industry (Imam et al. 2008). The constant growth approximation technique such as Gordon's growth model (Gordon and Shapiro 1956; Gordon 1959) is one of the best-known classes of dividend discount models. It assumes that dividends of a company will increase at a constant growth rate forever but less than the discount rate. Dutta et al. (2012) demonstrated the utility of fundamental analysis through the use of financial ratios to separate good stocks from poor stocks. The authors compared their one-year return against the benchmark—i.e., Nifty—which gives an accuracy of 74.6%. This is one of the few papers which focus on using fundamental features (i.e., company-specific ratios) to identify stocks for investments.

Furthermore, Hu et al. (2015) grouped the domains of technical analysis into sentiment, flow-of-funds, raw data, trend, momentum, volume, cycle, and volatility. Sentiment represents the behaviours of various market participants. Flow-of-funds is a type of indicator used to investigate the financial status of various investors to pre-evaluate their strength in terms of buying and selling stocks, then, corresponding strategies, such as short squeeze, can be adopted. Raw data include stock price series and price patterns such as K-line diagrams and bar charts. Trend and momentum are examples of price-based indicators, trend is used for tracing the stock price trends while momentum is used to evaluate the velocity of the price change and judge whether a trend reversal in stock price is about to occur. Volume is an indicator that reflects the enthusiasm of both buyers and sellers for investing, it is also a basis for predicting stock price movements. The cycle is based on the theory that stock prices vary periodically in the form of a long cycle of more than 10 years containing short cycles of a few days or weeks. Finally, volatility is often used to investigate the fluctuation range of stock prices and to evaluate risk and identify the level of support and resistance.

Sentiments can drive short-term market fluctuations which in turn cause disconnects between the price and true value of a company's shares but over long periods of time, however, the weighing machine kicks in as a company's fundamentals ultimately cause the value and market price of its shares to converge. A prominent example comes from the Nobel Laureate Robert Shiller, who showed that stock prices are extremely volatile over the short term but somewhat predictable by their price-to-earnings over long periods (Shiller 1980). Diamond (2000) explained what returns to expect from the stock markets considering the economic scenario and suggested that in the future, returns could be substantially lower. Shiller (2000) also suggested that stocks are overvalued, and the bubble will burst anytime. In the year 2000, rightly so, we witnessed the dotcom bubble burst.

Stock market price prediction is a tricky thing. Several theories regarding stock markets have been conceptualized over the years. They either try to explain the nature of stock markets or try to explain whether the markets can be beaten. One such popular and most debated theory given by Fama (1970) is the Efficient Market Hypothesis (EMH) which states that at any point in time, the market price of a stock incorporates all information about that stock. In other words, the stock is accurately valued until something changes. There are three variants of EMH (i) the weak form which is consistent with the random walk hypothesis (Fama 1995), and that stock prices move randomly while price changes are independent of each other hence, it is not possible to beat the market by earning abnormal returns on the basis of technical analysis; (ii) the semi-strong form which states that prices adjusted rapidly according to market and public information such as dividend, earnings announcements, and political or economic events, hence it is not possible to earn abnormal returns on the basis of fundamental analysis; and, finally, (iii) the strong form which states that prices reflect market, public, and private information as such no investor has monopolistic access to information (Naseer and Tariq 2015).

According to EMH, price changes are unpredictable and forecasting a financial market is a hopeless effort. However, (Abu-Mostafa and Atiya 1996) argued that the existence of so many price trends in financial markets and the undiscounted serial correlations among fundamental events and economic figures affecting the markets are two of many pieces of evidence against the EMH. Researchers and investors disagree with EMH both empirically and theoretically, thereby shifting the focus of discussion from EMH to the behavioural and psychological aspects of market players (Naseer and Tariq 2015). According to Zhong and Enke (2017), financial variables, such as stock prices, stock market index values, and the prices of financial derivatives are therefore thought to be predictable. Many widely accepted empirical studies show that financial markets are to some extent predictable (Chong et al. 2017). Criticism of EMH has given rise to an increasing number of studies that question the validity of EMH and introduce new and successful approaches that combine technical analysis indicators and chart patterns with methodologies from econometrics, statistics, data mining, and artificial intelligence (Arévalo et al. 2017).

Many new technologies and methods have been proposed over the years to try and predict stock prices via many avenues, thanks to the challenging and ever-changing landscape of stock markets (Chen and Chen 2016). In this paper, we focus on two topics, namely, stock analysis and stock prediction. We look at the research in the past, but mainly focus on modern techniques, highlighting some of the main challenges they pose and recent achievements for stock analysis and prediction. Finally, we discuss potential challenges and possible future research directions. We organize the rest of this paper as follows. Section 2 provides a background review and taxonomy of the various approaches to stock market analysis. Section 3 describes a literature study on stock markets analysis and prediction. Section 4 discusses and compares the approaches mentioned in Section 3. Section 5 provides an overview of challenges and additional areas for future research. Finally, Section 6 concludes the paper.

2. Taxonomy of Stock Market Analysis Approaches

Recent advancements in stock analysis and prediction fall under four categories—statistical, pattern recognition, machine learning (ML), and sentiment analysis. These categories mostly fall under the broader category of technical analysis, however, there are some machine learning techniques which also combine the broader categories of technical analysis with fundamental analysis approaches to predict the stock markets. Figure 1 shows a taxonomy of popular stock prediction techniques. These techniques have gained popularity and have shown promising results in the field of stock analysis in the recent past.

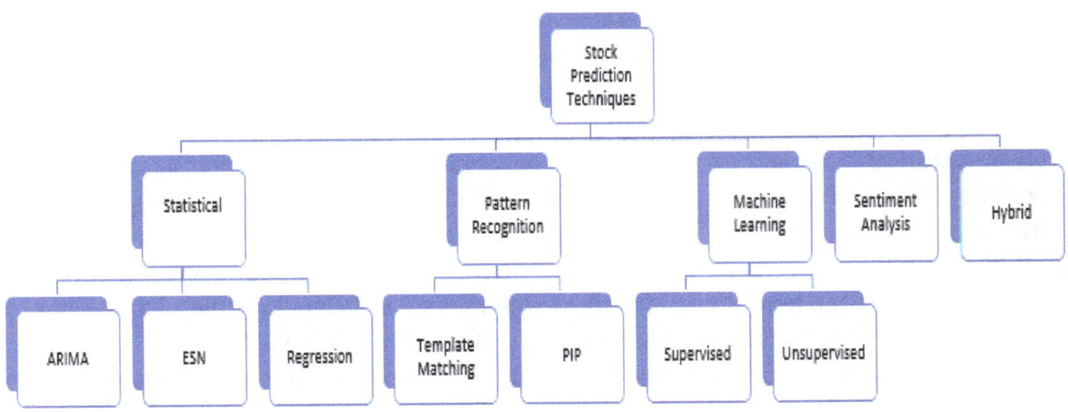

Figure 1. Taxonomy of stock prediction techniques.

Before the advent of machine learning techniques, statistical techniques which often assumes linearity, stationarity, and normality provided a way to analyse and predict stocks. Time series in stock market analysis is a chronological collection of observations such as daily sales totals and prices of stocks (Fu et al. 2005). According to Zhong and Enke (2017), one group of statistical approaches which fall into the category of univariate analysis, due to their use of time series as input variables, are the Auto-Regressive Moving Average (ARMA), the Auto-Regressive Integrated Moving Average (ARIMA), the Generalized Autoregressive Conditional Heteroskedastic (GARCH) volatility, and the

Smooth Transition Autoregressive (STAR) model. The ARIMA model is a widely used technique for stock market analysis (Hiransha et al. 2018). ARMA combines Auto-Regressive (AR) models which try to explain the momentum and mean reversion effects often observed in trading markets and Moving Average (MA) models which try to capture the shock effects observed in time series. A key limitation of the ARMA model is that it does not consider volatility clustering, a key empirical phenomenon in many financial time series. ARIMA is a natural extension to the class of ARMA models and can reduce a non-stationary series to a stationary series. The ARIMA (Box et al. 2015) is fitted to time series data to forecast future points. Zhong and Enke (2017) further describe another group of statistical approaches which usually utilize multiple input variables, these include Linear Discriminant Analysis (LDA), Quadratic Discriminant Analysis (QDA), and regression algorithms.

Pattern recognition is synonymous to machine learning but with respect to stock analysis, these two techniques are, however, applied in very different ways. Pattern recognition focuses on the detection of patterns and trends in data (Fu and Young 1986; Wang and Chan 2007; Parracho et al. 2010). Patterns in stock markets are recurring sequences found in Open-High-Low-Close (OHLC) candlestick charts which traders have historically used as buy and sell signals (Velay and Daniel 2018). Technical analysis relies on patterns found directly in stock data; it involves the visual analysis of charts constructed over time to show variations in price, volume, or other derived indicators such as price momentum (Nesbitt and Barrass 2004). Charting is a technique of technical analysis for comparing market price and volume history to chart patterns for predicting future price behaviour based on the degree of match (Leigh et al. 2002). Familiar chart patterns typically derived from their shapes are gaps, spikes, flags, pennants, wedges, saucers, triangles, head-and-shoulders, and various tops and bottoms (Park and Irwin 2007). Patterns of stock prices have the capacity to inform an investor of the future evolution of that stock (Parracho et al. 2010). Two widely used pattern recognition methods are Perceptually Important Points (PIP), which involve reducing time-series dimensions (i.e., the number of data point) by preserving the salient points and template matching, a technique used to match a given stock pattern with a pictographic image for object identification (Chen and Chen 2016). According to (Velay and Daniel 2018), many studies have found some correlation between patterns and future trends.

Machine learning has been extensively studied for its potentials in the prediction of financial markets (Shen et al. 2012). Machine learning tasks are broadly classified into supervised and unsupervised learning. In supervised learning, a set of labelled input data for training the algorithm and observed output data are available. However, in unsupervised learning, only the unlabelled or observed output data is available. The goal of supervised learning is to train an algorithm to automatically map the input data to the given output data. When trained, the machine would have learned to see an input data point and predict the expected output. The goal of unsupervised learning is to train an algorithm to find a pattern, correlation, or cluster in the given dataset. It can also act as a precursor for supervised learning tasks (Bhardwaj et al. 2015). Several algorithms have been used in stock price direction prediction. Simpler techniques such as the single decision tree, discriminant analysis, and naïve Bayes have been replaced by better-performing algorithms such as Random Forest, logistic regression, and neural networks (Ballings et al. 2015). With nonlinear, data-driven, and easy-to-generalize characteristics, multivariate analysis through the use of deep Artificial Neural Networks (ANNs) has become a dominant and popular analysis tool in the financial market analysis (Zhong and Enke 2017). Recently, deep nonlinear neural network topologies are beginning to attract attention in time series prediction (Bao et al. 2017).

Sentiment analysis is another approach which has lately been used for stock market analysis (Bollen et al. 2011). It is the process of predicting stock trends via automatic analysis of text corpuses such as news feeds or tweets specific to stock markets and public companies. The sentiment classification techniques are mainly divided into machine learning approach and lexicon-based approach which is further divided into dictionary-based or corpus-based approaches (Bhardwaj et al. 2015). Seng and Yang (2017) demonstrated the potential of using sentiment signals from an unstructured text for improving the efficiency of models for predicting volatility trends in the stock market.

The hybrid approach applies a combination of multiple different approaches for improved performance, for example, a hybrid of statistical and pattern recognition approaches, or a hybrid of statistical and machine learning approaches. The next section describes some of the recent work on different algorithms and methods under each class in Figure 1, and additionally discusses several hybrid approaches which have been used in stock market prediction.

3. Literature Survey

Based on the taxonomy shown in Figure 1, this paper presents a literature study on some of the most popular techniques that have been applied for stock prediction.

3.1. Statistical Approach

Numerous statistical techniques have been tried and tested for stock market analysis and prediction. The Exponential Smoothing Model (ESM) is a popular smoothing technique which is applied on time series data, it essentially uses the exponential window function for smoothing time series data and analyse the same (Billah et al. 2006). De Faria et al. (2009) compared the ANN and adaptive ESM model for predicting the Brazilian stock indices. Their experiment revealed the predictive power of ESM and the results for both methods show similar performances although the neural network model i.e., the multilayer feedforward network slightly outperformed the adaptive ESM in terms of the Root Means Square Error (RMSE). Dutta et al. (2012) took an interesting path by selecting the financial ratios as independent variables for a logistic regression model and then analysed the relationship between these ratios and the stock performances. The paper focused on a classification task for predicting companies which are good or poor based on their one-year performance. The results show that the financial ratios—like net sales, book value PE, price-to-book (P/B), EBITDA, etc.—classify the companies into good and poor classes with an accuracy of 74.6%, which is a good indication of why company health matters in stock analysis and prediction.

Devi et al. (2013) tried to address some issues not currently addressed in most of the stock analysis literature, such as the dimensionality and expectancy of a naïve investor. The authors essentially utilize the historical data of four Indian midcap companies for training the ARIMA model. The Akaike Information Criterion Bayesian Information Criterion (AICBIC) test was applied to predict the accuracy of the model. Testing the model on individual stocks and the Nifty 50 Index showed that the Nifty Index is the way to go for naïve investors because of low error and volatility.

Ariyo et al. (2014) explore the extensive process of building ARIMA models. To identify the optimal model out of all the ARIMA models generated, the authors chose criteria like the standard error of regression, adjusted R-square, and Bayesian information criteria. The best ARIMA model, based on the above criteria, did a satisfactory job in predicting the stock prices of Nokia and Zenith Bank. Furthermore, Ariyo et al. (2014) made a solid case not to undermine the powers of ARIMA models in terms of stock analysis because it can compete reasonably well against the emerging forecasting techniques available today for short term prediction.

Bhuriya et al. (2017) implemented variants of regression models to predict the stock price of Tata Consultancy Services stock based on five features i.e., open, high, low, close price, and volume. The paper compares the performances of the linear, polynomial, and Radial Basis Function (RBF) regression models based on the confidence values of the predicted results. In addition, Bhuriya et al. (2017) reported that the linear regression model outperformed the other techniques and achieved a confidence value of 0.97.

3.2. Pattern Recognition

Pattern recognition techniques do pattern matching to identify future trends based on historical templates. Fu et al. (2005) suggested an approach to identifying patterns in time series data more efficiently using human visualization concept of PIP. The results from their experiments suggest that the PIP approach not only reduces dimensionality but also allows for early detection of patterns when compared to template matching, because it uses a subsequence pattern matching approach by slicing time series data using the sliding window approach.

Leigh et al. (2008) challenged the EMH (Fama 1970) theory by showing that profits obtained using the heuristic method would be better than trading randomly. They utilized a bull flag pattern, which indicates a rise in prices in the near future and built a recognizer for identifying this pattern using template matching. The technique was applied on 9000 trading days of NYSE closing prices and the results show that the trading approach beats the average market profit most of the times, hence reinforcing the credibility of the technical analysis.

Parracho et al. (2010) proposed an approach to combine template matching with Genetic Algorithms (GA) for creating an algorithmic trading system. Template matching is utilized to identify upward trends and the GA helps in identifying the optimal values for the parameters used in template matching, i.e., fit buy, fit sell, noise removal, and window size. The trading strategy is trained on the S&P 500 stock data from 1998–2004 and tested on the 2005–2010 data. The results show that it outperforms the buy and hold strategy on an index and gets decent results for the individual stocks as well when compared to the buy and hold strategy.

Phetchanchai et al. (2010) proposed an innovative approach to analyse financial time series data by considering the zigzag movement in the data. In order to identify the Zigzag movements, the PIP technique was selected and the Zigzag based Mary tree (ZM-tree) was used for organizing these important points. The proposed technique illustrates a better performance in dimensionality reduction than existing techniques like Specialized Binary Trees (SB-Tree).

Cervelló-Royo et al. (2015) proposed a chart pattern based trading rule using the flag pattern. The study extends previous work by introducing two new parameters, stop loss and take profit, which allows the dynamic modelling of the closing of operations. It also employs intraday data to allow considerable width in the number of observations in the sample. Furthermore, Cervelló-Royo et al. (2015) considered both the opening and the closing prices to widen the information scope when deciding whether or not to start an operation. According to the authors, the results confirmed the positive performance of the flag pattern over the intraday data of the Dow Jones Industrial Average (DJIA) for a time horizon of more than 13 years. The results were also validated using two leading European indexes: the German stock index or Deutscher Aktienindex (DAX) and the Financial Times Stock Exchange (FTSE). It also provides empirical evidence which confronts the EMH (Fama 1970) indicating how it is possible to develop an investment strategy capable of beating the market in the mean-variance sense.

Chen and Chen (2016) proposed a hybrid approach to identify bull flag patterns on the Taiwan Capitalization Weighted Stock Index (TAIEX) and National Association of Securities Dealers Automated Quotations (NASDAQ) indices. The authors developed a methodology that combines the advantages of two traditional pattern recognition methods (PIP and template matching). Their proposed hybrid approach outperformed the other models like Rough Set Theory (RST), GA, and a hybrid model of GA and RST (Cheng et al. 2010) by a good margin in terms of total index returns.

Arévalo et al. (2017) offer a robust mechanism to dynamically trade DJIA based on filtered flag pattern recognition using template matching, based on the initial work of Cervelló-Royo et al. (2015). The authors impose multiple filters before considering the flag patterns as actionable for making trades, based on Exponential Moving Averages (EMA) and price ranges of the detected patterns. Their approach performs much better than the base approach of Cervelló-Royo et al. (2015) and the buy and hold strategy, resulting in higher profit and lower risk.

Kim et al. (2018) build a Pattern Matching Trading System (PMTS) based on Dynamic Time Warping (DTW) algorithm in order to trade index futures on the Korea Composite Stock Price Index (KOSPI 200). Taking the morning 9:00–12:00 p.m. time series data as input for the sliding windows, the authors then use DTW in order to match with known patterns. This forms the basis of the trading strategy to be carried in the afternoon's session on the same trading day. Their approach generates good annualized returns and shows that most patterns are more profitable near the clearing time.

3.3. *Machine Learning*

Many machine learning techniques have been explored for stock price direction prediction (Ballings et al. 2015). ANN and Support Vector Regression (SVR) are two widely used machine learning algorithms for predicting stock price and stock market index values (Patel et al. 2015). A literature survey of supervised and unsupervised machine learning methods applied in stock market analysis will be presented next.

3.3.1. Supervised Learning

Supervised learning techniques like Support Vector Machine (SVM) and Decision Trees can learn to predict stock market prices and trends based on historical data and provide meaningful analysis of historical price. Bernal et al. (2012) implemented a subclass of Recurrent Neural Networks (RNN) known as Echo State Networks (ESN) to predict S&P 500 stock prices using price, moving averages, and volume as features. The technique outperforms the Kalman Filter technique with a meagre test error of 0.0027. In order to generalize and validate their result, Bernal et al. (2012) examined the algorithm on 50 other stocks and reported that their results performed well against state of the art techniques.

Ballings et al. (2015) benchmark ensemble methods consisting of Random Forest, AdaBoost, and Kernel Factory against single classifier models such as Neural Networks, Logistic Regression, Support Vector Machines, and K-Nearest Neighbor using data from 5767 publicly listed European companies. The authors used five times two-fold cross-validation and Area Under the Curve (AUC) as a performance measure for predict long term stock price direction and reported Random Forest as the top algorithm.

Milosevic (2016) proposed an approach for long term prediction of stock market prices through a classification task where a stock is 'good' if the stock price increases by 10% in a year otherwise it is a 'bad'. Furthermore, Milosevic (2016) performed a manual feature selection, selected 11 relevant fundamental ratios, and applied several machine learning algorithms to stock prediction. It follows that Random Forest achieved the best F-Score of 0.751 against techniques such as SVM and Naïve Bayes.

Another technique that has grappled the attention of data scientists is the eXtreme Gradient Boosting (XGBoost). Dey et al. (2016) predicted the direction of stocks based on XGBoost algorithm using the technical indicators as the features. The results show that XGBoost beats the other techniques in performance achieving an accuracy of 87–99% for long term prediction of Apple and Yahoo stocks.

Long Short-Term Memory (LSTM) network have shown a lot of promises for time series prediction; Di Persio and Honchar (2017) applied three different Recurrent Neural Network models namely a basic RNN, the LSTM, and the Gated Recurrent Unit (GRU) on Google stock price to evaluate which variant of RNN performs better. It was evident from the results that the LSTM outperformed other variants with a 72% accuracy on a five-day horizon and the authors also explained and displayed the hidden dynamics of RNN. Roondiwala et al. (2017) implemented an LSTM network to predict Nifty prices with features like OHLC. Their results show that the LSTM achieves an RMSE of 0.00859 for the test data in terms of daily percentage changes.

Yang et al. (2017) proposed an ensemble of multi-layer feedforward networks for Chinese stock prediction. Three component networks were trained using training algorithms like backpropagation and Adam. The ensemble was formed using the bagging approach (Efron and Tibshirani 1994). The results obtained demonstrate that the Chinese markets are partially predictable and achieve a satisfactory accuracy, precision, and recall.

Zhang et al. (2018) propose a stock price trend prediction system that can predict both stock price movement and its interval of growth (or decline) rate within predefined prediction durations. They trained a random forest model from historical data from the Shenzhen Growth Enterprise Market (China) to classify multiple clips of stocks into four main classes (up, down, flat, and unknown) according to the shapes of their close prices. Their evaluation shows that the proposed system is robust to the market volatility and outperforms some existing predictions methods in terms of accuracy and return per trade.

Hossain et al. (2018) propose a deep learning-based hybrid model that consists of two well-known DNN architectures: LSTM and GRU. The authors trained a prediction model using S&P 500 time series dataset spanning about 66 years (1950 to 2016). The approach involves passing the input data to the LSTM network to generate a first level prediction and then passing the output of LSTM layer to the GRU layer to get the final prediction. The proposed network achieved a Mean Squared Error (MSE) of 0.00098 in prediction with outperforming previous neural network approaches.

Recently, Lv et al. (2019) synthetically evaluated various ML algorithms and observed the daily trading performance of stocks under transaction cost and no transaction cost. They utilized 424 S&P 500 index component stocks (SPICS) and 185 CSI 300 Index Component Stocks (CSICS) between 2010 and 2017 and compared traditional machine learning algorithms with advanced deep neural network (DNN) models. The traditional machine learning algorithms are SVM, Random Forest, Logistic Regression, naïve Bayes, Classification and Regression Tree (CART), and eXtreme Gradient Boosting while the DNN architectures include Multilayer Perceptron (MLP), Deep Belief Network (DBN), Stacked Autoencoders (SAE), RNN, LSTM, and GRU. Their results show that traditional machine learning algorithms have a better performance in most of the directional evaluation indicators without considering the transaction cost, however, DNN models show better performance considering transaction cost.

3.3.2. Unsupervised Learning

Unsupervised learning helps to identify correlations in an uncorrelated dataset like stock markets. Powell et al. (2008) drew a comparison between the supervised technique SVM and unsupervised technique K-means. They perform Principal Component Analysis (PCA) to reduce the dimensions or features. Both models are tested on S&P 500 data and the results show that both techniques have similar performance, SVM achieves 89.1% and K-means achieves 85.6% respectively. They also state how different distance measures for clustering affect the prediction accuracy and the best performance is shown by the Canberra distance metric.

Babu et al. (2012) proposed a clustering method called the HAK by combining the Hierarchical Agglomerative Clustering (HAC) and the reverse K-means clustering to predict the short-term impact on stocks after the release of financial reports. The study compared three different clustering techniques namely the HAC, K-means, and the reverse K-means. It also compared the proposed HRK against the three techniques and the SVM. Firstly, HAK takes financial reports and stock quotes as input and uses text analysis to convert each financial report into a feature vector. It then divides the feature vectors into clusters using HAC. Secondly, for each cluster, the K-means clustering method was applied to partition each cluster into sub-clusters and for each sub-cluster the centroids were computed. Finally, the centroids were used as the representative feature vectors to predict stock price movements. The experimental results show that the proposed technique outperforms SVM in terms of accuracy.

Wu et al. (2014) proposed a model based on the AprioriAll algorithm (association rule learning) and K-means. They converted stock data into charts using a sliding window and then the charts were clustered using K-means to extract chart patterns. Frequent patterns were extracted using AprioriAll to predict trends that are often associated (bought or sold together). The results show that their model outperforms other related work (Wang and Chan 2007; Chen 2011) in terms of average returns and also mutual funds.

Peachavanish (2016) proposes a clustering method to identify a group of stocks with the best trend and momentum characteristics at a given time, and therefore are most likely to outperform the market during a short time period. The author conducted an experiment on five-year historical price data of stocks listed on the Stock Exchange of Thailand (SET) and reported that the proposed method can outperform the market in the long run. Table 1 presents a summary of the existing literature on supervised ML approaches.

Table 1. Summary of literature on ML approaches applied to stock prediction.

Paper	Dataset	Features	Technique	Prediction Type	Metrics	Results
Leigh et al. (2008)	NYSE	Price	Template Matching	Daily	Average profits	3.1–4.59%
Bernal et al. (2012)	S&P 500	Price, MA, volume	ESN RNN	Daily	Test Error	0.0027
Milosevic (2016)	1700+ individual stocks	Price, 10 financial ratios	Random Forest vs. SVM vs. NB vs. Logistic Regression	Classification (good vs. bad)	Precision, Recall and F-score	0.751 (Random Forest)
Dey et al. (2016)	Apple, Yahoo	Technical indicators	XGBoost vs. SVM vs. ANN	Daily	Accuracy	85–99% (XGBoost)
Di Persio and Honchar (2017)	Google Stock	OHLCV	RNN vs. LSTM vs. GRU	Daily, Weekly	Log loss, accuracy	72%, 5 day (LSTM)
Yang et al. (2017)	Shanghai composite index	OHLCV	Ensemble of DNN's	Daily	Accuracy, relative error	71.34%
Zhang et al. (2018)	Shenzhen GE Market	Price trends	Random Forest	Classification (up, down, flat, and unknown)	Return per trade	75.1%

3.4. Sentiment Analysis

Sentiments can drive short-term market fluctuations which in turn causes a disconnect between the stock price and the true value of a company's share. Over long periods of time, however, the weighing machine kicks in as the fundamentals of a company ultimately cause the value and market price of its shares to converge. Sentiments are a big part of stock markets and the idea of analysing sentiments based on various data sources can give insights on how stock markets react to different kinds of news in the immediate and medium term. Hence a novel approach—sentimental analysis—has emerged which gauges the sentiment from data sources or sentiment behind the news to identify its impact on the markets.

Schumaker and Chen (2009) determined the effects of breaking news on stock prices within 20 min after the release. An SVM derivative model was proposed based on three different textual representations namely the Bag of Words (BoW) model, the Noun Phrases model, and the Named Entities model. First, news data was gathered and stored in a database using the three different textual representations. Next, the authors fetched the closing prices of the respective stocks for the last 60 min and used Support Vector Regression to predict the price for the next 20 min based on the price and sentiment analysis. The experiments showed that the model significantly outperformed the simple linear regression model in terms of closeness, directional accuracy and simulated trading. The authors also stated that noun phrases method performed much better when compared to the bag of words and named entities models.

Bollen et al. (2011) were one of the first studies to have considered Twitter data to predict stock trends. They analysed the Twitter data using Google Profile of Mood States (GPOMS) and Opinion Finder to understand correlations and predict DJIA closing prices. In addition, Bollen et al. (2011) cross-validated the Opinion Finder and GPOMS time series against popular events like presidential election and thanksgiving to gauge the public mood. They applied a granger causative analysis to determine whether one time series is dependent on another. After applying a Self-Organizing Fuzzy Neural Network (SOFNN) on a dataset of approximately 10 million tweets and DJIA closing prices from February to December 2008, the technique achieved an accuracy of 87.6% in predicting daily values of DJIA.

Mittal and Goel (2012) based their work on the study by Bollen et al. (2011), however they tested the proposed approach on a larger dataset of over 400+ million tweets. They preprocessed missing days data consisting of weekends and public holidays by replacing the missing values with the average value. They then applied a portfolio management strategy based on the Bollen et al. (2011) technique. They adjusted sharp rise and fall in prices to get a steady daily directional trend; they also removed data of volatile periods because of the inherent difficulty to predict such periods and made use of four classes of moods instead of two namely happy, alert, calm, and kind. Their technique achieved an accuracy of 75% and the portfolio management strategy achieved a decent profit over a 40-day testing period. Moreover, their work gave further insight that not only 'calmness' but also 'happiness' is granger causative over a range of three to four days.

Lee et al. (2014) proposed an approach to determine the importance of text analysis in stock market prediction. Form 8-K reports include important updates regarding the company. The authors created a system to predict whether a stock's price will go up, down, or stay the same by performing sentiment analysis on the 8-K reports of the respective stocks. Lee et al. (2014) ran their model first with only financial features and then again using financial and linguistic features (unigrams). It was observed that the most important feature was the 'earnings surprise' and that the text analysis helped to improve the model's accuracy by 10%. Their work also put forth an interesting finding that the effect of sentiment analysis on the 8-K reports diminishes quickly with time. Therefore, these would only be suitable for short term predictions.

Kalyanaraman et al. (2014) proposed a sentiment analysis model to gauge sentiments from news articles and feed the output from the model into two different machine learning algorithms. The authors made use of Bing API to get the news for a set of companies. They created their own dictionary to categorize positive and negative sentiments with respect to the stock market domain due to the lack of such open source dictionaries. The words in the article were compared against the dictionary and were tagged as positive and negative along with their frequencies. For example, a score of −3 would be assigned if a negative word appeared three times in the article. The output from the model was then fed into a linear regression model which used gradient descent for optimization. Results showed that the machine learning model using gradient descent was able to predict the sentiment of a news article with an accuracy of 60% when compared to manual analysis. Moreover, the ML model achieved an accuracy of 81.82% for predicting the actual stock prices.

Cakra and Trisedya (2015) tried to predict the price, price fluctuation, and margin percentage of Indonesian stocks using a simple sentiment analysis model coupled with classification techniques and a linear regression predictive model. The authors classified tweets into 'positive', 'negative', and 'neutral' classes. The work disregarded 'neutral' tweets as they were considered to be promotional and spam tweets. They retrieved lexicon sentiment semi-automatically from the data. First the corpus was tokenized into single words using the Indonesian dictionary. Next, formal words that were categorized as lexicons were chosen and informal words were manually checked by searching similar words. Then the positive and negative lexicons were separated. Their experiments suggested that the Random Forest algorithm produced the best result in classifying tweets amongst other algorithms with an accuracy of 60.39%. Cakra and Trisedya (2015) achieved an accuracy of 67.37% on price fluctuation prediction based on the classification of the tweets data using the Naive Bayes algorithm and 66.34% using the Random Forest algorithm.

Pagolu et al. (2016) implemented a sentiment analysis model based on Twitter data. The authors used N-gram and Word2vec (2-layer NN) to analyse the polarity of sentiments behind the tweets. They achieved an accuracy of around 70% and noted that the correlation between price and sentiments was 71.82%. The study concluded that with more data, the accuracy of the model would increase. Other approaches that utilized natural language and social media data include the study by Xu and Cohen (2018) which present StockNet, a neural network architecture for predicting stock price movement from tweets and historical stock prices. The model demonstrates a state-of-the-art performance and introduces recurrent, continuous latent variables for better treatment of stochasticity. Table 2 presents a summary of the literature study on sentiment analysis approaches.

Table 2. Summary of literature on sentiment analysis approaches applied to stock prediction.

Paper	Dataset	Technique	Prediction Type	Metrics	Results
Schumaker and Chen (2009)	News articles, S&P 500	Bag of words vs. noun phrases vs. noun entities → SVM	Daily	Returns, DA	2.57% (Noun phrases)
Bollen et al. (2011)	DJIA, Twitter data	Mood Indicators → SOFNN	Daily	Accuracy	87.14%
Lee et al. (2014)	8-K Reports, Stock prices, volatility	Ngram → Random Forest	Daily, long term	Accuracy	>10% (Increase in accuracy)
Kalyanaraman et al. (2014)	News articles (Bing API)	Dictionary approach → Linear Regression	Daily	Accuracy	81.82%
Pagolu et al. (2016)	MSFT price, Twitter data	Ngram + word vec → Random Forest	Daily	Accuracy	70.1%

3.5. Hybrid Approach

The hybrid approach applies a combination of multiple different approaches, for example, statistical and pattern recognition approaches, or statistical and machine learning approaches. Markowska-Kaczmar and Dziedzic (2008) implemented a supervised feedforward neural network technique to identify patterns in stock data and use the PIP technique to reduce the dimensionality and find only the important points of the patterns. The PIP technique was found to doing a fair job in discovering patterns on shortened time series datasets.

Tiwari et al. (2010) proposed an intriguing hybrid model by combining the statistical Hierarchical Hidden Markov model (HHMM) with supervised learning technique using decision trees to predict the Bombay Stock Exchange Sensitive Index (BSE SENSEX) trend based on its historical closing prices, dividends and earnings. After the extraction of features from the dataset, relevant features were selected by a decision tree. Then a set-based classifier was used for prediction while the HHMM was used to evaluate the predictions and for generating the final predictions which yield an accuracy of 92.1%.

Shen et al. (2012) proposed a prediction algorithm which combined statistical and SVM approaches. The technique exploits correlations amongst global markets and other products to predict the next day trend of stock prices. The authors chose varied datasets which might have an impact on each other such as the United States Dollar (USD), Japanese Yen (JPY), NASDAQ, gold, and oil prices, and drilled down important features via statistical methods like auto and cross correlation. Results of this study boasted a 77.6% prediction accuracy on the DJIA and up to 85% for longer-term predictions of more than 30 days.

Wang et al. (2012) present a Proposed Hybrid Model (PHM) which combines three models namely the ESM, ARIMA, and a Backpropagation Neural Network (BPNN) model, to leverage the strength of each model in predicting stock prices on a weekly basis. Results from this study show that the hybrid model outperforms the performances of the individual constituent sub-models and all traditional models when tested on the Shenzhen Integrated Index and DJIA with a directional accuracy of 70.16%.

Yoshihara et al. (2014) proposed an approach that considered the long-term effects of news events. The study employs a combination of the Recurrent Neural Networks Restricted Boltzmann Machine (RNN-RBM) and the Deep Belief Network (DBN) for predicting stock trends in a binary approach, i.e., up or down. Events represented as vectors using the bag of words model were given as inputs to the model. The results were compared against SVM and DBN and the proposed model achieved the lowest error rates amongst all.

Ding et al. (2015) proposed a hybrid approach which combined sentiment analysis and neural network models for the prediction of S&P 500 index. News events were represented as vectors and a deep Convolutional Neural Network (CNN) was trained to predict short and long-term influences of those events on the index. The study uses more than 10 million events over seven years and achieves an accuracy of 64.21% on the S&P 500 index and 65.48% on the individual stock price prediction.

Rather et al. (2015) proposed a hybrid model consisting of both the linear and non-linear approaches for predicting stock prices. The work combines the results of the component models namely the ARIMA, ESN, and the RNN models. The weights of each of the constituent models, which represent their effects on the prediction result were determined using a genetic algorithm. The proposed hybrid model achieves the lowest Mean Absolute Error (MAE) and MSE compared to the constituent models and outperforms the RNN in terms of price prediction.

Creighton and Zulkernine (2017) extended the original work of Wang et al. (2012) by applying the hybrid approach to daily stock price prediction and on different indices such as the S&P 400 and the S&P 500. The study by Creighton and Zulkernine (2017) showed that for the daily predictions, the hybrid model did not outperform its constituent models and the BPNN model gave the most accurate predictions. The statistical ARIMA and ESM models including the combined hybrid PHM could predict better for longer time range but suffered from price fluctuations when applied to the daily predictions. Table 3 presents a summary of the literature study on hybrid approaches.

Table 3. Summary of literature on hybrid approaches applied to stock prediction.

Paper	Dataset	Features	Technique	Prediction Type	Metrics	Results
Wang et al. (2012)	DJIA and SJI Index	Price	ESM + BPNN + ARIMA	Weekly	Directional Accuracy	70.16%
Tiwari et al. (2010)	Sensex + 3 stocks	Price, EPS and DPS	HHMM + Decision Trees	Daily	Accuracy	92.1%
Shen et al. (2012)	Indices, commodities	Asset prices	Auto, cross correlation + SVM	Daily, monthly	Accuracy	77.6%
Rather et al. (2015)	NSE stocks	Price, mean, SD	ARIMA + ESM + RNN + GA	Daily	Avg MSE, MAE	0.0009, 0.0127
Yoshihara et al. (2014)	Nikkei stocks, news articles	Word vectors	Bag of Words → DBN + RNN-RBM vs. SVM vs. DBN	Long term	Test error rates	39% (Lowest)
Ding et al. (2015)	S&P 500	Historical events	NN (event embeddings) + CNN	Weekly, Monthly	Accuracy & MCC	64.21%

4. Discussion

4.1. *Statistical*

It is evident from the surveyed literature that, despite the emergence of many techniques for stock prediction, statistical methods like ARIMA, ESM, Regression and their variants continue to be of interest for stock market forecasting due to their performance. For example, De Faria et al. (2009) provided a nice comparison between Adaptive ESM and NN which show that both models perform equally well except for the hit rates for forecasting stock direction where the NN does better. However, the study by De Faria et al. (2009) failed to provide information regarding the dataset and features used for the models. Nevertheless, it shows the power of statistical models and how they are still competing with emerging techniques like deep learning and hybrid models. Statistical models, in general, assume that there is a linear correlation structure in time series data. This is a limitation that emerging techniques are overcoming through combining statistical and machine learning or other techniques (Wang et al. 2012; Shen et al. 2012). One class of statistical model that is useful for understanding the risk or volatility in stock trading is ARIMA, this was demonstrated by Devi et al. (2013), that the Nifty index is a much better indicator of the volatility of stocks. Ariyo et al. (2014) predicted stock prices based on ARIMA and their results were convincing for stocks like Nokia and Zenith bank. However, the metrics that lead to the results could have been explained better and testing on more stocks would have provided a better picture.

4.2. Pattern Recognition

In general, pattern recognition techniques show promises but on their own do not give convincing results on stock prediction Velay and Daniel (2018). These techniques can be powerful for analysing and mining patterns rather than predicting the actual values. Therefore, instead of using pattern recognition techniques in isolation for stock prediction, it would be better if they were just used for identifying trends or in combination with prediction techniques. A recent pattern recognition model developed by Chen and Chen (2016) to ascertain the bull-flag patterns contained in historical stock patterns generated an unprecedented stock index return (TIR% and TIR) in forecasting the NASDAQ and TAIEX, indicating that the model can help stock analysts or stock investors to check stock patterns more carefully. This work seems to be promising and very thorough as they also consider the number of trades required for achieving such high TIR. However, their outperformance over other models seems to have two caveats. First, the proposed approach gives varying results depending upon the underlying index, which the authors address in the discussion section. Nonetheless, it would be valuable to see if their approach is able to generalize well for finding bull flag patterns across different stocks or indices and therefore achieve similar results as it did for TAIEX index. Second, it would have been interesting if the authors had shed more light as to why the 20-day holding variant was able to beat other models when compared to 5, 10, and 15-day holding variants.

Another interesting study that utilized a pattern recognition approach is the study by Arévalo et al. (2017) which suggest improvements to the trading strategy introduced by Cervelló-Royo et al. (2015). Arévalo et al. (2017) use the price ranges in which the detected bull/bear flag patterns lie in and test against the EMA (short and medium term) to successfully filter out patterns which would be worthwhile for making the trades in the first place. Most technical analysis studies do not take this into account. Arévalo et al. (2017) considered transaction costs and risk in order to determine the model's success. They apply robust and dynamic rules to make sure the take profit and stop loss levels for trade are not restricted to holding it for an x amount of days. Furthermore, they made sure that the take profit and stop loss levels are updated quarterly based on the best recent past performance of the trading rule. The authors use the OHLC dataset for DJIA and use intraday observations from 2000 to 2013 to test their trading strategy. The results indicate that their new and improved strategy performs better than the prior strategy (Cervelló-Royo et al. 2015) with higher profit and lesser risk which is commendable. The authors also test their strategy to make sure they pass the data snooping test (training on test data). Lastly, this study addresses all the parameters that Park and Irwin (2007) point out as being potential problems while determining profitability in technical analysis.

Most recently, Kim et al. (2018) propose a PMTS-based on dynamic time warping. The authors demonstrated how their PMTS performs with different parameters and found the most optimal set of parameters for trading resulting in higher Sharpe ratios. The strategy fetches above par annualized returns of about 9.58% returns with the most optimal parameter set. The authors claim that traders can use their PMTS to make more efficient trading decisions in order to help the markets to become more efficient. This claim seems to be a bit far-fetched because a lot of factors contribute to the market movements and their implicit assumption that the PMTS would always hold true for future market movements needs more evidence. Lastly, it would be interesting to see how their strategy would perform on normal stock trading instead of trading index futures and whether the later plays a role in the strategy's outcome.

4.3. Machine Learning

4.3.1. Supervised Learning

Machine Learning approaches, specifically supervised learning for stock prediction have shown great promises. Here we will discuss some recent and interesting results and highlighting their strengths or limitations. First, the study by Bernal et al. (2012) which evaluated an ESN network for stock prediction but do not give any reason behind comparing its performance against the Kalman Filter approach. Also, it is interesting to note that there is no increase in error as they forecast further into the future, which makes sense because the underlying dynamics of the stock were the same for the training and testing data. Thus, the paper does not consider the different dynamics that can prevail during the training and testing data periods respectively, which would render the approaches futile. A good way to work around the problem noted above would be to take a larger dataset which would cover a broader and varied set of stock market dynamics.

Another study by Milosevic (2016) applied a manual feature selection amongst financial ratios to understand identify optimal features. It is a wise approach because many ratios give little or no information regarding stock price movements. Furthermore, the author tests on 1700+ stocks and compared SVM, Naïve Bayes, and Logistic Regression with Random Forest; and found out that Random Forest outperforms the other approaches with a recall of 0.751. However, the methodology of classifying a stock as good or bad based on just one-year return being greater than 10% is not ideal. It should be compared with a benchmark, as done by Bernal et al. (2012) and Dutta et al. (2012).

Dey et al. (2016) explore a novel approach of Extreme Gradient Boosting (XGBoost) and compared it with SVM and ANN, in which XGBoost achieve superior results. However, the technique is tested on only two stocks and the model seems to be overfitting in the case where accuracy is 99% for Yahoo's stock prediction. Additional testing and transparency on overfitting would make a stronger case for their results. Di Persio and Honchar (2017) demonstrated why the LSTM variant is so popular and why it works better than the other RNN approaches. The authors further provided informative visualisations, which was able to explain how and when an RNN detects trends. This is a very interesting result. Another study that utilised LSTM is Roondiwala et al. (2017), however, the authors could not provide information about how they were able to prevent overfitting after training their LSTM network for 500 epochs.

Yang et al. (2017) used an ensemble of deep neural networks to predict Chinese stock markets. They utilized backpropagation and Adam training algorithms, however while training the network, the dataset was split into training and testing datasets only with no validation set, which is important for unbiased training of the network. The authors did not normalise the dataset (OHLC), which is also an important preprocessing step that can affect training algorithms as well as prediction results. Again, the ensemble model could not provide satisfactory predictions for an important feature i.e., closing prices of the indices. Nevertheless, the study highlights how an ensemble network performs better than its component networks for stock prediction. The model achieves an accuracy of 74.15% on high and low of Shanghai composite index and 73.95% and 72.34% respectively for the Shenzhen Stock Exchange component index. In terms of resources consumption, Bao et al. (2017) have observed that deep learning methods are time-consuming, and more attention should be paid to GPU-based and heterogeneous computing-based deep learning methods.

4.3.2. Unsupervised Learning

Unsupervised learning methods have been known to be equally strong for stock prediction. Powell et al. (2008) drew an effective comparison between SVM and K-means and explained which distance metric for K-means and which kernel function for SVM achieves best results. Additionally, for K-means it was observed that maximum accuracy is achieved with one feature, although they do not mention what other features were used, and which one feature worked out the best, post PCA.

Babu et al. (2012) proposed a clustering method called Hierarchical Agglomerative Clustering (HAC) and Reverse K-means clustering (HRK) to predict the short-term impact on stocks after the release of financial reports. Their experimental results show that the proposed technique outperforms K-means as well as the SVM in terms of accuracy, and the average profits for the HRK were 3.95% whereas SVM could only manage a profit of 1.46%. The paper nicely combines two clustering techniques to get the best features out of them and applied text analysis on financial reports to understand the impact of fundamental factors similar to Dutta et al. (2012).

Wu et al. (2014) proposed a model based on the AprioriAll algorithm (association rule learning) and K-means. This approach identifies patterns, initiates a buy position and then holds it until the end of the pattern. The results show that the proposed model outperforms the other related work (Wang and Chan 2007; Chen 2011) generating an average return of 2.22% compared to the 1.67% achieved by Wang and Chan (2007) and 1.5% achieved by Chen (2011) respectively. This is a particularly fascinating approach because not only does it outperform the other approaches, it does so with fewer trades and thus incurs lower trading costs. While comparing against mutual funds, the authors could not explain how they computed the annual returns from the 20-day return, because it seems to be outperforming the mutual funds by a huge margin. Another limitation is the assumption that the stock market patterns are repetitive, which may be true to some extent, but not always. Furthermore, if new patterns arise then the model needs to be retrained.

4.4. *Sentiment Analysis*

Sentiment analysis on social media is not an easy task because it is difficult to teach machines all the different contexts of how people express their emotions or opinions. For example, 'My flight has been delayed, Superb!', a human can quickly sense the sarcasm in this text, however a machine might identify this as a positive statement. For example, Bollen et al. (2011) used Twitter data to measure the correlations between the public comments and the changes in DJIA. The authors used an effective filtering technique to remove spam tweets, i.e., tweets are discarded if they contain the regular expression 'www.' or 'http://'. The 'calm' mood along with the historical prices as input to the SOFNN give 86.7% accuracy. However, the general assumption that the overall public mood affects the stock prices is naive because not all people who tweet invest in the stock markets (Pagolu et al. 2016). Hence a dataset of tweets pertaining to the general stock markets, specifically the DJIA, would be more indicative of the price changes in DJIA. The authors actually discussed these limitations and stated that by no means is the public mood is a good predictor of the changes in DJIA but that it may have some correlation. Mittal and Goel (2012) proposed their approach based on the work of Bollen et al. (2011). The difference between their work and Bollen et al. (2011) is that they chose a much larger dataset and observed that even 'happiness' is indicative of the DJIA prices. They also apply K-fold sequential cross-validation, which is apt for financial data and implemented a basic portfolio strategy which performs well. However, the accuracy achieved was lower than what Bollen et al. (2011) had reported.

Lee et al. (2014) proposed a text analysis model on the company's 8-K reports, which are more relevant compared to social media data. The authors demonstrated that text analysis helps to improve the prediction accuracy by 10%. According to Lee et al. (2014), the updates in 8-K reports have a short-term effect on stock prices, which makes sense because these reports contain company updates and a very few of them can affect the stock prices on a longer term.

Kalyanaraman et al. (2014) targeted a more reliable source of text data by creating their own dictionary to analyse sentiment polarity of sentences in news articles. The authors achieve an accuracy of 81.81% using linear regression with gradient descent optimisation. However, the accuracy is calculated over a long time period encompassing all selected news articles for each stock, and hence the results do not represent the true ability of the model to predict stock prices based on sentiment analysis of the news articles.

Cakra and Trisedya (2015) used five different algorithms for tweet classification, and the output is fed to a linear regression model for predicting Indonesian stock prices. A better alternative could be to try an ensemble of machine learning algorithms to better classify tweets and then feed it to a linear regressor model or a non-linear algorithm.

Finally, Pagolu et al. (2016) directly assessed tweets related to Microsoft's stock and its products and tried to predict the price of the stock for the next day. They achieved an accuracy of 71.82% with a small dataset containing only around 3000 tweets. The authors also addressed the issue that all Twitter participants are not in the stock market business, and plan to use a stock market specific social media platform to gather opinions of investors in their future work. This approach has two shortcomings; one, such techniques can be derailed by malicious or biased tweets; and two, Twitter data is already public and hence, provides an efficient and faster approach to access and process the tweets than other newly devised platforms. If not processed fast enough, social media data would already have influenced the stock prices, making the prediction useless.

4.5. Hybrid

Hybrid approaches combine multiple different approaches, for example, Markowska-Kaczmar and Dziedzic (2008) show how they effectively use the PIP approach for reducing dimensionality and identifying trends before they feed the data to a feedforward NN for prediction. A big disadvantage of PIP is that it would not accurately discover sequences if the time series has a high amplitude between two adjacent points.

Tiwari et al. (2010) proposed an intriguing hybrid model combining statistical Hierarchical Hidden Markov model (HHMM) with decision trees to predict BSE SENSEX trend which yields an accuracy of 92.1% making a strong point as to why hybrid approaches are powerful. However, the paper does not give detailed and transparent results, such as figures or tables describing how and why 92% accuracy was achieved. One of the results specified the predicted SENSEX value to be around 1.2567×10^3 i.e., 1256.7 in 2011 which should have been 12,567 instead. Again, the authors used a dataset with just 52 instances (yearly) partly because features like dividends and earnings are not declared daily, however using a quarterly approach would have given them a decent sized dataset to validate the results.

Wang et al. (2012) proposed a satisfactory PHM consisting of ARIMA, ESM and BPNN which give a directional accuracy of 70%. However, the results clearly demonstrated that BPNN outperforms statistical models like ARIMA and ESM for a weekly prediction of stock prices. Creighton and Zulkernine (2017) extended the work of Wang et al. (2012) for daily stock price prediction. Their results show that PHM is not as good in predicting daily prices compared to weekly prices and fortify the reasoning that daily price prediction is more difficult as it is susceptible to noise and price fluctuations including other factors. Both papers applied a genetic algorithm for deciding the weights of the component models in the PHM.

Shen et al. (2012) proposed a very good hybrid approach for feature selection based on statistical methods like auto and cross correlation, and use SVM algorithm to predict stock prices, which boasted a 77.6% prediction accuracy on the DJIA. For validation they predicted prices for the long term and got up to 85% accuracy. Also, to test the model's generalisability, the authors predicted on two other indices, the NASDAQ and the S&P 500. SVM in general is a powerful algorithm for a variety of problems, combining that with other statistical techniques like auto and cross correlation only makes it better as proposed by Shen et al. (2012).

Yoshihara et al. (2014) proposed a novel approach by combining DBN with RNN-RBM to better predict long term changes in stock prices based on significant events. The authors validated the distribution of data in train, test, and validation sets. The input to the model was the news events which were converted to vectors using the bag of words model. The results show that the hybrid model outperforms SVM and DBN achieving the lowest test error rate of 39%. The authors noted that if there are events which do not have long-term effects on stock prices then the proposed model's performance is similar to that of the DBN. Use of more performance metrics like accuracy or returns based on a trading strategy would have given more insights into the performances of their approach.

Ding et al. (2015) proposed a novel neural tensor network for learning event embeddings and used a deep CNN to model the influences of long and short-term events on stock price movements. The results show that event embedding based representations work better than other approaches. The performance is strongly validated as it is compared with other state-of-the-art approaches. Compared to other relevant work, the paper achieves a 6% improvement in predicting the S&P 500 index. The authors also simulated their approach for trading and the results outperformed other approaches in terms of returns by a good margin.

Rather et al. (2015) combined linear and non-linear approaches to design a hybrid model for stock prediction. The results show that their hybrid model outperforms RNN and is better able to predict rapid fluctuations in Indian stock prices. The authors, however, did not mention the motivation behind using genetic algorithms for selecting weights. Furthermore, the work chooses a 50:50 train–test split which is a little unusual for stock market datasets; therefore, it would have been better if they could provide any insights on the same.

Finally, it is important to take non-stationarity into consideration while evaluating forecasting models. Most of the literature today does not take non-stationarity into account. Shah et al. (2018) is a good example of how an LSTM-RNN based model is able to predict really well on non-stationary data. The work of Shah et al. (2018) shows that the LSTM model not only gives great results for daily predictions, i.e., one-day ahead but also gives more than decent results for predicting over longer-term horizons, i.e., 7-day ahead predictions just using daily price as a feature. The authors intentionally utilised a larger training dataset (20 years price data), since that period encompasses multiple up and down cycles of the market. Hence, this would allow the LSTM model to learn better and therefore have a fighting chance of being applicable to future time periods with similar market movements.

5. Challenges and Open Problems

Stock market analysis and prediction continue to be an interesting and challenging problem. As more data are becoming available, we face new challenges in acquiring and processing the data to extract knowledge and analyse the effect on stock prices. These challenges include issues of live testing, algorithmic trading, self-defeating, long-term predictions, and sentiment analysis on company filings.

Regarding live testing, most of the literature on stock analysis and prediction claim that the proposed techniques can be used in real time to make profits in the stock market. It is a big claim to make because an algorithm may work fine on backtesting in controlled environments, but the main challenge is live testing, because a lot of factors like price variations, and uneventful news and noise exist. One such example is the Knight Capital Tragedy[1] where the company suffered a loss of 440 million. Hence, a viable research direction would be to understand how some of the popular stock analysis techniques work in live or simulated environments.

Algorithmic trading systems have changed the way stock markets function. Most of the trading volumes in equity futures are generated by algorithms and not by humans. While algorithmic trading gives benefits like reduced cost, reduced latency, and no dependence on sentiments, it also brings up challenges for retail investors who do not have the necessary technology to build such systems. Today, it is common to see events where panic selling is triggered due to these systems and hence the markets overreact. As a result, it becomes more difficult to evaluate market behaviour. With new algorithms continuing to flood the markets every day, comparison of the efficacy and accuracy of these algorithms pose yet another challenge.

An interesting aspect of this research area on stock market prediction is its self-defeating nature. In simple words, if an algorithm can use a novel approach to generate high profits, then sharing it in any way to the market participants will render the novel approach useless. Thus, state of the art

1 https://dealbook.nytimes.com/2012/08/02/knight-capital-says-trading-mishap-cost-it-440-million/.

algorithms which are trading out there in the markets is proprietary and confidential. The research or methodology behind such algorithms is generally never published.

Researchers, analysts, and traders mostly focus on short term prediction of stock prices compared to longer term, i.e., weekly or monthly predictions based on historical data. Some good approaches to long term price prediction already exist such as the ARIMA. Stock markets are generally more predictable in the longer term. Several newer ANN approaches such as the LSTM and RNN are now being explored and compared against existing approaches in predicting long term dependencies in the data and the stock prices, which are equally valuable to the investors and data scientists.

Recently, due to the rising influence of social media on many aspects of our lives, a lot of attention is being given to sentiment analysis based on Twitter or news data. Social media data can be unreliable and difficult to process, and fake news is being posted on the web by multiple sources. A good alternative to these or additional resource would be the quarterly or annual reports filed by the companies (e.g., 10-Q and 10-K) for stock prediction to apply sentiment analysis. These documents, if decoded correctly, give a major insight into a company's status, which can help to understand the future trend of the stock.

6. Conclusions

Financial markets provide a unique platform for trading and investing, where trades can be executed from any device that can connect to the Internet. With the advent of stock markets, people have the opportunity to have multiple avenues to make their investment grow. Not only that, but it also gave rise to different types of funds like mutual funds, hedge funds and index funds for people and institutions to invest money according to their risk appetite. Governments of most countries invest a part of their healthcare, employment, or retirement funds into stock markets to achieve better returns for everyone. Online trading services have already revolutionised the way people buy and sell stocks. The financial markets have evolved rapidly into a strong and interconnected global marketplace. These advancements bring forth new opportunities and the data science techniques offer many advantages, but they also pose a whole set of new challenges. In this paper, we propose a taxonomy of computational approaches to stock market analysis and prediction, present a detailed literature study of the state-of-the-art algorithms and methods that are commonly applied to stock market prediction, and discuss some of the continuing challenges in this area that require more attention and provide opportunities for future development and research. Unlike traditional systems, stock market today are built using a combination of different technologies, such as machine learning, expert systems, and big data which communicate with one another to facilitate more informed decisions. At the same time, global user connectivity on the internet has rendered the stock market susceptible to customer sentiments, less stable due to developing news, and prone to malicious attacks. This is where further research can play an important role in paving the way how stock markets will be analysed and made more robust in the future. A promising research direction is to explore various algorithms to evaluate whether they are powerful enough to predict for the longer term, because markets act like weighing machines in the long run having less noise and more predictability. Hybrid approaches that combine statistical and machine learning techniques will probably prove to be more useful for stock prediction.

Author Contributions: Conceptualisation, D.S. and F.Z.; Methodology, D.S.; Literature survey, D.S., F.Z., and H.I.; Discussion, D.S. and H.I.; Writing—original draft preparation, D.S.; Writing—review and editing, F.Z., and H.I.; Supervision, F.Z.

Funding: This research received no external funding.

Conflicts of Interest: The authors declare no conflict of interest.

References

Abu-Mostafa, Yaser S., and Amir F. Atiya. 1996. Introduction to financial forecasting. *Applied Intelligence* 6: 205–13. [CrossRef]

Arévalo, Rubén, Jorge García, Francisco Guijarro, and Alfred Peris. 2017. A dynamic trading rule based on filtered flag pattern recognition for stock market price forecasting. *Expert Systems with Applications* 81: 177–92. [CrossRef]

Ariyo, Adebiyi A., Adewumi O. Adewumi, and Charles K. Ayo. 2014. Stock Price Prediction Using the Arima Model. Paper presented at the 2014 UKSim-AMSS 16th International Conference on Computer Modelling and Simulation (UKSim), Cambridge, UK, March 26–28.

Babu, M. Suresh, N. Geethanjali, and B. Satyanarayana. 2012. Clustering Approach to Stock Market Prediction. *International Journal of Advanced Networking and Applications* 3: 1281.

Ballings, Michel, Dirk Van den Poel, Nathalie Hespeels, and Ruben Gryp. 2015. Evaluating multiple classifiers for stock price direction prediction. *Expert Systems with Applications* 42: 7046–56. [CrossRef]

Bao, Wei, Jun Yue, and Yulei Rao. 2017. A deep learning framework for financial time series using stacked autoencoders and long-short term memory. *PLoS ONE* 12: e0180944. [CrossRef] [PubMed]

Bernal, Armando, Sam Fok, and Rohit Pidaparthi. 2012. *Financial Market Time Series Prediction with Recurrent Neural Networks*. State College: Citeseer.

Bhardwaj, Aditya, Yogendra Narayan, and Maitreyee Dutta. 2015. Sentiment analysis for Indian stock market prediction using Sensex and nifty. *Procedia Computer Science* 70: 85–91. [CrossRef]

Bhuriya, Dinesh, Girish Kausha, Ashish Sharma, and Upendra Singh. 2017. Stock Market Prediction Using a Linear Regression. Paper presented at the 2017 International Conference of Electronics, Communication and Aerospace Technology (ICECA), Coimbatore, India, April 20–22; vol. 2.

Billah, Baki, Maxwell L. King, Ralph D. Snyder, and Anne B. Koehler. 2006. Exponential Smoothing Model Selection for Forecasting. *International Journal of Forecasting* 22: 239–47. [CrossRef]

Bollen, Johan, Huina Mao, and Xiaojun Zeng. 2011. Twitter Mood Predicts the Stock Market. *Journal of Computational Science* 2: 1–8. [CrossRef]

Box, George E. P., Gwilym M. Jenkins, Gregory C. Reinsel, and Greta M. Ljung. 2015. *Time Series Analysis: Forecasting and Control*. Hoboken: John Wiley & Sons.

Cakra, Yahya Eru, and Bayu Distiawan Trisedya. 2015. Stock Price Prediction Using Linear Regression Based on Sentiment Analysis. Paper presented at the 2015 International Conference on Advanced Computer Science and Information Systems (ICACSIS), Depok, Indonesia, October 10–11.

Cervelló-Royo, Roberto, Francisco Guijarro, and Karolina Michniuk. 2015. Stock market trading rule based on pattern recognition and technical analysis: Forecasting the DJIA index with intraday data. *Expert Systems with Applications* 42: 5963–75. [CrossRef]

Chen, Tai-Liang. 2011. Forecasting the Taiwan Stock Market with a Stock Trend Recognition Model Based on the Characteristic Matrix of a Bull Market. *African Journal of Business Management* 5: 9947–60.

Chen, Tai-liang, and Feng-yu Chen. 2016. An intelligent pattern recognition model for supporting investment decisions in stock market. *Information Sciences* 346: 261–74. [CrossRef]

Cheng, Ching-Hsue, Tai-Liang Chen, and Liang-Ying Wei. 2010. A hybrid model based on rough sets theory and genetic algorithms for stock price forecasting. *Information Sciences* 180: 1610–29. [CrossRef]

Chong, Eunsuk, Chulwoo Han, and Frank C. Park. 2017. Deep learning networks for stock market analysis and prediction: Methodology, data representations, and case studies. *Expert Systems with Applications* 83: 187–205. [CrossRef]

Creighton, Jonathan, and Farhana H. Zulkernine. 2017. Towards Building a Hybrid Model for Predicting Stock Indexes. Paper presented at the 2017 IEEE International Conference on Big Data (Big Data), Boston, MA, USA, December 11–14.

De Faria, E. L., Marcelo P. Albuquerque, J. L. Gonzalez, J. T. P. Cavalcante, and Marcio P. Albuquerque. 2009. Predicting the Brazilian Stock Market through Neural Networks and Adaptive Exponential Smoothing Methods. *Expert Systems with Applications* 36: 12506–9. [CrossRef]

Devi, B. Uma, D. Sundar, and P. Alli. 2013. An Effective Time Series Analysis for Stock Trend Prediction Using Arima Model for Nifty Midcap-50. *International Journal of Data Mining & Knowledge Management Process* 3: 65.

Dey, Shubharthi, Yash Kumar, Snehanshu Saha, and Suryoday Basak. 2016. Forecasting to Classification: Predicting the Direction of Stock Market Price Using Xtreme Gradient Boosting. Working Paper. [CrossRef]

Di Persio, Luca, and Oleksandr Honchar. 2017. Recurrent Neural Networks Approach to the Financial Forecast of Google Assets. *International Journal of Mathematics and Computers in simulation* 11: 7–13.

Diamond, Peter A. 2000. What Stock Market Returns to Expect for the Future. *Social Security Bulletin* 63: 38.

Ding, Xiao, Yue Zhang, Ting Liu, and Junwen Duan. 2015. Deep Learning for Event-Driven Stock Prediction. Paper presented at the 24th International Conference on Artificial Intelligence (IJCAI), Buenos Aires, Argentina, July 25–31.

Dutta, Avijan, Gautam Bandopadhyay, and Suchismita Sengupta. 2012. Prediction of Stock Performance in Indian Stock Market Using Logistic Regression. *International Journal of Business and Information* 7: 105–36.

Efron, Bradley, and Robert J. Tibshirani. 1994. *An Introduction to the Bootstrap*. Boca Raton: CRC Press.

Fama, Eugene F. 1970. Efficient Capital Markets: A Review of Theory and Empirical Work. *The Journal of Finance* 25: 383–417. [CrossRef]

Fama, Eugene F. 1995. Random walks in stock market prices. *Financial Analysts Journal* 51: 75–80. [CrossRef]

Fu, King Sun, and Tzay Y. Young. 1986. *Handbook of Pattern Recognition and Image Processing*. Cambridge: Academic Press.

Fu, Tak-chung, Fu-lai Chung, Robert Luk, and Chak-man Ng. 2005. Preventing Meaningless Stock Time Series Pattern Discovery by Changing Perceptually Important Point Detection. Paper presented at the International Conference on Fuzzy Systems and Knowledge Discovery, Changsha, China, August 27–29.

Gordon, Myron J. 1959. Dividends, Earnings, and Stock Prices. *The Review of Economics and Statistics* 41: 99–105. [CrossRef]

Gordon, Myron J., and Eli Shapiro. 1956. Capital Equipment Analysis: The Required Rate of Profit. *Management Science* 3: 102–10. [CrossRef]

Hiransha, M., E. A. Gopalakrishnan, Vijay Krishna Menon, and Soman Kp. 2018. NSE stock market prediction using deep-learning models. *Procedia Computer Science* 132: 1351–62.

Hossain, Mohammad Asiful, Rezaul Karim, Ruppa K. Thulasiram, Neil D. B. Bruce, and Yang Wang. 2018. Hybrid Deep Learning Model for Stock Price Prediction. Paper presented at the 2018 IEEE Symposium Series on Computational Intelligence (SSCI), Bangalore, India, November 18–21.

Hu, Yong, Kang Liu, Xiangzhou Zhang, Lijun Su, E. W. T. Ngai, and Mei Liu. 2015. Application of evolutionary computation for rule discovery in stock algorithmic trading: A literature review. *Applied Soft Computing* 36: 534–51. [CrossRef]

Imam, Shahed, Richard Barker, and Colin Clubb. 2008. The Use of Valuation Models by Uk Investment Analysts. *European Accounting Review* 17: 503–35. [CrossRef]

Kalyanaraman, Vaanchitha, Sarah Kazi, Rohan Tondulkar, and Sangeeta Oswal. 2014. Sentiment Analysis on News Articles for Stocks. Paper presented at the 2014 8th Asia Modelling Symposium (AMS), Taipei, Taiwan, September 23–25.

Kim, Sang, Hee Soo Lee, Hanjun Ko, Seung Hwan Jeong, Hyun Woo Byun, and Kyong Joo Oh. 2018. Pattern Matching Trading System Based on the Dynamic Time Warping Algorithm. *Sustainability* 10: 4641. [CrossRef]

Lee, Heeyoung, Mihai Surdeanu, Bill MacCartney, and Dan Jurafsky. 2014. On the Importance of Text Analysis for Stock Price Prediction. Paper presented at the 9th International Conference on Language Resources and Evaluation, LREC 2014, Reykjavik, Iceland, May 26–31.

Leigh, William, Naval Modani, Russell Purvis, and Tom Roberts. 2002. Stock market trading rule discovery using technical charting heuristics. *Expert Systems with Applications* 23: 155–59. [CrossRef]

Leigh, William, Cheryl J. Frohlich, Steven Hornik, Russell L. Purvis, and Tom L. Roberts. 2008. Trading with a Stock Chart Heuristic. *IEEE Transactions on Systems, Man, and Cybernetics-Part A: Systems and Humans* 38: 93–104. [CrossRef]

Lv, Dongdong, Shuhan Yuan, Meizi Li, and Yang Xiang. 2019. An Empirical Study of Machine Learning Algorithms for Stock Daily Trading Strategy. *Mathematical Problems in Engineering*. [CrossRef]

Markowska-Kaczmar, Urszula, and Maciej Dziedzic. 2008. Discovery of Technical Analysis Patterns. Paper presented at the International Multiconference on Computer Science and Information Technology, 2008, IMCSIT 2008, Wisia, Poland, October 20–22.

Milosevic, Nikola. 2016. Equity Forecast: Predicting Long Term Stock Price Movement Using Machine Learning. *arXiv*.

Mittal, Anshul, and Arpit Goel. 2012. Stock Prediction Using Twitter Sentiment Analysis. *Standford University, CS229*. Available online: http://cs229.stanford.edu/proj2011/GoelMittal-StockMarketPredictionUsingTwitterSentimentAnalysis.pdf (accessed on 3 March 2019).

Naseer, Mehwish, and Yasir bin Tariq. 2015. The efficient market hypothesis: A critical review of the literature. *IUP Journal of Financial Risk Management* 12: 48–63.

Nesbitt, Keith V., and Stephen Barrass. 2004. Finding trading patterns in stock market data. *IEEE Computer Graphics and Applications* 24: 45–55. [CrossRef] [PubMed]

Nguyen, Thien Hai, Kiyoaki Shirai, and Julien Velcin. 2015. Sentiment Analysis on Social Media for Stock Movement Prediction. *Expert Systems with Applications* 42: 9603–11. [CrossRef]

Pagolu, Venkata Sasank, Kamal Nayan Reddy, Ganapati Panda, and Babita Majhi. 2016. Sentiment Analysis of Twitter Data for Predicting Stock Market Movements. Paper presented at the 2016 International Conference on Signal Processing, Communication, Power and Embedded System (SCOPES), Paralakhemundi, India, October 3–5.

Park, Cheol-Ho, and Scott H. Irwin. 2007. What do we know about the profitability of technical analysis? *Journal of Economic Surveys* 21: 786–826. [CrossRef]

Parracho, Paulo, Rui Neves, and Nuno Horta. 2010. Trading in Financial Markets Using Pattern Recognition Optimized by Genetic Algorithms. Paper presented at the 12th Annual Conference Companion on Genetic and Evolutionary Computation, Portland, OR, USA, July 7–11.

Patel, Jigar, Sahil Shah, Priyank Thakkar, and K. Kotecha. 2015. Predicting stock market index using fusion of machine learning techniques. *Expert Systems with Applications* 42: 2162–72. [CrossRef]

Peachavanish, Ratchata. 2016. Stock selection and trading based on cluster analysis of trend and momentum indicators. Paper presented at the International MultiConference of Engineers and Computer Scientists, Hong Kong, China, March 16–18.

Phetchanchai, Chawalsak, Ali Selamat, Amjad Rehman, and Tanzila Saba. 2010. Index Financial Time Series Based on Zigzag-Perceptually Important Points. *Journal of Computer Science* 6: 1389–95.

Powell, Nicole, Simon Y. Foo, and Mark Weatherspoon. 2008. Supervised and Unsupervised Methods for Stock Trend Forecasting. Paper presented at the 40th Southeastern Symposium on System Theory (SSST 2008), New Orleans, LA, USA, March 16–18.

Rather, Akhter Mohiuddin, Arun Agarwal, and V. N. Sastry. 2015. Recurrent Neural Network and a Hybrid Model for Prediction of Stock Returns. *Expert Systems with Applications* 42: 3234–41. [CrossRef]

Roondiwala, Murtaza, Harshal Patel, and Shraddha Varma. 2017. Predicting Stock Prices Using Lstm. *International Journal of Science and Research (IJSR)* 6: 1754–56.

Schumaker, Robert P., and Hsinchun Chen. 2009. Textual Analysis of Stock Market Prediction Using Breaking Financial News: The Azfin Text System. *ACM Transactions on Information Systems (TOIS)* 27: 12. [CrossRef]

Seng, Jia-Lang, and Hsiao-Fang Yang. 2017. The association between stock price volatility and financial news—A sentiment analysis approach. *Kybernetes* 46: 1341–65. [CrossRef]

Shah, Dev, Campbell Wesley, and Zulkernine Farhana. 2018. A Comparative Study of LSTM and DNN for Stock Market Forecasting. Paper presented at the 2018 IEEE International Conference on Big Data (Big Data), Seattle, WA, USA, December 10–13.

Shen, Shunrong, Haomiao Jiang, and Tongda Zhang. 2012. *Stock Market Forecasting Using Machine Learning Algorithms*. Stanford: Department of Electrical Engineering, Stanford University, pp. 1–5.

Shiller, Robert J. 1980. *Do Stock Prices Move Too Much to Be Justified by Subsequent Changes in Dividends?* Cambridge: National Bureau of Economic Research.

Shiller, Robert C. 2000. Irrational Exuberance. *Philosophy & Public Policy Quarterly* 20: 18–23.

Tiwari, Shweta, Rekha Pandit, and Vineet Richhariya. 2010. Predicting Future Trends in Stock Market by Decision Tree Rough-Set Based Hybrid System with Hhmm. *International Journal of Electronics and Computer Science Engineering* 1: 1578–87.

Velay, Marc, and Fabrice Daniel. 2018. Stock Chart Pattern recognition with Deep Learning. *arXiv*.

Wang, Jar-Long, and Shu-Hui Chan. 2007. Stock Market Trading Rule Discovery Using Pattern Recognition and Technical Analysis. *Expert Systems with Applications* 33: 304–15. [CrossRef]

Wang, Ju-Jie, Jian-Zhou Wang, Zhe-George Zhang, and Shu-Po Guo. 2012. Stock Index Forecasting Based on a Hybrid Model. *Omega* 40: 758–66. [CrossRef]

Wu, Kuo-Ping, Yung-Piao Wu, and Hahn-Ming Lee. 2014. Stock Trend Prediction by Using K-Means and Aprioriall Algorithm for Sequential Chart Pattern Mining. *Journal of Information Science and Engineering* 30: 669–86.

Xu, Yumo, and Shay B. Cohen. 2018. Stock movement prediction from tweets and historical prices. Paper Presented at the 56th Annual Meeting of the Association for Computational Linguistics, Melbourne, Australia, July 15–20.

Yang, Bing, Zi-Jia Gong, and Wenqi Yang. 2017. Stock Market Index Prediction Using Deep Neural Network Ensemble. Paper Presented at the 2017 36th Chinese Control Conference (CCC), Dalian, China, July 26–28.

Yoshihara, Akira, Kazuki Fujikawa, Kazuhiro Seki, and Kuniaki Uehara. 2014. Predicting Stock Market Trends by Recurrent Deep Neural Networks. Paper presented at the Pacific RIM International Conference on Artificial Intelligence, Gold Coast, Australia, December 1–5.

Zhang, Jing, Shicheng Cui, Yan Xu, Qianmu Li, and Tao Li. 2018. A novel data-driven stock price trend prediction system. *Expert Systems with Applications* 97: 60–69. [CrossRef]

Zhong, Xiao, and David Enke. 2017. Forecasting daily stock market return using dimensionality reduction. *Expert Systems with Applications* 67: 126–39. [CrossRef]

3

The Role of Canceled Warrants in the LME Market

Jaehwan Park

Commodity Research Center, Public Procurement Service, Daejeon 35208, Korea; drjppark@korea.kr

Abstract: This article visits the question of whether canceled warrants (CWs) have a positive effect on LME metal prices. To examine this question carefully, a regression model is applied. This paper finds a statistically significant positive link between CWs and LME metal prices, including aluminum, zinc, tin, and nickel. However, other metals such as copper and lead are not statistically significant. The second objective of the study is to identify the dynamic response of metal price returns for aluminum, zinc, tin, and nickel to an innovation in the CWs using VAR. It is found that the positive impact of the CWs on metal returns is transitory.

Keywords: LME spot price; canceled warrants; speculation; financialization

JEL Classification: C3; G1

---

1. Introduction

High cyclical fluctuations in commodity prices, with somewhat severe volatilities, have brought about a debate over the developments occurring in commodity markets (Singleton 2014). Recent years have seen a rapid growth in the participation of investors in the commodity market, in what is being called the 'financialization' of commodity markets (Cheng and Xiong 2014). This phenomenon has occurred where the commodity markets have become important, as institutional investors have come to regard commodities as an alternative asset class (Park 2019). Tang and Xiong (2012) concluded that the financialization of commodity markets through institutional investors' index funds has significantly impacted market dynamics and volatilities in commodity markets.

The LME (London Metal Exchange)[1] is the world's largest futures exchange in the metal industry, including for six base metals—copper, aluminum, lead, zinc, tin, and nickel—and is known for being quite correlated with the business cycle (Park 2018). Based on Bloomberg data, the LME is truly a global commodity exchange, as 95% of trades originate from overseas.

Producers of commodities do not have direct contract with the consumers who use their commodities in business activities (Otani 1983). The place for transactions of inventory stock between producers and consumers exists with middlemen, who deliver commodities from producers to consumers. Otani (1983) argued that the LME might be the most famous inventory stock market using its own warehouse system. Traders in LME can take physical deliveries of metals and sell excess inventory of over-supply in the market, which is possible due to peculiar LME warehouse regulations. There are more than 690 warehouses and storage facilities worldwide which are licensed by an LME authority. On a daily basis, LME reports the availability of the six base metal inventory at each of

---

1 The LME opened in 1877; it has continued strengthening since then, and became recognized as the global benchmark for the metal market. Major producers and consumers use LME contracts for hedging price risks, and for the reference price for spot and future prices. Park and Lim (2018) provided a good discussion of the LME. They found that the LME was an inefficient market due to financialization by institutional investors.

these warehouses. Most global sell-side brokers, such as Goldman Sachs, Macquarie and Societe Generale, report the variation of canceled warrants (CWs) in the LME market to focus on market trading momentum as a key factor.

The Metal Bulletin points out that "CWs[2] are important in that they represent the change in stockpiles of metal that may no longer be available at LME warehouses, and which are booked for removal or onward shipment. This information is an indicator of physical demand". Metals on warrants represent inventories in store at the LME's warehouse, while CWs imply metal earmarked for physical delivery soon. Investors cancel their warrants because they want to take it out of the LME warehouse. This is important signal for market demand/supply fundamentals. A rise in CWs suggests stronger market demand for the LME metals, and deliveries thereof. A warehouse inventory is the significant barometer to investors,[3] and there is an inverse relationship between inventories and prices as movement in stocks affect the future price direction. A sharp decline in inventories implies the demand is rising with less supply. Table 1 exhibits the possible stylized fact, which relates to dynamics between the CW ratio direction and the metal price direction. A rise in warehouse stocks or fall in the CW ratio suggests a negative direction for metal prices, while a fall in the inventory or rise in the CW ratio implies a positive trend for metal prices.

Table 1. Possible relationship between the CW ratio and effect on the metal price.

Inventories	CW Ratio	Effect on Metal Price
Up	Down	Negative
Down	Up	Positive

Note: the inverse relationship between inventories and CWs is held due to the definition of the CW calculation.

Investors may want to cancel their warrants because they take it out of the authorized LME warehouse to squeeze the market spread. These sequential investors' reactions have been strengthening through market expectation. This is possible because first, the middlemen are the commodity developers or smelters such as Glencore, Nyrstar and Rusal, and the warehouse companies such as Access World, C. Steinweg and Mitsubishi Logistics. They have a lot of market information, and are experienced professionals regarding metal market dynamics. I believe that the changes in CWs affect the investment sentiment and the financialization of the LME market. Second, the LME has very peculiar prompt dates. The LME provides spot (cash), futures (three month; benchmark) and various option contracts. The LME addresses daily rolling three month (3M) futures contracts that are different from those in other commodity markets, which are based on monthly prompt dates (Park and Lim 2018). This may convince traders, analysts, and index investors who have attributed the metal price direction to speculation that the fundamentals have indeed been improving. I develop my hypothesis as follows:

Hypothesis 1 (H1). *The rise in CWs increases the LME metal price.*

I consider pairs of variables; the first of each pair is the CWs, and the second is an LME metal price movement. Unfortunately, there is no previous study in the CWs area to the best of my knowledge, even though there are quite a few in LME market dynamics, such as on testing market efficiency (Arouri et al. 2011; Otto 2011; Park and Lim 2018) and measuring market volatility (Figuerola-Ferretti and Gilbert 2008). The purpose of this paper is to test the above hypothesis using daily LME market data from January 2006 to December 2018. This study uses a regression model and finds a statistically

[2] See details in Metal Bulletin (http://www.metalbulletin.com/Glossary.html). The CWs are the ratio of CWs to total warrants, where total warrants are the on warrants and canceled warrants.

[3] This information is a valuable investment factor of consumption trends, which can provide a meaningful implication of possible future price directions.

significant link between CWs and LME metal prices, including aluminum, zinc, tin and nickel, while the other metals are not statistically significant. Using the VAR model, it is found that the impact of a CW innovation on spot returns of aluminum, zinc, tin and nickel is transitory rather than permanent.

The paper is organized as follows. Section 2 reviews the previous literature about the LME. In Section 3, I present the research model and data with a summary of statistics and unit root test. Section 4 presents the main results. In the final section, I provide the summary and conclusion.

2. Literature Review

There is no direct study of CWs in the LME, or even in other commodity markets. This section reviews the previous studies in the LME-related-area. There are three different categories within LME studies. First, the testing of LME market efficiency is an important issue. However, there has not been consensus regarding the market efficiency of the LME. Canarella and Pollard (1986) and MacDonald and Taylor (1988) found that the LME was an efficient market, while Otto (2011) and Park and Lim (2018) found opposing results. Park and Lim (2018) argued that the financialization of commodities was growing.

Second, the financialization of the LME market has been debated. Koitsiwe and Adachi (2018) found that LME real copper spot prices had been characterized by structural changes, and its determinants vary in a distinct period. They showed that financial speculation had accentuated copper price moves during the last decade. Guzmán and Silva (2018) argued that, following the recent price boom, some dissent had arisen around the role played by non-fundamentals such as liquidity or money supply in major commodity markets. They found that some indications of financialization in the copper price explained the price dynamics using the VAR model. Park (2019) employed Granger causality tests to analyze the role of speculators using weekly COTR (Commitment of Traders Reports) data, and presented statistically significant evidence that the position changes of speculators, such as hedge funds, Granger-cause the prices of base metals, such as aluminum, copper and zinc among the six base metals.

Third, Figuerola-Ferretti and Gilbert (2008) studied the measurement of volatility in the LME market using realized volatility.[4] They examined the spot and three month aluminum and copper volatilities. They found that both spot and three month price volatilities of aluminum and copper followed a long memory process, caused by speculative traders.[5] They found no evidence that the volatilities processes were fractionally cointegrated. Park (2018) provided evidence of volatility transmission between oil and the base metals through the bivariate GARCH model. Within the results, he argued that hedging decisions across the oil and LME futures were feasible to deal with market risk. Park and Lim (2018) examined whether the price volatility of the LME changed within a sample period, to check the possibility of time-varying volatility due to the financialization of commodity markets. They showed the results from the difference-in-means tests of volatility difference in two sub-periods: pre-crisis (2000–2008) and post-crisis (2009–June 2016), which found that the LME's volatility was somewhat larger post-crisis when compared to pre-crisis, with a statistical significance of 1% for all base metals except nickel.

---

4 The LME does not report intra-day data and tick data. It is not possible to compute daily realized volatility measures for LME markets (Figuerola-Ferretti and Gilbert 2008). They used monthly rather realized volatility data.

5 Figuerola-Ferretti and Gilbert (2008) concluded that the LME aluminum and copper scedastic processes are both highly persistent. They argued that the strong symmetry of the two processes implied that the processes may be the outcome of common market microstructure factors.

3. Research Model and Data

3.1. Research Model

When examining the effect of CWs on base metal spot prices in LME, I developed a simple empirical framework. In its basic form, the following model determines the spot price returns of LME base metals with respect to CWs:

$$SR_{i,t} = \beta_0 + \beta_1 CW_{i,t} + \varepsilon_{i,t} \quad (1)$$

where $SR_{i,t}$ is the natural logarithm of the spot price return of base metal i against the previous day; $CW_{i,t}$ is the canceled warrant on the day of base metal i in the LME market; and $\varepsilon_{i,t}$ is the vector of independent and identically distributed (*i.i.d.*) errors of each of the $SR_{i,t}$s. If rising CWs tend to encourage the investment momentum upward, then $\beta_1 > 0$ is expected. Given the fact that LME investors tend to view CWs as a key variable, commodity funds such as hedge funds and CTAs (Commodity Trading Advisors) are likely to have a significant influence on metal prices.

3.2. Data

Daily data relating to the period of January 2006 to December 2018 are used for estimating Equation (1), providing N = 3284 observations through *Bloomberg*. In particular, to evaluate the effect of stockpiling on metal prices, I collected the available data on the LME metal stockpile. To measure the effect of the stockpile, CWs are used. Table 2 presents the descriptive statistics of returns and CWs. It is found that both the returns and CWs are strongly leptokurtic. The skewness and kurtosis measures show that the returns distributions are asymmetric and fat-tailed, which is known as excess kurtosis. The standard deviation of daily log returns as the volatility over the period shows that nickel is the largest, but aluminum is the lowest. Jarque–Bera statistics in Table 2 are for checking normal distribution, and reveal no normally distributed data within the considered data set. The conclusion for the data finds that the distributions for all returns and CWs are skewed and fat-tailed.

Table 2. Summary statistics. The total observation contains 3284 obs. (3 January 2006–31 December 2018; daily data). The natural logarithm data are applied in the returns calculations. The distributions for all returns and CWs are skewed and fat-tailed, as indicated by the high significance of the Jarque–Bera test for normality.

	Variable	Mean	Standard Deviation	Skewness	Maximum	Minimum	Kurtosis	Jarque-Bera
copper	cu_cw	0.1836	0.1564	1.0898	0.6742	0.0013	3.3818	458.75 (0.00)
	cu_r	0.0002	0.0182	0.1461	0.1244	−0.0980	6.8328	307.12 (0.00)
aluminum	al_cw	0.2194	0.1821	0.3844	0.5996	0.0037	1.7159	7548.3 (0.00)
	al_r	0.0005	0.0148	−0.0069	0.0660	−0.0752	4.7523	133.47 (0.00)
lead	pb_cw	0.1827	0.1792	0.9114	0.7752	0.0004	2.6438	364.71 (0.00)
	pb_r	0.0004	0.0221	−0.0028	0.1389	−0.1236	5.8982	228.62 (0.00)
zinc	zn_cw	0.1845	0.1797	1.1336	0.7610	0.0019	3.1896	474.37 (0.00)
	zn_r	0.0003	0.0209	−0.0039	0.1046	−0.1083	4.9927	154.59 (0.00)
tin	sn_cw	0.1435	0.1283	1.3391	0.6780	0.0000	4.4941	702.47 (0.00)
	sn_r	0.0005	0.0182	0.0856	0.1663	−0.1082	9.3753	443.00 (0.00)
nickel	ni_cw	0.1840	0.1504	0.5176	0.8586	0.0029	2.4871	197.66 (0.00)
	ni_r	0.0002	0.0237	0.1358	0.1423	−0.1284	5.6834	221.95 (0.00)

3.3. Stationarity Check: Unit Root Tests

To test the stationarity of the variables, this paper employs the ADF (Augmented Dickey Fuller) test and Phillip–Perron (PP) test, which are given in Table 3. Table 3 reports the unit root tests for all the variables (null hypothesis: there is a unit root). All the variables of the returns data have no unit root, therefore will not convert to be stationary by taking the first difference. However, the variables of the CW data are mixed. The CW variables, such as those for lead, tin and nickel, reveal stationary data, while those of aluminum and zinc were found to be non-stationary. Moreover, the CW variable of copper is not conclusive, because the ADF test indicates that it is non-stationary, but rejected the null hypothesis at the 5% significance level using the PP test. All the returns data use the level, and all of the CW data employ the level data, except aluminum and zinc.

Table 3. Unit root test results. The sample consists of 3284 observations. Table 3 presents the unit root tests for all the variables (null hypothesis: there is a unit root). The reported numbers represent test statistics. ***, ** and * indicate the rejection of the null hypothesis at the 1%, 5% and 10% level of significance, respectively.

	Variables	ADF		PP		Order of Integration
		Level	1st Diff	Level	1st Diff	
copper	cu_cw	−2.560		−3.155 **		not determine
	cu_r	−55.75 ***		−55.70 ***		I(0)
aluminum	al_cw	−0.993	−39.74 ***	−0.675	−39.91 ***	I(1)
	al_r	−53.19 ***		−53.20 ***		I(0)
lead	pb_cw	−2.582 *		−2.729 **		I(0)
	pb_r	−49.23 ***		−49.22 ***		I(0)
zinc	zn_cw	−2.013	−36.20 ***	−1.602	−36.01 ***	I(1)
	zn_r	−52.48 ***		−52.56 ***		I(0)
tin	sn_cw	−5.383 ***		−5.380 ***		I(0)
	sn_r	−50.18 ***		−50.19 ***		I(0)
nickel	ni_cw	−3.158 **		−3.271 **		I(0)
	ni_r	−51.66 ***		−51.75 ***		I(0)

4. Empirical Results

The main objective of this paper is to identify whether the CWs help explain the extent to which the LME market moves in a similar direction to the CWs. This paper uses daily data from January 2006 to December 2018, which covers the trading of the six base metals. The role of metal spot prices is mainly addressed through forward contracts in the LME market. The movement of spot prices gives the key indication of metal price levels for producers and demanders. Spot prices are known to be primarily affected by supply and demand, which is the market fundamental environment. In addition to this fundamental, this paper exhibits the impact of commodity fund activities.

Daily data relating to the period January 2006 to December 2018 are used for estimating Equation (1). Daily data can appropriately capture the arbitrage possibilities in the LME market (Park and Lim 2018).

4.1. Regression Results

In this section, I test whether changes in CWs have an effect on LME metal prices. My primary interest is in what happens to the coefficient of CWs increases, $SR_{i,t}$, in Table 4. The estimated elasticity of the CW increase is 0.0052 for tin and 0.0055 for nickel, indicating an immediate 0.52% increase in tin return and 0.55% increase in nickel return, respectively, given a 10% increase in both CWs. This is strongly significant, with t-statistics of 2.10 for tin and 2.01 for nickel, and verifies a positive relationship between increasing CWs and metal price returns. Furthermore, the first differenced variables, such as aluminum (0.1212) and zinc (0.0829), reveal stronger results at the 1% level which are statistically significant. This implies that the somewhat higher CWs, given a lower LME stockpile, impacts on the metal prices to motivate the commodity funds to boost investment sentiments (see Table 1). The positive effect of CWs on metal returns, such as aluminum, zinc, tin and nickel, indicates somewhat possible excess returns when investors consider CWs as a significant variable. Therefore, I conclude that CWs intensify the metal price direction, especially that of the aluminum, zinc, tin and nickel spot markets within the LME.

Table 4. Parameter estimates of Equation (1). The total observation contained 3284 obs. (January 2006–December 2018; daily data). The natural logarithm data were applied in the returns data. The reported numbers in parentheses represent t-statistics. *** and ** indicate statistical significance at the 1% and 5% levels. All the returns data use the level, and all the CW data employ the level, except aluminum and zinc, reflecting the unit root test results.

Commodity	β_0	β_1	R^2	F-Statistics	MSE
Copper	0.0001 (0.15)	0.0009 (0.46)	0.0001	0.21	0.0182
Aluminum	0.0002 (0.91)	0.1212 (2.89) ***	0.0032	8.37 ***	0.0147
Lead	0.0004 (0.84)	−0.0002 (−0.11)	0.0001	0.01	0.0222
Zinc	0.0004 (−0.45)	0.0829 (3.05) ***	0.0036	9.33 ***	0.0211
Tin	−0.0002 (−0.52)	0.0052 (2.10) **	0.0013	4.39 **	0.0182
Nickel	−0.0007 (−1.22)	0.0055 (2.01) **	0.0012	3.97 **	0.0236

Tang and Xiong (2012) showed that financialization by global institutional investors affected the market co-movement across commodity markets, and even equity markets. They argued that there was some possible link between financialization of a commodity market and trading volume. Park and Lim (2018) found that the LME futures market was inefficient because the financialization of commodities had been growing. Kang and Yoon (2016) examined the dynamic return and volatility spillovers between the Shanghai Futures Exchange (SFE) and the LME. They found that the LME had a significant impact on the SFE, and concluded that financial crises intensified both returns and volatility spillovers across base metals when considering aluminum, copper and zinc. Notice that their sample period was from August 2007 to April 2016, which is considered to be a somewhat strengthening period of financialization. Guzmán and Silva (2018) reported that the financialization of commodities appears to have a direct impact on the spot copper price, considering market liquidity as a non-fundamental variable. Koitsiwe and Adachi (2018) argued that the recent rise and fall in commodity prices were not determined by only the classical fundamental factors of supply and demand. These previous studies regarding the LME hinted at the financialization effect on the market price direction, and proved the possibility of abnormal returns.[6] I believe that CWs are one of important key parameters for LME investors to drive financial speculation of the market.

4.2. VAR Model Specifications and Impulse Response Results

In this section, to investigate the impact of CWs on metal returns among aluminum, zinc, tin and nickel in a dynamic manner, a vector autoregression (VAR) model is developed. In order to not

6 Koitsiwe and Adachi (2018) reported that commodity assets under management by financial investors dramatically increased in value, from about $13 billion in 2003 to $450 billion in 2011. Irwin and Sanders (2012) reported that a total of $161.2 billion was invested in commodity index investments as of 31 March 2010. A total of 78% of index investments were in the U.S. futures market, which invited major index funds with rising trading volumes.

impose a priori a theory of causality between the variables, a non-structural VAR is used. The VAR is a seemingly unrelated regression model with the same explanatory variables in each equation, when there are no constraints placed on the coefficients. The VAR can be written as:

$$Z_t = \left(\beta_1 L + \beta_2 L^2\right) Z_t + u_t \tag{2}$$

where $Z_t = (SR_{i,t}, CW_{i,t})'$, a vector of spot returns of aluminum, zinc, tin and nickel, and canceled warrants of aluminum, zinc, tin and nickel, respectively. L is the lag operator, β_1 and β_2 are 2X2 matrices of coefficients, and u_t is a 2X1 vector of white noise innovations. Two lags are appropriate based upon the Chi-squared test (likelihood-ratio test) and AIC value.

Rewriting and inverting Equation (2) allows Z_t to be expressed as an infinite order moving average representation:

$$Z_t = \sum_{i=0}^{\infty} \beth_i \mathfrak{C} \epsilon_{t-1} \tag{3}$$

where each $\beth_i$ is the 2X2 matrix of coefficients, $\mathfrak{C}\epsilon_{t-i} = u_{t-i}$, $\mathfrak{C}\mathfrak{C}'$ is a factorization of the covariance matrix of u, and ϵ_{t-i} is a matrix of orthogonalized innovations. Equation (3) can be used to identify the dynamic response of spot returns to the CW shocks, which is the impulse response function (g):

$$g_j = \frac{\partial Z_t}{\partial u_{t-j}} \tag{4}$$

The VAR shown in Equation (2) is then estimated using the Stata 12 software. The results for the parameters, as well as some statistics, are not reported in this paper, but we do present the impulse response results. The impulse responses to spot returns to CW shock are shown in Figure 1. It is found that the impact of a CW shock on spot returns of both tin and nickel has second period positive effects. The positive effect on metal returns holds for the contemporaneous and first two lags following an increase in CWs, and then the positive effect on spot returns of a CW shocks fades after the second period. In Figure 2 there are the impulse responses to spot price returns of aluminum and zinc to CW shocks, which implies one more period impact compared to tin and nickel. In conclusion, the positive impact of the CWs to metal returns is transitory.

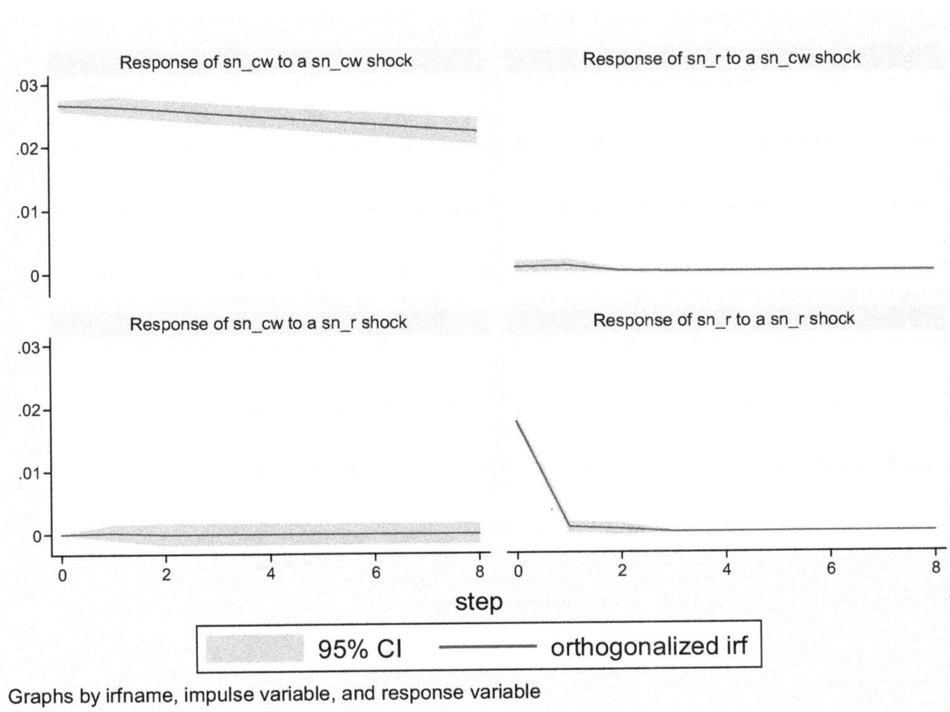

Figure 1. *Cont.*

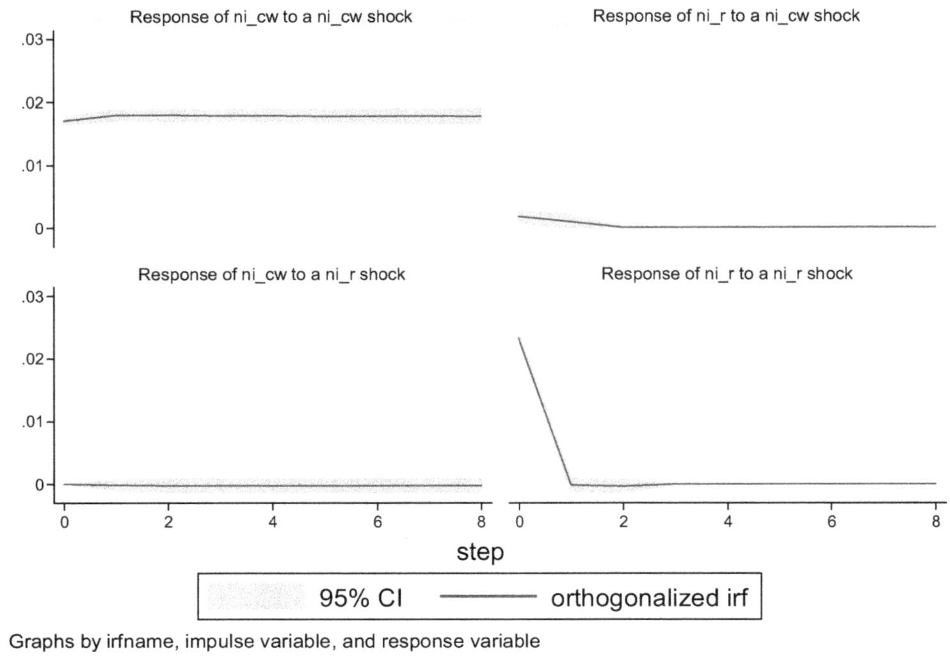

Figure 1. Plot of impulse response results: tin and nickel. Notes: The solid line is the orthogonalized impulse response, while the grey area is the 95% confidence interval. The responses of spot returns to a CW shock show that they are very short lived within the second period.

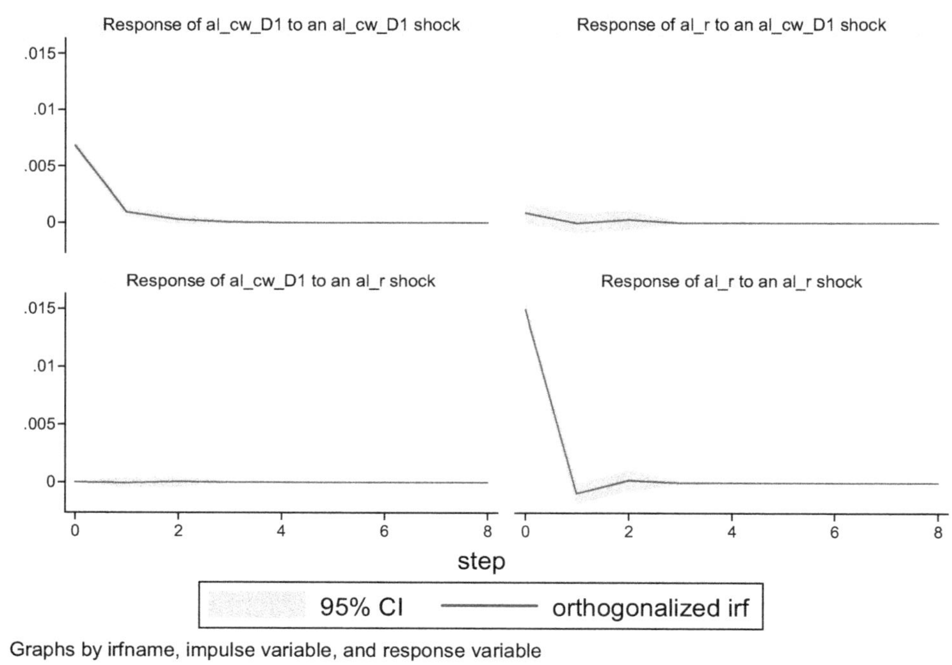

Figure 2. *Cont.*

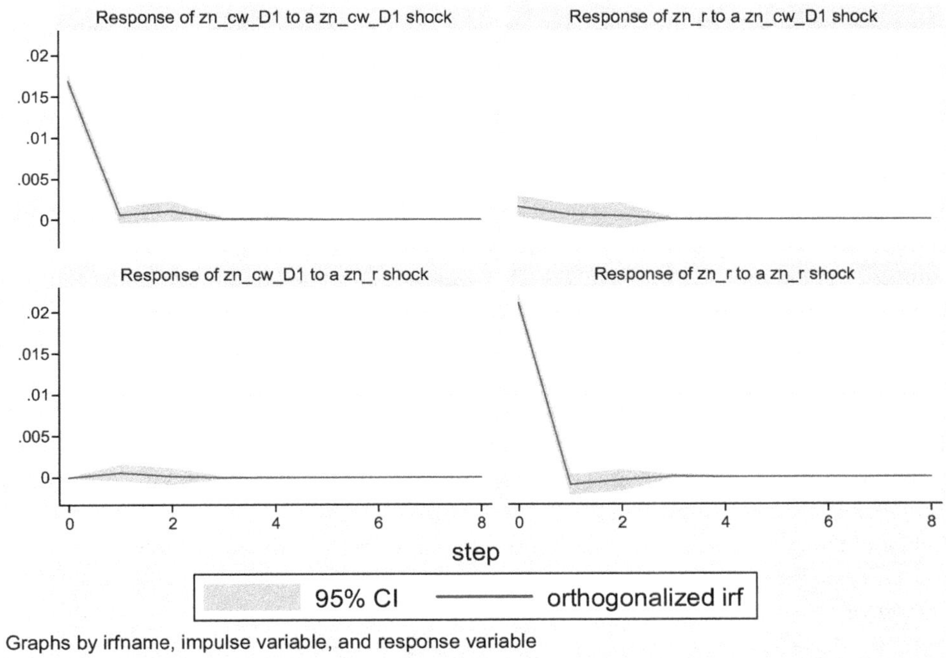

Figure 2. Plot of impulse response results: aluminum and zinc. Notes: The solid line is the orthogonalized impulse response, while the grey area is the 95% confidence interval. The responses of spot returns to a CW shock show that they are very short lived within the third period. al_cw_D1 and zn_cw_D1 indicate the first differenced variables.

Guzmán and Silva (2018) found similar result for the copper market using error variance decomposition. They reported that more than 19% of variance was associated with financial speculation, such as the long positions in the futures market during the period over August 2003 and September 2008. However, different periods, such as April 1995–March 2003 and October 2003–October 2015, showed a somewhat lowered effect.

5. Summary and Conclusions

Particular interest has been growing recently in the potential role of the financialization of commodity markets. This study establishes a hypothesis concerning whether the rise in CWs is associated with LME metal price increases. The CWs variable is important, because it encompasses two factors—fundamentals and non-fundamentals. It is a fundamentals variable because it relates to the market inventory. It is also a non-fundamentals variable because it deals with global sell-side brokers' reports and affects investors' sentiments. Using 13 years of daily data, first, this paper observes that there is a statistically significant positive link between CWs and LME metal prices, especially aluminum, zinc, tin, and nickel. I conclude that CWs intensify the aluminum, zinc, tin, and nickel spot prices direction. Second, the impulse response to a CW shock shows that the positive impact of the metal returns for aluminum, zinc, tin, and nickel is transitory rather than permanent, so that the effect of a unit shock in CWs eventually converges to zero. Indeed, after the second period, the positive effect on spot returns of a CW innovation dies out.

The link between CWs and spot prices has important implications for the pricing of the LME market, and ex post analysis of the reasons behind LME base metal prices. In the light of these results, it would be useful to test the effect of CW changes within various LME warehouses, such as Rotterdam, Vlissingen, New Orleans, Johor, and Busan, even though collecting data is somewhat difficult.

Funding: This research received no external funding.

Acknowledgments: Tae Seok Park, my colleague, provides the data set and gives useful comments.

Conflicts of Interest: The author reports no conflicts of interest. The author alone is responsible for the content and writing of the paper.

References

Arouri, Mohamed El Hedi, Fredj Jawadi, and Prosper Mouak. 2011. The Speculative Efficiency of the Aluminum Market: A Nonlinear Investigation. *International Economics* 126–27: 73–89. [CrossRef]

Canarella, Giorgio, and Stephen K. Pollard. 1986. The "Efficiency" of the London Metal Exchange: A Test with Overlapping and Non-Overlapping Data. *Journal of Banking and Finance* 10: 575–93. [CrossRef]

Cheng, Ing-Haw, and Wei Xiong. 2014. Financialization of Commodity Markets. *Annual Review of Financial Economics* 6: 419–41. [CrossRef]

Figuerola-Ferretti, Isabel, and Christopher L. Gilbert. 2008. Commonality in the LME Aluminum and Copper Volatility Processes through a FIGARCH Lens. *The Journal of Futures Markets* 28: 935–62. [CrossRef]

Guzmán, Juan Ignacio, and Enrique Silva. 2018. Copper Price Determination: Fundamentals versus Non-fundamentals. *Mineral Economics* 31: 283–300. [CrossRef]

Irwin, Scott H., and Dwight R. Sanders. 2012. Testing the Masters Hypothesis in commodity futures markets. *Energy Economics* 34: 256–69. [CrossRef]

Kang, Sang Hoon, and Seong-Min Yoon. 2016. Dynamic Spillovers between Shanghai and London Nonferrous Metal Futures Markets. *Finance Research Letters* 19: 181–88. [CrossRef]

Koitsiwe, Kegomoditswe, and Tsuyoshi Adachi. 2018. The Role of Financial Speculation in Copper Prices. *Applied Economics and Finance* 5: 87–94. [CrossRef]

MacDonald, Ronald, and Mark Taylor. 1988. Metal Prices, Efficiency and Cointegration: Some Evidence from the LME. *Bulletin of Economic Research* 40: 235–39. [CrossRef]

Otani, Kiyoshi. 1983. The Price Determination in the Inventory Stock Market: A Disequilibrium Analysis. *International Economic Review* 24: 709–19. [CrossRef]

Otto, Sascha Werner. 2011. A Speculative Efficiency Analysis of the London Metal Exchange in a Multi-Contract Framework. *International Journal of Economics and Finance* 3: 3–16. [CrossRef]

Park, Jaehwan. 2018. Volatility Transmission between Oil and LME Futures. *Applied Economics and Finance* 5: 65–72. [CrossRef]

Park, Jaehwan. 2019. Effect of Speculators' Position Changes in the LME Futures Market. Working Paper. under review.

Park, Jaehwan, and Byungkwon Lim. 2018. Testing Efficiency of the London Metal Exchange: New Evidence. *International Journal of Financial Studies* 6: 32. [CrossRef]

Singleton, Kenneth J. 2014. Investor Flows and the 2008 Boom/Bust in Oil Prices. *Management Science* 60: 300–18. [CrossRef]

Tang, Ke, and Wei Xiong. 2012. Index Investment and the Financialization of Commodities. *Financial Analysts Journal* 68: 54–74. [CrossRef]

4

Is the External Audit Report Useful for Bankruptcy Prediction? Evidence Using Artificial Intelligence

Nora Muñoz-Izquierdo [1,*], María-del-Mar Camacho-Miñano [2], María-Jesús Segovia-Vargas [2] and David Pascual-Ezama [2]

[1] CUNEF—Colegio Universitario de Estudios Financieros, Leonardo Prieto Castro, 2, Ciudad Universitaria, 28040 Madrid, Spain

[2] Facultad de Ciencias Económicas y Empresariales, Complutense University of Madrid, Campus de Somosaguas, Pozuelo de Alarcón, 28223 Madrid, Spain; marcamacho@ccee.ucm.es (M.-d.-M.C.-M.); mjsegovia@ccee.ucm.es (M.-J.S.-V.); david.pascual@ccee.ucm.es (D.P.-E.)

* Correspondence: nmunoz@cunef.edu

Abstract: Despite the number of studies on bankruptcy prediction using financial ratios, very little is known about how external audit information can contribute to anticipating financial distress. A handful of papers have shown that a combination of ratios and audit data is significant for predictive purposes, but only one recent paper provided a predictive accuracy of 80% solely by using the disclosures contained in audit reports. This study was complemented by simplifying the analysis of audit reports for prediction purposes and the same predictive accuracy was achieved. By applying three artificial intelligence techniques (PART algorithm, random forest, and support vector machine), the predictive ability of more easily extracted information from the report was examined and a practical implication suggested for each user. Simply by (1) finding the audit opinion, (2) identifying if a matter section exists, and (3) the number of comments disclosed, any user may predict a bankruptcy situation with the same accuracy as if they had scrutinized the whole report. In addition, an extended literature review is included, on previous studies on the interaction between bankruptcy prediction and the external audit information.

Keywords: bankruptcy prediction; audit report; artificial intelligence; PART algorithm

JEL Classification: G33; M40; M41; M42; C14

---

1. Introduction

During the last 70 years, the development of bankruptcy prediction models has been a challenging research topic worldwide (Sun et al. 2014; Cultrera and Brédart 2016; Altman 2018). Despite the number of studies in this field, recent literature indicates there is still a need to improve the accuracy of the prediction models (Balcaen and Ooghe 2006; Du Jardin 2015; Bauweraerts 2016) and there is a call to apply different sources of data and techniques, such as non-parametric techniques, to tackle this issue (Calderon and Cheh 2002; Zięba et al. 2016; Amani and Fadlalla 2017). This paper aimed to contribute to this line of research by examining the bankruptcy predictive ability of the external audit report using artificial intelligence methodologies.

The objective of this study was two-fold. First, it examined whether or not the audit report provided significant explanatory power when predicting bankruptcy by applying three artificial intelligence classifiers: the Projective Adaptive Resonance Theory (PART) algorithm, random forest, and support vector machine. Second, by testing the predictive ability of the audit report, a practical implication could be provided for each user, as it was easy to extract information from the report to make decisions related to a firm's viability. It was proposed that the three variables found without any difficulty in the audit report—the audit opinion, the type of paragraphs disclosed, and the number of comments included in those paragraphs—are significant variables to improve the detection of bankruptcy.

While considerable research has been devoted to bankruptcy prediction using financial ratios (Altman et al. 2017), very little is known about how external audit information can contribute to anticipating a firm's precarious financial condition. Considering that the auditing profession ensures the quality of financial statements with the issuance of an opinion in the audit report (Lennox 1999), it seems reasonable to expect that the information extracted from the report can represent a good indicator of a firm's insolvency.

Only a handful of papers have combined accounting ratios and some audit variables for predictive purposes (Altman and McGough 1974; Hopwood et al. 1989; Laitinen and Laitinen 2009; Altman et al. 2010; Piñeiro-Sánchez et al. 2013; Cenciarelli et al. 2018). Altman and McGough (1974) were pioneers in using audit information to predict bankruptcy. Hopwood et al. (1989) focused on some audit qualifications, finding that there was an association between bankruptcy and consistency, going concern, and other "subject to" qualifications. Altman et al. (2010) suggested that the audit opinion had high predictive power, and that firms with audit qualifications, such as severe qualifications or going concern, were more likely to fail, since the auditor was questioning its viability. Others, such as Piñeiro-Sánchez et al. (2013), examined the predictive ability of different auditor characteristics. According to their evidence, the auditor rotation, qualified reports, and non-compliance with deadlines (regarding approval and filing of financial statements) presented relevant differences between bankrupt and non-bankrupt firms. Similarly, Cenciarelli et al. (2018) posited that firms audited by industry-expert, large, and long-tenured auditors were less likely to fail. They also found that prediction models were more effective when the auditor attributed complementary financial characteristics.

A paper by Muñoz-Izquierdo et al. (2019) is the only one that has not combined audit data with accounting ratios to explain business failures. They anticipated the causes of business failure by solely applying external audit variables, namely, the narrative disclosures of the audit report. Narrative disclosures are the comments that auditors mention in the paragraphs regarding accounting and environmental issues that occur in the audited firms. They suggested that failure can be explained by specific internal causes, such as asset valuation and a firm's real and potential debts, as well as the external circumstances like the regulatory framework or changes in the market. However, obtaining this information from the audit report is not quick and easy. It takes time to interpret every comment, and users should have extended accounting or auditing knowledge to be able to understand the content of all disclosures. Therefore, the current paper contributes by simplifying the task of detecting business failure for the users of the audit report, so that stakeholders interested in the business's future viability will not need to scrutinize the complete report.

The current paper is a follow-up study to that of Muñoz-Izquierdo et al. (2019), and also uses information from the audit report in isolation (not combined with financial data) for bankruptcy estimation purposes. As previously stated, the aim of this paper was different because it attempted to anticipate bankruptcy, that is, to find an accurate percentage of prediction and not the particular causes of the bankruptcy situation. Furthermore, the aim was to do so by using the minimum number of variables extracted from the audit report, and those easiest to identify by any user. New variables were introduced that users could obtain without being experts on the valuation of assets and liabilities, policy changes, or the markets in which the firms operate.

The results of this study suggest that three easily extracted audit report variables could provide a reasonably accurate bankruptcy predictive power, similar to the one obtained in prior works that combined accounting with auditing variables. These variables are the audit opinion, the matter sections disclosed in the audit reports, and the number of comments included in the matter sections and qualification paragraphs. Thus, the findings indicate that there is a positive relationship between the propensity to file for bankruptcy and the issuance of qualified reports with a high number of comments disclosed by the auditors. There was even a positive relationship between the bankruptcy filing and unqualified reports with comments disclosed in the matter paragraphs. Since the audit report is a standardized and regulated document, these variables are easily detected by any user without the need to scrutinize the whole report or having any special accounting or auditing knowledge.

This empirical evidence shows a practical implication for the users of the audit report—a simple identification of the opinion, the type of paragraphs disclosed, and the number of auditors' comments represents a substantive approach to detect and estimate bankruptcy. A contribution to the bankruptcy prediction literature was made by applying three different artificial intelligence methodologies, which have never applied before with auditing variables. Lastly, this study also provides an extensive review of the research into the interaction between bankruptcy and auditing research, thus contributing to both areas of knowledge.

2. Literature Review and Research Question

Auditors are required to express in the audit report if the likelihood of default is high during the one-year period following the issuance of the document (McKee 2003). Although the role of auditors is not expected to be a predictor of bankruptcy, stakeholders might be dissatisfied if a firm fails immediately after receiving an unqualified opinion. This issue has persisted for many years, and the auditing literature has considered audit quality from the viewpoint of the users of the financial statements. Indeed, during the last global financial crisis, companies sought financial support within a short period after receiving an unqualified opinion (Sikka 2009). Since then, researchers have paid more attention to the association between bankruptcy and the auditing profession, suggesting that the propensity to issue going concern opinions prior to bankruptcy increases after a crisis (Geiger et al. 2014). However, evidence about the auditors' ability to warn investors about upcoming failures is not unanimous, as other prior studies have suggested that investors perceive audit reports as informative (Dopuch et al. 1987; Piñeiro-Sánchez et al. 2013), emphasizing that audit opinions provide explanatory power for predicting bankruptcy (Kim et al. 2008; Altman et al. 2010).

A systematic literature review was conducted to present the state-of-the-art literature regarding the relationship between the external audit information and the prediction of bankruptcy, and to show the contribution of the current study.

2.1. Systematic Literature Review: Scope of the Review

All of the academic papers from the Institute for Scientific Information (ISI) Web of Knowledge database as of December 2018 were compiled according to two keywords: "audit" and "bankruptcy". The preliminary search identified many papers focused on the broad domains of bankruptcy. The process of reading the abstracts and introductions of the articles led to the further elimination of studies outside the scope of this research. After filtering the results, 86 articles on the integration between auditing and bankruptcy remained for this study. With the purpose of systematizing and organizing the literature, these papers were assembled and classified according to their main themes, by dividing them into four lines of research: the effects of auditing; audit quality and auditor independence; audit opinion prediction; and bankruptcy prediction using auditing. The contribution of the current study will fall into this fourth category, although all four lines are absolutely interconnected. A list of the reviewed articles appears in Table 1, explaining their samples, methodologies, and key findings.

Table 1. Literature review of bankruptcy and auditing.

Studies/Year	Sample (Country/Type of Firms/Years/Number)	Key Findings/Methodology
Line of research: Effects of auditing		
Lowe and Reckers (1994)	US/92 prospective jurors	Outcome knowledge biases jurors' evaluations of the auditor's judgement/Experiment
Menon and Williams (1994)	US/Public/1990/100 L&H clients and 4523 non-L&H clients	The disclosure of bankruptcy has an adverse effect on market prices and the market does not react to an auditor's replacement/Multivariate test (OLS)
Chen and Church (1996)	US/Public/1980–1988/98 bankrupt	Firms receiving GCOs experience less negative excess returns in the period surrounding bankruptcy filings than those receiving clean opinions/Multivariate test (logit)
Buchman and Collins (1998)	US/Public/1977/60 with qualified opinions for litigation uncertainty and 331 with unqualified	Qualified opinions are useful for financial statement users in predicting material litigation losses/Multivariate test (logit)
Charitou et al. (2007)	US/Public/1986–2004/859 bankrupt and 859 non-bankrupt	Managers of highly distressed firms shift earnings downward before filing for bankruptcy/Multivariate test (earnings management accrual models)
Blay et al. (2011)	US/Public/1989–2006/431 with GCO and 431 without	GCOs represent a risk communication to the equity market and result in a shift of the market's perception of distressed firms/Multivariate test (models based on Barth et al. 1998)
Van Caneghem and Van Campenhout (2012)	Belgium/Private/2007/79,097 SMEs	The amount and quality of financial statement information is positively related to the SMEs' financial structures (leverage)/Multivariate test (OLS)
Stanisic et al. (2013)	Serbia/2007–2011/163 audit reports of 33 banks	Special attention should be paid to banks with explanatory paragraphs or qualifications on their auditors' reports/Univariate analyses
Amin et al. (2014)	US/Public/2000–2010/114 firm-year observations with GCOs and 5343 without	There is a positive relationship between the issuance of a GCO and the firm's subsequent cost of equity capital/Multivariate test (models based on Khurana and Raman (2006) and Ogneva et al. (2007))
Eutsler et al. (2016)	US/Public/1995–2012/314 fraud	Auditors are penalized for documenting their awareness of fraud risk if subsequent financial statements are fraudulent/Multivariate test (probit)
Chen et al. (2016)	US/Public/1992–2009/5377	Loan contracts incorporate information contained in qualifications/Multivariate test (OLS and probit)
Kausar and Lennox (2017)	UK/Public/1994–2008/120 bankrupt	Conservative audit reporting compensates less conservative balance sheets where book values of assets exceed their liquidation values/Multivariate test (logit and OLS)
Kausar et al. (2017)	US and UK/Public/1995–2002/823 US and 123 UK first-time GCOs	Investors in a creditor-friendly bankruptcy regime (UK) react more adversely to a first-time GCO than investors in a debtor-friendly regime (US)/Multivariate test (OLS)
Myers et al. (2018)	US/Public/2003–2014/897 new GCOs	Market responses to GCOs are statistically weak and smaller in economic magnitude than has been suggested in prior literature/Multivariate test (OLS)
Line of research: Auditor independence and audit quality		
Schwartz and Menon (1985)	US/Public/1974–1982/132 failed and 132 non-failed	Greater tendency for failed firms to switch auditors than non-failed firms; neither qualifications nor management changes are associated with auditor displacement in failing firms/Univariate analysis
McKeown et al. (1991)	US/Public/1974–1985/134 failed and 160 non-failed	Auditors are less likely to modify opinions of failed firms that are large, have ambiguous probabilities of bankruptcy, or have shorter lags between fiscal year end and audit opinion dates/Multivariate test (logit)
Pratt and Stice (1994)	US/243 responses	The financial conditions of poorer firms are associated with higher levels of litigation risk, more audit evidence, and higher audit fees/Questionnaires to Big 6 partners
Carcello et al. (1995)	US/Public/1972–1992/446	Increase in the propensity to modify bankruptcy-related opinions after the issuance of SAS No. 34 but not after SAS No. 59/Multivariate test (logit)

Table 1. *Cont.*

Studies/Year	Sample (Country/Type of Firms/Years/Number)	Key Findings/Methodology
Raghunandan and Rama (1995)	US/Public/1987–1991/174 and 188 distressed from pre- and post-SAS No. 59 periods, respectively	After SAS No. 59 became effective, auditors were more likely to issue GCOs for distressed non-bankrupt firms and for bankrupt firms prior to failure/Multivariate test (logit)
Ragothaman et al. (1995)	US/Public/1960–1980/34 error and 58 non-error	A prototype expert system that evaluates material errors and potential fraud classifies firms into error and non-error categories correctly/Rule induction
Daily (1996)	US/Large/1988–1993/53 bankrupt and 53 non-bankrupt	No association between affiliated director representation on audit committees or institutional holdings and the incidence of bankruptcy/Multivariate test (logit)
Carcello et al. (1997)	US/Public/1985–1991/248 bankrupt and 440 non-bankrupt	Any evidence of a significant SAS No. 59 effect is highly dependent on the transition period treatment/Multivariate test (logit)
Krishnan and Krishnan (1997)	US/Public/1986–1994/141 auditor resignation firms	Resignation firms differ from dismissal firms along dimensions that capture the likelihood of litigation: distress, the variance of abnormal returns, auditor independence, tenure, and GCOs/Multivariate test (logit)
Louwers (1998)	US/Public and private/1984–1991/808 distressed	When issuing GCOs, auditors focus on the client's financial condition and other indicators of financial distress, and not on factors related to litigation or loss of revenues/Multivariate test (logit)
Louwers et al. (1999)	US/Public/1984–1994/210 first-time GCOs	The "self-fulfilling prophecy" effect has little impact on future company prospects/Multivariate test (logit)
Carcello and Neal (2000)	US/Public/1994/223 distressed	The greater the percentage of affiliated directors on the audit committee, the lower the likelihood of receiving a GCO/Multivariate test (logit)
Vanstraelen (2000)	Belgium/Large/1992–1996/398 distressed and 398 non-distressed	Long-term auditor-client relationships increase the likelihood of an unqualified opinion/Multivariate test (logit)
Citron and Taffler (2001)	UK/Public/1986–1993/99 with GCOs and 99 without	No empirical support for the self-fulfilling prophecy in the UK/Multivariate test (logit)
Geiger and Raghunandan (2001)	US/Public/1991–1998/383 bankrupt	The likelihood of issuing prior GCOs for bankrupt firms decreased after the Private Securities Litigation Reform Act (1995)/Multivariate test (logit)
DeFond et al. (2002)	US/Public/2000/1158 distressed	There is no association between non-audit service fees and impairment of auditor independence/Multivariate test (logit)
Vanstraelen (2002)	Belgium/Large/1992–1996/392 bankrupt, 392 distressed non-bankrupt and 392 non-distressed non-bankrupt firms	In a limited litigious environment, the likelihood of issuing GCOs decreases with higher audit fees and higher proportions of client losses/Multivariate test (logit)
Geiger and Raghunandan (2002)	US/Public/1996–1998/117 distressed	There is an inverse relationship between audit tenure and audit reporting failures/Multivariate test (logit)
Carcello and Neal (2003)	US/Public/1988–1999/124 with GCOs and 250 without	Audit committees with greater independence are more effective in protecting auditors from dismissal after the issuance of first-time GCOs; moreover, the association between committee independence and auditor protection from dismissal has grown stronger over time; finally, the turnover rate for independent committee members increases after auditor dismissals/Multivariate test (logit)
Joe (2003)	US/90 in-charge auditors from an international public accounting firm	Negative press coverage increases the auditors' perceptions of the client's probability of failure, leading to more qualified opinions/Experiment
Ruiz-Barbadillo et al. (2004)	Spain/Public/1991–2000/1199 firm-year observations of distressed firms	For a distressed company, the audit quality affects the likelihood of receiving a GCO/Multivariate test (logit)
Geiger et al. (2005)	US/Public/2000–2003/226 distressed	Auditors were more likely to issue GCOs in the period after December 2001, with the number increasing even more in 2002–03 due to the Sarbanes–Oxley Act (2002)/Multivariate test (logit)

Table 1. *Cont.*

Studies/Year	Sample (Country/Type of Firms/Years/Number)	Key Findings/Methodology
Carey and Simnett (2006)	Australia/Public/1995/1021	For long audit partner tenure, there is a deterioration in audit quality, measured by a lower propensity to issue GCOs/Multivariate test (logit)
Cunnigham (2006)	-	Financial statement insurance could be a way to restructure the auditing industry, so large audit firms can leave without upsetting the financial system/Theoretical study
Knechel and Vanstraelen (2007)	Belgium/Large/1992–1996/309 distressed bankrupt and 309 distressed non-bankrupt	Auditors are not less independent over time, nor do they become better at predicting the failures of companies/Multivariate test (logit)
Carey et al. (2008)	Australia/Public/1994–1997/68 with first-time GCOs and 68 without	Audit switching is positively associated with the issuance of GCOs; moreover, the issuance of a first-time GCO leads to a loss of clients; however, there is no evidence of the self-fulfilling prophecy/Multivariate test (logit)
Gaeremynck et al. (2008)	Belgium/Public and private/1997/200 distressed	While solvency characteristics of an audit-firm portfolio are positively associated with the financial reporting quality amongst firms, there is no association between reporting quality and the portfolio size/Multivariate test (logit)
Robinson (2008)	US/Public/2001–2004/209 bankrupt	There is a positive association between the level of tax services fees and the likelihood of correctly issuing a GCO prior to bankruptcy filing/Multivariate test (logit)
Callaghan et al. (2009)	US/Public/2001–2005/92 bankrupt	There is no connection between the issuance of GCOs and audit and non-audit fees/Multivariate test (logit)
Feldmann and Read (2010)	US/Public/2000–2008/565 bankrupt	While the issuance of GCOs increased sharply in 2002–03 when compared to 2000–01, the number decreased immediately after returning to the pre-Enron level/Multivariate test (logit)
Lim and Tan (2010)	US/Public/2000–2005/12,783 firm-year observations	Audit quality is higher for firms audited by industry specialists relative to non-specialists when auditor tenure increases/Multivariate test (qualified discretionary accruals model (McNichols 2002)
Stanley (2011)	US/Public/2000–2008/31,057 firm-year observations	There is little evidence of an association between audit fees and changes in the clients' solvency, including bankruptcy/Multivariate test (audit fee model, adapted from DeFond et al. (2002) and others)
Arnedo-Ajona et al. (2012)	Spain/Public and private/1992–2002/236 bankrupt and 236 non-bankrupt	Significant increases in the probability of bankruptcy following a GCO are limited to those cases in which the opinion was considered unexpected/Multivariate test (OLS)
Carey et al. (2012)	Australia/Public/1995–1996 and 2004–2005/142 with GCOs	Auditors maintained the reporting accuracy of GCOs before and after corporate collapses in 2001/Multivariate test (logit)
Basioudis et al. (2012)	US/Public/2000–2007 10,394 firm-year observations of distressed firms	High non-audit fees affect auditor independence only when audit tenure is long or when auditor quality is poor/Multivariate test (logit)
Chen et al. (2013)	US/Public and private/2000–2007/801 firm-year observations with first-time GCOs and 11,528 without	The likelihood of receiving a GCO is negatively associated with the level of insider trading/Multivariate test (logit, probit, and OLS)
García-Blandón and Argiles-Bosch (2013)	Spain/Public/2001–2009/881 firm-year observations	The probability of issuing audit qualifications decreases with audit tenure/Multivariate test (logit)
Geiger et al. (2014)	US/Public/2004–2010/414 bankrupt	The propensity of issuing a GCO prior to bankruptcy increased after the GFC/Multivariate test (logit)
Rodríguez-López et al. (2014)	Galicia (Spain)/Private/1990–1997/60 distressed and 60 non-distressed	Distress prediction models that use financial ratios show higher performance rates than audit-based forecast models/Multivariate test (MDA and logit) and neural networks
Aguiar-Díaz and Díaz-Díaz (2015)	Spain/Private/2007–2010/733 distressed	Auditor behaviors change depending on the client size, suggesting that larger auditors provide higher audit quality for larger clients/Multivariate test (probit) and simultaneous equation model
Kuhn et al. (2015)	One firm (Frontier Airlines, a low-cost US airline)	The development of a systems design theory for continuous auditing systems/Case study

Table 1. *Cont.*

Studies/Year	Sample (Country/Type of Firms/Years/Number)	Key Findings/Methodology
Kumar and Lim (2015)	US/Public/1996–2000/4669 Andersen clients and 17,793 other Big 5 clients	Andersen's audit quality did not differ materially from its peers prior to its failure/Multivariate tests (earnings response coefficients, magnitudes of abnormal accruals, propensity to issue GCOs, the usefulness of GCOs in predicting bankruptcy) and frequency of AAER
Shu et al. (2015)	Taiwan/Public/1999–2010/9876 firm-year observations	The level and volatility of the audit report lag is positively related to the clients' credit risk/Multivariate test (logit)
Carson et al. (2016)	Australia/Public/2005–2013/15,855	GCOs have increased beyond the GFC in Australian publicly listed companies/Univariate test
Read and Yezegel (2016)	US/Public/2002–2008/401 bankrupt	There is no association between audit tenure and the Big 4 firms not issuing prior GCOs to bankrupt firms, and there is a non-linear association for non-Big 4 firms/Multivariate test (logit)
Cao et al. (2017)	US/Public/2000–2010/11,056 distressed firms that distributed income	When issuing GCOs, auditors underreact to corporate payout decreases (negative signals) but react appropriately to payout increases/Multivariate test (logit)
Chen et al. (2017)	US/Public/2000–2013/4322 firm-year observations of distressed firms	Auditors issue fewer GCOs and more material weakness opinions to firms following innovative prospector strategies than cost-leadership defenders/Multivariate test (probit)
Cohen et al. (2017)	Italy/Local governments/2003–2012/44 distressed and 53 non-distressed	Personnel expenses over revenues, short-term liabilities over revenues, and the reliance on subsidies are discriminators of financial distress/Multivariate test (logit)
Hope et al. (2017)	US/Public/2000–2013/1610 firms (538 pilot firms and 1072 non-pilot firms)	Audit fees increase when auditors are concerned about bankruptcy risk or when managers are less likely to be disciplined by short sellers/Multivariate test (OLS)
Koh and Lee (2017)	US/Public/2000–2009/1157 bankrupt	Greater CEO risk-decreasing incentives are positively related to a lower probability of bankruptcy and a lower tendency to issue GCOs/Multivariate test (logit and OLS)
Lennox and Kausar (2017)	US/Public/2000–2013/51,882 firm-year observations	Estimation risk significantly affects auditor behavior/Multivariate test (regressions)
Muñoz-Izquierdo et al. (2017)	Spain/Private/2004–2014/404 bankrupt	Audit reports of bankrupt firms vary depending on auditor size, client industry, and financial condition and the stage of insolvency legal proceedings/Univariate test
Berglund et al. (2018)	US/Public/2000–2013/933 first-time GCOs and 8334 distressed clients with no GCOs	Controlling for the firms' financial health, there is a positive relationship between auditor size and the issuance of GCOs/Multivariate test (logit)
Pedrosa Rodríguez and López-Corrales (2018)	Spain/Private/pre-GFC period (2006–2007) and GFC period (2008–2010)	The propensity to issue GCOs increased during the GFC for both Big 4 and non-Big 4 auditors/Multivariate test (logit)
Read and Yezegel (2018)	US/Public/2006–2015/340 bankrupt	The propensity to issue GCOs significantly increased following the GFC, but decreased to GFC levels after two post-GFC recovery periods/Multivariate test (logit)
Line of research: Audit opinion prediction		
McKeown et al. (1991)	US/Public/1974–1985/134 bankrupt and 160 non-bankrupt	Firms that do not receive qualified opinions are more likely to have ambiguous bankruptcy probabilities, to be larger, and to have shorter time periods between their fiscal year ends and audit report dates than those that do receive GCOs. Additionally, hidden fraud does not explain the auditors' failure to modify opinions of distressed companies that go bankrupt/Multivariate test (logit)
Lenard et al. (1995)	US/Public/1982–1987/40 with GCO and 40 without	Neural networks are proposed as a robust alternative for auditors to support their issuance of GCOs/Neural networks and multivariate test (logit)
McKee (1995)	US/Public/1986–1989/30 with GCO and 30 without	Induction algorithm predicts bankruptcy using a simple and theoretically consistent model with 97% accuracy/Inductive inferencing algorithm
Lundberg and Nagle (2002)	US/55 professional auditors	Professional auditors edit crucial signals, but the extent of the post-decision editing depends on the task and the presence/absence of feedback/Experiment

Table 1. *Cont.*

Studies/Year	Sample (Country/Type of Firms/Years/Number)	Key Findings/Methodology
Zdolsek and Jagric (2011)	UK and Ireland/Public/1997–2002/265 with qualified opinion and 265 with non-qualified	Development of a model to identify qualified opinions using accounting ratios/Multivariate test (logit)
Cassell et al. (2013)	US/Public/2004–2009/6702 firm-year observations with comment letter	Low profitability, high complexity, engaging a small audit firm, and weaknesses in governance are positively associated with the receipt of SEC comment letters/Multivariate tests (logit and OLS)
Ittonen et al. (2017)	US/Public/2003–2015/5146 non-financial firms obtained from Compustat	GCOs should be issued when there is an 8% chance (or higher) that the client is bankrupt/Shannon entropy from information theory
Line of research: Bankruptcy prediction using auditing		
Casterella et al. (2000)	US/Public/1982–1992/100 bankrupt	Auditors do not appear to be able to predict either bankruptcy filings or resolutions/Multivariate analysis (logit)
McKee (2003)	US/Public/1991–1997/146 bankrupt and 145 non-bankrupt	Rough set models do not provide a significant comparative advantage regarding prediction accuracy over auditors' methodologies/Artificial intelligence (rough sets)
Kim et al. (2008)	Republic of Korea/1991–2003/35 firms that recovered from financial distress and 24 non-recovered	Audit opinion, client risk, and client size are accurate predictors of the survival prospects of distressed firms/Multivariate test (logit)
Altman et al. (2010)	UK/Private/2000–2007/5.8 million SMEs, of which 66,000 failed	Creditors' legal actions, company filing histories, comprehensive audit reports, and audit opinions contribute to increasing the default prediction power of risk models for SMEs/Multivariate test (logit)
Piñeiro-Sánchez et al. (2012)	Galicia (Spain)/Private/1998–2008/101 distressed and 101 non-distressed	The accumulation of qualified opinions and high auditor rotation rates are reliable measures of credit risk and predictors of bankruptcy/Multivariate test (logit)
Piñeiro-Sánchez et al. (2013)	Galicia (Spain)/Private/1998–2008/98 distressed	High auditor rotation, qualified reports, and non-compliance with the publication deadlines of financial statements are accurate indicators of financial distress/Multivariate test (logit)
Van Peursem and Chan (2014)	New Zealand/Public/2001–2010/25 failed and 25 non-failed	There are significant differences between failing and non-failing firms that can be detected using financial ratios and audit data/Univariate analysis
Appiah and Amon (2017)	UK/Public/1994–2011/98 insolvent and 269 solvent	There is a negative association between meetings and the independence of the audit committee/Multivariate test (logit)
Armeanu et al. (2017)	Romania/Public/2013/69	Business failure is negatively influenced by CEO gender, board size, and audit committee/Multivariate test (principal components)
Desai et al. (2017)	US/Public/1995–2015/All distressed firms in the SEC's EDGAR database	The survival rate of first-time GCOs is much lower using delisting as a measure of financial viability than bankruptcy/Search engine technology (textual analysis)

In Table 1, AAER: Accounting and Auditing Enforcement Releases; GCO: going concern opinion; GFC: global financial crisis; L&H: Laventhol and Horwath; MDA: multiple discriminant analysis; OLS: ordinary least squares; SAS: Statement on Auditing Standards; SEC: Securities and Exchange Commission; SMEs: small and medium-sized enterprises; UK: United Kingdom; US: United States.

2.1.1. Line of Research: Effects of Auditing

Qualified opinions issued by auditors can have an impact in different ways. Audited financial statements with qualifications, or even Emphasis of Matter paragraphs, should be reviewed more carefully than unqualified audit reports (Stanisic et al. 2013). This advice is especially salient when qualifications are related to going concern uncertainties. For example, loan contracts include information regarding qualifications (Chen et al. 2016). However, it is not only qualifications that impact debt contracting. Going concern opinions can be interpreted as a communication of risk to the equity market (Blay et al. 2011), as they have an adverse effect on market prices (Menon and Williams 1994) and can cause an increase in the subsequent cost of capital (Amin et al. 2014). In particular, Kausar et al. (2017) found that the reaction to a first-time going concern opinion is more adverse in a creditor-friendly regime, such as that in the UK, than in a debtor-friendly regime, such as that in the US. However, recent evidence has shown that market reactions to going concern opinions are statistically weaker than has been suggested in prior literature (Myers et al. 2018).

2.1.2. Line of Research: Auditor Independence and Audit Quality

As evidenced in the review of the research, many studies have evaluated audit quality. Audit quality is one of the most relevant issues facing the auditing profession, and it depends on the auditor's competence and independence (Vanstraelen 2000). Competence relies on the auditor's knowledge and technological capabilities, and prior studies have shown that auditors can discover errors in the accounting system (Kida 1980).

Since audit quality is crucial for the effectiveness of the auditing profession (Vanstraelen 2000), factors that can impact independence, such as the pricing of audit services (Vanstraelen 2002; Robinson 2008; Callaghan et al. 2009; Stanley 2011; Basioudis et al. 2012; Hope et al. 2017), auditor tenure (Geiger and Raghunandan 2002; Carey and Simnett 2006; Knechel and Vanstraelen 2007; Read and Yezegel 2016), audit report lags (Shu et al. 2015), auditors' decisions to resign (Krishnan and Krishnan 1997), auditor switching (Schwartz and Menon 1985; Carey et al. 2008), or the composition of the audit committee (Carcello and Neal 2000, 2003) have been extensively studied. The issuance of going concern opinions has also been accepted as a measure of auditor independence and quality throughout the literature (Carey and Simnett 2006; Robinson 2008; DeFond and Zhang 2014; Koh and Lee 2017; Berglund et al. 2018). As auditor independence is difficult to assess directly, other common proxies used in the literature have been linked to the characteristics of clients, such as their size (McKeown et al. 1991; Aguiar-Díaz and Díaz-Díaz 2015), financial condition (Pratt and Stice 1994; Louwers et al. 1999; Muñoz-Izquierdo et al. 2017), strategies (Chen et al. 2017), corporate payouts (Cao et al. 2017), and CEO incentives (Koh and Lee 2017).

Although the empirical evidence is not unanimous, many studies have supported auditor independence. For instance, Louwers et al. (1999) confirmed that their assessments focused on the client's financial condition and other indicators of financial distress, and not on factors related to litigation risk or loss of clients. Additionally, DeFond et al. (2002) did not find an association between non-audit fees and impairment of independence, and Knechel and Vanstraelen (2007) stated that independence was maintained over time.

Additionally, audit quality has received increased attention after regulatory changes, corporate collapses, or economic crises. Carcello et al. (1995) found that qualified opinions increased after the issuance of Statement of Auditing Standard (SAS) No. 34 and not after SAS No. 59, while Feldmann and Read (2010) argued that the likelihood of going concern opinions increased sharply immediately after the Enron collapse, and Carey et al. (2012) showed that the likelihood of these opinions returned to pre-Enron level shortly thereafter. Pedrosa Rodríguez and López-Corrales (2018) posited that the propensity to issue going concern opinions increased during the recent global financial crisis in Spain, and similar evidence was found using publicly listed Australian firms by Carson et al. (2016). After the crisis, Geiger et al. (2014) indicated that going concern opinions kept increasing, but Read and Yezegel (2018) pointed out that they decreased to the crisis levels after two post recovery periods.

All this evidence shows that qualifications are interpreted as external signals of potential financial instabilities (Buchman and Collins 1998), and they also communicate information about audit quality (Piñeiro-Sánchez et al. 2013). The current study added more evidence to this line of research about the independence of auditors as they disclosed signals of bankruptcy in their audit reports before, during, and after the global financial crisis.

2.1.3. Line of Research: Audit Opinion Prediction

Prior research has shown that auditors signal bankruptcy in approximately half of the cases in which companies subsequently file for bankruptcy (McKee 2003; Laitinen and Laitinen 2009).

Ittonen et al. (2017) suggested that going concern opinions should be issued when there is an 8% chance that the firm is bankrupt. McKeown et al. (1991) found that auditors issued less qualified opinions to larger firms, firms with shorter time lags between the fiscal year end and the audit opinion dates, and when the probability of bankruptcy was ambiguous. Additionally, empirical evidence has also shown that accounting data can be used to identify qualified opinions. Different methodologies, such as logistic regression (Zdolsek and Jagric 2011), neural networks (Lenard et al. 1995), or inductive inferencing algorithms (McKee 1995) have been applied for this purpose.

2.1.4. Line of Research: Bankruptcy Prediction Using Auditing

Prior works have found associations between audit quality, financial distress, and qualified reports (Blay 2005; Arnedo-Ajona et al. 2012). However, there seems to be no consensus on the accuracy of auditing information for predicting bankruptcy or the survival of firms. On one hand, it can be argued that auditors are not able to predict either bankruptcy filings or resolutions (Casterella et al. 2000). On the other hand, some researchers have agreed with the idea that differences between failing and non-failing firms might be detected using financial ratios and audit data (Van Peursem and Chan 2014). Some audit information contributes to an increase in default prediction power, such as the recurrent issuance of qualified opinions, high auditor rotation or lack of meetings, and the lack of independence of the audit committee (Kim et al. 2008; Altman et al. 2010; Piñeiro-Sánchez et al. 2012, 2013; Appiah and Amon 2017; Armeanu et al. 2017). The present study contributes to this research line by examining the predictive ability of information easily extracted from the audit report, which has resulted in variables never tested before in prediction literature.

2.2. Research Question Development

Although the auditing profession ensures the credibility of a firm's financial statements in the audit report, it seems that the audit report has not been well studied as a measure of bankruptcy prediction. Research opportunities remain in this area, and the present study has attempted to fill this gap.

The main role of external auditors is to guarantee the reliability of the financial statements presented by any company. Thus, it seems that the information included in audit reports is likely to improve the accuracy of bankruptcy prediction modeling. Based on this reasoning, audit report information should be incorporated as explanatory variables in statistical models. With this in mind, the research question to be investigated is specified as follows:

Research question: What information in the external audit report can accurately predict bankruptcy?

It is expected that information from the audit report will provide accurate bankruptcy predictive power, and therefore this work may complement previous studies. This is the first study to have applied the audit report in isolation as a bankruptcy predictor. Additionally, due to the vast number of audit report users (who do not necessarily need to be experts in auditing), the explanatory variables that could best anticipate the event of bankruptcy have been simplified. The variables investigated were the most accurate variables and were also the easiest to detect by any user of the report interested in a firm's insolvency. Finally, this study used novel techniques in the area of auditing for bankruptcy prediction: the non-parametric methodologies of the PART algorithm, random forest, and support vector machine.

3. Methodology

3.1. Sample and the Dependent Variable

As in previous bankruptcy studies, the present work applied a matched sample of bankrupt and non-bankrupt firms (Schwartz and Menon 1985; Carcello and Neal 2003; Knechel and Vanstraelen 2007; Blay et al. 2011). An ad-hoc sample of 808 Spanish private non-financial audited firms was manually selected and prepared from the entire population of firms in the Spanish Bureau Van Dijk (hereafter BVD) database. The sample was evenly divided between bankrupt and non-bankrupt firms.

A company was considered to be bankrupt if it had filed for bankruptcy protection (Piñeiro-Sánchez et al. 2013). Thus, all bankrupt firms included in the database that had filed for bankruptcy proceedings as of 30 January 2015 were identified (1821 firms), and their financial and audit data extracted from this source for the fiscal year prior to the bankruptcy filing date. The filing dates were also manually collected from the "Registro Público Concursal" (the official Spanish source of bankruptcy data), as they did not appear in the BVD database. All of the bankruptcy filing dates along the sample belonged to the 2004–2014 period. Out of the 1821 firms, the final bankrupt sample consisted of 404 observations, with the remaining firms being removed due to missing data.

Subsequently, each bankrupt observation was manually matched with a non-bankrupt firm. For each non-bankrupt firm, financial and audit data was extracted from the BVD database[1] for the fiscal year prior to the bankruptcy filing date of its bankrupt pair. The matching procedure was performed according to year, firm size—using the measure of total assets—and industry, as in the prior literature (Schwartz and Menon 1985; Knechel and Vanstraelen 2007). Therefore, the process resulted in a total sample of 808 firms: 404 bankrupt, which were then matched with 404 non-bankrupt firms.

Following prior literature, a dummy variable was used (*BANKRUPT*) as the dependent variable (Piñeiro-Sánchez et al. 2013), because it represents the start of court bankruptcy proceedings, and therefore provides a legal, objective, and narrow definition of bankruptcy. The variable *BANKRUPT* takes the value of 1 if the firm has filed for bankruptcy proceedings; otherwise, it is 0.

3.2. Independent Variables: Audit Report Variables

In this paper, the independent (or explanatory) variables of bankruptcy were related to the audit report. A summarized definition of all variables is presented in Table 2. The first variable tested was the audit opinion issued in the period prior to bankruptcy, or in the corresponding year for the non-bankrupt firms. The role of the opinion in predicting bankruptcy was examined, using a dummy variable (*AUDIT_OP*) with the following two categories: unqualified (0) and qualified (1) opinion. An opinion is unqualified when the auditor determines that the financial statement gives a true and fair view in accordance with the reporting framework used for the preparation of the annual accounts. An opinion is qualified when the auditor points out that the financial statement is materially misstated, or when the auditor is unable to obtain evidence regarding any transaction or disclosure. The audit opinion dummy variable was chosen as it has been the most studied audit variable in prior bankruptcy literature (Altman and McGough 1974; Laitinen and Laitinen 2009). It was expected that the opinion would contribute to distinguishing between bankrupt and non-bankrupt firms, according to prior findings (Piñeiro-Sánchez et al. 2013). According to Altman et al. (2010), there is a positive relationship between the likelihood of filing for bankruptcy and the issuance of a qualified report.

The second and third independent variables of this study represent the type of paragraph that auditors include in the report (if any). The dummy variable *EMPHASIS* takes the value of 1 if an Emphasis of Matter paragraph is included in the report, and 0 otherwise. Auditors disclose matter paragraphs when it is necessary to mention significant uncertainties, appropriately included in the notes to the financial statements. Emphasis sections point out fundamental matters for the users' understanding. These paragraphs do not qualify as the opinion, but represent concerns for the auditor and relevant signals regarding the likelihood of the firm's survival (Blay 2005).

Similarly, the categorical variable *SCOPE_VIOLATIONS* has a value of 1 when either a qualification regarding a scope violation or a qualification due to a violation of generally accepted accounting

---

1 The audit data available in the BVD database is a section called the "Auditor's opinion". It consists of a maximum of 991 characters of the report representing emphasis paragraphs, qualification paragraphs, or both. From this field, we extracted the audit opinion (unqualified or qualified), the type of paragraphs disclosed, and the number of comments in those paragraphs. We identified the comments manually by reading and labeling the content of each report.

principles (GAAP) is included; 2 when both qualifications are issued in the report; and 0 when none are disclosed. It was hypothesized that the inclusion of any of these paragraphs in the audit report reveals a sign of possible bankruptcy, as indicated by the auditor. This expectation is in line with the rationale of the *AUDIT_OP* variable, because prior evidence suggests that prediction accuracy increases once the audit report (unqualified or qualified) is included in the estimation models (Altman et al. 2010).

Table 2. Classification and description of the audit report variables in this study.

AUDIT OPINION	*AUDIT_OP*	Dummy variable with a value of 1 if the auditor's report is qualified, and 0 if it is unqualified.
TYPE OF PARAGRAPH	*EMPHASIS*	Dummy variable with a value of 1 if the auditor's report has an Emphasis of Matter paragraph, 0 otherwise.
	SCOPE_VIOLATIONS	Categorical variable with a value of 0 if no qualifications appear in the report, 1 if the audit report has a qualification due to a scope limitation or due a GAAP violation, and 2 if the report shows both.
NUMBER OF COMMENTS	*NUMBER_COMM*	Categorical variable with a value of 0 if no comments are disclosed in the report, and 1 to 6 according to the number of comments shown.

Table 2 summarizes the independent variables used in this study and the audit report variables.

Furthermore, not only did was the type of paragraphs disclosed in the audit report tested, but also the number of comments mentioned by auditors in them. A categorical variable (*NUMBER_COMM*) was incorporated that had the value of 0 when no comments were disclosed, and otherwise 1 to 6 in agreement with the number of comments shown. Six comments was the maximum number found in a few firms in the database. Most comments were related to accounting elements, such as the valuation of assets, liabilities, accumulated losses, or negative working capital, but auditors also write about regulatory issues, concerns regarding markets in which firms operate, or companies being involved in legal processes[2]. A positive association was hypothesized between an increase in the number of comments and the propensity to file for bankruptcy, which was based on the idea that more comments might point to higher chances of bankruptcy and more concerns for users when reading the audit report. A contribution was made to the literature by adding this variable to the estimation models as, to our knowledge, the predictive power of the accumulation of auditor comments has not been tested thus far.

3.3. *Artificial Intelligence Methodology: The PART Algorithm*

Despite the popularity of parametric models (such as the commonly used multivariate discriminant analysis or the logit regression model) for bankruptcy prediction, another current research approach to tackle financial problems is based on non-parametric techniques such as artificial intelligence

2 To illustrate the process of identifying the comments in the audit report, here is one example of a firm included in our sample. This firm filed for bankruptcy in 2008 and issued an unqualified audit report with an emphasis on the matter paragraph in the same year. According to the BVD database, this paragraph said: "The company incurred a net loss of 3128 thousand of euros during the year ended 31 December 2008. Also, as of that date, its current liabilities exceeded its total assets so that the company may be unable to convert its assets into funds that can be used to meet its financial obligations. Additionally, as stated in Note 16 in the financial statements, the company holds significant investments in group companies under serious financial distress. These events or conditions indicate that a material uncertainty exists that may cast significant doubt on the company's ability to continue as a going concern. Although the financial statements were prepared on a going concern basis, the company may be unable to realize its assets, specially the tax credit, and discharge its liabilities in the normal course of business." Therefore, the comments of the report basically total six in number: accumulated losses, negative working capital, short-term and long-term financial investments, going concern, and deferred tax assets. These are the comments that we took into consideration in our sample, so the independent variable *NUMBER_COMM* for this firm took the value of six. For this firm, the other three independent dummy variables of the study took the following values: *AUDIT_OP* value of 0 (unqualified), *EMPHASIS* takes the value of 1 (matter paragraph disclosed), and *SCOPE_VIOLATIONS* is 0 (no qualifications).

(Calderon and Cheh 2002; Zięba et al. 2016; Amani and Fadlalla 2017). While parametric techniques have shown satisfactory results, they have a drawback when applied to real bankruptcy data, as some hypotheses required are not satisfied (especially if outliers exist). However, artificial intelligence techniques, which are non-parametric, do not require the data to satisfy any concrete assumptions. This advantage allows them to predict bankruptcy more accurately. Indeed, artificial intelligence methods have already been used to explain insolvency risk (Kumar and Ravi 2007; Wu 2010; Koyuncugil and Ozgulbas 2012; Kirkos 2015) and prior research has also applied these methods for anticipating going concern issues (Lenard et al. 1995; Yeh et al. 2014).

In this paper, the PART algorithm was used as the main artificial intelligence technique. Additionally, the validity of the results was tested by applying two other machine learning methodologies, namely random forest and support vector machine, as robustness checks.

The PART algorithm is a rule induction classifier developed by Frank and Witten (1998) that generates rules by incorporating a modified form of the J48 decision tree and eliminating some of the paths found in an initial decision tree structure. This algorithm builds partial decision trees instead of fully explored ones. Once the algorithm finds the partial tree, the tree-building stops and a rule is generated with the leaf that represents the greatest number of situations. Due to the fact that it is based on partial decision trees, the main advantage of the PART algorithm is its simplicity. However, its performance is similar to that of other machine learning algorithms. Consequently, this explicative technique was chosen because of the simplicity of its rules, with no loss of accuracy. The results are easier to interpret when compared to other classifiers as they are expressed in logical if/else statements (Díaz-Martínez et al. 2009). Additionally, the usefulness of this methodology has been corroborated in business studies (Camacho-Miñano et al. 2015), although it has not been applied before for bankruptcy prediction using audit report variables.

The rules created by the PART algorithm classify objects into decision classes depending on a series of variables or conditions. These rules are expressed in logical statements with the following form: IF < conditions are fulfilled > THEN < the object belongs to a given decision class >.

In this study, the objects were firms, the two decision classes were bankrupt and non-bankrupt, and the conditions were all audit report variables or independent variables. Thus, the PART algorithm was applied to classify firms (objects) into bankrupt and non-bankrupt (decision classes) depending on a set of audit report variables (conditions).

4. Results and Discussion

4.1. *Summary Statistics*

Summary statistics of the sample are provided in Table 3. Bankrupt and non-bankrupt firms had the same frequency per industry due to the matching technique used. The total sample included a variety of industries, with construction and real-estate firms making up the largest group (35%), mainly due to the impact of the housing bubble during the global financial crisis in Spain (Conefrey and Gerald 2010). Accordingly, along with the matching procedure, this study controlled for firm size in its statistical analyses, by measuring by the firms' total assets in thousands of euros.

Table 3. Descriptive statistics.

Frequency of Industries by Bankruptcy Classification				
	Bankrupt firms	Non-bankrupt firms	Total	Total (%)
Construction and real-estate	141	141	282	35%
Manufacturing	110	110	220	27%
Commercial	79	79	158	20%
Services	70	70	140	17%
Primary	4	4	8	1%
Total	404	404	808	100%

Table 3. *Cont.*

Means and Standard Deviations by Bankruptcy Classification				
	Bankrupt firms		Non-bankrupt firms	
	Mean	S.D.	Mean	S.D.
Age (years)	22	13	23	14
Size (total assets)	84,352	276,969	84,431	293,514
WCTA	−0.090	0.401	0.239	0.307
EBITTA	−0.169	0.329	0.026	0.104
BVETL	0.278	1.098	1.728	3.015
# of obs.	404		404	

Table 3 presents the summary statistics of the sample. The total sample comprised 808 firms, 404 of which had filed for bankruptcy legal proceedings. The rest, or non-bankrupt group, were manually selected to match the year, size (total assets), and industry of one of the bankrupt observations. Industries of the sample were created based on NACE (Nomenclature of Economic Activities) codes. The age of the sample was expressed in years and the size in thousands of euros. WCTA stands for "Working capital divided by total assets", EBITTA for "Earnings before interest and taxes divided by total assets", and BVETL for "Book value of equity divided by total liabilities". Data used to calculate the financial ratios was winsorized at 1% and 99%. Finally, # of obs. is the number of observations.

Regarding the financial condition of the sample, bankrupt companies are generally more illiquid (lower working capital to total assets ratio), less profitable (lower return on assets ratio), and more leveraged (higher book value of equity to total liabilities ratio) than non-bankrupt firms, which is consistent with prior studies (Bellovary et al. 2007; Tascón-Fernández and Castaño-Gutiérrez 2012; Altman et al. 2017).

4.2. The Results of the PART Algorithm

4.2.1. PART Algorithm: Model 1

Results of the estimation models using the PART algorithm are presented below. Model 1 is based on the audit opinion (*AUDIT_OP*) as the only explanatory variable of bankruptcy (see Figure 1). The classification power of the model was 68.20% (31.80% incorrectly classified cases). According to this model, this dummy variable classified 513 firms as non-bankrupt with 36% error (183 errors) and 295 as bankrupt (25% error). This result suggests that, in isolation, the audit opinion anticipated the financial condition of two-thirds of the sample accurately. Although this prediction does not appear to be very precise, it is relevant, considering that the model only includes one variable. This evidence complements previous studies where the audit opinion was a bankruptcy predictor (Hopwood et al. 1989; Laitinen and Laitinen 2009; Altman et al. 2010; Piñeiro-Sánchez et al. 2012, 2013) and those that interpreted qualifications as external signals of potential financial instabilities (Buchman and Collins 1998). However, this variable solely has never before been used 23 March 2019, probably due to the number of incorrectly classified cases obtained. In the following models, more explanatory variables were included, to increase the predictive accuracy.

If AUDIT_OP* (audit opinion) = Unqualified, *then
: Non-bankrupt firms (correctly/incorrectly classified cases: 513/183)
: Bankrupt firms (correctly/incorrectly classified cases: 295/74)

Number of Rules: 2

=== Stratified cross-validation ===
Correctly Classified Instances 551 68.1931 %
Incorrectly Classified Instances 257 31.8069 %
Total Number of Instances 808

Figure 1. Model 1: The audit opinion PART model.

4.2.2. PART Algorithm: Model 2

As the prediction was relatively low in Model 1, Model 2 added the two dummy variables of the type of paragraphs disclosed in the audit report (*EMPHASIS* and *SCOPE_VIOLATIONS*) to the initial model, when those paragraphs existed in the firms (see Figure 2). As mentioned previously, auditors place their comments in the audit report, either in the Emphasis of Matter sections that do not qualify the opinion (*EMPHASIS*) or in qualification paragraphs (*SCOPE_VIOLATIONS*). In Model 2, the predictive power increased to 76.49% (23.51% incorrectly classified cases). This result showed the relevance of the type of paragraph for explaining bankruptcy, as the prediction improved by 8% when compared to Model 1. Even more importantly, it provided evidence of the importance of Matter sections when predicting bankruptcy. The existence of qualifications did not appear in the model as it is embedded in the qualified opinion (when the opinion is qualified, a qualification paragraph is disclaimed), that is, when the dummy variable *AUDIT_OP* takes the value of 1.

If *AUDIT_OP* (audit opinion) = Unqualified *and EMPHASIS* = 0 (no emphasis of matter paragraph), *then*
: Non-bankrupt firms (correctly/incorrectly classified cases: 324/55)
: Bankrupt firms (correctly/incorrectly classified cases: 484/135)

Number of Rules: 2

=== Stratified cross-validation ===
Correctly Classified Instances 618 76.4851 %
Incorrectly Classified Instances 190 23.5149 %
Total Number of Instances 808

Figure 2. Model 2: The audit opinion and type of paragraphs PART model.

As per Model 2, if the audit opinion was unqualified (*AUDIT_OP* = 0), the viability of the firm was determined by the existence of a Matter section. Without an Emphasis of Matter paragraph, the model classified the firms as non-bankrupt (*AUDIT_OP* = 0 and *EMPHASIS* = 0) in 324 cases (17% error). Interestingly, even when the opinion was unqualified, the algorithm classified a firm as bankrupt when a Matter section was disclosed (*AUDIT_OP* = 0 and *EMPHASIS* = 1), and this rule codified 484 firms (28% error). This empirical evidence validates prior studies that suggest that auditors issued unqualified reports to some bankrupt firms during the recent global financial crisis (Sikka 2009). However, the role of external auditors during that period could not be fully questioned, as their main task was to guarantee the reliability of the firms' financial statements and, according to the results of this study, were at least issuing Matter sections emphasizing their financial concerns about soon-to-be-bankrupt firms.

4.2.3. PART Algorithm: Model 3

In Model 3, the number of comments in the paragraphs was aggregated to the PART algorithm as a new independent and categorical variable (see Figure 3). This model strongly codified firms as non-bankrupt when there were no paragraphs, so in the absence of comments *NUMBER_COMM* = 0. This rule classified 324 firms as non-bankrupt (17% error). The same classification was provided by the algorithm when one comment was disclosed but the opinion was unqualified, so the comment was disclosed in a Matter section (55 firms classified as non-bankrupt, 20% error).

If NUMBER_COMM **(number of comments) = 0,** ***then***
: Non-bankrupt firms (correctly/incorrectly classified cases: 324/55)

If NUMBER_COMM **= 1** ***and AUDIT_OP*** **= qualified,** ***then*** **bankrupt firms (correctly/incorrectly classified cases: 121/48)**

If NUMBER_COMM **= 2,** ***then*** **bankrupt firms (correctly/incorrectly classified cases: 115/27)**

If NUMBER_COMM **= 3,** ***then*** **bankrupt firms (correctly/incorrectly classified cases: 87/8)**

If NUMBER_COMM **= 4,** ***then*** **bankrupt firms (correctly/incorrectly classified cases: 70/7)**

If NUMBER_COMM **= 1,** ***then*** **non-bankrupt firms (correctly/incorrectly classified cases: 55/10)**

: Bankrupt firms (correctly classified cases: 36)

Number of Rules: 7

=== Stratified cross-validation ===
Correctly Classified Instances 653 80.8168 %
Incorrectly Classified Instances 155 19.1832 %
Total Number of Instances 808

Figure 3. Model 3: The audit opinion, type of paragraphs, and number of comments in the PART model.

However, with one comment in a qualification paragraph (*NUMBER_COMM* = 1 and *AUDIT_OP* = 1), the classification already moved to bankruptcy (121 bankrupt firms, 40% error). From one comment onwards (*NUMBER_COMM* = 2; 3; 4), there was a prevailing discrimination toward bankruptcy with a low percentage of error. In line with prior studies that incorporated different qualifications in their estimations (Hopwood et al. 1989; Piñeiro-Sánchez et al. 2012), the inclusion of the number of comments increased the predictive ability of the model (in this study, the classification went up 5%, from 76.49% to 80.82%), indicating that if auditors disclose several concerns in their reports, it is very plausible that the viability of the firm is being questioned. Thus, these results indicate that there is a positive relationship between the propensity of a firm to file for bankruptcy and a high number of comments disclosed in the audit report. The evidence from this model complemented the prior literature because this is the first time in which the accumulation of auditors' comments was tested for bankruptcy predictive purposes.

In conclusion, after analyzing the findings of the three models, the research question could be answered. The audit report information—mainly consisting of the easily extracted variables of the audit opinion, the disclosure of a Matter paragraph, and the number of comments shown—represents accurate measures for predicting bankruptcy. Thus, there is a positive relationship between these audit report disclosures and the propensity of a firm to file for bankruptcy.

4.2.4. Robustness: Random Forest and SVM

To ensure the reliability of the empirical evidence in this study, two robustness checks were performed, using other artificial intelligence methodologies. These checks examined whether the correctly classified instances remained constant, using random forest and support vector machine. These two methods were chosen because they are widely applied in the bankruptcy and going concern prediction literature (Min and Lee 2005; Min et al. 2006; Yeh et al. 2014). Random Forest is a machine learning classifier that uses a combination of independent decision trees to model data (Yeh et al. 2014). The trees are built using bootstrap samples, not all data are applied to build a tree, and features are randomly selected at each node. Therefore, Random Forest is one of the most accurate and efficient classifiers, even in large datasets with missing data, as it generates an unbiased estimate of the generalization error as the forest building progresses.

Support vector machine is a learning algorithm that applies a linear model to implement nonlinear classes through vectors into a high-dimensional space (Min and Lee 2005). It finds a maximum margin hyperplane that provides the maximum separation between decision classes. The support vectors are the examples used for defining the classes, and are the closest to the hyperplane. Support vector machine has been used in bankruptcy prediction because the results are easy to analyze, less theory-driven and more data-driven, and more distribution-free than conventional statistical techniques (Min and Lee 2005).

Motivated by these studies, random forest and support vector machine were applied to check the robustness of the results of the PART algorithm. The untabulated evidence of this study suggests that the confusion matrixes obtained by the random forest and the support vector machine revealed the same percentages of correctly-classified cases as the PART algorithm. For Models 1, 2, and 3, the percentages of classification accuracy were 68.2%, 76.5%, and 80.8%, respectively. Therefore, according to other machine learning algorithms, the ability to anticipate bankruptcy for the audit report variables of this study was robust. When auditors issue their reports, users may pay attention to the type of opinion, the existence of a Matter paragraph, and other comments included in qualification paragraphs, as these pieces of information represent signs of a firm's bankruptcy.

5. General Conclusions

The aim of this paper was to examine the explanatory power of the external audit report when predicting the bankruptcy situation of firms. New prediction models were introduced using artificial intelligence methodologies—the PART algorithm, random forest, and support vector machine—which had never been applied before in bankruptcy prediction models using data from audit reports. The evidence indicates that the information extracted from the audit report is useful for analyzing the probability of filing for bankruptcy and anticipating precarious financial conditions with high accuracy. Specifically, using the PART algorithm, classification rules were found where the most significant variables that distinguished between bankrupt and non-bankrupt firms were the audit opinion, the Matter sections disclosed in the audit reports, and the number of comments included in the Matter sections and qualification paragraphs. This evidence shows the positive relationship between the tendency of a firm to file for bankruptcy and the issuance of a qualified report with a high number of comments disclosed by the auditors. Interestingly, our results even corroborated the positive relationship between the bankruptcy filing and an unqualified report issued with comments disclosed in a matter paragraph.

Some implications can be drawn from these results. A contribution was made to the literature of bankruptcy prediction. This is the first study that used three non-parametric methodologies with only variables extracted from the audit report (the audit opinion, type of paragraphs, and number of comments in the report) to forecast a bankruptcy situation. The only study that was closely related to the present study was that by Muñoz-Izquierdo et al. (2019). However, the objectives of both papers were different. Muñoz-Izquierdo et al. (2019) used the content of the audit report to explain the specific causes of business failure, that is, they focused on justifying the reasons why firms failed, such as internal causes like accumulated losses or high debts, or external causes such as changes in the market in which they operate or policy changes that affect them. The current paper looked for an accurate percentage of prediction, and not the particular causes of the bankruptcy. It also attempted to find the minimum number of variables from the audit report that achieved the most accurate bankruptcy predictive power possible, and these variables also needed to be the easiest for any user to obtain without any specific knowledge. Therefore, the current work is a follow-up study of the aforementioned paper, with practical implications for the users of the report. A user can strongly benefit from this study, because it found that there was no need to be an expert in the accounting and auditing domains to be able to use the audit report to detect if a firm was going bankrupt. Simply by identifying the type of opinion, whether or not a Matter section was disclosed by the auditor, and the number of comments included in the section or in a qualification paragraph, any user could quickly and easily predict the chances of bankruptcy with the same accuracy as if they had scrutinized the complete audit report. Therefore, this result may save costs in terms of time and effort to financial analysts, creditors, firms' stakeholders, and other potential users of the audit reports.

Finally, the auditing profession might also benefit from this paper because the results confirmed that, during the global financial crisis, there was an important number of bankrupt firms that issued qualified reports or, at least, a warning in a Matter section about their imminent failure, whereas non-bankrupt companies issued unqualified reports. Thus, even though the role of auditors is to ensure the reliability of the financial information provided to stakeholders, the audit report can also be a "first glance" signal to evaluate a firm's probability of bankruptcy.

The limitations of this study are mainly related to the sample. First, the non-bankrupt group was selected based on a matching process, using the variables of firm size, year, and industry, in accordance with prior literature. Nevertheless, it seems reasonable to think that other variables could have been chosen. Second, this study focused on Spanish private non-financial firms, so some results might have been driven by the specific socio-demographic characteristics of the sample. For instance, due to the Spanish context, the frequency of firms in the different industries of the sample varied significantly. For comparison purposes, future research could focus on an extension of the study to other regulatory contexts and periods of time. Although this line of research could lead to very interesting results, the preparation of the dataset might be time consuming given that every audit report must be manually codified.

Author Contributions: Conceptualization, N.M.-I. and M.d.-M.C.-M.; Data curation, N.M.-I.; Formal analysis, N.M.-I. and M.d.-M.C.-M.; Investigation, N.M.-I.; Methodology, software and validation, M.-J.S.-V.; Project administration and supervision, M.-d.-M.C.-M. and D.P.-E.; Writing—original draft, N.M.-I. and M.-d.M.C.-M.; Writing—review & editing, All.

Funding: This research received no external funding.

Acknowledgments: This paper is part of an ongoing project of the Research Group UCM 950025 "Risk in insurance, finance, financial distress, and entrepreneurship". We wish to thank our universities for their support and we are also very grateful to the participants of the EAA 40th Annual Congress 2017 for their helpful comments.

Conflicts of Interest: The authors declare no conflict of interest.

References

Aguiar-Díaz, Inmaculada, and Nieves L. Díaz-Díaz. 2015. Audit quality, second-tier and size: Effect on the Spanish private distressed firms. *Spanish Journal of Finance and Accounting* 44: 24–46.

Altman, Edward I. 2018. Applications of distress prediction models: What have we learned after 50 years from the Z-Score models? *International Journal of Financial Studies* 6: 70. [CrossRef]

Altman, Edward I., and Thomas P. McGough. 1974. Evaluation of a company as a going-concern. *Journal of Accountancy* 138: 50–57.

Altman, Edward I., Gabriele Sabato, and Nicholas Wilson. 2010. The value of non-financial information in small and medium-sized enterprise risk management. *Journal of Credit Risk* 2: 95–127. [CrossRef]

Altman, Edward I., Małgorzata Iwanicz-Drozdowska, Erkki K. Laitinen, and Arto Suvas. 2017. Financial distress prediction in an international context: A review and empirical analysis of Altman's Z-Score model. *Journal of International Financial Management and Accounting* 28: 131–71. [CrossRef]

Amani, Farzaneh A., and Adam M. Fadlalla. 2017. Data mining applications in accounting: A review of the literature and organizing framework. *International Journal of Accounting Information Systems* 24: 32–58. [CrossRef]

Amin, Keval, Jagan Krishnan, and Joon Sun Yang. 2014. Going concern opinion and cost of equity. *Auditing: A Journal of Practice and Theory* 33: 1–39. [CrossRef]

Appiah, Kingsley Opoku, and Chizema Amon. 2017. Board audit committee and corporate insolvency. *Journal of Applied Accounting Research* 18: 298–316. [CrossRef]

Armeanu, Daniel Ştefan, Georgeta Vintilă, Ştefan Cristian Gherghina, and Dan Cosmin Petrache. 2017. Approaches on correlation between board of directors and risk management in resilient economies. *Sustainability* 9: 173. [CrossRef]

Arnedo-Ajona, Laura, Fermín Lizarraga-Dallo, Santiago Sánchez-Alegría, and Emiliano Ruiz-Barbadillo. 2012. User's expectations before audit going concern opinions. Empirical evidence of self-fulfilling prophecy in the Spanish case. *Spanish Journal of Finance and Accounting* 41: 263–89.

Balcaen, Sofie, and Hubert Ooghe. 2006. 35 years of studies on business failure: An overview of the classic statistical methodologies and their related problems. *The British Accounting Review* 38: 63–93. [CrossRef]

Barth, Mary E., William H. Beaver, and Wayne R. Landsman. 1998. Relative valuation roles of equity book value and net income as a function of financial health. *Journal of Accounting and Economics* 25: 1–34. [CrossRef]

Basioudis, Ilias G., Ferdinand A. Gul, and Anthony C. Ng. 2012. Non-Audit fees, Auditor Tenure, and Auditor Independence. Working Paper. Available online: https://papers.ssrn.com/sol3/papers.cfm?abstract_id=2043311 (accessed on 3 April 2019).

Bauweraerts, Jonathan. 2016. Predicting bankruptcy in private firms: Towards a stepwise regression procedure. *International Journal of Financial Research* 7: 147–53. [CrossRef]

Bellovary, Jodi L., Don E. Giacomino, and Michael D. Akers. 2007. A review of bankruptcy prediction studies: 1930 to present. *Journal of Financial Education* 33: 1–42.

Berglund, Nathan R., John Daniel Eshleman, and Peng Guo. 2018. Auditor size and going concern reporting. *Auditing: A Journal of Practice & Theory* 37: 1–25.

Blay, Allen D. 2005. Independence threats, litigation risk, and the auditor's decision process. *Contemporary Accounting Research* 22: 759–89. [CrossRef]

Blay, Allen D., Marshall A. Geiger, and David S. North. 2011. The auditor's going-concern opinion as a communication of risk. *Auditing: A Journal of Practice and Theory* 30: 77–102. [CrossRef]

Buchman, Thomas A., and Denton Collins. 1998. Uncertainty about litigation losses and auditors' modified audit reports. *Journal of Business Research* 43: 57–63. [CrossRef]

Calderon, Thomas G., and John J. Cheh. 2002. A roadmap for future neural networks research in auditing and risk assessment. *International Journal of Accounting Information Systems* 3: 203–36. [CrossRef]

Callaghan, Joseph, Mohinder Parkash, and Rajeev Singhal. 2009. Going-concern audit opinions and the provision of nonaudit services: Implications for auditor independence of bankrupt firms. *Auditing: A Journal of Practice and Theory* 28: 153–69. [CrossRef]

Camacho-Miñano, Maria-del-Mar, Maria-Jesus Segovia-Vargas, and David Pascual-Ezama. 2015. Which characteristics predict the survival of insolvent firms? An SME reorganization prediction model. *Journal of Small Business Management* 53: 340–54. [CrossRef]

Cao, Jian, Thomas R. Kubick, and Adi N.S. Masli. 2017. Do corporate payouts signal going-concern risk for auditors? Evidence from audit reports for companies in financial distress. *Review of Quantitative Finance and Accounting* 49: 599–631. [CrossRef]

Carcello, Joseph V., and Terry L. Neal. 2000. Audit committee composition and auditor reporting. *The Accounting Review* 75: 453–67. [CrossRef]

Carcello, Joseph V., and Terry L. Neal. 2003. Audit committee characteristics and auditor dismissals following "new" going-concern reports. *The Accounting Review* 78: 95–117. [CrossRef]

Carcello, Joseph V., Dana R. Hermanson, and H. Fenwick Huss. 1995. Temporal changes in bankruptcy-related reporting. *Auditing: A Journal of Practice and Theory* 14: 133–43.

Carcello, Joseph V., Dana R. Hermanson, and H. Fenwick Huss. 1997. The effect of SAS No. 59: How treatment of the transition period influences results. *Auditing: A Journal of Practice and Theory* 16: 114–23.

Carey, Peter, and Roger Simnett. 2006. Audit partner tenure and audit quality. *The Accounting Review* 81: 653–76. [CrossRef]

Carey, Peter J., Marshall A. Geiger, and Brendan T. O'Connell. 2008. Costs associated with going-concern-modified audit opinions: An analysis of the Australian audit market. *Abacus* 44: 61–81. [CrossRef]

Carey, Peter, Stuart Kortum, and Robyn Moroney. 2012. Auditors' going-concern-modified opinions after 2001: Measuring reporting accuracy. *Accounting and Finance* 52: 1041–59. [CrossRef]

Carson, Elizabeth, Neil Fargher, and Yuyu Zhang. 2016. Trends in auditor reporting in Australia: A synthesis and opportunities for research. *Australian Accounting Review* 26: 226–42. [CrossRef]

Cassell, Cory A., Lauren M. Dreher, and Linda A. Myers. 2013. Reviewing the SEC's review process: 10-K comment letters and the cost of remediation. *The Accounting Review* 88: 1875–908. [CrossRef]

Casterella, Jeffrey R., Barry L. Lewis, and Paul L. Walker. 2000. Modeling the audit opinions issued to bankrupt companies: A two-stage empirical analysis. *Decision Sciences* 31: 507–30. [CrossRef]

Cenciarelli, Velia Gabriella, Giulio Greco, and Marco Allegrini. 2018. External audit and bankruptcy prediction. *Journal of Management and Governance* 22: 1–28. [CrossRef]

Charitou, Andreas, Neophytos Lambertides, and Lenos Trigeorgis. 2007. Earnings behaviour of financially distressed firms: The role of institutional ownership. *Abacus* 43: 271–96. [CrossRef]

Chen, Kevin C. W., and Bryan K. Church. 1996. Going concern opinions and the market's reaction to bankruptcy filings. *The Accounting Review* 71: 117–28.

Chen, Chen, Xiumin Martin, and Xin Wang. 2013. Insider trading, litigation concerns, and auditor going-concern opinions. *The Accounting Review* 88: 365–93. [CrossRef]

Chen, Peter F., Shaohua He, Zhiming Ma, and Derrald Stice. 2016. The information role of audit opinions in debt contracting. *Journal of Accounting and Economics* 61: 121–44. [CrossRef]

Chen, Yu, John Daniel Eshleman, and Jared S. Soileau. 2017. Business strategy and auditor reporting. *Auditing: A Journal of Practice & Theory* 36: 63–86.

Citron, David B., and Richard J. Taffler. 2001. Ethical behaviour in the UK audit profession: The case of the self-fulfilling prophecy under going-concern uncertainties. *Journal of Business Ethics* 29: 353–63. [CrossRef]

Cohen, Sandra, Antonella Costanzo, and Francesca Manes-Rossi. 2017. Auditors and early signals of financial distress in local governments. *Managerial Auditing Journal* 32: 234–50. [CrossRef]

Conefrey, Thomas, and John Fitz Gerald. 2010. Managing housing bubbles in regional economies under EMU: Ireland and Spain. *National Institute Economic Review* 211: 91–108. [CrossRef]

Cultrera, Loredana, and Xavier Brédart. 2016. Bankruptcy prediction: The case of Belgian SMEs. *Review of Accounting and Finance* 15: 1–23. [CrossRef]

Cunnigham, Lawrence A. 2006. Too big to fail: moral hazard in auditing and the need to restructure the industry before it unravels. *Columbia Law Review* 106: 1–68.

Daily, Catherine M. 1996. Governance patterns in bankruptcy reorganizations. *Strategic Management Journal* 17: 355–75. [CrossRef]

DeFond, Mark, and Jieying Zhang. 2014. A review of archival auditing research. *Journal of Accounting and Economics* 58: 275–326. [CrossRef]

DeFond, Mark L., Kannan Raghunandan, and K. R. Subramanyam. 2002. Do non-audit service fees impair auditor independence? Evidence from going concern audit opinions. *Journal of Accounting Research* 40: 1247–74. [CrossRef]

Desai, Vikram, Joung W. Kim, Rajendra P. Srivastava, and Renu V. Desai. 2017. A study of the relationship between a going concern opinion and its financial distress metrics. *Journal of Emerging Technologies in Accounting* 14: 17–28. [CrossRef]

Díaz-Martínez, Zuleyka, Alicia Sanchís-Arellano, and María Jesús Segovia-Vargas. 2009. Analysis of Financial Instability by Means of Decision Trees and Lists. In *Emerging Topics in Macroeconomics*. Edited by Richard O. Bailly. New York: Editorial Nova Publishers, pp. 303–27.

Dopuch, Nicholas, Robert W. Holthausen, and Richard W. Leftwich. 1987. Predicting audit qualifications with financial and market variables. *The Accounting Review* 62: 431–54.

Du Jardin, Philippe. 2015. Bankruptcy prediction using terminal failure processes. *European Journal of Operational Research* 242: 286–303. [CrossRef]

Eutsler, Jared, Erin Burrell Nickell, and Sean W. G. Robb. 2016. Fraud Risk Awareness and the Likelihood of Audit Enforcement Action. *Accounting Horizons* 30: 379–92. [CrossRef]

Feldmann, Dorothy A., and William J. Read. 2010. Auditor conservatism after Enron. *Auditing: A Journal of Practice and Theory* 29: 267–78. [CrossRef]

Frank, Eibe, and Ian H. Witten. 1998. *Generating Accurate Rule Sets without Global Optimization*. Working Paper. Hamilton: University of Waikato, Department of Computer Science.

Gaeremynck, Ann, Sofie Van Der Meulen, and Marleen Willekens. 2008. Audit-firm portfolio characteristics and client financial reporting quality. *European Accounting Review* 17: 243–70. [CrossRef]

García-Blandón, Josep, and Josep Maria Argiles-Bosch. 2013. Audit tenure and audit qualifications in a low litigation risk setting: An analysis of the Spanish market. *Estudios de Economía* 40: 133–56. [CrossRef]

Geiger, Marshall A., and Kanan Raghunandan. 2001. Bankruptcies, audit reports, and the reform act. *Auditing: A Journal of Practice and Theory* 20: 187–95. [CrossRef]

Geiger, Marshall A., and Kanan Raghunandan. 2002. Auditor tenure and audit reporting failures. *Auditing: A Journal of Practice and Theory* 21: 67–78. [CrossRef]

Geiger, Marshall A., Kanan Raghunandan, and Dasaratha V. Rama. 2005. Recent changes in the association between bankruptcies and prior audit opinions. *Auditing: A Journal of Practice and Theory* 24: 21–35. [CrossRef]

Geiger, Marshall A., Kanan Raghunandan, and William Riccardi. 2014. The Global Financial Crisis: US bankruptcies and going-concern audit opinions. *Accounting Horizons* 28: 59–75. [CrossRef]

Hope, Ole-Kristian, Danqi Hu, and Wuyang Zhao. 2017. Third-party consequences of short-selling threats: The case of auditor behavior. *Journal of Accounting and Economics* 63: 479–98. [CrossRef]

Hopwood, William, James McKeown, and Jane Mutchler. 1989. A test of the incremental explanatory power of opinions qualified for consistency and uncertainty. *The Accounting Review* 64: 28–48.

Ittonen, Kim, Per C. Tronnes, and Leon Wong. 2017. Substantial doubt and the entropy of auditors' going concern modifications. *Journal of Contemporary Accounting & Economics* 13: 134–47.

Joe, Jennifer R. 2003. Why press coverage of a client influences the audit opinion. *Journal of Accounting Research* 41: 109–33. [CrossRef]

Kausar, Asad, and Clive S. Lennox. 2017. Balance sheet conservatism and audit reporting conservatism. *Journal of Business Finance & Accounting* 44: 897–924.

Kausar, Asad, Richard J. Taffler, and Christine E. L. Tan. 2017. Legal regimes and investor response to the auditor's going-concern opinion. *Journal of Accounting, Auditing & Finance* 32: 40–72.

Khurana, Inder K., and Kris K. Raman. 2006. Do investors care about the auditor's economic dependence on the client? *Contemporary Accounting Research* 23: 977–1016. [CrossRef]

Kida, Thomas. 1980. An investigation into auditors' continuity and related qualification judgments. *Journal of Accounting Research* 18: 506–23. [CrossRef]

Kim, Minchoul, Minho Kim, and Ronald D. McNiel. 2008. Predicting survival prospect of corporate restructuring in Korea. *Applied Economics Letters* 15: 1187–90. [CrossRef]

Kirkos, Efstathios. 2015. Assessing methodologies for intelligent bankruptcy prediction. *Artificial Intelligence Review* 43: 83–123. [CrossRef]

Knechel, W. Robert, and Ann Vanstraelen. 2007. The relationship between auditor tenure and audit quality implied by going concern opinions. *Auditing: A Journal of Practice and Theory* 26: 113–31. [CrossRef]

Koh, Wei-Chem, and Kin-Wai Lee. 2017. Do Auditors Recognize Managerial Risk-Taking Incentives? *International Journal of Business* 22: 206–29.

Koyuncugil, Ali Serhan, and Nermin Ozgulbas. 2012. Financial early warning system model and data mining application for risk detection. *Expert Systems with Applications* 39: 6238–53. [CrossRef]

Krishnan, Jagan, and Jayanthi Krishnan. 1997. Litigation risk and auditor resignations. *The Accounting Review* 72: 539–60.

Kuhn, John R., James F. Courtney, and Bonnie Morris. 2015. A theory of complex adaptive inquiring organizations: Application to continuous assurance of corporate financial information. *The Knowledge Engineering Review* 30: 265–96. [CrossRef]

Kumar, Krishna, and Lucy Lim. 2015. Was Andersen's audit quality lower than its peers? A comparative analysis of audit quality. *Managerial Auditing Journal* 30: 911–62. [CrossRef]

Kumar, P. Ravi, and Vadlamani Ravi. 2007. Bankruptcy prediction in banks and firms via statistical and intelligent techniques: A review. *European Journal of Operational Research* 180: 1–28. [CrossRef]

Laitinen, Erkki K., and Teija Laitinen. 2009. Effect of accruals on financial, non-financial, and audit information in payment default prediction. *International Journal of Accounting, Auditing and Performance Evaluation* 5: 353–83. [CrossRef]

Lenard, Mary Jane, Pervaiz Alam, and Gregory R. Madey. 1995. The application of neural networks and a qualitative response model to the auditor's going concern uncertainty decision. *Decision Sciences* 26: 209–27. [CrossRef]

Lennox, Clive S. 1999. The accuracy and incremental information content of audit reports in predicting bankruptcy. *Journal of Business Finance and Accounting* 26: 757–78. [CrossRef]

Lennox, Clive S., and Asad Kausar. 2017. Estimation risk and auditor conservatism. *Review of Accounting Studies* 22: 185–216. [CrossRef]

Lim, Chee-Yeow, and Hun-Tong Tan. 2010. Does auditor tenure improve audit quality? Moderating effects of industry specialization and fee dependence. *Contemporary Accounting Research* 27: 923–57. [CrossRef]

Louwers, Timothy J. 1998. The relation between going-concern opinions and the auditor's loss function. *Journal of Accounting Research* 36: 143–55. [CrossRef]

Louwers, Timothy J., Frank M. Messina, and Michael D. Richard. 1999. The auditor's going-concern disclosure as a self-fulfilling prophecy: A discrete-time survival analysis. *Decision Sciences* 30: 805–24. [CrossRef]

Lowe, D. Jordan, and Philip M. J. Reckers. 1994. The effects of hindsight bias on jurors' evaluations of auditor decisions. *Decision Sciences* 25: 401–26. [CrossRef]

Lundberg, C. Gustav, and Brian M. Nagle. 2002. Post-decision inference editing of supportive and counter indicative signals among external auditors in a going concern judgment. *European Journal of Operational Research* 136: 264–81. [CrossRef]

McKee, Thomas E. 1995. Predicting bankruptcy via induction. *Journal of Information Technology* 10: 26–36. [CrossRef]

McKee, Thomas E. 2003. Rough sets bankruptcy prediction models versus auditor signalling rates. *Journal of Forecasting* 22: 569–86. [CrossRef]

McKeown, James C., Jane F. Mutchler, and William Hopwood. 1991. Towards an explanation of auditor failure to modify the audit opinions of bankrupt companies. *Auditing: A Journal of Practice and Theory* 10: 1–13.

McNichols, Maureen F. 2002. Discussion of the quality of accruals and earnings: The role of accrual estimation errors. *The Accounting Review* 77: 61–69. [CrossRef]

Menon, Krishnagopal, and David D. Williams. 1994. The insurance hypothesis and market prices. *The Accounting Review* 69: 327–42.

Min, Jae H., and Young-Chan Lee. 2005. Bankruptcy prediction using support vector machine with optimal choice of kernel function parameters. *Expert Systems with Applications* 28: 603–14. [CrossRef]

Min, Sung-Hwan, Jumin Lee, and Ingoo Han. 2006. Hybrid genetic algorithms and support vector machines for bankruptcy prediction. *Expert Systems with Applications* 31: 652–60. [CrossRef]

Muñoz-Izquierdo, Nora, María-del-Mar Camacho-Miñano, and David Pascual-Ezama. 2017. The content of the audit report in the year prior to bankruptcy filing. Empirical evidence from Spain. *Spanish Journal of Finance and Accounting* 46: 92–126.

Muñoz-Izquierdo, Nora, María Jesús Segovia-Vargas, María-del-Mar Camacho-Miñano, and David Pascual-Ezama. 2019. Explaining the causes of business failure using audit report disclosures. *Journal of Business Research* 98: 403–14. [CrossRef]

Myers, Linda A., Jonathan E. Shipman, Quinn T. Swanquist, and Robert L. Whited. 2018. Measuring the market response to going concern modifications: The importance of disclosure timing. *Review of Accounting Studies* 23: 1512–42. [CrossRef]

Ogneva, Maria K., Raghunandan Subramanyam, and Kannan Raghunandan. 2007. Internal control weakness and cost of equity: Evidence from SOX Section 404 disclosures. *The Accounting Review* 82: 1255–97. [CrossRef]

Pedrosa Rodríguez, M. Áurea, and Francisco López-Corrales. 2018. Autors' response to the global financial crisis: Evidence from Spanish non-listed companies. *Spanish Journal of Finance and Accounting* 47: 400–31.

Piñeiro-Sánchez, Carlos, Pablo de Llano-Monelos, and Manuel Rodríguez-López. 2012. Evaluation of the likelihood of financial failure. Empirical contrast of the informational content audit of accounts. *Spanish Journal of Finance and Accounting* 46: 565–87.

Piñeiro-Sánchez, Carlos, Pablo de Llano-Monelos, and Manuel Rodríguez-López. 2013. A parsimonious model to forecast financial distress, based on audit evidence. *Contaduría y Administración* 58: 151–73. [CrossRef]

Pratt, Jamie, and James D. Stice. 1994. The effects of client characteristics on auditor litigation risk judgments, required audit evidence, and recommended audit fees. *The Accounting Review* 69: 639–56.

Raghunandan, Kannan, and Dasaratha V. Rama. 1995. Audit reports for companies in financial distress: Before and after SAS No. 59. *Auditing: A Journal of Practice and Theory* 14: 50–63.

Ragothaman, Srinivasan, Jon Carpenter, and Thomas Buttars. 1995. Using rule induction for knowledge acquisition: An expert systems approach to evaluating material errors and irregularities. *Expert Systems with Applications* 9: 483–90. [CrossRef]

Read, William J., and Ari Yezegel. 2016. Auditor tenure and going concern opinions for bankrupt clients: Additional evidence. *Auditing: A Journal of Practice and Theory* 35: 163–79. [CrossRef]

Read, William J., and Ari Yezegel. 2018. Going-concern opinion decisions on bankrupt clients: Evidence of long-lasting auditor conservatism? *Advances in Accounting* 40: 20–26. [CrossRef]

Robinson, Dahlia. 2008. Auditor independence and auditor-provided tax service: Evidence from going-concern audit opinions prior to bankruptcy filings. *Auditing: A Journal of Practice and Theory* 27: 31–54. [CrossRef]

Rodríguez-López, Manuel, Carlos Piñeiro-Sánchez, and Pablo de Llano-Monelos. 2014. Financial risk determination of failure by using parametric model, artificial intelligence and audit information. *Estudios de Economía* 41: 187–217.

Ruiz-Barbadillo, Emiliano, Nieves Gómez-Aguilar, Cristina De Fuentes-Barberá, and María Antonia García-Benau. 2004. Audit quality and the going-concern decision-making process: Spanish evidence. *European Accounting Review* 13: 597–620. [CrossRef]

Schwartz, Kenneth B., and Krishnagopal Menon. 1985. Auditor switches by failing firms. *The Accounting Review* 60: 248–61.

Shu, Pei-Gi, Tsung-Kang Chen, and Wen-Jye Hung. 2015. Audit duration quality and client credit risk. *Asia-Pacific Journal of Accounting and Economics* 22: 137–62. [CrossRef]

Sikka, Prem. 2009. Financial crisis and the silence of the auditors. *Accounting, Organizations and Society* 34: 868–73. [CrossRef]

Stanisic, Milovan, Danka Stefanovic, Nada Arezina, and Vule Mizdrakovic. 2013. Analysis of auditors' reports and bankruptcy risk in banking sector in the Republic of Serbia. *The Amfiteatru Economic Journal* 15: 431–41.

Stanley, Jonathan D. 2011. Is the audit fee disclosure a leading indicator of clients' business risk? *Auditing: A Journal of Practice and Theory* 30: 157–79. [CrossRef]

Sun, Jie, Hui Li, Qing-Hua Huang, and Kai-Yu He. 2014. Predicting financial distress and corporate failure: A review from the state-of-the-art definitions, modelling, sampling, and featuring approaches. *Knowledge-Based Systems* 57: 41–56. [CrossRef]

Tascón-Fernández, María T., and Francisco J. Castaño-Gutiérrez. 2012. Variables and models for the identification and prediction of business failure: Revision of recent empirical research advances. *Spanish Accounting Review* 15: 7–58.

Van Caneghem, Tom, and Geert Van Campenhout. 2012. Quantity and quality of information and SME financial structure. *Small Business Economics* 39: 341–58. [CrossRef]

Van Peursem, Karen, and Yi Chiann Chan. 2014. Forecasting New Zealand corporate failures 2001–10: Opportunity lost? *Australian Accounting Review* 24: 276–88. [CrossRef]

Vanstraelen, Ann. 2000. Impact of renewable long-term audit mandates on audit quality. *European Accounting Review* 9: 419–42. [CrossRef]

Vanstraelen, Ann. 2002. Auditor economic incentives and going-concern opinions in a limited litigious continental European business environment: Empirical evidence from Belgium. *Accounting and Business Research* 32: 171–86. [CrossRef]

Wu, Wei-Wen. 2010. Beyond business failure prediction. *Expert Systems with Applications* 37: 2371–76. [CrossRef]

Yeh, Ching-Chiang, Der-Jang Chi, and Yi-Rong Lin. 2014. Going-concern prediction using hybrid random forests and rough set approach. *Information Sciences* 254: 98–110. [CrossRef]

Zdolsek, D., and T. Jagric. 2011. Audit opinion identification using accounting ratios: Experience of United Kingdom and Ireland. *Actual Problems of Economics* 115: 285–310.

Zięba, Maciej, Sebastian K. Tomczak, and Jakub M. Tomczak. 2016. Ensemble boosted trees with synthetic features generation in application to bankruptcy prediction. *Expert Systems with Applications* 58: 93–101. [CrossRef]

5

Flobsion—Flexible Option with Benefit Sharing

Nikolay Khabarov [1,*], Ruben Lubowski [2], Andrey Krasovskii [1] and Michael Obersteiner [1]

1 Ecosystems Services and Management Program (ESM), International Institute for Applied Systems Analysis (IIASA), Schlossplatz 1, A-2361 Laxenburg, Austria; krasov@iiasa.ac.at (A.K.); oberstei@iiasa.ac.at (M.O.)
2 Environmental Defense Fund, 1875 Connecticut Ave NW #600, Washington, DC 20009, USA; rlubowski@edf.org
* Correspondence: khabarov@iiasa.ac.at

Abstract: Global environmental goals and the Paris agreement declared the need to avoid dangerous climate change by reducing emissions of greenhouse gases with an ultimate goal to transform today's policies and reach climate neutrality before the end of the century. In the medium to long-term, climate policies imply rising CO_2 price and consequent financial risk for carbon-intensive producers. In this context, there is a need for tools to buffer CO_2 prices within the period of transition to greener technologies when the emission offsetting markets expose high volatility. Contracts for optional future purchase of carbon credits could provide emitters with a cost-efficient solution to address existing regulatory risks. At the same time, this would help to create much needed financing for the projects generating carbon credits in the future. This work presents the concept of a *flobsion*—a flexible option with benefit sharing—and demonstrates its advantages in terms of risk reduction for both seller and buyer as compared to both a "do nothing" strategy (offsetting at future market price) and a traditional option with a fixed strike price. The results are supported analytically and numerically, employing as a benchmark the dataset on historical CO_2 prices from the European Emission Trading Scheme. Flobsion has the potential to extend the traditional option in financial applications beyond compliance markets.

Keywords: CO_2; emissions offsetting; options; financial risk; benefit sharing; climate policy

---

1. Introduction

The sustainable development agenda United Nations Development Programme (2016) and the need to restrain climate change UNFCCC (2015) limit greenhouse gas (GHG) emissions into the Earth's atmosphere and thus constrain the future use of fossil fuel. While concrete mechanisms of achieving these goals are not yet in place, there is a clear move in this direction. On the technological side, there is a substantial progress on electric vehicles that were considered as a potential future development a decade ago and already in 2016 the global electric car stock surpassed two million vehicles after crossing the 1 million threshold in 2015; the registrations of electric cars hit a record in 2016, with over 750 thousand sales worldwide International Energy Agency (2017). The energy used by the industry and households (also to recharge car's batteries) is coming partially from renewable sources, and that share is increasing, so between 2010 and 2014, renewable energy consumption of the top countries has effectively doubled from 168 million tons to 316 million tons of oil equivalent WordAtlas (2018). However, in the energy sector that is responsible for about 40% of global GHG emissions The Shift Project Data Portal (2019), there is still a big (over 80%) share of fossil fuels in total energy production BP p.l.c. (2018). The main reason for that is apparently lower costs, but also other considerations e.g., electric grid stabilization needs as wind mills can generate fluctuations of capacity Hannele Holttinen et al. (2006), societal attitude to avoid operation and construction of new nuclear power plants U.S. Congress, Office of Technology Assessment (1984). Although one may foresee drastic changes in the energy generation technologies in the coming decades, it seems that fossil fuel-based (i.e., CO_2 intensive technologies) will maintain a reasonable share in the total power generation mix throughout that transitional period.

The mechanisms for CO_2 pricing are not established yet beyond regional scale and the legal background is missing with the exception for the European Emission Trading Scheme (EU–ETS) and the Cap-and-Trade Program in California, USA. However, in the mid– to long–term, the CO_2 price is likely to upscale to a larger geographical extent, be it in a form of a carbon tax, cap-and-trade, or a mix thereof. This would inevitably create a distortion in the energy sector, with the highest impact on those companies that have large share of fossil fuel in their power generation technologies mix. Because of the system role of those companies, they would need to be supported with enough supply of emission allowances/offsets. Creating such a supply by legal/policy means would raise a question on diminishing the purpose of the CO_2 price geographical upscaling, while subsidizing these companies would mean spending taxpayers money against the principles they were spent to support renewable technologies in the previous period. From this perspective, there seem to be a need for tools supporting a smooth transition from a few regional CO_2 pricing models to a larger scale implementation.

In this context, contracting at current relatively low price levels the future delivery of CO_2 credits is one of the possibilities to reduce regulatory risk for carbon-intensive emitters that have limited possibilities of technological change. These carbon credits could be supplied in the future by projects on reducing emissions in the industry and energy sectors UNFCCC (2012).

As the future development of the CO_2 price is highly uncertain, a hedging strategy protecting a regulated entity from excessive price peaks seems to be a reasonable approach for managing the associated risk. One of the potential candidates from available financial instruments to provide hedging capabilities is a traditional call option Collins and Fabozzi (2008), which (in our setting) is the right purchased in advance to buy in the future a specified amount of carbon credits at a specified price. The call option provides financing to the seller before the actual delivery, which is advantageous in the context of financing a project implementation that is needed to generate carbon credits.

The contribution of this paper is in the introduction and proofs of analytical properties of a new financial instrument—a flexible option with a benefit sharing mechanism, a flobsion in short, which is an extension of a call option concept combined with the idea of benefit (and loss) sharing between the contracting parties explored in earlier publications Krasovskii et al. (2016, 2017). A flobsion has advantages in terms of risk reduction for both buyer and seller as compared to a "do nothing" strategy (offsetting at future market price) and a traditional option with a fixed strike price. We illustrate analytical results with benchmarking examples employing historical data on CO_2 prices in the European Emission Trading Scheme (EU-ETS).

2. Literature Review and Motivation

There is a rich set of literature sources devoted to the multiple concepts that we employed in this manuscript: risk management in general and that connected to an uncertain future CO_2 price for emissions offsetting in particular; principles of indifference prices, benefit sharing, and optionality to address future uncertainty. In this section we provide a condensed review of selected publications in order to position our manuscript and provide the reader with an entry point to the relevant literature.

In the general risk management context a key role plays a notion of a risk measure and in particular a "coherent" measure of risk that possesses desirable properties Artzner et al. (1999). While there exist many risk measures used in practice e.g., variance, value-at-risk, conditional value-at-risk—not all of them are coherent. In practice, there are deficiencies associated also with coherent risk measures e.g., inability to differentiate between market risk and model uncertainty Cont (2006). As a proxy for risk associated with the future asset market price we use variance and to address risk associated with a potential price model uncertainty, in the spirit of Cont (2006), demonstrate that flobsion (as compared to an option) has a lower sensitivity to a wrong assumption on a price scenario.

The employed idea of benefit (revenue) and risk sharing is rather general and was earlier explored within various contexts e.g., revenue-risk-sharing for public-private partnerships in construction Rouhani et al. (2018), game theoretic setting for contracts in electricity market Ma et al. (2019), coordination of supply chains Liu et al. (2017), emission offsetting context for a forward contract Krasovskii et al. (2017). In this paper, we merge the concept of benefit sharing with a financial option to create a new instrument.

There is an vast body of literature starting from early works Black and Scholes (1973); Cox and Ross (1976) further developed and summarized in comprehensive books on extensive treatment of theoretical and computational aspects of options-style derivatives pricing Detemple (2005); Pierre Henry-Labordere (2009). In these works a stochastic price process has to belong to a specific family (e.g., Brownian motion) and the problem of derivatives' pricing requires specific treatment depending on the time moment when an option can be executed (American or European option). We employ a different and a more general approach that deals with a rather generic form of a discrete price distribution and does not specify the instrument's execution date.

Financial instruments including those of option-type are becoming increasingly important for risk management in particular in electricity markets due to uncertainty of consumption and limited fungibility of energy Kudryavtsev and Zanette (2013). The link to volatile emission permit markets leads to more complexity in risk management as the permits may expose features that are distinctive from other financial assets Medina and Pardo (2013). An earlier research on pricing European emission allowances Chesney and Taschini (2012) suggested a closed-form formula for option-pricing, while admitting its rather limited utility because of the specific model assumptions. Our results are less price-centric due to the established link to existing options pricing and more oriented towards risk reduction properties of a flobsion.

With regard to risk reduction, a paper Andrew and Chen (2017) examines the effect of imposing various permit price-containment policies on spot market such as a price ceiling, floor, or collar within an electricity market context. While addressing the same problem of market volatility, unlike the paper Andrew and Chen (2017), we suggest an instrument that is bilateral and does not require market-level intervention by a regulator. From this perspective, the two approaches are complementary to each other.

The motivation of this research is in the high uncertainty and risks associated with the future CO_2 prices in the context of emissions offsetting of regulated entities. The research question was whether it is possible to reduce these risks even further as compared to a traditional option respecting the concerns of both regulated entity (buyer) and the offset supplier (seller). In parallel to suggesting a new financial instrument, our work is addressing the need of evaluating "the new contractual forms that are constantly emerging in response to evolving economic conditions and regulations" Detemple (2005).

3. Flobsion Description

There exist two flavors of an option—"put" and "call", and for the purposes of the manuscript we will only use the call-option, further referring to it for simplicity as just "option". An option for an asset (e.g., for an emission offset) implies that a buyer pays an amount p_1 to the seller of the option for the future possibility to purchase the asset at an agreed "strike" price s_1. The owner of the option decides in the future whether to make such a purchase or not, so for them it is a possibility, but not an obligation. The time component of an option is specified in the contract and can be e.g., a specific day on which the purchase of the asset can be executed a "European option", or a time period within which that purchase can be made an "American option". Our discussion below is applicable to both cases as we do not explicitly model dynamic prices and instead refer to two time moments: (1) the time of purchase of an option and (2) the time of executing the option.

A flobsion is similar, yet has a more general construction than the option. A buyer pays the amount p_d to the seller of a flobsion for the future possibility to purchase the asset at the agreed "strike" price s_d plus the discounted difference between the asset's market price x and s_d, if that difference is positive (or just s_d otherwise). So, in case if the flobsion holder decides to make a purchase of an asset within the period of validity of a flobsion, they would pay the amount

$$a_d = \begin{cases} s_d + (1-d) \times (x - s_d), & \text{if} \quad x > s_d \\ x, & \text{if} \quad x \le s_d \end{cases}, \tag{1}$$

meaning that an asset is being purchased at a market price x and the flobsion is not being executed if $x \le s_d$. Here $0 \le d \le 1$ is a discount to the market price using s_d as a base. In case of a flobsion, a future asset purchase is still optional for the buyer as in case of a standard option. The price for future purchase of an asset in case of a flobsion is not fixed, yet tied to the market price, so based on this general trait, the flobsion is a new, so far unknown, member of a loosely defined set of financial instruments commonly called "exotic options" Buchen (2012); Collins and Fabozzi (2008).

Remark 1. *For $d = 1$, a flobsion turns into an option, so that the amount paid for an underlying asset in the future conditional on the market price x would be*

$$a_1 = \begin{cases} s_1, & \textit{if} \quad x > s_1 \\ x, & \textit{if} \quad x \le s_1 \end{cases}. \tag{2}$$

Remark 2. *For $d = 0$ the amount paid in the future for an underlying asset equals the market price x, which corresponds to the "do nothing" alternative (naturally assuming $p_d = 0$ i.e., nothing was paid for a zero future discount to the market price).*

4. Analytical Results

Below, we present the proofs for a probabilistic market price x described for simplicity by a discrete distribution in the form

$$\{x_i\}, \qquad \mathbb{P}(x_i) = 1/N, \qquad i = 1, ..., N, \tag{3}$$

which is practical for numerical modeling and is sufficient for our application. Analytical results on discrete approximations of continuous distributions are available in the literature Kennan (2006).

Definition 1. *The price p_d is a "fair price" of a flobsion with the strike price s_d if the expected total amount paid for an asset by a flobsion holder equals the expected market price of the asset:*

$$\mathbb{E}(p_d + a_d) = \mathbb{E}x. \tag{4}$$

Theorem 1. *Let $s_1 = s_d$, where s_1 is the strike price of an option and s_d that one of a flobsion. Then the fair prices of an option p_1 and a flobsion p_d are connected through the flobsion's discount to the future market price d:*

$$p_d = dp_1. \tag{5}$$

Proof. First, we denote by a_d^i the amount a_d defined by Equation (1) and paid in case of a particular market price $x = x_i$. Second, the fairness condition Equation (5) for p_1 and p_d implies

$$\mathbb{E}(p_1 + a_1) = \mathbb{E}x = \mathbb{E}(p_d + a_d), \tag{6}$$

hence

$$\begin{aligned}0 &= \mathbb{E}(p_d + a_d) - \mathbb{E}(p_1 + a_1) = p_d - p_1 + \mathbb{E}(a_d - a_1) = \\ &= p_d - p_1 + \sum_{i=1}^{N}(a_d^i - a_1^i) = \\ &= p_d - p_1 + \sum_{i:\, x_i \le s_1}(a_d^i - a_1^i) + \sum_{i:\, x_i > s_1}(a_d^i - a_1^i) = \{s_1 = s_d\} = \\ &= p_d - p_1 + \sum_{i:\, x_i \le s_1}(x_i - x_i) + \sum_{i:\, x_i > s_1}(s_d + (1-d) \times (x_i - s_d) - s_d) = \\ &= p_d - p_1 + (1-d)\sum_{i:\, x_i > s_1}(x_i - s_d).\end{aligned} \tag{7}$$

From the left equality in Equation (6) it follows that

$$\sum_{i=1}^{N} x_i \equiv \mathbb{E}x = \mathbb{E}(p_1 + a_1) \equiv p_1 + \sum_{i:\, x_i \le s_1} x_i + \sum_{i:\, x_i > s_1} s_1$$

and hence

$$p_1 = \sum_{i=1}^{N} x_i - \sum_{i:\, x_i \le s_1} x_i - \sum_{i:\, x_i > s_1} s_1 = \sum_{i:\, x_i > s_1} x_i - \sum_{i:\, x_i > s_1} s_1 = \sum_{i:\, x_i > s_1}(x_i - s_1). \tag{8}$$

Employing Equation (7) and substituting p_1 from Equation (8) we obtain

$$\begin{aligned}p_d &= p_1 - (1-d)\sum_{i:\, x_i > s_1}(x_i - s_d) = \\ &= \sum_{i:\, x_i > s_1}(x_i - s_1) - (1-d)\sum_{i:\, x_i > s_1}(x_i - s_d) = \{s_1 = s_d\} = \\ &= d\sum_{i:\, x_i > s_1}(x_i - s_1) = \{\text{Equation (8)}\} = dp_1.\end{aligned}$$

□

Theorem 2. *Let $s_d = s_1$ be the strike prices of a flobsion and an option, and p_d and p_1 the corresponding fair prices for the same price distribution Equation (3). Then for any alternative price distribution $\{y_j\}$, $j = 1, ..., K$, $\mathbb{P}(y_j) = 1/K$, the following equality holds:*

$$\mathbb{E}(p_d + a_d) - \mathbb{E}y = d\left[\mathbb{E}(p_1 + a_1) - \mathbb{E}y\right],$$

where the expectation is calculated over the price distribution $\{y_j\}$.

Proof.

$$\begin{aligned}&\mathbb{E}(p_d + a_d) - \mathbb{E}y - d\left[\mathbb{E}(p_1 + a_1) - \mathbb{E}y\right] = \{p_d = dp_1 \text{ (Theorem 1)}, s_d = s_1\} = \\ &= dp_1 + \sum_{j:\, y_j \le s_1} y_j + \sum_{j:\, y_j > s_1}\left[(1-d)(y_j - s_1) + s_1\right] - \mathbb{E}y - \\ &- dp_1 - d\sum_{j:\, y_j \le s_1} y_j - d\sum_{j:\, y_j > s_1} s_1 + d\mathbb{E}y = \\ &= (1-d)\sum_{j:\, y_j \le s_1} y_j + (1-d)\sum_{j:\, y_j > s_1} y_j - (1-d)\mathbb{E}y = \\ &= (1-d)\left[\sum_{j=1}^{K} y_j - \mathbb{E}y\right] = 0.\end{aligned}$$

□

Remark 3. *In Theorem 2, the prices p_d, s_d (also respective ones for an option, if $d = 1$) while being fair for the price distribution Equation (3) are not necessarily fair for the alternative price distribution $\{y_j\}$, so that generally speaking*

$$\mathbb{E}(p_d + a_d) \neq \mathbb{E}y$$

and the meaning of the term

$$\mathbb{E}(p_d + a_d) - \mathbb{E}y$$

is the average expected profit or loss as compared to "do nothing" approach where no flobsions/options are contracted and only the market price for an asset is being paid. The practical implication of Theorem 2 is that the flobsion is less sensitive to a wrong assumption on price distribution than the option in terms of reducing both expected profit and loss (both contradict the principle of a fair price) under an alternative price scenario.

Definition 2. *We would call a function $f(\cdot) : \mathbb{R} \to \mathbb{R}$ a compressing transform of a distribution $\{x_i\}$ Equation (3) if there exist a number $\xi \in \mathbb{R}$ such that*

$$|f(x_i) + \xi - \bar{x}| \leq |x_i - \bar{x}|, \quad \textit{for all} \quad i = 1, ..., N. \tag{9}$$

where $\bar{x} = \mathbb{E}x$.

Definition 3. *We would call a function $g(\cdot) : \mathbb{R} \to \mathbb{R}$ a pair-wise compressing transform of a distribution Equation (3) with additionally ordered values $x_1 \leq ... \leq x_N$ if*

$$0 \leq g(x_{i+1}) - g(x_i) \leq x_{i+1} - x_i, \quad \textit{for all} \quad i = 1, ..., N-1. \tag{10}$$

Lemma 1. *A flobsion is a pair-wise compressing transform of the price distribution Equation (3).*

Proof. Let us denote $g(x) \equiv a_d(x)$, where a_d is defined in Equation (1). Without changing connotation we may assume that the values $\{x_i\}$ are ordered, so that $x_i \leq x_{i+1}$, for all $i = 1, ..., N$. Let us consider all three possible options for any fixed $i = 1, ..., N-1$:

- if $x_{i+1} \leq s_d$, then $g(x_{i+1}) - g(x_i) = x_{i+1} - x_i$ i.e., Equation (10) is true;
- if $x_i \leq s_d < x_{i+1}$, then $g(x_{i+1}) - g(x_i) = s_d + (1-d) \times (x_{i+1} - s_d) - x_i = x_{i+1} - x_{i+1} + s_d + (1-d) \times (x_{i+1} - s_d) - x_i = x_{i+1} - x_i - d\,(x_{i+1} - s_d)$ i.e., Equation (10) is true as
  - $x_{i+1} - x_i - d\,(x_{i+1} - s_d) \leq \{d \geq 0,\ s_d < x_{i+1}\} \leq x_{i+1} - x_i$, and
  - $x_{i+1} - x_i - d\,(x_{i+1} - s_d) > \{d < 1\} > x_{i+1} - x_i - x_{i+1} + s_d = s_d - x_i \geq 0$;
- finally, if $s_d < x_i$, then $g(x_{i+1}) - g(x_i) = s_d + (1-d) \times (x_{i+1} - s_d) - s_d - (1-d) \times (x_i - s_d) = (1-d) \times (x_{i+1} - x_i)$ i.e., Equation (10) is true as
  - $(1-d) \times (x_{i+1} - x_i) \leq \{d \geq 0\} \leq x_{i+1} - x_i$, and
  - $(1-d) \times (x_{i+1} - x_i) \geq \{d \leq 1\} \geq 0$.

□

Lemma 2. *Any pair-wise compressing transform in the sense of Definition 3 is a compressing transform in the sense of Definition 2.*

Proof. Let us denote the distribution under consideration as $\{x_i\}$ and the transform as $f(x)$. Then from Definition 3 it follows that

$$0 \leq f(x_{i+1}) - f(x_i) \leq x_{i+1} - x_i, \text{ for all } i = 1, ..., N. \tag{11}$$

Let us consider the value of the index $i = i_*$ such that

$$i_* : x_{i_*} \leq \bar{x} \leq x_{i_*+1}, \text{ where } \bar{x} = \mathbb{E}x. \tag{12}$$

From Equation (11) it follows that

$$0 \leq f(x_{i_*+1}) - f(x_{i_*}) \leq x_{i_*+1} - x_{i_*} \tag{13}$$

and hence there exist such a shifting parameter ξ, such that the following inclusion of the intervals is valid:

$$[f(x_{i_*}) + \xi, f(x_{i_*+1}) + \xi] \subseteq [x_{i_*}, x_{i_*+1}], \tag{14}$$

furthermore, because of Equation (12) $\bar{x} \in [x_{i_*}, x_{i_*+1}]$ and the value of shifting parameter ξ in Equation (14) can be refined in such a way that $\bar{x}$ also belongs to the interval $[f(x_{i_*}) + \xi, f(x_{i_*+1}) + \xi]$ implying the following chain of inequalities:

$$x_{i_*} \leq f(x_{i_*}) + \xi \leq \bar{x} \leq f(x_{i_*+1}) + \xi \leq x_{i_*+1},$$

that for easier reference we split into a set of inequalities:

$$\begin{aligned}
x_{i_*} &\leq f(x_{i_*}) + \xi, && (15)\\
f(x_{i_*}) + \xi &\leq \bar{x}, && (16)\\
\bar{x} &\leq f(x_{i_*+1}) + \xi, && (17)\\
f(x_{i_*+1}) + \xi &\leq x_{i_*+1}. && (18)
\end{aligned}$$

Let us fix an arbitrary index i and consider two cases:

$$\begin{aligned}
&\text{Case "A":} \quad i \leq i_*, \quad \text{and} && (19)\\
&\text{Case "B":} \quad i \geq i_* + 1. && (20)
\end{aligned}$$

Let us start with the case "A":

$$\begin{aligned}
&|f(x_i) + \xi - \bar{x}| = \\
&= \{i \leq i_*, Equation\ (19), f(x_i) \leq f(x_{i_*}), Equation\ (11), Equation\ (16) \Rightarrow f(x_i) + \xi - \bar{x} \leq 0\} = \\
&= \bar{x} - f(x_i) - \xi = \bar{x} - \xi - f(x_i) = \\
&= \bar{x} - \xi - f(x_i) + f(x_{i+1}) - f(x_{i+1}) + ... + f(x_{i_*-1}) - f(x_{i_*-1}) + f(x_{i_*}) - f(x_{i_*}) \leq \\
&\leq \{Equation\ (11)\} \leq \\
&\leq \bar{x} - \xi - x_i + x_{i+1} - x_{i+1} + ... + x_{i_*-1} - x_{i_*-1} + x_{i_*} - f(x_{i_*}) = \\
&= \bar{x} - \xi - x_i + x_{i_*} - f(x_{i_*}) = \bar{x} - x_i + x_{i_*} - f(x_{i_*}) - \xi \leq \{Equation\ (15)\} \leq \bar{x} - x_i = \\
&= \{i \leq i_*, Equation\ (19), x_i \leq x_{i_*}, Equation\ (12) \Rightarrow x_i \leq \bar{x}\} = |x_i - \bar{x}|.
\end{aligned}$$

So, the lemma is proven for the case "A". Equation (9) holds for $i \le i_*$. Let us consider also the case "B":

$$
\begin{aligned}
&|f(x_i) + \xi - \bar{x}| = \\
&= \{i \ge i_* + 1, \mathit{Equation}\ (20), f(x_i) \ge f(x_{i_*+1}), \mathit{Equation}\ (11), \mathit{Equation}\ (17) \Rightarrow f(x_i) + \xi - \bar{x} \ge 0\} = \\
&= f(x_i) + \xi - \bar{x} = \\
&= f(x_i) - f(x_{i-1}) + f(x_{i-1}) - \ldots - f(x_{i_*+2}) + f(x_{i_*+2}) - f(x_{i_*+1}) + f(x_{i_*+1}) + \xi - \bar{x} \le \\
&\le \{\mathit{Equation}\ (11)\} \le \\
&\le x_i - x_{i-1} + x_{i-1} - \ldots - x_{i_*+2} + x_{i_*+2} - x_{i_*+1} + f(x_{i_*+1}) + \xi - \bar{x} = \\
&= x_i - x_{i_*+1} + f(x_{i_*+1}) + \xi - \bar{x} = x_i - \bar{x} - x_{i_*+1} + f(x_{i_*+1}) + \xi \le \{\mathit{Equation}\ (18)\} \le x_i - \bar{x} = \\
&= \{i \ge i_* + 1, \mathit{Equation}\ (20), x_i \ge x_{i_*+1}, \mathit{Equation}\ (12) \Rightarrow x_i \ge \bar{x}\} = |x_i - \bar{x}|.
\end{aligned}
$$

The lemma is proven also for the case "B": Equation (9) holds for $i \ge i_* + 1$. □

Lemma 3. *If* $f(\cdot) : \mathbb{R} \to \mathbb{R}$ *is a* compressing transform *of a distribution* $\{x_i\}$ *Equation (3), then the following inequality holds:*

$$\mathrm{Var} f(x) \le \mathrm{Var}(x). \tag{21}$$

Proof. Let us denote $\bar{f} = \mathbb{E}f(x)$ and $\bar{x} = \mathbb{E}x$, then

$$
\begin{aligned}
\mathrm{Var} f(x) &= \sum_{i=1}^{N} [f(x_i) - \bar{f}]^2 = \{\text{taking } \xi \text{ from Definition 2}\} = \\
&= \sum_{i=1}^{N} [f(x_i) + \xi - \xi - \bar{f}]^2 = \sum_{i=1}^{N} [f(x_i) + \xi - (\bar{f} + \xi)]^2 = \\
&= \{(\bar{f} + \xi) = \mathbb{E}(f(x) + \xi),\ \mathbb{E}z = \operatorname*{argmin}_{w} \sum_{i=1}^{N} (z_i - w)^2,\ \forall z_i\} \le \\
&\le \sum_{i=1}^{N} (f(x_i) + \xi - \bar{x})^2 \le \{\text{Definition 2}\} \le \sum_{i=1}^{N} (x_i - \bar{x})^2 = \mathrm{Var}(x).
\end{aligned}
$$

□

Theorem 3. *A flobsion reduces risk (decreases cost variance) for any future discount d, strike price $s_d = s_1$, and flobsion price p_d:*

$$\mathrm{Var}(p_d + a_d) \le \mathrm{Var}(x), \tag{22}$$

where the amount a_d paid in the second period is conditional on the market price and is defined in Equation (1).

Proof. According to Lemma 1, a flobsion is a pair-wise compressing transform of the price distribution Equation (3), hence, by Lemma 2, a flobsion is a compressing transform of the price distribution, hence for the function $f(\cdot)$ transforming the market price into a price paid for an underlying asset by a flobsion owner the Lemma 3 is valid and hence Equation (21) holds where $f(x) \equiv a_d$, that implies the validity of Equation (22) as $\mathrm{Var}(p_d + a_d) \equiv \mathrm{Var}(a_d)$ for any p_d (a constant defined in the first time period). □

Remark 4. *In Theorem 3 the flobsion price p_d does not have to be the fair price as* $\mathrm{Var}(p_d + a_d) \equiv \mathrm{Var}(a_d)$ *for any p_d (a constant defined in the first time period).*

Remark 5. *The Theorem 3 allows for making an even stronger statement: if a strict inequality* $s_d < \max\{x_i\}$ *holds and* $d > 0$*, then there is at least one strict inequality in Equation (10), hence in Equation (9), hence in Equation (21), implying a strict inequality in Equation (22).*

Theorem 4. *Let the prices of a flobsion* p_d *and an option* p_1 *satisfy the same equation Equation (5) as the fair prices. Then in terms of total cost of offsets, a flobsion with the strike price s and a discount d is equivalent to a portfolio of* v_m *offsets to be purchased in the future at a market price and* v_o *options with the same strike price s, and* $d = \frac{v_o}{v_o+v_m}$.

Proof. We denote the total cost of v offsets when acquiring them on the market, via option, and via flobsion as $T_m(v)$, $T_o(v)$, and $T_d(v)$ respectively. For any offset price x materialized in the future, we consider two possible cases: case A: $x < s$ that implies

$$\begin{aligned}
T_o(v_o) &= p_1 v_o + x v_o, \\
T_m(v_m) &= x v_m, \quad \text{and} \\
T_d(v_o+v_m) &= p_d(v_o+v_m) + x(v_o+v_m) = \{Equation\ (5)\} = \\
&= d p_1(v_o+v_m) + x(v_o+v_m) = \{d = \frac{v_o}{v_o+v_m}\} = \\
&= p_1 v_o + x v_o + x v_m \equiv T_o(v_o) + T_m(v_m).
\end{aligned}$$

Case B: $x \geq s$ that implies

$$\begin{aligned}
T_o(v_o) &= p_1 v_o + s v_o, \\
T_m(v_m) &= x v_m, \quad \text{and} \\
T_d(v_o+v_m) &= p_d(v_o+v_m) + s(v_o+v_m) + (x-s)(1-d)(v_o+v_m) = \\
&= (v_o+v_m)\left[p_d + s + (x-s)(1-d)\right] = \{Equation\ (5)\} = \\
&= (v_o+v_m)\left[d p_1 + s + (x-s)(1-d)\right] = \{d = \frac{v_o}{v_o+v_m}\} = \\
&= (v_o+v_m)\left[\frac{v_o}{v_o+v_m} p_1 + s + (x-s)\frac{v_m}{v_o+v_m}\right] = \\
&= (v_o+v_m)\left[\frac{p_1 v_o + s(v_o+v_m) + (x-s)v_m}{v_o+v_m}\right] = \\
&= p_1 v_o + s(v_o+v_m) + (x-s)v_m = \\
&= p_1 v_o + s v_o + x v_m \equiv T_o(v_o) + T_m(v_m).
\end{aligned}$$

□

Remark 6. *The prices in Theorem 4 for a flobsion and an option do not necessarily have to be fair prices, yet naturally the theorem holds for fair prices.*

5. Benchmarking Results

For numerical illustration we employ the dataset on historical CO_2 prices (emission allowances, EUA) from the European Emission Trading Scheme (ETS) Fusion Media (2018) spanning the time period August 2005–February 2018 (further referred to as the "historical period"). These prices are presented in Figure 1.

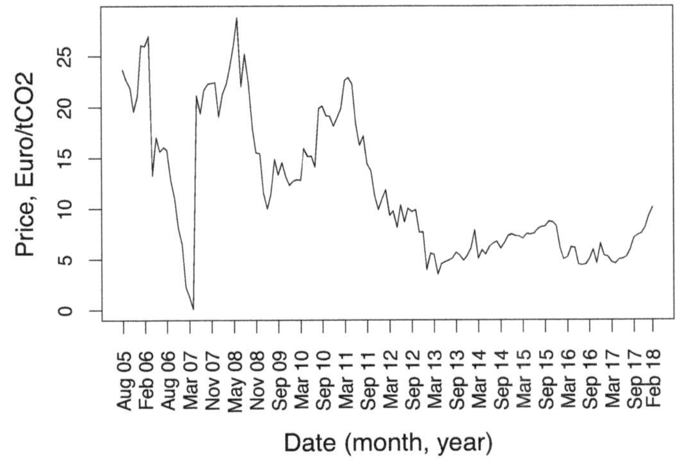

Figure 1. Historical CO_2 prices from the European Emission Trading Scheme (ETS) Fusion Media (2018).

For the purposes of benchmarking a flobsion against an option, we consider a hypothetic scenario where both an option and a flobsion for EUA were purchased before August 2005 and were executed (or expired without execution) at a random date uniformly distributed within the historical period. The market price distribution at the time of execution/expiration of a flobsion/option is shown in the form of a histogram in Figure 2.

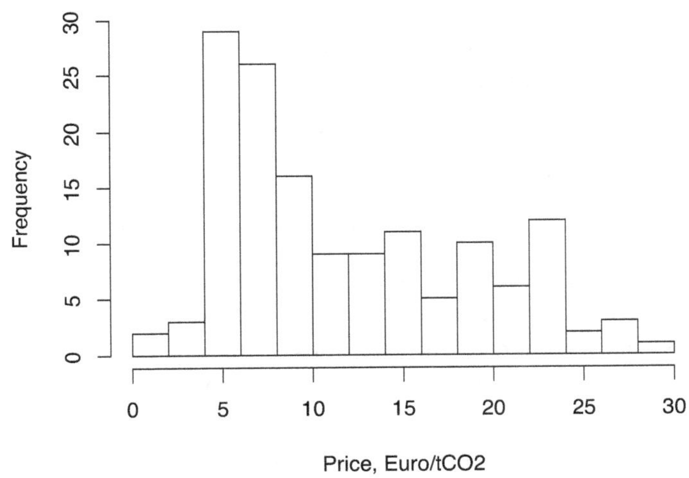

Figure 2. CO_2-price distribution from the EU ETS for the period August 2005–February 2018.

We assume that the contracted volume of allowances was actually used to offset emissions either through an option (flobsion) or via direct purchase on the market, so that the total price paid per one ton of emitted CO_2 is the sum of the option (flobsion) price plus either market price (in case the option/flobsion was not executed) or the option's strike price (flobsion's strike price plus discounted market price).

For the purposes of numerical calculations we arbitrarily set the flobsion's discount d to 0.5 and the strike price to 8 Euro/tCO_2 (both for the option and the flobsion). The total amount that was paid in three possible cases: just paying actual market price for emissions, using a flobsion or an option is presented in Figure 3 for three price scenarios: original historical prices, those doubled, and halved, where the initial purchase prices for both option and flobsion are "fair" for the original (historical) price distribution. The total amount paid per unit of emissions when flobsion is involved for all possible market prices stays between those of an option and the market price as illustrated in Figure 3.

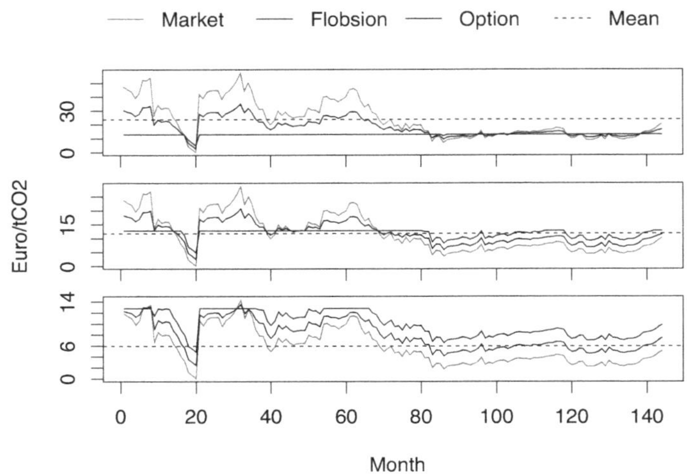

Figure 3. The total amount paid for emissions offsetting depending on the date (month since August 2005) in three cases: just paying a market price, using an option or a flobsion for three price scenarios: original historical prices (middle panel), those doubled (top panel), and halved (bottom panel).

The expected deviations from zero-expected profit (loss) in case of an option and a flobsion are presented in Table 1. The smaller scale of profits and losses provided by a flobsion numerically illustrates the analytical results obtained in Theorem 2.

Table 1. Expected deviations from zero-expected profit (loss) in Euro/tCO_2 in case of an option and a flobsion. Positive numbers are profits, negative numbers are losses.

Price Scenario	Option	Flobsion
Doubled	10.97	5.48
Halved	−4.05	−2.02

The flobsion's and option's reduction in offset cost variance for the original market price scenario is presented in Table 2. According to Theorem 4, purchasing a flobsion was similar to buying an option for a share of needed offsets and then actual emissions offsetting in the future using that option and purchasing the rest of needed offsets at a market price. The variance of the total cost of emissions offsetting supported by a flobsion is between that of an option and the "do nothing in advance" approach. Table 2 illustrates numerically the results of Theorem 3 i.e., the variance of the offsetting cost supported by a flobsion is smaller than the "original" variance of the market price ($15.58 < 46.21$).

Table 2. Variance of the emission offsetting costs for the historical price distribution and three alternatives: paying just the marked price ("do nothing"), contracting a flobsion, and an option.

Do nothing	Flobsion	Option
46.21	15.58	2.28

The numbers in Tables 1 and 2 indicate a trade-off between lower sensitivity to a wrong assumption on the price scenario (lower absolute values for flobsion in Table 1) and higher variance of offsetting costs within a fixed price scenario (higher value for flobsion than for option in Table 2). This links to the concepts of "model uncertainty" and "market risk" discussed earlier in Section 2 and illustrates the fact that a better performance in the sense of "model uncertainty" (price scenario) comes at the expense of lower performance in the sense of "market risk". At the same time, contracting a flobsion is better than buying an option if the price scenario is uncertain (Table 1) and better than "do nothing" if a price scenario is fixed (Table 2).

6. Discussion

The construction of a flobsion possesses universal properties that make it advantageous (or at least more flexible) as compared to contracting an option or "doing nothing" (implying a future purchase at a market price). This flexibility allows for shaping financial risk of an economic entity (flobsion buyer) in the face of future uncertain marked developments and in a sense "soft" hedging against unfavorable situation where the flobsion's underlying asset price increases. While this risk is not fully absorbed by a flobsion (as opposed to an option), it allows for a flexibility on flobsion's seller side who would like to avoid finding themselves in a situation where they have to sell an underlying asset to the option holder at the pre-defined strike price regardless of how high the market price turns out to be in the future. The flobsions' discount construction allows for balancing the benefit (between buyer and seller) created by a possible future price increase. So, in case if such an increase materializes in the future, the buyer and seller are factually sharing profits stemming from the discount to the actual market price. In case if the market price stays below the flobsions' strike price, the instrument is not being executed and there is no difference with the option.

A similar idea of controlling the volatility of the final price paid for an underlying asset, however under more specific conditions imposed on the stochastic price process, was explored earlier for the barrier options and capped options Detemple (2005). The fobsion's concept of a discount seems to be a "smoother" way of controlling that volatility as compared to barrier/capped options which are inherently controlled by respective thresholds. A quantitative comparison of these approaches within a problem-specific stochastic price processes may be useful in potential applications.

Selection of a particular risk measure is application-specific, depends on a particular problem context, and involves consideration of the complexity in interpretation of the risk measure and tractability of the resulting risk minimization problem. We have chosen variance for our analysis despite its known limitations Rockafellar et al. (2002) in addressing fat-tails and equal penalty to ups and downs of a distribution. While latter seems of a smaller problem in our setting that is intended to address the concerns of both buyer and seller (ups for a seller are downs for a buyer and vice versa), the fat-tail limitation is accepted assuming the interpretation of variance as a risk proxy employed for benchmarking rather than a risk measure used in an application-specific formulation of an optimization problem.

The options-style derivatives pricing Detemple (2005); Pierre Henry-Labordere (2009) assume a specific family of the stochastic price process to estimate the derivative's price. Our approach, based on a rather generic form of a discrete price distribution, allows us to capitalize on existing results for options pricing (both American and European style) and reduce the flobsion's pricing problem to those extensively explored earlier for options. To make the link between a traditional option and a flobsion we employ the "fair price" principle, which is similar to the utility-indifference pricing concept Hobson (2005) and the no-arbitrage principle widely used in the options pricing literature Buchen (2012); Chesney and Taschini (2012); Cox and Ross (1976); Detemple (2005).

As stated by Theorem 4, flobsion is similar to a portfolio with fixed shares of offsets to be purchased in the future at a market price and those covered by an option. Although mathematically, flobsion delivers the same distribution of the total cost of offsetting as such a portfolio, it allows for a legal contract for the whole amount of offsets, not only those covered by an option. In the sense of a portfolio-style point of view, this seems to be similar to the result obtained for the problem of pricing and hedging using oil and copper futures and forward contracts Kenichiro Shiraya et al. (2016), where the authors found that using three different futures contracts to hedge long-term contracts outperformed the traditional hedge based on a single futures position.

Here for simplicity, we have considered the properties of emission costs associated with the CO_2 price employing financial instruments independently from other emission costs reduction options that may be available to a concerned emitter, e.g., energy producers who have a portfolio of technologies varying in emission rates (per produced energy unit) may have a flexibility in adapting to an increased CO_2 price by adjusting the shares of individual technologies used in production

Krasovskii et al. (2016, 2017). So, the cost structure of an energy producer may change for higher CO_2 prices as these would lead to a different ranking of technologies in the total production portfolio. Therefore, the construction of a flobsion has to be applied to such cases and studied in more detail. As energy producers who have only CO_2-intensive technologies in their portfolios lack this flexibility, they are largely limited in managing their costs to financial instruments including a flobsion.

A more complex problem setting than that considered in this paper, could include the case of asymmetric information where the flobsion buyer and seller have different views on the future CO_2 prices, so their fair price estimates would be different. Depending on the mathematical sign of that difference, it can make it easier or more difficult to come to a purchase agreement Krasovskii et al. (2017). A similar consideration is valid in the context of risk preferences of a buyer and a seller (risk taking or risk averse attitudes). We expect that the risk context would influence the flobsion price in a similar way as it influences the price of a forward contract, however, this has to be proven by a numerical modeling similar to earlier works Krasovskii et al. (2016).

In this paper, we carried out an indicative benchmarking of a flobsion's performance employing a historical dataset with real market prices to avoid the complexity of price process modeling. As demonstrated in the earlier literature (see e.g., Fortin et al. (2008); Fuss et al. (2012)), the price process can be represented by a multi-parametric family of distributions, where the parameters of a distribution determine the results of numerical modeling. In this study we illustrated possible outcomes of contracting flobsions employing original historical data (and simple transformations thereof) to avoid the necessity of finding a suitable distribution family and prove its fit to historical prices.

The flobsion concept carries potential for supporting initiatives on reducing emissions from deforestation and forest degradation (REDD), while the problem associated with the acceptance of REDD-based offsets for emission reduction compliance at both national and international levels is still open and the future fungibility of REDD-based offsets with emission allowances and clean development mechanism (CDM) offsets is unknown Beltran et al. (2013); Dooley and Gupta (2017). This uncertainty creates additional risk associated with contracting REDD-offsets that a flobsion might help to mitigate.

7. Conclusions

Analytical results on the flobsion's properties presented in this paper cover a rich enough family of discrete price distributions and make this work complete for practical applications. These applications can be more general and not necessarily connected to the current and future CO_2 markets and the emission offsetting context.

The simple relation between the option and flobsion price based on Theorem 1 allows for easy determination of the flobsion price for any given discount based on the price of an option which is familiar to many market players. Flobsion's reduction of cost variance is less than that provided by the option, however, in case that the initially assumed price scenario turns out to be wrong, flobsion leads to smaller implied losses and gains, which reduces the risk for both buyer and seller.

While the flobsion construct is apparently applicable more universally, we see its good fit within the emission offsetting context. Despite technical details of potential future regulation remain uncertain, there is a progress towards more climate-aware policies. As policy changes can create not only opportunities, but also risks for certain market players, there is a need to accommodate and alleviate those risks. The flobsion's properties presented in this paper prove it to be a potential candidate helping in addressing these challenges and ultimately enabling or accelerating the implementation of new policies.

Further research might be directed towards exploration of a flobsion in more general financial risk management contexts as well as in the context of more detailed economic models that inherently include a regulated entity's possibility to adapt to rising CO_2 prices e.g., by adjusting technological portfolios.

Author Contributions: N.K. designed the study. N.K. and R.L. developed the concept of a flobsion. N.K., R.L., A.K., and M.O. discussed preliminary results. N.K. obtained analytical results, carried out numerical experiments, and wrote the manuscript with contributions from all the authors.

Funding: This work was supported by the project "Delivering Incentives to End Deforestation: Global Ambition, Private/Public Finance and Zero-Deforestation Supply Chains" funded by the Norwegian Agency for Development Cooperation under agreement number QZA-0464, QZA-16/0218.

Acknowledgments: Nikolay Khabarov would like to acknowledge Elena Moltchanova from the University of Canterbury, New Zealand, for help, useful discussions, and motivating the work in analytical direction. The authors express their gratitude to Michaela Rossini from the IIASA Library for supporting this work. The authors are thankful to two anonymous reviewers whose critical feedback and constructive suggestions helped to improve the manuscript.

Conflicts of Interest: The authors declare no conflict of interest.

Abbreviations

EUA	emission allowances from the European Emission Trading Scheme
EU ETS	European Emission Trading Scheme
CDM	Clean Development Mechanism

References

Andrew, L. Liu, and Yihsu Chen. 2017. Price containment in emissions permit markets: Balancing market risk and environmental outcomes. *IISE Transactions* 49: 1129–49. [CrossRef]

Artzner, Philippe, Freddy Delbaen, Jean-Marc Eber, and David Heath. 1999. Coherent measures of risk. *Mathematical Finance* 9: 203–28. [CrossRef]

Beltran, Angelica Mendoza, Arild Angelsen, Michel den Elzen, Caroline Wang Gierløff, and Hannes Böttcher. 2013. Analysing the Options and Impacts of Including REDD Credits in Carbon Markets. Technical Report, PBL Working Paper 17. Available online: https://www.pbl.nl/sites/default/files/cms/publicaties/pbl-2013-working-paper-analysing-the-options-and-impacts-of-including-redd-credits-in-carbon-markets.pdf (accessed on 17 September 2018).

Black, Fischer, and Myron Scholes. 1973. The pricing of options and corporate liabilities. *Journal of Political Economy* 81: 637–54. [CrossRef]

BP p.l.c.. 2018. BP Statistical Review of World Energy 2018. Available online: https://www.bp.com/content/dam/bp/en/corporate/pdf/energy-economics/statistical-review/bp-stats-review-2018-full-report.pdf (accessed on 17 September 2018).

Buchen, Peter. 2012. *An Introduction to Exotic Option Pricing*. Boca Raton: CRC Press.

Chesney, Marc, and Luca Taschini. 2012. The endogenous price dynamics of emission allowances and an application to co2 option pricing. *Applied Mathematical Finance* 19: 447–75. [CrossRef]

Collins, B., and F. J. Fabozzi. 2008. Financial Markets and Instruments (Chapter 15). In *OTC Equity Derivatives*. Hoboken: John Wiley & Sons, vol. 1, pp. 181–89.

Cont, Rama. 2006. Model uncertainty and its impact on the pricing of derivative instruments. *Mathematical Finance* 16: 519–47. [CrossRef]

Cox, John C., and Stephen A. Ross. 1976. The valuation of options for alternative stochastic processes. *Journal of Financial Economics* 3: 145–66. [CrossRef]

Detemple, Jerome. 2005. *American-Style Derivatives*. Boca Raton: CRC Press.

Dooley, Kate, and Aarti Gupta. 2017. Governing by expertise: The contested politics of (accounting for) land-based mitigation in a new climate agreement. *International Environmental Agreements: Politics, Law and Economics* 17: 483–500. [CrossRef]

Fortin, Ines, Sabine Fuss, Jaroslava Hlouskova, Nikolay Khabarov, and Michael Obersteiner. 2008. An integrated CVaR and real options approach to investments in the energy sector. *The Journal of Energy Markets* 1: 61–85. [CrossRef]

Fusion Media. 2018. Carbon Emissions Futures Historical Data. Available online: https://www.investing.com/commodities/carbon-emissions-historical-data (accessed on 18 September 2018).

Fuss, Sabine, Jana Szolgayová, Nikolay Khabarov, and Michael Obersteiner. 2012. Renewables and climate change mitigation: Irreversible energy investment under uncertainty and portfolio effects. *Energy Policy* 40: 59–68. [CrossRef]

Hannele Holttinen, Peter Meibom, Antje Orths, Frans Van Hulle, Cornel Ensslin, Lutz Hofmann, John McCann, Jan Pierik, John Olav Tande, Ana Estanqueiro, and et al. 2006. Design and Operation of Power Systems with Large Amounts of Wind Power. Available online: https://www.webcitation.org/61DCFd3dj?url=http://www.ieawind.org/AnnexXXV/Meetings/Oklahoma/IEA%20SysOp%20GWPC2006%20paper_final.pdf (accessed on 17 September 2018).

Hobson, D. G. 2005. Bounds for the utility-indifference prices of non-traded assets in incomplete markets. *Decisions in Economics and Finance* 28: 33–52. [CrossRef]

International Energy Agency. 2017. Global EV Outlook 2017. Available online: https://www.iea.org/publications/freepublications/publication/GlobalEVOutlook2017.pdf (accessed on 17 September 2018).

Kenichiro Shiraya, Akihiko Takahashi, M. A. H. Dempster, and Ke Tang, eds. 2016. *Pricing and Hedging of Long-Term Futures and Forward Contracts with a Three-Factor Model*. Boca Raton: CRC Press, Taylor & Francis Group, pp. 31–52, ISBN 978-1-4987-1233-0.

Kennan, John. 2006. A note on Discrete Approximations of Continuous Distributions. Available online: http://www.ssc.wisc.edu/~{}jkennan/research/DiscreteApprox.pdf (accessed on 18 September 2018).

Kudryavtsev, Oleg, and Antonino Zanette. 2013. Efficient pricing of swing options in Lévy-driven models. *Quantitative Finance* 13: 627–35. [CrossRef]

Krasovskii, Andrey, Nikolay Khabarov, and Michael Obersteiner. 2016. Fair pricing of REDD-based emission offsets under risk preferences and benefit-sharing. *Energy Policy* 96: 193–205. [CrossRef]

Krasovskii, Andrey, Nikolay Khabarov, and Michael Obersteiner. 2017. CO_2-intensive power generation and REDD-based emission offsets with a benefit-sharing mechanism. *Energy Systems* 8: 857–83. [CrossRef]

Liu, Xiaofang, Jian Li, Jun Wu, and Guoqing Zhang. 2017. Coordination of supply chain with a dominant retailer under government price regulation by revenue sharing contracts. *Annals of Operations Research* 257: 587–612. [CrossRef]

Ma, Kai, Congshan Wang, Jie Yang, Changchun Hua, and Xinping Guan. 2019. Pricing mechanism with noncooperative game and revenue sharing contract in electricity market. *IEEE Transactions on Cybernetics* 49: 97–106. [CrossRef] [PubMed]

Medina, Vicente, and Angel Pardo. 2013. Is the eua a new asset class? *Quantitative Finance* 13: 637–53. [CrossRef]

Pierre Henry-Labordere. 2009. *Analysis, Geometry, and Modeling in Finance: Advanced Methods in Option Pricing*. Boca Raton: CRC Press.

Rockafellar, R. Tyrrell, Stanislav P. Uryasev, and Michael Zabarankin. 2002. Deviation Measures in Risk Analysis and Optimization. *SSRN* 2002-7. [CrossRef]

Rouhani, Omid M., Richard R. Geddes, Wooseok Do, H. Oliver Gao, and Arash Beheshtian. 2018. Revenue-risk-sharing approaches for public-private partnership provision of highway facilities. *Case Studies on Transport Policy* 6: 439–48.. [CrossRef]

The Shift Project Data Portal. 2019. Breakdown of World GHG Emissions by Sector in 2010. Available online: http://www.tsp-data-portal.org/Breakdown-of-GHG-Emissions-by-Sector#tspQvChart (accessed on 22 February 2019).

UNFCCC. 2012. Kyoto Protocol CDM Passes One Billionth Certified Emission Reduction Milestone. Available online: https://cdm.unfccc.int/CDMNews/issues/issues/I_P0QZOY6FWYYKFKOSAZ5GYH2250DRQK/viewnewsitem.html (accessed on 22 February 2019).

UNFCCC. 2015. Cop 21 Paris Climate Conference. Available online: http://www.cop21paris.org/about/cop21 (accessed on 7 June 2018).

United Nations Development Programme. 2016. Sustainable Development Goals. Available online: http://www.undp.org/content/undp/en/home/sustainable-development-goals.html (accessed on 4 May 2018).

U.S. Congress, Office of Technology Assessment. 1984. *Nuclear Power in an Age of Uncertainty. Chapter 8: Public Attitudes Toward Nuclear Power*. Washington: U.S. Government Printing Office, pp. 211–251. Available online: http://govinfo.library.unt.edu/ota/Ota_4/DATA/1984/8421.PDF (accessed on 17 September 2018).

WordAtlas. 2018. Renewable Energy by Country: China, the United States, Brazil, and Canada Lead the World in Renewable Energy Production. Available online: https://www.worldatlas.com/articles/top-15-countries-using-renewable-energy.html (accessed on 17 September 2018).

6

The Effects of Quantitative Easing Announcements on the Mortgage Market: An Event Study Approach

Gang Wang

Department of Economics, The College of Wooster, 206 Morgan Hall, Wooster, OH 44691, USA; gangwang419@outlook.com

Abstract: This paper uses event study analysis to estimate the impact of the United States Federal Reserve Bank's (Fed) quantitative easing (QE) announcements on the mortgage market during the zero lower bound (ZLB) period. A total of 35 QE announcements are identified and their effects are evaluated. The best-fitting integrated generalized autoregressive conditional heteroskedasticity (IGARCH) model with skewed t distribution is used to measure the QE announcement effects on daily changes of the 30-year mortgage rate, the 30-year Treasury rate and the spread between them. Announcements suggesting the start of a new round of QE reduced the mortgage rate tremendously, while the effects of further news diminished. Announcements of an increase in mortgage-backed security purchases decreased the mortgage rate more than the Treasury rate and reduced the credit risk of holding mortgage securities over Treasury securities. The delayed effects of QE announcements on the mortgage rate were less than short-run effects but persistent. We also find that the previous literature overestimates QE effects on interest rates in general.

Keywords: event studies; the Fed; GARCH; Monetary Policy; mortgage; Quantitative Easing

JEL Classification: E52; E58; G21

---

1. Introduction

Unconventional monetary policy instruments have been widely employed by central banks in major developed economies (i.e., U.S., U.K., euro area and Japan) since the 2007–2008 financial crisis. Among these instruments, quantitative easing (QE) was most widely used by central banks and discussed by researchers. In the U.S., during the zero lower bound (ZLB) period[1], the Federal Reserve Bank (Fed) frequently implemented several rounds of QE such as large-scale asset purchase (LSAP) and operation twists[2] (OT). Although the types and quantities of assets purchased by the Fed were not the same during each round, the aim of the Fed's QEs was that by increasing the prices and decreasing the yields of government and agency assets through Fed's purchases, investors were more willing to buy private assets. As a result, better liquidity and less credit constraints were achieved in the market. Mortgage-backed securities (MBSs) were among the securities purchased by the Fed and thus the yields of MBSs and mortgage rates were expected to be reduced in the course of QEs. The former chairman of the Fed Ben Bernanke said in his Jackson Hole Speech on 31 August 2012: "The QE program … has been linked to substantial reductions in MBS yields and retail mortgage rates".

---

1 ZLB period started at the end of 2008 when the Fed reduced the federal funds rate to be in the range of 0 to 0.25 percent, and concluded at late 2015 when the Fed decided to increase the federal funds rate to be in the range of 0.25 to 0.5 percent.

2 Also known as maturity extension program (or MEP).

While QE effects on asset prices in general are broadly studied, few researchers (Hancock and Passmore 2011, 2012, 2015) have looked into the mortgage market. In the broad QE literature, the vector autoregressive (VAR) model is most commonly used to estimate the co-movement of mortgage rates and other asset yields, but the effects of QE announcements on mortgage rates on event day or in an event window have not been investigated until this paper.

The purpose of this paper is to analyze the QE announcement effects on the mortgage rate and the spread over the Treasury rate. By contrast with Hancock and Passmore (2011, 2012, 2015) who treat the announcements in the same round of QE as the same event, we consider all 35 announcements as different events and evaluate their effects on the mortgage rate respectively.

In general, we find that announcements of an increase in MBS purchases decreased the mortgage rate more than the Treasury rate and narrowed the spread between the mortgage rate and the Treasury rate. This is consistent with the finding in Di Maggio et al. (2016): Mortgage rates decreased more in QE1 than in QE2 since the Fed only purchased Treasury bonds in QE2.

Our analysis has several advantages compared to the prior literature. Our data set are updated to the end of 2015 which includes all the Fed's QE announcement events during the ZLB period. Using regression-based event studies to account for the effects reduces concerns regarding endogeneity and overlapping event windows. We use the generalized autoregressive conditional heteroskedasticity (GARCH) model to control for the serial correlation and heteroskedasticity within the data series for better estimating the pure effect of events. We summarize primarily formal methods and econometric evidence in QE announcement effect literature and compare their results with ours. We find the QE announcement effects on the mortgage rate in the short run (i.e., on event day and in event windows) and in long run (i.e., assume a steady state). Finally, we categorize the QE announcements by type and summarize their distinct effects.

The outline of the paper is as follows: Section 1 gives the background and introduction. Section 2 presents the literature review. Section 3 describes the data sources and descriptive statistics. Section 4 shows the event study methodology and model selection. Section 5 discusses the results. Section 6 analyzes the case when QE events are grouped by the type of announcements and the round of QE. Section 7 demonstrates two robustness checks and Section 8 concludes the findings.

2. Literature Review

2.1. Quantitative Easing (QE) Announcement Effects on Interest Rates and Asset Prices

A large amount of literature focuses on estimating the direct effects of QE announcements on long-term interest rates and term premia. Wright (2012) finds that although QE shocks had effects on both long-term interest rates and corporate bond yields, the effect decayed really fast. Li and Wei (2012) conclude that QE1, QE2 and OT combined result in a decrease of about 100 basis points on the 10-year Treasury yield. Jarrow and Li (2014) evaluate the effects of the Fed's QE1 and QE2 on US term premia of interest rates.

Hancock and Passmore (2011) evaluate effects of the Fed's MBS purchase program in 2008 (part of QE1) on mortgage rates and MBS yields. They run linear regression of mortgage rates on the determinants and period dummies to conclude that the program lowered the mortgage rates. Hollifield (2011) points out two drawbacks in the research of Hancock and Passmore (2011), which are a non-linear relationship between MBS yields and their determinants, and endogenous right-hand side regression variables to the Fed's MBS purchase program. Hancock and Passmore (2012) extend the data to include QE2 and OT, modify the determination models of mortgage rates and MBS yields, and model the relation between these two variables. Hancock and Passmore (2015) use a co-integrated, error-correction model to estimate the "stock" and "flow" effect[3] of Fed's LSAP on MBS yields and mortgage rates. Different from their previous researches, they account for the separate QE rounds (QE1, QE2, OT and QE3) by defining a dummy for each round. They conclude that "portfolio rebalancing" channel is a more important consideration for QE transmission than other channels. They also indicate that the "stock" effect dominates the "flow" effect of the Fed's QE on MBS yields and mortgage rates.

Di Maggio et al. (2016) use micro-level mortgage market data to analyze the interest rate movements and the origination volumes of assets in different rounds of QE. They find that the interest rates and origination volumes depend on the segmentation of the market and the types of assets purchased. Adalid and Falagiarda (2018) claim that the boom of mortgage loan origination can be partially explained by the effectiveness of the European Central Bank's (ECB) non-standard monetary policy on lowering the mortgage rate in the euro area.

2.2. QE Announcement Effects Analysis Using Event Studies

A few researchers incorporate event studies[4] to analyze QE effects. Swanson et al. (2011) uses event study to examine the QE announcement effects on Treasury yields during "Operation Twist" in the 1960s and QE2. Glick and Leduc (2012) consider the first principal component of yield changes of 2-, 5-, 10- and 30-year U.S. bond futures in a 2-hour window (Wright 2012) as the Fed's QE announcement shock and employ event studies to analyze QE announcement effects on the financial market. Patrabansh et al. (2014) use the event study method to show how the 10-year Treasury yield responded to the Fed's QE announcement. Kozicki et al. (2015) incorporate event studies with GARCH (1,1) model to analyze the Fed's LSAP announcement effects on commodity prices and international spillovers.

Falagiarda and Reitz (2015) employ event studies to access the different instruments of the ECB's unconventional monetary policy announcements and their distinctive effects on the sovereign spreads of five European countries. Szczerbowicz (2015) uses a similar strategy to gauge the correlation between the announcements and banks' financing costs. Altavilla et al. (2015) perform an event study assessment on the ECB's Asset Purchase Programme (APP) announcements' impacts on the bond yields of European countries. They add dummy variables in the regressions to control for the macroeconomic news releases. Using the same methodology, Altavilla et al. (2016) investigate the responses on sovereign bond yields of four European countries to the ECB's Outright Monetary Transaction (OMT) announcements. Eser and Schwaab (2016) use a panel regression to evaluate the effects of the ECB's Securities Markets Programme (SMP) on five European sovereign bond markets. In additional to the announcement effects, they examine a negative linear relationship between the change of bond yields and the value amount of bond purchased across time.

3. Data

We analyze the 30-year fixed mortgage rate (FRM)[5] as the indicator for the cost of financing a single-family house. The corresponding benchmark- 30-year Treasury rate is also evaluated. Figure 1 shows these two data series along with the daily Freddie Mac 30-year current coupon yield from 3 January 2000 to 31 December 2015. To eliminate the federal funds rate effect[6] on the mortgage rate, we only use data from 2 January 2008 to 31 December 2015 which covers the whole ZLB period.

---

3 The stock effect means the effect of increases in the Fed's asset holdings, while the flow effect means the effect of QE announcements.

4 Event study literature and methodology are discussed in the Supplemental Materials, Part 1.

5 Specifically, the mortgage rate is the daily overnight 30-year US home mortgage national average from the bank rate. We only estimate the 30-year mortgage rate here since 60–70 percent mortgages originated during ZLB period were 30-year FRMs. The 30-year mortgage rate is a good reflection of the general borrowing cost of mortgages.

6 It is known as the effect of traditional monetary policy.

Figure 1. Mortgage rates, Treasury rates and mortgage-backed securities (MBS) yields. This figure shows time series of the 30-year mortgage rate, the 30-year Treasury rate and the 30-year Freddie Mac MBS current coupon yield from 3 January 2000 to 31 December 2015. The different rounds of quantitative easing (QE) are marked by different colors. Source: Bloomberg and U.S. Treasury.

Before the initiation of QE, all three yields stayed in high levels. Then they all tumbled during the initiation of QE1, QE2 and OT, rallied to relatively high levels when OT ended, and were gradually declining in QE tapering. During each round of QE, the rates dropped sharply when purchase programs were announced. There is a clear evidence that QE announcements had influences on long-term interest rates and spreads. The summary statistics are reported in Table A1.

4. Methodology

4.1. QE Announcement Dates for Event Study

The QE announcement events take several forms including announcements after the Federal Open Market Committee (FOMC) meetings, Fed testimonies, Fed chairman's speeches, press conference reports and Fed minutes released. An announcement is identified as a QE announcement based on two criteria. First, the announcement should mention the QE program, either as an indication of launching a new round of QE or the types and quantities of assets the Fed planned to purchase. Second, the announcement should contain news to the market other than mentioning the same thing as in the last QE announcement.

Without the official version of QE announcement events timeline published by the Fed, we identify the events from previous literature. There is a consensus among previous researchers (Gagnon et al. 2011; Woodford 2012; Hancock and Passmore 2015; Hattori et al. 2016; Altavilla and Giannone 2017; Glick and Leduc 2015) that there were a total of 13 QE announcements during QE1 and QE2. We include all 13 events during QE1 and QE2 in this paper. For the OT (a.k.a. MEP) period, we identify three events mentioned in Bowman et al. (2015) and Borrallo et al. (2016), and one event mentioned in Hancock and Passmore (2015). Among these four events, two hinted at the possible OT program and the other two were official announcements of launching OT. For QE3, we combine the events mentioned in Bowman et al. (2015) and Hancock and Passmore (2015) and delete one "irrelevant" event[7] to a total of four events. For the QE tapering period, the first four events are taken from Altavilla and Giannone (2017), three of which indicated the decreasing pace of asset purchases and one was the official announcement of tapering. We update the data to include another 10 events concerning stepwise QE tapering procedure until the end of QE program on 29 October 2014. Finally, a total of 35 events is identified and reported in Table A2.

4.2. Event Window, Issues and GARCH

To measure the effect of QE announcements on the mortgage rate using event studies, we choose three different event window sizes (i.e., 1-day, 3-day and 5-day)[8] for each of the 35 events and run regressions according to each window size. Specifically, the 1-day window only identifies the event day on which there was a QE announcement; the 3-day window consists of one pre-event day, the event day and one post-event day; 5-day window is comprised of two pre-event days, the event day and two post-event days. The augmented Dickey–Fuller unit root tests[9] on levels and changes of variables (i.e., 30-year mortgage rate, 30-year Treasury rate, and the spread between these two) validate that the changes of these variables are covariance stationary and not over differenced.

Instead of finding the abnormal return (AR) as the difference between the observed and predicted returns in the traditional way with non-overlapping event windows, we use regression-based event study methodology to allow for overlapping event windows[10]. The coefficient of the event dummy

---

7 The announcement on 20 March 2013 is considered irrelevant to QE since it only remarked on the improved economic and labor market conditions. It was treated as an unconventional monetary policy announcement (i.e., forward guidance) in Bowman et al. (2015), but should not be regarded as a QE announcement here.

8 Event windows larger than five days are not considered in my study to avoid the effects of other news.

9 The test results can be found in Table S1 in the Supplementary Materials.

10 From the data, the windows for event on 11/25/2008 and the one on 12/1/2008 overlapped.

corresponding to event k on day t is the abnormal return[11] (AR_{kt}) of the left hand side variable. We run four different regressions and adjust for three different event window sizes (5-day, 3-day and 1-day). The four regressions are:

$$\Delta MR_t = \gamma_{1,0} + \gamma_{1,1}\Delta TR_t + \phi_1' D_t + \varepsilon_{1,t}, \tag{1}$$

$$\Delta MR_t = \gamma_{2,0} + \phi_2' D_t + \varepsilon_{2,t}, \tag{2}$$

$$\Delta TR_t = \gamma_{3,0} + \phi_3' D_t + \varepsilon_{3,t}, \tag{3}$$

$$\Delta Spread_t = \gamma_{4,0} + \phi_4' D_t + \varepsilon_{4,t}, \tag{4}$$

where ΔMR_t is the change of 30-year mortgage rate from day $t-1$ to day t, ΔTR_t is the change of 30-year Treasury rate from day $t-1$ to day t, and $\Delta Spread_t$ is the change of spread between 30-year mortgage rate and Treasury rate from day $t-1$ to day t. The Spread measures the perceived riskiness of holding mortgages over Treasury bonds (i.e., the risk premium). D_t is a $L \times 1$ column vector of event dummies taking value 1 on that day and 0 on other days. L equals to 35 for 1-day window, 105 for 3-day window and 175 for 5-day window. Equation (1) indicates a "market model" regression[12] that the Treasury rate is the market rate which determines the mortgage rate. The vector of coefficients ϕ_1 measure the daily abnormal returns of the mortgage rate on day t. Equation (2) is a "constant mean return" regression without ΔTR_t. This regression can be regarded as a robustness check for Equation (1). Equation (3)[13] estimates the relation between ΔTR_t and D_t. Equation (4) combines ΔMR_t and ΔTR_t as one dependent variable. Although someone would argue that Equation (4) is a restricted version of Equation (1), it would not be the case when GARCH terms are added into the model.

Our analysis[14] shows that the dependent variables in Equation (1) to (4) are serially correlated and heteroskedastic, the characteristics that are typically modelled using GARCH models. We first select a GARCH model that best fits each of the return series (ΔMR_t, ΔTR_t, and $\Delta Spread_t$), and then add the controls and event dummies to build the full model. To better capture the patterns of error terms, we suppose them following skewed t distributions (Makenzie et al. 2004).

After adding autoregressive moving average (ARMA) and GARCH items to Equation (1) to (4), the complete model is specified as

$$\Delta MR_t = \gamma_{1,0} + \gamma_{1,1}\Delta TR_t + \sum_{i=1}^{7} \lambda_{1,i}\Delta MR_{t-i} + \phi_1' D_t + \pi_1' X_t + \varepsilon_{1,t}, \tag{5}$$

$$\varepsilon_{1,t} = e_{1,t}\sigma_{1,t}, \quad e_{1,t} \sim skewed - t(0,1;\vartheta_1, r_1),$$
$$\sigma_{1,t}^2 = \alpha_1\sigma_{1,t-1}^2 + \beta_1\varepsilon_{1,t-1}^2 + (1-\alpha_1-\beta_1)\varepsilon_{1,t-2}^2;$$

$$\Delta MR_t = \gamma_{2,0} + \sum_{i=1}^{7} \lambda_{2,i}\Delta MR_{t-i} + \phi_2' D_t + \pi_2' X_t + \varepsilon_{2,t}, \tag{6}$$

$$\varepsilon_{2,t} = e_{2,t}\sigma_{2,t}, \quad e_{2,t} \sim skewed - t(0,1;\vartheta_2, r_2),$$
$$\sigma_{2,t}^2 = \alpha_2\sigma_{2,t-1}^2 + \beta_2\varepsilon_{2,t-1}^2 + (1-\alpha_2-\beta_2)\varepsilon_{2,t-2}^2;$$

---

11 Usually return means the percentage change of a variable, here I name change of rate as return since mortgage and Treasury rates are already in percent. Also, since "abnormal return" is widely used by researchers doing event studies, it is used in this paper instead of "abnormal change" to avoid confusions.

12 The name "market model regression" can be found in Degryse et al. (2009).

13 A constant mean return regression is preferred to a market model regression for estimating the Treasury rate because there is no single reference series (market rate) that simulates or determines the Treasury rate.

14 The identification of issues, ARMA and GARCH selections, and the skewed t distribution analysis are discussed in the Supplementary Materials, Part 2.

$$\Delta TR_t = \gamma_{3,0} + \sum_{j=1}^{5} \lambda_{3,j}\Delta TR_{t-j} + \phi_3' D_t + \pi_3' X_t + \varepsilon_{3,t}, \tag{7}$$

$$\varepsilon_{3,t} = e_{3,t}\sigma_{3,t}, \quad e_{3,t} \sim skewed - t(0,1;\vartheta_3, r_3),$$

$$\sigma_{3,t}^2 = \alpha_3\sigma_{3,t-1}^2 + (1-\alpha_3)\varepsilon_{3,t-1}^2;$$

$$\Delta Spread_t = \gamma_{4,0} + \sum_{i=1}^{6} \lambda_{4,i}\Delta Spread_{t-i} + \phi_4' D_t + \pi_4' X_t + \varepsilon_{4,t}, \tag{8}$$

$$\varepsilon_{4,t} = e_{4,t}\sigma_{4,t}, \quad e_{4,t} \sim skewed - t(0,1;\vartheta_4, r_4),$$

$$\sigma_{4,t}^2 = \alpha_4\sigma_{4,t-1}^2 + (1-\alpha_4)\varepsilon_{4,t-1}^2.$$

In the model, $e_{j,t}$ is the standardized innovation following standard skewed t distribution with degree of freedom ϑ_i and skewness r_j in regression j. The variance $\sigma_{j,t}^2$ of innovation $\varepsilon_{j,t}$ in regression j at time t is conditional on past values of the squared innovations (ARCH) and variances (GARCH). X_t is a vector of control variables including unexpected changes of macroeconomic variables and mortgage rate determinants. As the control variables have a minor impact[15] on dependent variables, X_t is not included in the regressions here.

For 5-day and 3-day window cases, we add up the abnormal return (AR_{kt}) for each day t from an event window of event k to get the cumulative abnormal return (CAR_k), which can be expressed as

$$CAR_k = \sum_{t=t_1}^{t_2} AR_{kt}, \tag{9}$$

where t_1 and t_2 represent the lower and upper bounds of days in an event window. For a 1-day window, CAR_k is the same as AR_k.

5. Results

5.1. Individual Events

The regression results are reported in Tables 1–3 for 1-day, 3-day and 5-day event window cases. we report abnormal returns (ARs) on event days for 1-day window case and cumulative abnormal returns (CARs) in event windows for 3-day and 5-day window cases.[16] Most of the ARs in 1-day window and CARs in 3-day and 5-day windows for the same event followed the similar signs and significances with few exceptions. The magnitudes of CARs in 3-day and 5-day windows were not always greater than those of ARs on event days for the same event, which suggests the high volatility of ARs within an event window.

15 The trivial impacts are mentioned by Altavilla and Giannone (2017), we found similar results in robustness check part.

16 The ARs for calculating CARs can be found in the Supplementary Materials, Tables S3 and S4.

Table 1. Abnormal returns (ARs) in 1-day windows. We run four regressions (Equations (5) to (8)) with 1-day event window. For each regression, the ARs and standard errors (SEs) on QE event days are reported in Panel A. Coefficient estimates and SEs of control variables and GARCH components are reported in Panel B.

	Panel A							
	(5)		(6)		(7)		(8)	
	Mortgage Rate		Mortgage Rate		Treasury Rate		Spread	
	AR	SE	AR	SE	AR	SE	AR	SE
Mean Model								
11/25/2008	−0.121 **	0.048	−0.165 ***	0.052	−0.166 *	0.095	0.002	0.079
12/1/2008	0.011	0.046	−0.053	0.044	−0.220 **	0.093	0.205 ***	0.076
12/16/2008	0.039	0.043	0.008	0.040	−0.127	0.091	0.129*	0.077
1/28/2009	−0.066	0.043	−0.012	0.043	0.214 ***	0.078	−0.225 ***	0.078
3/18/2009	0.064 **	0.028	−0.005	0.026	−0.239 ***	0.072	0.202 ***	0.076
8/12/2009	−0.027	0.031	−0.001	0.038	0.085	0.073	−0.068	0.054
9/23/2009	0.051 *	0.030	0.055	0.034	0.006	0.064	0.054	0.052
11/4/2009	0.026	0.035	0.047	0.037	0.083	0.054	−0.050	0.055
8/10/2010	0.043 **	0.018	0.044 *	0.022	−0.013	0.062	0.052	0.047
8/27/2010	−0.175 ***	0.017	−0.134 ***	0.019	0.165 ***	0.053	−0.266 ***	0.050
9/21/2010	0.000	0.059	−0.002	0.057	−0.079	0.060	0.036	0.069
10/15/2010	0.117 **	0.055	0.156 ***	0.051	0.088 *	0.051	0.028	0.069
11/3/2010	−0.055	0.044	−0.014	0.047	0.171 ***	0.050	−0.152 **	0.060
8/9/2011	0.040 ***	0.015	0.002	0.019	−0.122*	0.072	0.151 **	0.060
8/26/2011	−0.017	0.023	−0.032	0.029	−0.054	0.090	0.039	0.062
9/21/2011	0.020	0.018	−0.024	0.020	−0.161 **	0.075	0.161 ***	0.057
6/20/2012	0.016	0.016	0.014	0.017	−0.004	0.051	0.016	0.037
8/22/2012	−0.048 **	0.020	−0.061 ***	0.023	−0.071	0.046	0.001	0.031
8/31/2012	0.022	0.017	0.007	0.019	−0.061	0.039	0.061 *	0.033
9/13/2012	−0.046 ***	0.016	−0.034*	0.020	0.047	0.040	−0.104 ***	0.034
12/12/2012	−0.026 ***	0.010	−0.003	0.013	0.080 **	0.032	−0.084 ***	0.023
5/1/2013	−0.010	0.016	−0.024	0.019	−0.040	0.035	0.020	0.026
5/22/2013	0.068 ***	0.017	0.091 ***	0.024	0.074 *	0.040	0.025	0.026
6/19/2013	0.036	0.037	0.055	0.044	0.084 **	0.041	−0.002	0.045
12/18/2013	0.012	0.023	0.019	0.027	0.030	0.034	−0.001	0.028
1/29/2014	−0.003	0.020	−0.022	0.025	−0.055*	0.032	0.029	0.027
3/19/2014	0.045 ***	0.017	0.053 **	0.023	0.037	0.036	0.030	0.031
4/30/2014	−0.024	0.037	−0.037	0.042	−0.020	0.035	−0.003	0.048
5/7/2014	−0.026	0.046	−0.002	0.044	0.020	0.035	−0.063	0.053
6/18/2014	0.009	0.031	0.005	0.033	−0.009	0.035	0.010	0.040
7/15/2014	0.016	0.027	0.023	0.024	0.006	0.035	0.005	0.037
7/30/2014	−0.106 **	0.042	−0.091 **	0.044	0.093 **	0.035	−0.148 **	0.059
8/22/2014	0.009	0.050	−0.007	0.058	−0.028	0.036	0.046	0.058
9/17/2014	0.008	0.041	0.015	0.046	0.017	0.039	−0.013	0.049
10/29/2014	0.013	0.038	0.020	0.034	0.009	0.032	0.004	0.049
	Panel B							
	(5)		(6)		(7)		(8)	
	Estimate	SE	Estimate	SE	Estimate	SE	Estimate	SE
Mean Model								
Intercept	−0.001 ***	0.001	−0.002 ***	0.001	−0.001	0.001	0.000	0.001
ΔTR_t	0.280 ***	0.013						
ΔMR_{t-1}	−0.094 ***	0.023	−0.004	0.023				
ΔMR_{t-2}	−0.032	0.020	−0.033	0.021				
ΔMR_{t-3}	−0.031	0.021	−0.052 **	0.021				
ΔMR_{t-4}	−0.018	0.021	−0.044 **	0.020				
ΔMR_{t-5}	−0.041 *	0.021	−0.024	0.022				
ΔMR_{t-6}	−0.009	0.021	0.014	0.021				
ΔMR_{t-7}	−0.037 *	0.020	−0.048 **	0.021				
ΔTR_{t-1}					−0.044 *	0.023		
ΔTR_{t-2}					−0.041 *	0.023		
ΔTR_{t-3}					−0.028	0.023		
ΔTR_{t-4}					−0.050 **	0.023		
ΔTR_{t-5}					−0.048 **	0.023		
$\Delta Spread_{t-1}$							−0.234 ***	0.023
$\Delta Spread_{t-2}$							−0.056 **	0.023
$\Delta Spread_{t-3}$							−0.033	0.023
$\Delta Spread_{t-4}$							−0.060 **	0.023
$\Delta Spread_{t-5}$							−0.082 ***	0.023
$\Delta Spread_{t-6}$							−0.062 ***	0.022

Table 1. *Cont.*

Panel B								
	(5)		(6)		(7)		(8)	
	Estimate	SE	Estimate	SE	Estimate	SE	Estimate	SE
Variance Model								
σ^2_{t-1}	0.084 ***	0.016	0.103 ***	0.015	0.039 ***	0.006	0.047 ***	0.000
ε^2_{t-1}	0.403 *	0.211	0.249 *	0.128	0.961 ***	NA	0.953 ***	NA
ε^2_{t-2}	0.513 ***		0.649 ***					
Quality of Model								
Log Likelihood	3720.612		3484.149		2939.588		2950.285	
AIC	−3.678		−3.442		−2.900		−2.910	
BIC	−3.544		−3.311		−2.777		−2.784	

Note: ***, ** and * indicate statistical significance at 0.01, 0.05, 0.1 levels.

Table 2. Cumulative abnormal returns (CARs) in 3-day windows. We run four regressions (Equations (5) to (8)) with 3-day event window (i.e., $t = -1, 0, 1$). For each regression, the CARs and standard errors (SEs) on QE event days are reported in Panel A. Coefficient estimates and SEs of control variables and GARCH components are reported in Panel B.

Panel A								
	(5)		(6)		(7)		(8)	
	Mortgage Rate		Mortgage Rate		Treasury Rate		Spread	
	CAR	SE	CAR	SE	CAR	SE	CAR	SE
Mean Model								
11/25/2008	−0.149 **	0.065	−0.202 ***	0.077	−0.199	0.140	0.006	0.108
12/1/2008	0.005	0.063	−0.098	0.076	−0.342 **	0.132	0.274 **	0.106
12/16/2008	−0.146 ***	0.053	−0.270 ***	0.063	−0.387 ***	0.121	0.150	0.097
1/28/2009	−0.084	0.056	−0.020	0.062	0.265 **	0.116	−0.284 ***	0.097
3/18/2009	−0.006	0.036	−0.037	0.036	−0.094	0.118	0.040	0.095
8/12/2009	−0.065	0.043	−0.079	0.054	−0.070	0.115	−0.003	0.076
9/23/2009	0.036	0.047	0.011	0.057	−0.060	0.101	0.090	0.073
11/4/2009	0.029	0.057	0.076	0.066	0.164*	0.090	−0.105	0.079
8/10/2010	−0.017	0.020	−0.035	0.022	−0.069	0.093	0.057	0.060
8/27/2010	−0.127 ***	0.023	−0.121 ***	0.030	0.030	0.080	−0.134 **	0.064
9/21/2010	−0.140 **	0.063	−0.177 **	0.078	−0.138	0.091	−0.015	0.090
10/15/2010	−0.007	0.075	0.037	0.085	0.128	0.079	−0.109	0.090
11/3/2010	−0.014	0.065	0.010	0.078	0.070	0.074	−0.088	0.082
8/9/2011	−0.057 ***	0.017	−0.135 ***	0.029	−0.282 **	0.112	0.176 ***	0.064
8/26/2011	0.017	0.028	0.020	0.044	0.015	0.136	0.031	0.080
9/21/2011	0.002	0.021	−0.111 ***	0.031	−0.392 ***	0.113	0.300 ***	0.081
6/20/2012	−0.001	0.022	0.003	0.028	0.022	0.078	−0.010	0.053
8/22/2012	−0.118 ***	0.023	−0.151 ***	0.032	−0.112	0.071	−0.029	0.043
8/31/2012	0.003	0.023	−0.014	0.029	−0.053	0.061	0.037	0.044
9/13/2012	−0.080 ***	0.020	−0.007	0.030	0.265 ***	0.069	−0.272 ***	0.041
12/12/2012	−0.008	0.014	0.027	0.020	0.124 **	0.050	−0.089 ***	0.033
5/1/2013	0.016	0.024	0.004	0.030	−0.034	0.055	0.029	0.039
5/22/2013	0.114 ***	0.025	0.131 ***	0.037	0.046	0.062	0.088 ***	0.034
6/19/2013	0.246 ***	0.051	0.290 ***	0.065	0.165 ***	0.063	0.129 **	0.056
12/18/2013	0.053	0.037	0.065	0.046	0.034	0.055	0.037	0.040
1/29/2014	−0.016	0.031	−0.025	0.038	−0.016	0.054	−0.012	0.036
3/19/2014	0.118 ***	0.028	0.127 ***	0.038	0.030	0.057	0.097 **	0.040
4/30/2014	0.020	0.054	0.000	0.066	−0.049	0.047	0.066	0.067
5/7/2014	−0.127 **	0.056	−0.092	0.063	0.046	0.051	−0.170 *	0.067
6/18/2014	0.019	0.039	0.037	0.046	0.065	0.053	−0.024	0.051
7/15/2014	0.002	0.038	0.002	0.043	0.004	0.053	0.011	0.050
7/30/2014	0.008	0.061	0.032	0.070	0.068	0.053	−0.042	0.079
8/22/2014	0.042	0.074	0.014	0.089	−0.075	0.052	0.069	0.080
9/17/2014	0.005	0.057	0.008	0.074	0.037	0.060	−0.035	0.072
10/29/2014	−0.009	0.053	0.002	0.059	0.026	0.052	−0.029	0.070

Table 2. *Cont.*

Panel B								
	(5)		(6)		(7)		(8)	
	Estimate	SE	Estimate	SE	Estimate	SE	Estimate	SE
Mean Model								
Intercept	−0.001 ***	0.001	−0.002 ***	0.001	−0.001	0.001	0.000	0.001
ΔTR_t	0.280 ***	0.013						
ΔMR_{t-1}	−0.098 ***	0.023	0.000	0.023				
ΔMR_{t-2}	−0.031	0.020	−0.034	0.021				
ΔMR_{t-3}	−0.026	0.021	−0.054 **	0.022				
ΔMR_{t-4}	−0.007	0.021	−0.039 *	0.021				
ΔMR_{t-5}	−0.052 **	0.021	−0.029	0.022				
ΔMR_{t-6}	−0.011	0.021	0.013	0.021				
ΔMR_{t-7}	−0.044 **	0.020	−0.055 **	0.021				
ΔTR_{t-1}					−0.040 *	0.023		
ΔTR_{t-2}					−0.045 *	0.024		
ΔTR_{t-3}					−0.030	0.024		
ΔTR_{t-4}					−0.054 **	0.024		
ΔTR_{t-5}					−0.047 *	0.024		
$\Delta Spread_{t-1}$							−0.233 ***	0.023
$\Delta Spread_{t-2}$							−0.042 *	0.023
$\Delta Spread_{t-3}$							−0.032	0.024
$\Delta Spread_{t-4}$							−0.069 ***	0.023
$\Delta Spread_{t-5}$							−0.090 ***	0.023
$\Delta Spread_{t-6}$							−0.074 ***	0.023
Variance Model								
σ^2_{t-1}	0.087 ***	0.016	0.105 ***	0.016	0.036 ***	0.006	0.039 ***	0.008
ε^2_{t-1}	0.268	0.170	0.176 *	0.095	0.964 ***		0.961 ***	
ε^2_{t-2}	0.645 ***		0.718 ***					
Quality of Model								
Log Likelihood	3795.506		3550.227		2982.218		3005.344	
AIC	−3.683		−3.438		−2.873		−2.895	
BIC	−3.352		−3.110		−2.553		−2.572	

Note: ***, ** and * indicate statistical significance at 0.01, 0.05, 0.1 levels.

Large effects on the mortgage rate were found during the days when new rounds of QE or QE tapering were hinted, the effects from any further news conveying a continuation of the current QE policy dwindled. For example, when QE1 was first announced on 11/25/2008 for purchasing GSE debts and MBSs, ARs and CARs were significantly negative for all three window sizes. Specifically, AR was −0.121 percent on event day and CAR was −0.149 percent in the 3-day window. For other QE events that followed,[17] AR and CARs were all negative but in smaller magnitudes. On 5/22/2013, when Bernanke remarked the potential tapering of asset purchases during his speech, AR went up to 0.068 percent on event day, and CARs were 0.114 and 0.120 in 3-day and 5-day windows. For other QE tapering events that followed,[18] AR and CARs were all positive but in smaller magnitudes. Significant ARs and CARs were also found in other announcement dates suggesting new rounds of QE.[19]

The macroeconomic news largely deviating from market expectation contaminate the QE announcement effects on the Treasury rate more than on the mortgage rate. For example, when Bernanke mentioned additional QE "should further action" on 8/27/2010, there was supposed to be downward pressure on both Treasury rate and mortgage rate. However, event day AR and 3-day CAR of mortgage rate were significant and negative at −0.175 and −0.127 percent, while those of Treasury rate were significant and positive at 0.165 and 0.030 percent. Only when we increase the window size to 5-day, the CARs of the Treasury rate switch to negative. The positive AR and CARs of the Treasury

[17] Events on 1/28/2009 and 3/18/2009. Events on 12/1/2008 and 12/16/2008 are not counted since they both focused on Treasury bond purchases.

[18] Events on 6/19/2013 and 12/18/2013.

[19] They are 8/27/2010 for QE2, 8/9/2011 for OT, 8/22/2012 for QE3.

rate can be attributed to a better-than-expected report on U.S. economic growth by the Department of Commerce,[20] which had little effect on the mortgage.

Table 3. Cumulative abnormal returns (CARs) in 5-day windows. We run four regressions (Equations (5) to (8)) with 5-day event window (i.e., t = −2, −1, 0, 1, 2). For each regression, the CARs and standard errors (SEs) on QE event days are reported in Panel A. Coefficient estimates and SEs of control variables and GARCH components are reported in Panel B. The CARs for 11/25/2008 and 12/1/2008 are not reported since they are overlapped.

Panel A.								
	(5)		(6)		(7)		(8)	
	Mortgage Rate		Mortgage Rate		Treasury Rate		Spread	
	CAR	SE	CAR	SE	CAR	SE	CAR	SE
Mean Model								
11/25/2008	N/A	N/A	N/A	N/A	N/A	NA	N/A	N/A
12/1/2008	N/A	N/A	N/A	N/A	N/A	N/A	N/A	N/A
12/16/2008	−0.090	0.067	−0.232 ***	0.073	−0.484 ***	0.137	0.253 **	0.115
1/28/2009	−0.082	0.067	0.020	0.079	0.367 **	0.145	−0.358 ***	0.109
3/18/2009	−0.005	0.046	0.002	0.047	0.043	0.146	−0.051	0.107
8/12/2009	−0.095 **	0.047	−0.142 **	0.062	−0.152	0.139	0.029	0.091
9/23/2009	0.087*	0.050	0.050	0.059	−0.115	0.121	0.165*	0.086
11/4/2009	−0.053	0.064	−0.003	0.071	0.185*	0.109	−0.179 **	0.090
8/10/2010	0.002	0.025	−0.028	0.026	−0.101	0.110	0.109	0.072
8/27/2010	−0.133 ***	0.029	−0.142 ***	0.033	−0.018	0.095	−0.093	0.076
9/21/2010	−0.104	0.079	−0.149*	0.090	−0.147	0.106	0.010	0.108
10/15/2010	−0.073	0.086	−0.026	0.097	0.154*	0.090	−0.204 **	0.104
11/3/2010	−0.029	0.077	0.021	0.089	0.176 **	0.086	−0.154	0.097
8/9/2011	−0.108 ***	0.019	−0.086 **	0.035	0.067	0.143	−0.073	0.079
8/26/2011	0.023	0.032	0.042	0.044	0.081	0.131	−0.005	0.085
9/21/2011	−0.013	0.023	−0.130 ***	0.032	−0.381 ***	0.118	0.279 ***	0.084
6/20/2012	−0.008	0.026	0.010	0.033	0.066	0.097	−0.033	0.061
8/22/2012	−0.067 ***	0.024	−0.088 **	0.036	−0.102	0.085	0.015	0.050
8/31/2012	−0.010	0.021	−0.016	0.030	−0.015	0.072	−0.002	0.051
9/13/2012	−0.045 **	0.022	0.021	0.032	0.230 ***	0.081	−0.208 ***	0.046
12/12/2012	0.009	0.018	0.035	0.025	0.100*	0.060	−0.063	0.039
5/1/2013	0.039	0.030	0.074 **	0.037	0.120*	0.063	−0.048	0.041
5/22/2013	0.120 ***	0.030	0.133 ***	0.043	0.052	0.067	0.086 **	0.037
6/19/2013	0.361 ***	0.064	0.448 ***	0.078	0.296 ***	0.075	0.152 **	0.066
12/18/2013	0.041	0.043	0.038	0.051	−0.021	0.064	0.056	0.047
1/29/2014	−0.047	0.034	−0.049	0.041	−0.022	0.063	−0.028	0.041
3/19/2014	0.121 ***	0.031	0.127 ***	0.041	0.015	0.064	0.110 **	0.047
4/30/2014	0.204 ***	0.066	0.190 ***	0.072	−0.066	0.053	0.232 ***	0.076
5/7/2014	−0.181 ***	0.058	−0.149 **	0.064	0.110 **	0.055	−0.262 ***	0.070
6/18/2014	0.017	0.044	0.028	0.050	0.035	0.058	−0.003	0.055
7/15/2014	0.296 ***	0.040	0.270 ***	0.045	−0.096*	0.052	0.352 ***	0.054
7/30/2014	−0.010	0.049	0.006	0.054	0.062	0.054	−0.047	0.066
8/22/2014	0.011	0.075	0.015	0.092	−0.043	0.058	0.003	0.080
9/17/2014	0.071	0.069	0.065	0.080	−0.022	0.067	0.062	0.075
10/29/2014	0.023	0.063	0.041	0.072	0.057	0.061	−0.020	0.078

20 Department of Commerce reported real GDP growth of 1.6 percent in second quarter of 2010, which was higher than the consensus value of 1.3 percent. From Bloomberg, no other significant macroeconomic news was announced on the same dates as the QE announcement dates.

Table 3. *Cont.*

	Panel B							
	(5)		(6)		(7)		(8)	
	Estimate	SE	Estimate	SE	Estimate	SE	Estimate	SE
Mean Model								
Intercept	−0.002 ***	0.001	−0.002 ***	0.001	−0.001	0.001	0.000	0.001
ΔTR_t	0.280 ***	0.013						
ΔMR_{t-1}	−0.085 ***	0.022	0.007	0.022				
ΔMR_{t-2}	−0.035 *	0.020	−0.043 **	0.021				
ΔMR_{t-3}	−0.023	0.021	−0.052 **	0.022				
ΔMR_{t-4}	−0.005	0.020	−0.030	0.021				
ΔMR_{t-5}	−0.073 ***	0.022	−0.046 **	0.022				
ΔMR_{t-6}	−0.004	0.022	0.020	0.022				
ΔMR_{t-7}	−0.048 **	0.021	−0.065 ***	0.021				
ΔTR_{t-1}					−0.029	0.023		
ΔTR_{t-2}					−0.046 *	0.024		
ΔTR_{t-3}					−0.031	0.024		
ΔTR_{t-4}					−0.054 **	0.025		
ΔTR_{t-5}					−0.038	0.025		
$\Delta Spread_{t-1}$							−0.220 ***	0.023
$\Delta Spread_{t-2}$							−0.043 *	0.023
$\Delta Spread_{t-3}$							−0.027	0.023
$\Delta Spread_{t-4}$							−0.060 **	0.024
$\Delta Spread_{t-5}$							−0.099 ***	0.024
$\Delta Spread_{t-6}$							−0.075 ***	0.024
Variance Model								
σ^2_{t-1}	0.080 ***	0.017	0.099 ***	0.018	0.036 ***	0.007	0.039 ***	0.009
ε^2_{t-1}	0.309 *	0.161	0.203*	0.106	0.964 ***		0.961 ***	
ε^2_{t-2}	0.611 ***		0.699 ***					
Quality of Model								
Log Likelihood	3853.002		3608.316		3031.920		3062.150	
AIC	−3.673		−3.429		−2.854		−2.884	
BIC	−3.151		−2.910		−2.344		−2.370	

Note: ***, ** and * indicate statistical significance at 0.01, 0.05, 0.1 levels.

Market expectations before QE announcements had a strong effect on both mortgage rate and Treasury rate. For example, the Fed on 9/13/2012 announced an increase in purchases of MBSs, although the public expected the purchase to be mix of MBSs and Treasury bonds[21]. On the event day, a significant and negative AR of mortgage rate at −0.046 percent coexisted with an insignificant and positive AR of Treasury rate at 0.047 percent, while 3-day and 5-day CARs of the mortgage rate were −0.080 and −0.045 percent compared to those of the Treasury rate at 0.265 and 0.230 percent.

If no other events happened on the same day, an unexpected announcement of increase in MBS purchases shocked the mortgage rate more than the Treasury rate, while an unexpected announcement of increase in Treasury purchases shocked the Treasury rate more than the mortgage rate.[22] For instance, on 12/1/2008, when Bernanke mentioned possible longer-term Treasury bond purchases, the Treasury rate declined tremendously but the mortgage rate did not. Specifically, AR and 3-day CAR of Treasury rate were significant at −0.166 and −0.342 percent, while those of the mortgage rate were both insignificant at 0.011 and 0.005 percent. Different signs of AR or CAR of the mortgage rate and the Treasury rate led to large and positive AR and CAR of the spread. Similar phenomena were found in 3/18/2009 when the Fed officially announced Treasury bond purchase in QE1, 8/10/2010 when the

[21] See Bloomberg article 9/13/2012.

[22] An exception is the first QE announcement on 11/25/2008 which announced only the MBS purchase, but both mortgage rate and Treasury rate had significantly large and negative ARs and CARs.

Fed announced it would reinvest principal payments from MBSs in Treasury bonds, 9/21/2011 when the Fed announced to purchase long-term and sell same amount of short-term Treasury bonds, and 9/13/2012 when the Fed announced the additional purchase of MBSs in QE3.

The signs and magnitudes of ARs and CARs were not consistent for a few events. When market took days after the QE announcement to absorb the news or the news had been already priced in the days leading up to the announcement, insignificant AR and significant CARs were found for that event (e.g., events on 8/12/2009 and 7/15/2014). When the effect of QE announcement was transitory, significant AR and insignificant CARs were found for that event (e.g., events on 12/12/2012 and 7/30/2014).

5.2. Delayed Effects

Since there are right-hand side lagged dependent variables in all four regressions (i.e., Equations (5)–(8)), the announcement effects on dependent variables will last into the future through them. In long run, if we assume a steady state $\Delta MR_t = \Delta MR_{t-1} = \cdots = \Delta MR_{t-7}$, from Equation (5) or (6), the total AR of the mortgage rate for event k can be calculated as:

$$TAR_k = \frac{\phi_{1,k}}{1 - \sum_{i=1}^{7} \lambda_{1,i}} = \frac{AR_k}{1 - \sum_{i=1}^{7} \lambda_{1,i}}, \tag{10}$$

and total CAR of the mortgage rate for event k as:

$$TCAR_k = \frac{\sum_{t=t_1}^{t_2} \phi_{1,t}}{1 - \sum_{i=1}^{7} \lambda_{1,i}} = \frac{CAR_k}{1 - \sum_{i=1}^{7} \lambda_{1,i}}. \tag{11}$$

Total abnormal returns (TARs) and total cumulative abnormal returns (TCARs) of the Treasury rate and spread could also be derived by similar strategy from Equations (7) and (8). Given that both TARs and TCARs are non-linear transformations of regression parameters, we incorporate the Delta method[23] to find the asymptotic standard errors for them. Table 6 reports the estimates and standard errors of TARs and 3-day and 5-day TCARs from four regressions.

From Table 4, TARs and TCARs for the same event had less magnitudes than AR and CARs, while the signs and significances did not vary so much. That being said, although the delayed effects of QE announcement on the mortgage rate shrunk, the directions of delayed effects stayed the same as short-run effects. The muted delayed effects are due to the negative autocorrelations and partial autocorrelations within the data series as we found earlier. Moreover, the delayed effects were less volatile than short-run effects since the standard errors of TAR and TCARs for the same event decreased compared to those of AR and CARs.

---

23 The Delta method estimates the standard errors of 1st order Taylor expansion of $f(\beta)$, which can be expressed as $SE(f(\beta)) \approx \sqrt{\nabla f(\beta)^T \cdot Cov(\beta) \cdot \nabla f(\beta)}$. In the equation, $f(\beta)$ is a transformation of regression parameter vector β and $\nabla f(\beta)$ is the gradient of $f(\beta)$. Here, $f(\beta)$ is TAR or TCAR.

Table 4. Delayed effects of QE announcement.

	(5)						(6)						(7)						(8)					
	Mortgage Rate						Mortgage Rate						Treasury Rate						Spread					
	1-day		3-day		5-day		1-day		3-day		5-day		1-day		3-day		5-day		1-day		3-day		5-day	
Date	TAR	SE	TCAR	SE	TCAR	SE	TAR	SE	TCAR	SE	TCAR	SE	TAR	SE	TCAR	SE	TCAR	SE	TAR	SE	TCAR	SE	TCAR	SE
11/25/2008	−0.096 **	0.038	−0.118 *	0.062	N/A	N/A	−0.139 **	0.044	−0.169 **	0.073	N/A	N/A	−0.137 *	0.078	−0.163	0.132	N/A	N/A	0.001	0.051	0.004	0.097	N/A	N/A
12/1/2008	0.008	0.036	0.004	0.058	N/A	N/A	−0.044	0.037	−0.082	0.073	N/A	N/A	−0.181 **	0.077	−0.281 **	0.125	N/A	N/A	0.134 ***	0.050	0.178*	0.094	N/A	N/A
12/16/2008	0.031	0.034	−0.115 *	0.050	−0.071	0.065	0.007	0.034	−0.225 ***	0.061	−0.192 ***	0.071	−0.105	0.075	−0.318 ***	0.115	−0.404 ***	0.133	0.084*	0.050	0.097	0.088	0.166	0.109
1/28/2009	−0.052	0.034	−0.066	0.053	−0.064	0.065	−0.010	0.036	−0.017	0.059	0.016	0.076	0.177 ***	0.064	0.218 **	0.109	0.306 **	0.142	−0.147 ***	0.051	−0.184 **	0.087	−0.235 **	0.103
3/18/2009	0.050 **	0.023	−0.005	0.033	−0.004	0.044	−0.004	0.022	−0.031	0.034	0.002	0.045	−0.197 ***	0.061	−0.077	0.113	0.035	0.141	0.132 ***	0.050	0.026	0.085	−0.033	0.100
8/12/2009	−0.022	0.025	−0.051	0.040	−0.074	0.046	−0.001	0.032	−0.066	0.052	−0.117*	0.060	0.070	0.061	−0.057	0.108	−0.126	0.135	−0.044	0.036	−0.002	0.068	0.019	0.085
9/23/2009	0.041*	0.024	0.028	0.044	0.069	0.048	0.046	0.028	0.009	0.054	0.042	0.057	0.005	0.052	−0.050	0.095	−0.096	0.117	0.035	0.034	0.058	0.065	0.108	0.082
11/4/2009	0.021	0.028	0.023	0.053	−0.041	0.062	0.039	0.032	0.063	0.063	−0.003	0.069	0.069	0.045	0.135	0.085	0.154	0.105	−0.033	0.036	−0.068	0.071	−0.117	0.086
8/10/2010	0.034 **	0.014	−0.013	0.019	0.001	0.024	0.037 **	0.019	−0.029	0.021	−0.023	0.026	−0.010	0.051	−0.057	0.088	−0.084	0.107	0.034	0.031	0.037	0.054	0.071	0.067
8/27/2010	−0.139 ***	0.015	−0.100 ***	0.021	−0.104 ***	0.028	−0.112 **	0.017	−0.101 ***	0.028	−0.118 ***	0.032	0.136 ***	0.044	0.024	0.076	−0.015	0.092	−0.174 ***	0.034	−0.087	0.058	−0.061	0.070
9/21/2010	0.000	0.046	−0.110*	0.059	−0.081	0.077	−0.002	0.048	−0.148 **	0.073	−0.123	0.087	−0.065	0.050	−0.114	0.086	−0.123	0.103	0.024	0.045	−0.010	0.081	0.007	0.101
10/15/2010	0.092 **	0.044	−0.006	0.070	−0.057	0.083	0.131 **	0.043	0.031	0.081	−0.020	0.095	0.073*	0.042	0.106	0.074	0.128	0.087	0.018	0.045	−0.071	0.081	−0.134	0.098
11/3/2010	−0.044	0.035	−0.011	0.061	−0.023	0.074	−0.012	0.040	0.008	0.074	0.017	0.087	0.141 ***	0.042	0.057	0.070	0.146 *	0.084	−0.099 **	0.040	−0.057	0.074	−0.101	0.091
8/9/2011	0.032 ***	0.012	−0.045 ***	0.016	−0.085 ***	0.018	0.002	0.016	−0.112 ***	0.027	−0.071 **	0.034	−0.101*	0.059	−0.232 **	0.104	0.056	0.141	0.099 **	0.040	0.114 **	0.058	−0.048	0.075
8/26/2011	−0.013	0.018	0.014	0.026	0.018	0.031	−0.027	0.024	0.017	0.042	0.035	0.042	−0.045	0.075	0.012	0.129	0.068	0.126	0.026	0.041	0.020	0.072	−0.003	0.079
9/21/2011	0.016	0.014	0.002	0.019	−0.010	0.022	−0.020	0.017	−0.093 ***	0.030	−0.107 ***	0.032	−0.133 **	0.062	−0.322 ***	0.107	−0.318 ***	0.115	0.105 ***	0.038	0.195 ***	0.073	0.183 **	0.078
6/20/2012	0.012	0.013	−0.001	0.020	−0.006	0.025	0.012	0.014	0.002	0.026	0.008	0.032	−0.003	0.042	0.018	0.073	0.055	0.094	0.011	0.024	−0.006	0.047	−0.022	0.057
8/22/2012	−0.038 **	0.016	−0.093 ***	0.022	−0.052 **	0.023	−0.051 ***	0.019	−0.126 ***	0.031	−0.073 **	0.035	−0.059	0.038	−0.092	0.067	−0.085	0.083	0.001	0.020	−0.019	0.039	0.010	0.047
8/31/2012	0.017	0.014	0.002	0.021	−0.008	0.021	0.006	0.016	−0.012	0.028	−0.013	0.029	−0.050	0.032	−0.043	0.057	−0.012	0.070	0.040 *	0.022	0.024	0.040	−0.001	0.048
9/13/2012	−0.036 ***	0.013	−0.063 ***	0.019	−0.035*	0.021	−0.029 *	0.017	−0.005	0.028	0.017	0.031	0.039	0.033	0.218 ***	0.065	0.191 **	0.079	−0.068 ***	0.022	−0.177 ***	0.037	−0.136 ***	0.044
12/12/2012	−0.020 ***	0.008	−0.006	0.013	0.007	0.017	−0.003	0.011	0.022	0.019	0.029	0.024	0.066 **	0.026	0.102 **	0.047	0.084	0.058	−0.055 ***	0.015	−0.057 *	0.030	−0.041	0.036
5/1/2013	−0.008	0.013	0.013	0.022	0.031	0.029	−0.020	0.016	0.004	0.029	0.061*	0.037	−0.033	0.029	−0.028	0.052	0.100	0.062	0.013	0.017	0.019	0.034	−0.032	0.039
5/22/2013	0.054 ***	0.013	0.090 ***	0.023	0.094 ***	0.029	0.076 ***	0.021	0.109 ***	0.035	0.110 ***	0.042	0.061*	0.033	0.038	0.059	0.043	0.065	0.017	0.017	0.057 *	0.030	0.056	0.035
6/19/2013	0.028	0.029	0.194 ***	0.048	0.284 ***	0.062	0.046	0.037	0.242 ***	0.062	0.371 ***	0.076	0.069 **	0.033	0.136 **	0.060	0.247 ***	0.073	−0.001	0.030	0.084 *	0.050	0.100	0.063
12/18/2013	0.009	0.018	0.042	0.034	0.032	0.042	0.016	0.023	0.055	0.044	0.032	0.050	0.025	0.028	0.028	0.052	−0.018	0.063	0.000	0.018	0.024	0.036	0.037	0.044
1/29/2014	−0.002	0.016	−0.013	0.029	−0.037	0.033	−0.018	0.021	−0.021	0.037	−0.040	0.040	−0.045 *	0.027	−0.013	0.052	−0.019	0.061	0.019	0.018	−0.008	0.032	−0.019	0.038
3/19/2014	0.036 ***	0.014	0.093 ***	0.027	0.095 ***	0.030	0.044 **	0.020	0.106 ***	0.036	0.105 ***	0.040	0.030	0.030	0.025	0.053	0.013	0.062	0.020	0.021	0.063 *	0.036	0.072	0.044
4/30/2014	−0.019	0.029	0.016	0.051	0.160 **	0.064	−0.031	0.036	0.000	0.062	0.157 **	0.071	−0.017	0.029	−0.041	0.045	−0.055	0.052	−0.002	0.031	0.043	0.060	0.152 **	0.072
5/7/2014	−0.021	0.036	−0.100 *	0.053	−0.142 **	0.056	−0.001	0.037	−0.076	0.060	−0.123 *	0.061	0.016	0.029	0.038	0.048	0.092 *	0.053	−0.041	0.034	−0.110 *	0.060	−0.172 **	0.067
6/18/2014	0.007	0.024	0.015	0.037	0.013	0.042	0.004	0.028	0.031	0.044	0.023	0.049	−0.007	0.029	0.053	0.050	0.029	0.056	0.007	0.026	−0.016	0.046	−0.002	0.052
7/15/2014	0.013	0.021	0.002	0.036	0.232 ***	0.040	0.019	0.021	0.001	0.041	0.223 ***	0.045	0.005	0.029	0.003	0.050	−0.080	0.050	0.003	0.024	0.007	0.045	0.231 ***	0.051
7/30/2014	−0.084 **	0.034	0.006	0.057	−0.008	0.047	−0.076 **	0.037	0.027	0.066	0.006	0.052	0.077 ***	0.029	0.056	0.050	0.052	0.052	−0.097 **	0.039	−0.027	0.070	−0.031	0.061
8/22/2014	0.007	0.040	0.033	0.069	0.009	0.071	−0.006	0.048	0.012	0.085	0.012	0.092	−0.023	0.030	−0.062	0.050	−0.036	0.057	0.030	0.038	0.045	0.072	0.002	0.074
9/17/2014	0.006	0.033	0.004	0.054	0.056	0.067	0.012	0.039	0.007	0.070	0.054	0.078	0.014	0.032	0.031	0.057	−0.018	0.065	−0.008	0.032	−0.023	0.065	0.041	0.071
10/29/2014	0.011	0.030	−0.007	0.050	0.018	0.061	0.017	0.029	0.002	0.056	0.034	0.070	0.007	0.027	0.021	0.049	0.047	0.059	0.003	0.032	−0.019	0.062	-0.013	0.073

The estimates and standard errors (SEs) of total abnormal returns (TARs) for 1-day window and total cumulative abnormal returns (TCARs) for 3-day window and 5-day window are reported in the table. Standard errors (SEs) are asymptotic standard errors calculated by the Delta method. The TCARs for two events with overlapped event windows on 11/25/2008 and 12/1/2008 are invalid and denoted as N/A. Note: ***, ** and * indicate statistical significance at 0.01, 0.05, 0.1 levels.

5.3. Comparing the Results with Literature

Next, we aggregate the ARs in each round of QE to find the cumulative effects of announcements. Table 5 reports the cumulative effects[24] for 1-day, 3-day and 5-day window cases from my estimation and those from other studies. My estimation is consistent with other studies that cumulative effects on both the mortgage rate and the Treasury rate were greater in QE1 than in other rounds of QE. However, the magnitudes of the effects in QE1 in my study were only half of those in other studies.[25] The evidence suggests that event studies using OLS without controlling for the serial correlation and the conditional heteroscedasticity within the data series overestimate the QE announcement effects on interest rates in general. The spread between the mortgage rate and the Treasury rate increased around days of announcements cumulatively in all rounds of QE except for QE3, which were expected to boost the risk-taking behaviors of investors as a goal of the Fed's QE.

Table 5. Cumulative effects of QE announcements on the mortgage rate and Treasury rate. Row 1 reports the cumulative abnormal returns of the 30-year mortgage rate, the 30-year Treasury rate and the spread between them across all announcements in each round of QE with 1-day, 3-day and 5-day event windows from my estimation. As a comparison, the cumulative effects on mortgage rates and MBS yields found in other literature are reported. The cumulative changes of the 30-year MBS yield and the 30-year Treasury rate are found in Krishnamurthy and Vissing-Jorgensen (2011) and Di Maggio et al. (2016), all other studies report cumulative changes of the 10-year MBS yield and the 10-year Treasury rate. For comparison purposes, we only focus on "easing" announcements, four events of decrease in purchases of assets are not used for calculation. In line with the events used in other studies, four events on 8/27/2010, 11/3/2010, 6/20/2012 and 12/12/2012 are excluded from my calculation.

Study	Event Window Size	Round of QE	Mortgage Rate (Market Model)	Mortgage Rate (Constant Mean Return Model)	Treasury Rate	Spread
My Estimation in this paper	1-day, 3-day, 5-day	QE1	−7, −38, −37	−23, −63, −56	−54, −76, −58	31, 19, 10
		QE2	4, −16, −10	4, −21, −18	−9, −21, −25	9, 4, 12
		OT	4, −4, −10	−5, −23, −17	−34, −66, −23	35, 51, 20
		QE3	−7, −20, −12	−9, −17, −8	−9, 10, 11	−4, −26, −19
		Tapering	5, 49, 107	10, 60, 124	22, 35, 48	−6, 21, 64
Gagnon et al. (2011)	1-day, 2-day	QE1		−113, −115	−91, −105	
Krishnamurthy and Vissing-Jorgensen (2011)	2-day for QE1, 1-day and 2-day for QE2	QE1		−107	−73	
		QE2		−9, −8	−9, −21	
Christensen and Rudebusch (2012)	1-day	QE1			−100	
Neely (2015)	1-day	QE1			−100	
Altavilla and Giannone (2017)	2-day	QE1			−104	
		QE2			−29	
		OT			−43	
		QE3			−4	
		Tapering			40	
Bowman et al. (2015)	2-day	QE1			−99	
		QE2			−28	
		OT			−41	
		QE3			−9	
		Tapering			37	
Borrallo et al. (2016)	2-day	QE1			−104	
		QE2			−29	
		OT			−37	
		QE3			−10	
		Tapering			42	
Di Maggio et al. (2016)	3-month, 6-month	QE1			−117, −140	
		QE2			−37, −47	
		OT			−46, −63	
		QE3			−18, −32	
		Tapering			26, −53	

Note: Events on 8/27/2010 and 11/3/2010 (both in QE2) are not picked by Krishnamurthy and Vissing-Jorgensen (2011), and events on 6/20/2012 (in OT) and 12/12/2012 (in QE3) are not picked by Bowman et al. (2015) and Borrallo et al. (2016). In fact, as discussed in Section 5, these four events are also the events either contaminated by the economy report release or are already expected by the market.

24 The cumulative effects are graphed in the Supplementary Materials, Figure S4.

25 The cumulative abnormal returns of the mortgage rate and the Treasury rate for the 1-day window in my study were −23 and −54 basis points, while those in other studies were all around −100 basis points.

6. Events Grouped by Announcement Type and QE Round

6.1. Regressions with Grouped Event Dummies

In order to generalize QE announcement effects on the mortgage rate, we next group all QE events[26] by type of asset purchased (i.e., the MBSs, the Treasury securities or both as shown in Table 2, Column 5), increase or decrease of purchase (i.e., as shown in Table A2, Column 5), and round of QE (i.e., QE1, QE2, OT, QE3 and tapering as shown in Table A2, Column 2). Dummy variables are created with value 1 on days of grouped event and 0 on other days. For example, the dummy variable "QE1_MBS_Increase" has value 1 on the days when Fed announced an increase of MBS purchases during QE1 and 0 on other days. We replace the individual event dummies in Equations (5) to (8) by the new dummies and run four regressions. The regression results for 1-day, 3-day and 5-day windows are reported in Table 6.

Table 6. Abnormal returns (ARs) and cumulative abnormal returns (CARs) for event groups. A total of 31 QE events are grouped by type of asset purchased, increase or decrease of purchase, and QE round. ARs are reported for the 1-day window and CARs are reported for 3-day and 5-day windows. The ARs used to calculate CARs are not reported for 3-day and 5-day window cases, but can be found in Supplementary Materials, Table S5.

Panel A. 1-day window

	(5)		(6)		(7)		(8)	
	Mortgage Rate		Mortgage Rate		Treasury Rate		Spread	
	AR	SE	AR	SE	AR	SE	AR	SE
QE1_MBS_Increase	−0.095 ***	0.033	−0.086	0.052	0.004	0.079	−0.130 **	0.066
QE1_T_Increase	0.010	0.046	−0.056	0.045	−0.223 **	0.100	0.210 ***	0.079
QE1_Both_Increase	0.055 **	0.024	−0.001	0.024	−0.198 ***	0.060	0.164 ***	0.057
QE1_MBS_Decrease	0.038*	0.023	0.051 **	0.025	0.045	0.041	0.000	0.041
QE1_T_Decrease	−0.027	0.032	−0.001	0.039	0.085	0.075	−0.069	0.054
QE2_T_Increase	0.038 *	0.021	0.038 *	0.023	−0.050	0.044	0.047	0.040
QE2_T_Decrease	0.117 **	0.058	0.157 ***	0.053	0.087	0.057	0.029	0.073
OT_T_Increase	0.020	0.018	−0.023	0.021	−0.162 **	0.077	0.161 ***	0.058
OT_Both_Increase	0.013	0.030	−0.014	0.021	−0.094	0.059	0.092 *	0.054
QE3_MBS_Increase	−0.046 ***	0.018	−0.034 *	0.020	0.047	0.040	−0.104 ***	0.035
QE3_Both_Increase	−0.019	0.031	−0.025	0.025	−0.066 **	0.031	0.027	0.027
Tapering	0.006	0.010	0.001	0.012	0.008	0.011	0.009	0.011

Panel B. 3-day window

	(5)		(6)		(7)		(8)	
	Mortgage Rate		Mortgage Rate		Treasury Rate		Spread	
	CAR	SE	CAR	SE	CAR	SE	CAR	SE
QE1_MBS_Increase	−0.116 **	0.049	−0.101	0.072	−0.018	0.120	−0.178 *	0.103
QE1_T_Increase	0.004	0.067	−0.107	0.081	−0.358 **	0.154	0.311 ***	0.118
QE1_Both_Increase	−0.048	0.045	−0.082 *	0.048	−0.268 **	0.104	0.082	0.078
QE1_MBS_Decrease	0.024	0.037	0.031	0.045	0.052	0.068	−0.013	0.061
QE1_T_Decrease	−0.064	0.042	−0.079	0.056	−0.068	0.120	−0.006	0.079
QE2_T_Increase	−0.025	0.023	−0.044 *	0.026	−0.109	0.069	0.036	0.056
QE2_T_Decrease	−0.006	0.084	0.038	0.092	0.128	0.087	−0.108	0.101
OT_T_Increase	0.004	0.025	−0.109 ***	0.036	−0.393 ***	0.119	0.299 ***	0.086
OT_Both_Increase	0.034	0.034	−0.021	0.051	−0.161 *	0.095	0.114 *	0.066
QE3_MBS_Increase	−0.079 ***	0.023	−0.004	0.033	0.264 ***	0.072	−0.271 ***	0.044
QE3_Both_Increase	−0.066	0.046	−0.087 **	0.039	−0.085 *	0.049	0.004	0.035
Tapering	0.021	0.017	0.016	0.020	0.009	0.017	0.028	0.018

[26] A total of 31 events are in the sample at this part. As we discuss in Part 5, the event on 8/27/2010 is excluded since it is contaminated by the better economy report on the same day. Event on 11/3/2010, 6/20/2012 and 12/12/2012 are excluded given that these 3 events were well expected by the market. In fact, plenty of other researchers exclude those four events in their studies as well. After the deletion, my sample of events is consistent with Krishnamurthy and Vissing-Jorgensen (2011), Bowman et al. (2015) and Borrallo et al. (2016).

Table 6. *Cont.*

Panel C. 5-day window								
	(5)		(6)		(7)		(8)	
	Mortgage Rate		Mortgage Rate		Treasury Rate		Spread	
	CAR	SE	CAR	SE	CAR	SE	CAR	SE
QE1_MBS_Increase	−0.115 *	0.065	−0.050	0.087	0.220	0.154	−0.318 ***	0.114
QE1_T_Increase	−0.049	0.089	−0.231 **	0.108	−0.651 ***	0.220	0.505 ***	0.161
QE1_Both_Increase	−0.035	0.052	−0.035	0.053	−0.263 **	0.130	0.066	0.100
QE1_MBS_Decrease	0.010	0.053	0.012	0.054	0.031	0.084	−0.020	0.078
QE1_T_Decrease	−0.095 *	0.048	−0.144 **	0.066	−0.149	0.148	0.027	0.096
QE2_T_Increase	−0.005	0.028	−0.035	0.029	−0.132	0.085	0.083	0.069
QE2_T_Decrease	−0.066	0.101	−0.022	0.109	0.160	0.105	−0.203 *	0.118
OT_T_Increase	−0.010	0.029	−0.127 ***	0.039	−0.375 ***	0.137	0.279 ***	0.096
OT_Both_Increase	0.011	0.040	0.000	0.052	−0.005	0.122	0.041	0.099
QE3_MBS_Increase	−0.042	0.029	0.024	0.040	0.230 ***	0.088	−0.208 ***	0.051
QE3_Both_Increase	−0.059	0.048	−0.067	0.043	−0.060	0.059	0.002	0.040
Tapering	0.032 *	0.019	0.028	0.024	0.000	0.022	0.034	0.022

Note: ***, ** and * indicate statistical significance at 0.01, 0.05, 0.1.

Consistent with the result in Section 5, the events of increase in MBS purchases reduced the mortgage rate more than the Treasury rate, while the events of increase in Treasury purchases reduced the Treasury rate more than the mortgage rate on event days or in event windows.[27] From Table 6, Panel A, on event days of increase in MBS purchases in QE1 and QE3, ARs of the mortgage rate were large and negative at −0.095 and −0.046 percent, while ARs of the Treasury rate were small and positive at 0.004 and 0.047 percent. In longer window cases from Table 6, Panel B and C, CARs of the mortgage rate were significantly negative at −0.166 and −0.079 percent for the 3-day window, and −0.115 and −0.042 percent for the 5-day window, while CARs of the Treasury rate were small or even positive at −0.018 and 0.264 percent for the 3-day window, and 0.220 and 0.230 percent for 5-day window. On the other hand, large and negative ARs and CARs of the Treasury rate were found during events of increase in Treasury purchases, but the mortgage rate was not significantly affected. For example, the AR on event day and 3-day and 5-day CARs of the Treasury rate for events of increase in Treasury purchases in QE1 were large and negative at −0.223, −0.358 and −0.651 percent, while those of the mortgage rate were minute and event-positive at 0.010, 0.004 and −0.049 percent. The similar results were found in other rounds of QE[28] as well.

The different responses of the mortgage rate and the Treasury rate for those two types of events led to different movements of mortgage-Treasury rate spread. Generally, the spread narrowed during events of increase in MBS purchases, while the spread widened during events of increase in Treasury purchases. For the 5-day window case, CARs of the spread were −0.318 and −0.208 percent for events of increase in MBS purchases in QE1 and QE3 respectively. In contrast, CARs of the spread were 0.505, 0.083 and 0.279 percent for events of increase in Treasury purchases in QE1, QE2 and OT correspondingly. Similar results were found in 1-day or 3-day windows. In other words, the credit risk of holding MBSs over Treasury securities were reduced when the Fed announced to increase MBSs purchases, while the risk was intensified when Fed announced to increase Treasury purchases.

The events of decrease in MBS purchases and decrease in Treasury purchases were not quite consistent with increased purchases. Although the event of decrease in MBS purchases in QE1 led to positive ARs and CARs of both the mortgage rate and the Treasury rate, the AR on event day and CARs in 3-day and 5-day event windows of the mortgage rate were all less than those of the Treasury rate. Moreover, CARs of the mortgage rate and the Treasury rate were both negative in 3-day and 5-day windows for the event of decrease in Treasury purchases in QE1.

27 ARs and CARs of mortgage rate here are from market model regressions.
28 Events of only increasing Treasury purchases happened in QE2 and OT periods too.

QE tapering events enhanced both the mortgage rate and the Treasury rate, however, the effects were limited. The AR and 3-day and 5-day CARs of the mortgage rate for tapering events were only 0.006, 0.021 and 0.032 percent, while those of the Treasury rate stayed as low as 0.008, 0.009 and 0.000 percent. As we showed in Section 5, although significant and positive AR on the event day and CARs in 3-day and 5-day windows of the mortgage rate and the Treasury rate existed during the first few events in the tapering period, the insignificant and smaller AR and CARs during latter events diluted the average effects of tapering events.

6.2. Evolution of Cumulative Abnormal Returns (CARs) for Grouped QE Events

To see how the mortgage rate, the Treasury rate and the spread moved on each day in a 5-day event window of grouped events, the evolutions of CARs in a 5-day event window are shown in Figure 2.

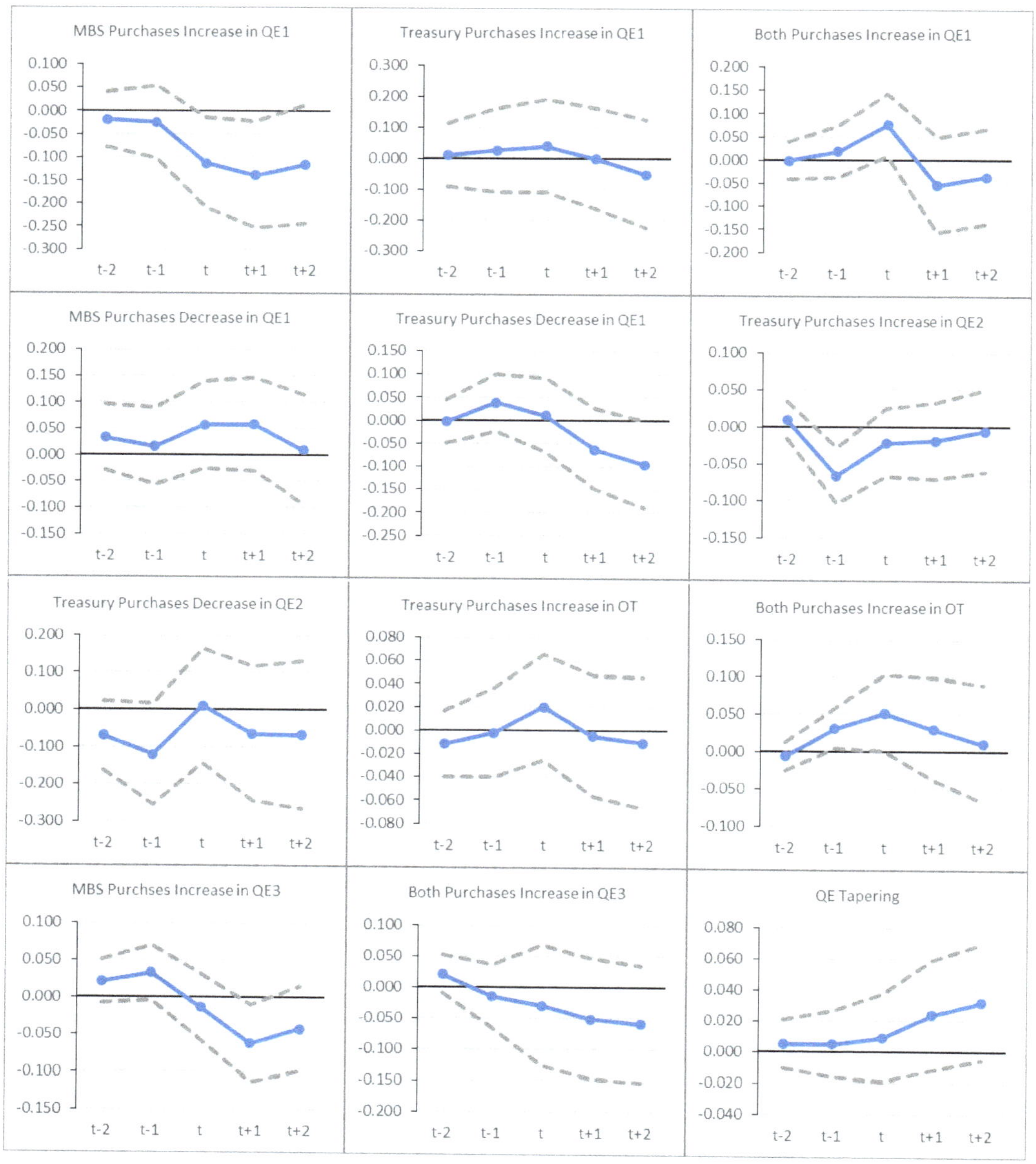

(A)

Figure 2. *Cont.*

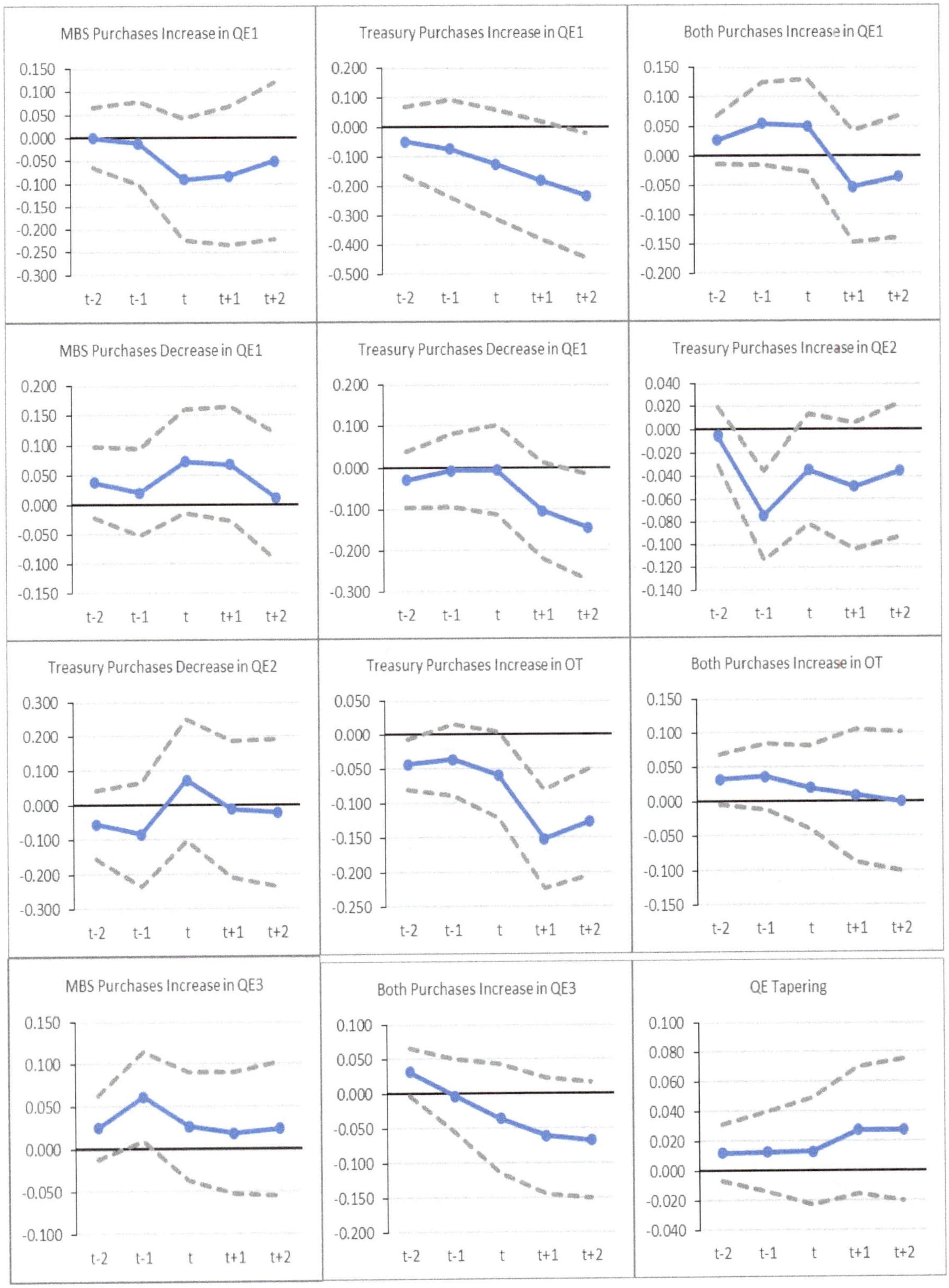

(B)

Figure 2. *Cont.*

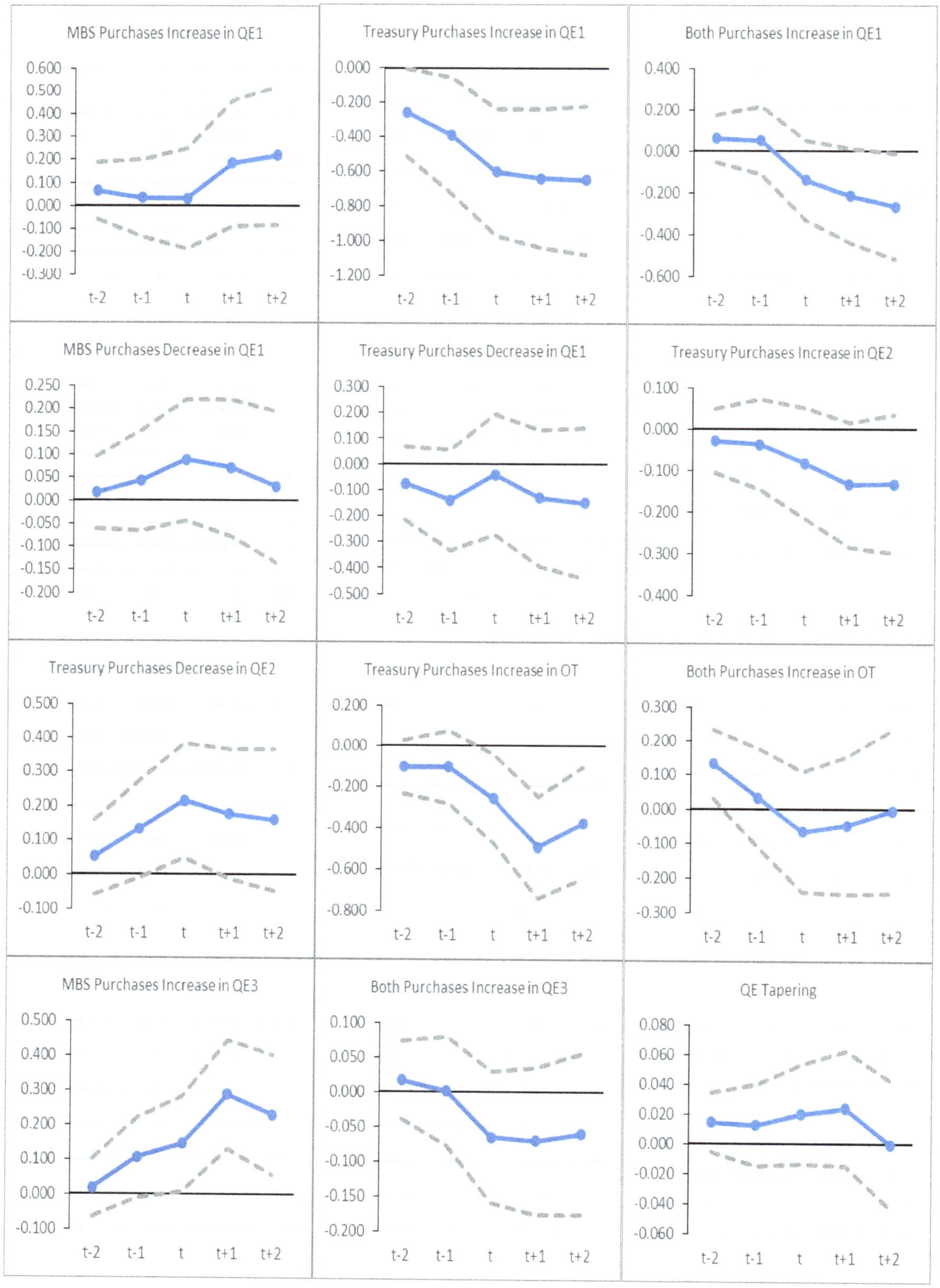

(C)

Figure 2. *Cont.*

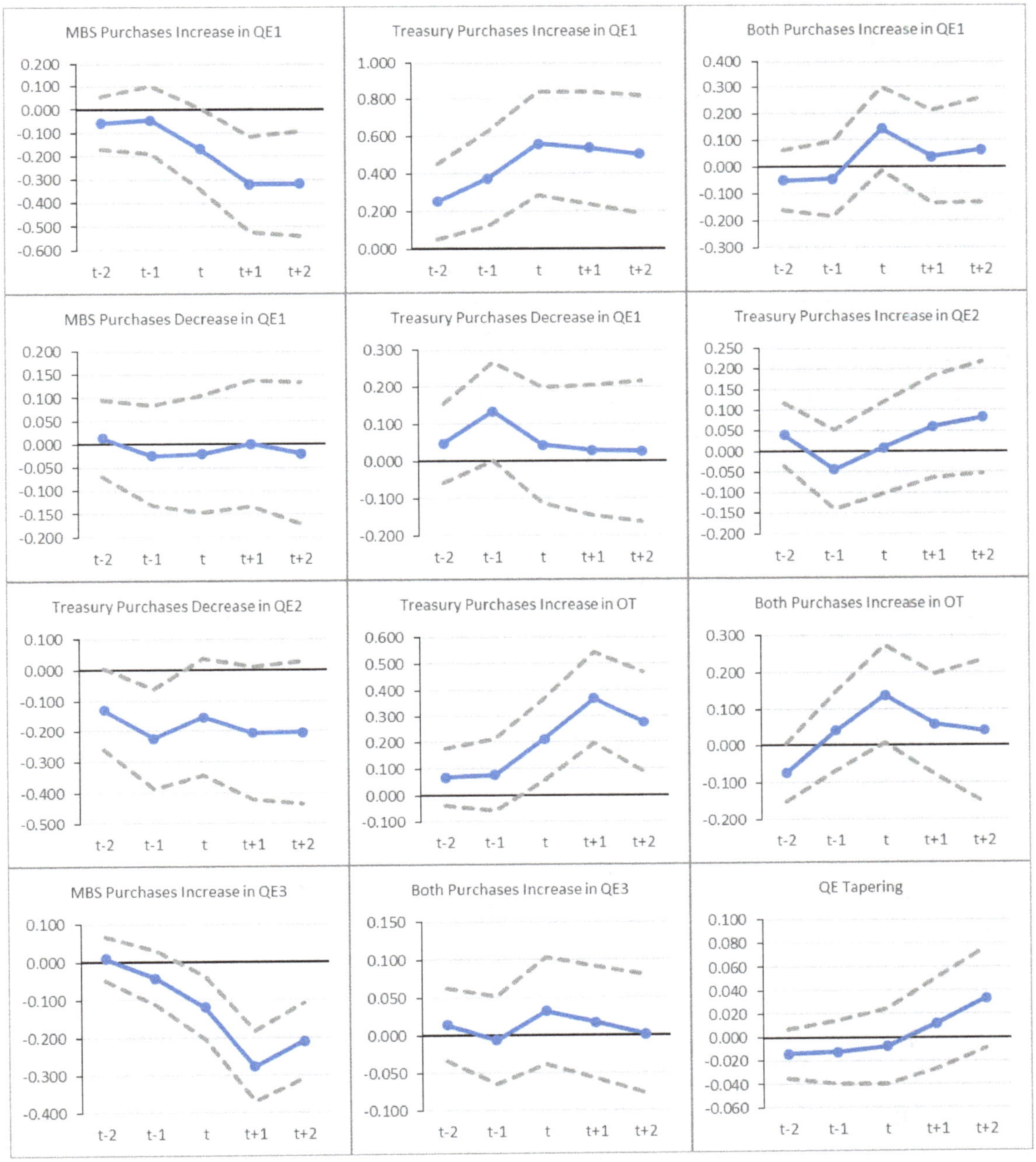

(D)

Figure 2. Cumulative abnormal returns (CARs) on days in a 5-day window of grouped event. The CAR on each day inside a 5-day event window for grouped events are reported in the figure. Each CAR is calculated as a summation of abnormal returns from two days before the event day ($t - 2$) to the day interested. The region between two dash lines in each graph is the 95 percent confidence interval of ARs. t indicates the event day. Panel (**A**) CARs of 30-year mortgage rate (market regression); Panel (**B**) CARs of 30-year mortgage rate (constant mean return regression); Panel (**C**) CARs of 30-year Treasury rate; Panel (**D**) CARs of spread between 30-year mortgage rate and Treasury rate.

For QE events targeting at both MBS and Treasury purchases (i.e., in QE1, OT and QE3), the mortgage rate and the Treasury rate decreased either on event days or one day after event days. The decrease of the Treasury rate was larger in magnitude than the decrease of the mortgage rate, which is in accordance with Wright's (2012) finding of smaller effects on private sector rates than on Treasury yields of QE shocks. Thus, on average the mortgage-Treasury rate spread expanded on event days and then narrowed the days after.

From Figure 2, Panel A, during events of increase in MBS purchases (i.e., in QE1 and QE3), the mortgage rate declined considerably on event day and one day after the event day. Specifically, CARs of the mortgage rate one day after the event day slumped to −0.14 and −0.06 percent for events in QE1 and QE3 respectively. However, from Figure 2, Panel C, during the same event, the Treasury rate increased on event day and one day after the event. Specifically, CARs of the Treasury rate one day after the event day surged to 0.19 and 0.29 percent for events in QE1 and QE3.

In contrast, from Figure 2, Panel A, during events of an increase in Treasury purchases (i.e., in QE1, QE2 and OT), the mortgage rate barely declined or even rose up a bit on event day and days after the event day. CARs of the mortgage rate one day after the event day remained 0.00, −0.02 and −0.01 percent for events in QE1, QE2 and OT, respectively. Again, from Figure 2, Panel C, during the same event, the Treasury rate dropped sharply on the event day and after. CARs of the Treasury rate one day after the event day collapsed to −0.61, −0.13 and −0.50 percent for events in QE1, QE2 and OT. The evidence strongly supports the previous conclusion that events of increase in MBS purchases lowered the mortgage rate more than the Treasury rate, while events of increase in Treasury purchases lowered the Treasury rate more than the mortgage rate around event days.

From Figure 2, Panel D, the mortgage-Treasury rate spread went down largely after increases in MBS purchases and went up after increases in Treasury purchases. The graphs show significant and negative CARs at −0.31 and −0.29 percent one day after the event day for events of MBS purchases in QE1 and QE3, while significant and positive CARs at 0.55, 0.06 and 0.38 percent one day after the event day for events of Treasury purchases in QE1, QE2 and OT. The results are in line with the previous conclusion from regression analysis that announcements of an increase in MBS purchases lessened the credit risk of holding mortgages over Treasury securities, while announcements of an increase in Treasury security purchases augmented the risk.

Section 6.1 shows that the tapering announcements had limited effects on the mortgage rate and the Treasury rate. This result also applies to where the CARs of both rates were trending up in small magnitudes. In addition, Figure 2 shows that the upward movement of the mortgage rate after tapering announcements was more persistent than that of the Treasury rate, which boosted the spread and increased the risk of holding mortgages over Treasury securities.

7. Robustness Checks

7.1. Adding More Controls into the Model

We check if our model is better fitted by adding more control variables. First, macroeconomic surprises are thought to have an impact on the interest rate. Patrabansh et al. (2014) and Thornton (2017) mention the abnormal changes of Treasury rate were attributed to both QE announcements and macroeconomic news. However, Altavilla and Giannone (2017) show that the effects of macroeconomic shock were "marginal" on average and the estimation results did not change so much with the inclusion of surprise components.[29] We pick unexpected changes of Consumer Price Index(CPI) and unexpected changes of the unemployment rate (UER) to identify macroeconomic surprises[30].

Second, shocks to the determinants of mortgage rates and MBS yields might affect the mortgage rate. Hancock and Passmore (2011, 2012, 2015) propose some determinants of mortgage rates and MBS yields, from which we select the control variables by using two criteria. One is that the variables

[29] They claim that since only important events are considered, the effect of which were tremendous and take over macroeconomic news within the event window.

[30] An unexpected change of GDP growth is another indicator of macroeconomic surprises. However, it is hard to estimate since quarterly GDP growth rate would be revised several times in a long time span by the Bureau of Economic Analysis (or U.S. Department of Commerce).

selected should not be significantly affected by QE announcements. The other is that the variables should contain news about mortgage rates. Only two variables from their study are in line with these two standards, which are the Case–Shiller Home Price Index (HPI) and unemployment rate (UER). From Hancock and Passmore (2011, 2012), HPI measures the costs of origination and servicing. Along with UER, they both reflect the credit risk of mortgage.

Although the values of three control variables (i.e., $\Delta Ln(CPI)$, $\Delta Ln(HPI)$ and ΔUER) are reported monthly, the data are identified with respect to the dates they are announced. Since all three variables do not have unit root,[31] we use ARMA models to estimate the expected values of them. Then the unexpected part of these three variables equals to the value of original data minus the expected value. Based on AIC, the best models fitting these three control variables are ARMA(3,2), ARMA(2,0) and ARMA(1,5) respectively[32].

Next, we run the four regressions as Equations (5) to (8) by adding $\Delta Ln(CPI)_t$, $\Delta Ln(HPI)_t$, ΔUER_t, $\Delta Ln(CPI)_{t-1}$, $\Delta Ln(HPI)_{t-1}$, ΔUER_{t-1}, $\Delta Ln(CPI)_{t-2}$, $\Delta Ln(HPI)_{t-2}$,ΔUER_{t-2} to the right-hand side of equations with 1-day, 3-day and 5-day windows. From the results, we find that values and significances of ARs and CARs with controls are similar to what we found without controls for all three window sizes. For that reason, we only report the coefficient estimates of these newly added control variables in the regressions for the 5-day window[33] in Table A3. From the table, most of the coefficient estimates are statistically insignificant and have small magnitudes and standard errors. Specifically, one unit change of control variables only accounts for less than 0.05 percent change of each dependent variable. In conclusion, the effects of control variables identifying the macroeconomic shock and determining that mortgage rate are trivial, thus we are not worried about not including them in the model.

7.2. Using 10-Year instead of 30-Year Treasury Rate

Since most of the 30-year mortgages are paid off or refinanced within 10 years, the 10-year Treasury rate is widely regarded as the risk-free rate determining the 30-year mortgage rate rather than the 30-year Treasury rate. In the period of our interest from 1/1/2008 to 12/31/2015, the correlation between the 30-year mortgage rate and the 10-year Treasury rate is 0.912, which is greater than the correlation between the 30-year mortgage rate and the 30-year Treasury at 0.807.

To compare the results, we replace the 30-year Treasury rate with the 10-year Treasury rate in Equation (5) and run the regression to find ARs and CARs of the 30-year mortgage rate for grouped events. The CARs of mortgage rates from regressions controlling for the 10-year and 30-year Treasury rate separately are reported in Table A4.

There is no major difference between the results of regressions controlling for the 10-year Treasury rate and the 30-year Treasury rate. Both the value and standard error of CAR for same grouped events were similar in magnitude except for events of increase in Treasury purchases in QE1 and increases in both purchases in OT. In fact, CARs for these two grouped events were insignificant and had small values in terms of both regressions with different controls.

Some authors (Sirmans et al. 2015) propose that the 10-year LIBOR swap rate is superior to the 10-year Treasury rate as determination. We replace the 30-year Treasury rate by the 10-year swap rate in my model and find that the results do not vary so much both statistically and economically. In conclusion, there is not much difference between choosing the 10-year and 30-year Treasury rate as the market rate in my model.

---

31 Dickey–Fuller unit root test results are found in the Supplementary Materials, Table S1.

32 All three ARMA models are sufficient. From the Supplementary Materials, Figures S5 and S6, we can see that the autocorrelation function (ACF) and the partial autocorrelation function (PACF) of residuals in three models for all lags are insignificant.

33 Similar studies using 1-day and 3-day window sizes are done and result in the similar outcomes as the ones without including these 3 determinants in the models, and we don't report the results in this paper.

8. Conclusions

This paper uses event study methodology to estimate the effects of the Fed's QE announcements on the 30-year mortgage rate. In the analysis, we apply an autoregressive model with IGARCH errors following skewed t distribution to run the regressions with three different window sizes.

We find that although the QE announcements suggesting the start of a new QE round or tapering affected the mortgage rate enormously, the effects from further news conveying a continuation of the current QE policy diminished. Macroeconomic news largely different from the market expectation on the same day of a QE event obscured the QE announcement effect on the Treasury rate, but did not shadow the QE announcement effect on the mortgage rate so much. If the market expectation was in the same direction as a QE announcement, the effect of this announcement on the mortgage rate would be minimized and vice versa. Signs and magnitudes of AR and CARs for the same event might not be confirmative if the announcement effect was transitory or the news had already been priced into mortgage rate before the announcement day. The calculation of TCARs tells us that although delayed effects of QE announcements were less than short-run effects, they did not fade away too much. We also find that event studies without controlling for serial correlation and conditional heteroscedasticity within data series overemphasize the QE effects on interest rates in general.

After grouping QE events by the announcement type and the QE round, we conclude that the mortgage rate decreased more than the Treasury rate and the spread narrowed during the events of increase in MBS purchases. Meanwhile, the Treasury rate decreased more than the mortgage rate and the spread expanded during the events of increase in Treasury security purchases. Finally, although QE tapering events had limited effects on both the mortgage rate and the Treasury rate on average, they boosted the credit risk of holding mortgage assets instead of Treasury bonds.

The findings of this paper have important implications for policy makers when they are considering launching another round of QE in future. As the QE announcements are more effective at the beginning of a QE program than later, the policy makers might want to announce a larger amount of asset purchases or combine QE with other policy instruments at a later stage. To fulfill the policy goal, policy makers should think of other news and the market expectation ahead of decision making. Again, the announcements of increase in MBS purchases were effective in stabilizing the housing market by pushing down the mortgage rate and narrowing the spread. Building on this result, the Fed might consider to expand its toolbox by targeting on other financial assets in addition to Treasury bonds and MBSs.

Future research could be done in different directions. First, we can use higher frequency data and narrower event windows to better estimate the QE announcement effects on the mortgage rate. Second, as the 30-year mortgage rate is not the whole picture of the mortgage market, there is an incentive to look at the yields on other types of mortgages such as 15-year FRM, 10-year ARM, jumbo mortgages, and so on. Again, the regression model will have better estimation power by adding new variables identifying macroeconomic news and market expectations.

Funding: This research received no external funding.

Conflicts of Interest: The author declares no conflicts of interest.

Appendix A

Table A1. Summary of data. This table reports the descriptive statistics of the variables used in this paper. All the rates are in percentage and the indices are in level. The sample period spans from 1/1/2008 to 12/31/2015.

	Obs.	Frequency	Mean	Median	SD	Min	Max	Skewness	Kurtosis
30-year Mortgage Rate	1998	Daily	4.52	4.34	0.75	3.36	6.51	0.65	−0.38
30-year Treasury Rate	1998	Daily	3.63	3.61	0.67	2.25	4.85	0.08	−1.34
10-year Treasury Rate	1998	Daily	2.72	2.63	0.71	1.43	4.27	0.24	−1.14
Freddie Mac 30-year MBS Current Coupon	1998	Daily	3.674	3.438	0.959	1.522	6.177	0.680	−0.121
Consumer Price Index	96	Monthly	225.859	227.196	8.892	211.398	238.302	−0.131	−1.497
Case-Shiller House Price Index	96	Monthly	155.62	148.02	14.85	137.08	184.03	0.45	−1.34
Unemployment Rate	96	Monthly	7.57	7.75	1.63	4.90	10.00	−0.15	−1.35

Note: Data of the 30-year mortgage rates and the Freddie Mac 30-year MBS current coupon yield come from Bloomberg; Data of the 30-year Treasury rate and the 10-year Treasury rate come from the U.S. Department of Treasury; Data of the consumer price index, the Case-Shiller house price index and the unemployment rate come from Federal Reserve Bank of St. Louis.

Table A2. The Federal Reserve Bank's quantitative easing (QE) announcements. This table reports the QE announcement events ordered by event date. There are 35 events in total, and each of them is assigned to a certain QE program, event type and event group. "Increase", "Decrease" and "Com" tell us if the event is about increasing asset purchases, decrease asset purchases or only a communication to the market.

Date	Program	Event	Announcement	Group
11/25/2008	QE1	FOMC Meeting	The FOMC "will purchase $100 billion in GSE debt and $500 billion in GSE MBS."	MBS_Increase
12/1/2008	QE1	Bernanke Speech	He stated Fed "could purchase longer-term Treasury or agency securities."	T_Increase
12/16/2008	QE1	FOMC Meeting	The Fed cut federal funds rate target from 1 percent to 0–0.25 percent, was "ready to expand its purchases of agency debt and MBSs as conditions warrant", and suggested of extending QE to Treasury purchases.	Both_Increase
1/28/2009	QE1	FOMC Meeting	The Fed was ready to expand the quantity and duration of MBS purchases.	MBS_Increase,
3/18/2009	QE1	FOMC Meeting	The FOMC "will purchase up to an additional $750 billion of agency MBSs with a total of $1.25 trillion, up to $100 billion agency debt this year with a total of $200 billion and up to $300 billion longer-term Treasury securities over the next six months."	Both_Increase
8/12/2009	QE1	FOMC Meeting	The FOMC "decided to gradually slow the pace" of Treasury purchases.	T_Decrease
9/23/2009	QE1	FOMC Meeting	The FOMC "will gradually slow the pace" of MBS purchases.	MBS_Decrease
11/4/2009	QE1	FOMC Meeting	The FOMC "will purchase a total of $175 billion of agency debt" instead of $200 billion. It also "will gradually slow the pace of its purchases of agency debt and MBSs and these transactions will executed by the end of first quarter of 2010."	MBS_Decrease

Table A2. *Cont.*

Date	Program	Event	Announcement	Group
8/10/2010	QE2	FOMC Meeting	The FOMC "will keep constant the Fed's holdings of securities . . . by reinvesting principal payments from agency debt, agency MBSs in longer-term Treasury securities." It also "will continue roll over Treasury securities holdings."	T_Increase
8/27/2010	QE2	Bernanke Speech	He suggested additional QE "should further action prove necessary."	T_Increase
9/21/2010	QE2	FOMC Meeting	The FOMC "is prepared to provide additional accommodation if needed."	T_Increase
10/15/2010	QE2	Bernanke Speech	Bernanke commented the drawbacks of large scale asset purchases.	T_Decrease
11/3/2010	QE2	FOMC Meeting	The FOMC "intends to purchase a further $600 billion of longer term Treasury securities by the end of second quarter of 2011, at a pace of about $75 billion per month."	T_Increase
8/9/2011	OT	FOMC Meeting	The FOMC "is prepared adjust those (securities) holdings as appropriate."	Both_Increase
8/26/2011	OT	Bernanke Speech	He announced "employ its tools . . . to promote a stronger economic recovery."	Both_Increase
9/21/2011	OT	FOMC Meeting	The FOMC "intends to purchase, by the end of June 2012, $400 billion of Treasury securities with remaining maturities of 6 years to 30 years and sell an equal amount of Treasury securities with remaining maturities of 3 years or less".	T_Increase
6/20/2012	OT	FOMC Meeting	The FOMC decided to "continue through the end of the year its program to extend average maturity of its holdings of securities."	T_Increase
8/22/2012	OT/QE3	FOMC Minutes Released	FOMC members "judged that additional monetary accommodation would likely be warranted fairly soon."	Both_Increase
8/31/2012	OT/QE3	Bernanke Speech	He remarked about unconventional monetary policy tools.	Both_Increase
9/13/2012	OT/QE3	FOMC Meeting	The FOMC "will purchase additional agency MBSs at a pace of $40 billion per month", along with OT will together increase "holdings of longer-term securities by about $85 billion each month through the end of the year."	MBS_Increase
12/12/2012	OT/QE3	FOMC Meeting	The FOMC "will purchase longer—term Treasury securities after OT is completed at the end of the year, initially at a pace of $45 billion per month."	T_Increase
5/1/2013	Tapering	FOMC Meeting	The FOMC "is prepared to increase or reduce the pace of its purchase."	Tapering
5/22/2013	Tapering	Bernanke Speech and testimony	He remarked about a potential "step down" in the pace of asset purchases.	Tapering
6/19/2013	Tapering	Bernanke's Press Conference	He said "If the incoming data are broadly consistent with this forecast, . . . be appropriate to moderate the monthly pace of purchases later this year."	Tapering
12/18/2013	Tapering	FOMC Meeting	The FOMC "Beginning in January . . . will add to its holdings of agency MBSs . . . $35 billion rather than $40 billion per month, long-term Treasury securities . . . $40 billion rather than $45 billion per month."	Tapering
1/29/2014	Tapering	FOMC Meeting	The FOMC "Beginning in February . . . will add to its holdings of agency MBSs . . . $30 billion rather than $35 billion per month, long-term Treasury securities . . . $35 billion rather than $40 billion per month."	Tapering

Table A2. *Cont.*

Date	Program	Event	Announcement	Group
3/19/2014	Tapering	FOMC Meeting	The FOMC "Beginning in April . . . will add to its holdings of agency MBSs . . . $25 billion rather than $30 billion per month, long-term Treasury securities . . . $30 billion rather than $35 billion per month."	Tapering
4/30/2014	Tapering	FOMC Meeting	The FOMC "Beginning in May . . . will add to its holdings of agency MBSs . . . $20 billion rather than $25 billion per month, long-term Treasury securities . . . $25 billion rather than $30 billion per month."	Tapering
5/7/2014	Tapering	Yellen Testimony	She said "further measured reductions in asset purchases were appropriate."	Tapering
6/18/2014	Tapering	FOMC Meeting	The FOMC "Beginning in July . . . will add to its holdings of agency MBSs . . . $15 billion rather than $20 billion per month, long-term Treasury securities . . . $20 billion rather than $25 billion per month."	Tapering
7/15/2014	Tapering	Yellen Testimony	She said "will make further measured reductions in the pace of asset purchases at upcoming meetings."	Tapering
7/30/2014	Tapering	FOMC Meeting	The FOMC "Beginning in August . . . will add to its holdings of agency MBSs . . . $10 billion rather than $15 billion per month, long-term Treasury securities . . . $15 billion rather than $20 billion per month."	Tapering
8/22/2014	Tapering	Yellen Speech	She said "we have reduced our pace of asset purchases and expect to complete this program in October."	Tapering
9/17/2014	Tapering	FOMC Meeting	The FOMC "Beginning in October . . . will add to its holdings of agency MBSs . . . $5 billion rather than $10 billion per month, long-term Treasury securities . . . $10 billion rather than $15 billion per month."	Tapering
10/29/2014	Tapering	FOMC Meeting	The FOMC "decided to conclude its asset purchase program this month." It is also "maintaining its existing policy of reinvesting principal payments from its holdings of agency debt and agency MBSs in agency MBSs and of rolling over maturing Treasury securities at auction."	Tapering

Note: The event on 8/27/2010 coincided with the better economy report released by Department of Commerce on the same day. Events on 11/3/2010, 6/20/2012 and 12/12/2012 were well anticipated by the market.

Table A3. Coefficient estimates of additional control variables in regressions. The change of log unexpected CPI, the change of log unexpected Case-Shiller House Price Index (HPI), the change of unexpected unemployment rate (UER), and the lagged variables (2 lags for each of these 3 variables) are added to each of the 4 models as independent variables. This table only reports the estimates and standard errors of coefficients associated with these newly added variables by using the 1-day event window. ARs, CARs and coefficient estimates of other independent variables are not reported in this table since the values and significances of them are similar to the case without including these control variables.

	Dependent Variable							
	ΔMR_30_t		ΔMR_30_t		ΔT_30_t		$\Delta Spread_t$	
Control Variables	Estimate	SE	Estimate	SE	Estimate	SE	Estimate	SE
$\Delta \ln(CPI)_t$	−0.008	0.014	−0.012	0.015	0.013	0.026	−0.021	0.021
$\Delta \ln(CPI)_{t-1}$	0.013	0.012	0.019	0.014	0.026	0.024	0.033	0.021
$\Delta \ln(CPI)_{t-2}$	−0.003	0.012	0.006	0.014	0.014	0.022	0.011	0.022
$\Delta \ln(HPI)_t$	−0.009	0.011	−0.012	0.012	−0.018	0.018	0.005	0.018
$\Delta \ln(HPI)_{t-1}$	−0.016	0.011	−0.022	0.014	0.013	0.021	−0.050 **	0.020
$\Delta \ln(HPI)_{t-2}$	0.010	0.012	0.006	0.012	0.006	0.018	0.021	0.017
ΔUER_t	−0.028	0.020	−0.020	0.027	0.026	0.032	−0.010	0.032
ΔUER_{t-1}	0.009	0.018	0.024	0.020	−0.019	0.031	0.022	0.030
ΔUER_{t-2}	0.031*	0.018	0.026	0.021	0.019	0.031	0.016	0.030

Note: ***, ** and * indicate statistical significance at 0.01, 0.05, 0.1 levels.

Table A4. Differences in regression results by using 10-year Treasury rate instead of 30-year Treasury rate. Values and standard deviations (SEs) for CAR of mortgage rate from regressions controlling for 10-year Treasury rate and 30-year Treasury rate respectively are reported.

	Mortgage Rate (Controlling for 10-year Treasury Rate)		Mortgage Rate (Controlling for 30-year Treasury Rate)	
	CAR	SE	CAR	SE
QE1_MBS_Increase	−0.124 **	0.061	−0.115 *	0.065
QE1_T_Increase	−0.024	0.082	−0.049	0.089
QE1_Both_Increase	−0.038	0.051	−0.035	0.052
QE1_MBS_Decrease	0.010	0.047	0.010	0.053
QE1_T_Decrease	−0.044	0.042	−0.095 *	0.048
QE2_T_Increase	0.032	0.026	−0.005	0.028
QE2_T_Decrease	−0.059	0.094	−0.066	0.101
OT_T_Increase	−0.063 **	0.027	−0.010	0.029
OT_Both_Increase	−0.011	0.040	0.011	0.040
QE3_MBS_Increase	−0.046 *	0.027	−0.042	0.029
QE3_Both_Increase	−0.048	0.035	−0.059	0.048
Tapering	0.022	0.017	0.032 *	0.019

Note: ***, ** and * indicate statistical significance at 0.01, 0.05, 0.1 levels.

References

Adalid, Ramón, and Matteo Falagiarda. 2018. How Repayments Manipulate Our Perceptions about Loan Dynamics after a Boom. Working Paper Series No. 2211; Frankfurt, Germany: European Central Bank.

Altavilla, Carlo, and Domenico Giannone. 2017. The Effectiveness of Nonstandard Monetary Policy Measures: Evidence from Survey Data. *Journal of Applied Econometrics* 32: 952–64. [CrossRef]

Altavilla, Carlo, Giacomo Carboni, and Roberto Motto. 2015. *Asset Purchase Programmes and Financial Markets: Lessons from the Euro Area*. Working Paper Series No. 1864; Frankfurt, Germany: European Central Bank.

Altavilla, Carlo, Domenico Giannone, and Michele Lenza. 2016. The financial and macroeconomic effects of the OMT announcements. *International Journal of Central Banking* 12: 29–57.

Borrallo, Fructuoso, Ignacio Hernando, and Javier Valles. 2016. *The Effects of US Unconventional Monetary Policies in Latin America*. Working Papers, No. 1606. Madrid, Spain: Banco de España.

Bowman, David, Juan Londono, and Horacio Sapriza. 2015. U.S. Unconventional Monetary Policy and Transmission to Emerging Market Economies. *Journal of International Money and Finance* 55: 27–59. [CrossRef]

Christensen, Jens, and Glenn Rudebusch. 2012. The response of interest rates to US and UK quantitative easing. *The Economic Journal* 122: F385–414.

Degryse, Hans, Moshe Kim, and Steven Ongena. 2009. *Microeconometrics of Banking*. Oxford: Oxford University Press.

Di Maggio, Marco, Christopher Palmer, and Amir Kermani. 2016. *How Quantitative Easing Works: Evidence on the Refinancing Channel*. NBER Working Paper 22638. Cambridge, MA, USA: National Bureau of Economic Research.

Eser, Fabian, and Bernd Schwaab. 2016. Evaluating the impact of unconventional monetary policy measures: Empirical evidence from the ECB's Securities Markets Programme. *Journal of Financial Economics* 119: 147–67. [CrossRef]

Falagiarda, Matteo, and Stefan Reitz. 2015. Announcements of ECB unconventional programs: Implications for the sovereign spreads of stressed euro area countries. *Journal of International Money and Finance* 53: 276–95. [CrossRef]

Gagnon, Joseph, Matthew Raskin, Julie Remache, and Brian Sack. 2011. The Financial Market Effects of the Federal Reserve's Large-Scale Asset Purchases. *International Journal of Central Banking* 7: 3–43.

Glick, Reuven, and Sylvain Leduc. 2012. Central bank announcements of asset purchases and the impact on global financial and commodity markets. *Journal of International Money and Finance* 31: 2078–101. [CrossRef]

Glick, Reuven, and Sylvain Leduc. 2015. Unconventional Monetary Policy and the Dollar: Conventional Signs, Unconventional Magnitudes. *International Journal of Central Banking* 14: 103–52. [CrossRef]

Hancock, Diana, and Wayne Passmore. 2011. Did the Federal Reserve's MBS Purchase Program Lower Mortgage Rates? *Journal of Monetary Economics* 58: 498–514. [CrossRef]

Hancock, Diana, and Wayne Passmore. 2012. *The Federal Reserve's Portfolio and Its Effects on Mortgage Markets (March 6, 2012)*; FEDS Working Paper No. 2012-22. Washington, DC, USA: Board of Governors of the Federal Reserve System.

Hancock, Diana, and Wayne Passmore. 2015. How Does the Federal Reserve's Large-Scale Asset Purchase (LSAPs) Influence Mortgage-Backed Securities (MBS) Yields and U.S. Mortgage Rates? *Real Estate Economics* 43: 855–90. [CrossRef]

Hattori, Masazumi, Andreas Schrimpf, and Vladyslav Sushko. 2016. The Response of Tail Risk Perceptions to Unconventional Monetary Policy. *American Economic Journal: Macroeconomics* 8: 111–36. [CrossRef]

Hollifield, Burton. 2011. Comments on 'Did the Federal Reserve's MBS Purchase Program Lower Mortgage Rates?'. *Journal of Monetary Economics* 58: 515–17. [CrossRef]

Jarrow, Robert, and Hao Li. 2014. The Impact of Quantitative Easing on the U.S. Term Structure of Interest Rates. *Review of Derivatives Research* 17: 287–321. [CrossRef]

Kozicki, Sharon, Eric Santor, and Lena Suchanek. 2015. *Large-Scale Asset Purchases: Impact on Commodity Prices and International Spillover Effects*. Bank of Canada Working Paper, No. 2015-21. Ottawa, ON, Canada: Bank of Canada.

Krishnamurthy, Arvind, and Annette Vissing-Jorgensen. 2011. *The Effects of Quantitative Easing on Interest Rates: Channels and Implications for Policy*. Brookings Paper on Economic Activity, NBER Working Paper No. 17555. Cambridge, MA, USA: National Bureau of Economic Research.

Li, Canlin, and Min Wei. 2012. *Term Structure Modelling with Supply Factors and the Federal Reserve's Large Scale Asset Purchase Programs*; FEDS Working Paper, No. 2012-37. Washington, DC, USA: Board of Governors of the Federal Reserve System.

Makenzie, Andrew M., Michael R. Thomsen, and Bruce L. Dixon. 2004. The Performance of Event Study Approaches Using Daily Commodity Futures Returns. *Journal of Futures Markets* 24: 533–55. [CrossRef]

Neely, Christopher. 2015. Unconventional monetary policy had large international effects. *Journal of Banking and Finance* 52: 101–11.

Patrabansh, Saty, William Doerner, and Samuel Asin. 2014. *The Effects of Monetary Policy on Mortgage Rates*; FHFA Working Papers 14-2. Washington, DC, USA: The Federal Housing Finance Agency.

Sirmans, Stace, Stanley Smith, and Stacy Sirmans. 2015. Determinants of Mortgage Interest Rates: Treasuries versus Swaps. *Journal of Real Estate and Financial Economics* 50: 34–51. [CrossRef]

Swanson, Eric, Lucrezia Reichlin, and Jonathan Wright. 2011. Let's Twist Again: A High-Frequency Event-Study Analysis of Operation Twist and Its Implications for QE2. *Brookings Papers on Economic Activity* 2011: 151–207. [CrossRef]

Szczerbowicz, Urszula. 2015. The ECB Unconventional Monetary Policies: Have They Lowered Market Borrowing Costs for Banks and Governments? *International Journal of Central Banking* 11: 91–127.

Thornton, Daniel. 2017. Effectiveness of QE: An Assessment of Event-Study Evidence. *Journal of Macroeconomics* 52: 56–74. [CrossRef]

Woodford, Michael. 2012. Methods of Policy Accommodation at the Interest-Rate Lower Bound. Presented at the Jackson Hole Symposium "The Changing Policy Landscape", Jackson, WY, USA, August 31–September 1.

Wright, Jonathan. 2012. What Does Monetary Policy Do to Long-Term Interest Rates at the Zero Lower Bound? *The Economic Journal* 122: F447–66. [CrossRef]

7

Effect of Speculators' Position Changes on the LME Futures Market

Jaehwan Park

Commodity Research Center, Public Procurement Service, Daejeon 35208, Korea; drjppark@korea.kr

Abstract: This paper employs Granger causality tests to analyze the role of speculators using weekly COTR (commitment of traders reports) data covering the period of August 2014 to July 2017. The paper presents statistically significant evidence that the position changes of speculators, such as hedge funds and CTAs (commodity trading advisors), unidirectionally Granger-cause the prices of base metals, such as aluminum, copper, and zinc. This finding is a result of causality going from the levels of net futures positions of money managers to futures price changes on the London Metal Exchange (LME). However, producers' and swap dealers' speculative roles in price-formation are rejected in Granger causality tests. This paper presents clear results with important market implications.

Keywords: COTR; non-commercial traders; money managers; Granger causality test

JEL Classification: C3; G1

1. Introduction

Traditional discussion of commodity futures markets is in terms of hedgers and speculators (Gilbert 2010). The commodity futures markets have become important as investors regard commodity futures as an alternative asset class, comparable with equity and bonds (Tang and Xiong 2012). The coincidental and rapid rise in the prices of commodities and the increased number of financial investors in commodities futures markets between 2000 and 2008 have led certain observers to question whether speculators have distorted commodity prices. The key argument is whether the financialization (Cheng and Xiong 2014) of commodities markets distorts commodities prices[1]. Substantial attention from legislators (US Senate Permanent Subcommittee on Investigations USPSI[2]), academia, and news media have intensified the debate. Buyuksahin et al. (2009) reported that the rise in investments by non-commercial traders contributed to concurrent oil price increases in energy. Gilbert (2010) observed a statistically significant relationship between index fund trading and food prices in agriculture.

Alternatively, Sanders et al. (2010) observed that long-only index funds in agricultural futures markets might benefit from short hedging pressure but there was no strong implication that speculators drove agricultural commodities prices. Irwin and Sanders (2012) observed little evidence that

---

1 This is called the "Masters Hypothesis" by Irwin and Sanders (2012), in which long-only index investment was a major driver of the 2007–2008 spikes in commodities futures. Masters, a hedge fund manager, argued that massive buy-side 'demand' from index funds created a bubble in commodities prices in U.S. congressional hearings. He insisted that the recent speculators' behavior differed from that of traditional speculators. First, new investors took positions across the entire range of commodity futures, not in specific futures as traditional speculators did. Second, new investors were almost only long, whereas traditional speculators might equally be long or short.

2 The USPSI (US Senate Permanent Subcommittee on Investigations USPSI) concluded that there was significant evidence from the wheat futures market that one of the major reasons for unusual market price spikes is the high level of speculation by commodity index traders.

speculators in commodities markets caused market prices to spike and determined no statistical causal links between returns and the positions of large energy exchange-traded index funds.

Most previous studies in this research area employed COT (commitments of traders) data, which are reported by the CFTC (commodity futures trading commission). The COT provides market data and position information on market participants who have positions in a specific futures market. Unlike energy and agricultural commodities, base metals are excluded from the COT data. This exclusion is the main reason why no previous study of base metals has been conducted in this study area.

The purpose of this paper is to examine data from the COTR (commitment of traders reports) to test the relationship between LME (London metal exchange)[3] futures prices and the trading positions of various types of investors. This study conducts Granger causality tests and identifies a statistically significant link between money managers' position changes and subsequent returns in the LME market using weekly data from August 2014 to July 2017. Notice that the LME provides the market positioning data on a weekly basis beginning in August 2014. The empirical results suggest that the position changes of speculators have an unidirectionally strong Granger-cause on the LME futures prices. However, there is no evidence that producers' and swap dealers' position changes have a Granger-cause on the LME futures prices. There is statistically significant evidence: first, the evidence of a link between money managers' net position changes for aluminum, copper, and zinc prices, and second, the evidence of a link between money managers' net position changes to volatilities for only copper and zinc. Within this empirical result, it was found that copper and zinc face a somewhat higher risk among the LME's major six base metals from the speculators' trading pattern.

The rest of the paper is organized as follows. Section 2 reviews the previous literature. In Section 3, the model is presented and a discussion is provided regarding how the Granger-causality hypothesis was set. In Section 4, the data set is illustrated and the main results are presented. Section 5 details the conclusions.

2. Literature Review

The role of speculators in commodity markets has been an issue of considerable interest and controversy (Brunetti et al. 2015). There has been no consensus about the impact of speculators on commodity futures markets. Singleton (2014), Buyuksahin and Robe (2009), Buyuksahin et al. (2009), and Gilbert (2010) found that speculators' impacts had a statistically significant effect on commodity futures prices, while Buyuksahin and Harris (2011), Sanders et al. (2010), and Irwin and Sanders (2012) found opposing results.

Singleton (2014) found that the largest impacts on futures prices were from intermediate-term growth rates of index positions and managed-money spread positions in oil futures markets. He also found that hedge fund trading in spread positions in futures influenced the shape of the term structure of oil futures prices. Buyuksahin and Robe (2009) showed that energy–equity co-movements increase amid greater participation in energy markets by, for example, hedge funds, but the impact of hedge fund activity is subdued during periods of financial turmoil. Buyuksahin et al. (2009) provided evidence for causal connections between non-commercial traders and oil prices. They found that the rise in participation by non-commercial traders during the preceding eight years (2000–2008) increased concurrent oil prices. Gilbert (2010) found that massive index-based investments in agricultural futures markets were seen as a major transmission channel through which macroeconomic and monetary factors generated the rapid food price rises between 2007 and 2008 using Granger causality analysis.

On the other hand, Buyuksahin and Harris (2011) highlighted that the role of speculators was the subject of heated debate, as oil futures price peaked at $147/barrel in July 2008. They employed COT

---

3 The LME is the world's largest futures exchange in the metal industry, including base metals and spot (cash), futures (3M), and various option contracts. Park and Lim (2018) provided a good discussion of the LME. They found that the LME was an inefficient market.

data from US CFTC to test the relationship between oil prices and the trading positions of various types of traders in the oil futures market. They found little evidence that the speculators' position changes Granger-cause oil price changes. Irwin and Sanders (2012) found no statistically significant causal links between daily returns or volatility in the crude oil, and even natural gas futures markets and the positions for two large sample energy exchange-traded index funds using a Granger causality test. Brunetti and Buyuksahin (2009) did not find a statistical link between swap dealers' positions (a proxy for commodity index fund positions) and returns or volatility in the crude oil, natural gas, and corn futures markets using a Granger causality test. Sanders et al. (2010) showed that traditional speculation in agricultural futures markets using COT data did not influence returns. However, the long-only index funds might be beneficial, thanks to investments by speculators.

Park (2018) found that the evidence of volatility transmission between oil and base metals was somewhat strong, with a 1% significant level. He argued that considering this result, the behavior of volatility in oil and LME futures prices applied to hedge decisions across the commodity market was useful. Park and Lim (2018) reported that the LME market was not efficient due to the false premise that the financialization of commodities had been growing. This result implied that the LME futures market could generate somewhat possible excess returns, which could attract speculators such as hedge funds and CTAs (commodity trading advisors). Park (2019) argued that the canceled warrants (CWs) in the LME market were key indicators to explain the financialization effect in the market price directly. He pointed out that the CWs variable was crucial because it encompassed two factors—fundamentals and non-fundamentals. He found that the rise in CWs increased the LME metal prices, including aluminum, zinc, tin, and nickel. He found that the positive impact of the CWs on metal returns was transitory.

Arouri et al. (2011) exhibited the speculative efficiency of the aluminum contract traded in the LME using cointegration approaches. They found that futures aluminum prices were found to be cointegrated with spot prices and they were the biased estimators of future spot prices. In a somewhat different aspect, Figuerola-Ferretti and Gilbert (2008) reported the volatilities characteristics of aluminum and copper in LME. They found that aluminum and copper volatilities follow statistically long memory process, which were caused by speculative traders.

3. Methodology

Most previous articles in this study area have employed Granger causality tests to examine the effect of non-commercial traders on specific commodity market prices (Buyuksahin et al. 2009; Brunetti and Buyuksahin 2009; Gilbert 2010; Buyuksahin and Harris 2011; Irwin and Sanders 2012). The Granger causality test is based on a bivariate VAR (vector autoregressions) representation of stationary time series $\{X_t\}$ and $\{Y_t\}$:

$$X_t = A(L)X_t + B(L)Y_t + \varepsilon_{X,t} \tag{1}$$

$$Y_t = C(L)X_t + D(L)Y_t + \varepsilon_{Y,t} \tag{2}$$

where A(L), B(L), C(L), and D(L) are lag polynomials. The null hypothesis is that "lagged Y does not Granger-cause X", while the alternative hypothesis is that "lagged Y causes X". The null hypothesis will be rejected if the coefficients on the lagged Y's are jointly significantly different from zero. Specification issues arise in relation to the choice of lag length because test results are sensitive to lag selection. To determine the optimal lag to be used in the VAR estimation, this paper employs the AIC (akaike information criterion) and SIC (Schwarz information criterion).

4. Empirical Results

4.1. Data

The main objective of this paper is to identify whether participation by some types of traders explains the extent to which the market moves as a consequence of investment money flows. This paper uses weekly COTR[4] data from August 2014 to July 2017, which includes the trading positions of various types of investors, such as a money manager (mm), broker-dealer/index trader (bd), producer/merchant/user (pm), and other reportable parameters. Money managers are engaged in managing LME contracts on behalf of clients, while broker–dealer/index traders are engaged in transactions and use the LME to manage or hedge the risk associated with those transactions (see details in the LME disaggregated reports). These data are used to compute net futures positions and evaluate percent changes against the previous week. For example, the variable mm_al is the weekly percent change in net position changes in the aluminum markettrackingcopper (cu), aluminum (al), lead (pb), zinc (zn), tin (sn), and nickel (ni). The benchmark futures price for base metals is that of a contract expiring after three months (3M), as obtained from Reuters over the same the period and computed using Thursday–Thursday[5] log returns to 3M futures prices. For example, the variable r_al denotes the weekly log returns in the aluminum market.

4.2. Empirical Results

Granger causality tests require variables to be stationary. To test stationarity, this paper employs the ADF (augmented dickey fuller) unit root test. Table 1 reports the ADF test results[6]. The table confirms that all variables are I (0), that is, stationary data. Therefore, the VARs (vector autoregressions) were ran in levels, rather than first differencing. The differencing non-stationary variables usually render them stationary.

Table 1. Unit root test results.

Metals	Variables	Statistics	Metals	Variables	Statistics
Aluminum	r_al	−14.09	Copper	r_cu	−12.60
	mm_al	−13.18		mm_cu	−12.86
	bd_al	−14.23		bd_cu	−12.57
	pm_al	−9.935		pm_cu	−12.15
Zinc	r_zn	−13.32	Lead	r_pb	−11.61
	mm_zn	−9.293		mm_pb	−11.92
	bd_zn	−12.24		bd_pb	−9.940
	pm_zn	−12.07		pm_pb	−11.74
Tin	r_sn	−13.55	Nickel	r_ni	−14.28
	mm_sn	−12.69		mm_ni	−13.10
	bd_sn	−12.33		bd_ni	−13.13
	pm_sn	−13.02		pm_ni	−12.41

Notes: There are 153 observations. (August 2014–July 2016; weekly data). Natural logarithms are used to calculate returns (r_al, r_cu, r_zn, r_pb, r_sn, and r_ni). The commitment of traders reports' (COTR's) position data are percent changes from the previous week (for example, mm_al: aluminum position changes of money managers, bd_al: aluminum position changes of broker-dealers, and pm_al: aluminum position changes of producers. Most previous studies utilized this method). The one percent critical value is −3.493. The unit root tests show that all variables are I (0).

This paper analyzes Granger causality between weekly metal price changes and net position changes by including money managers, swap dealers, and producer groups, respectively. An initial hypothesis of Granger causality between LME metal price changes and position changes of only a money manager, rather than a broker–dealer/index trader or producer/merchant/user like most previous studies (Buyuksahin et al. 2009; Brunetti and Buyuksahin 2009; Gilbert 2010; Buyuksahin and

4 Six major base metals reports are published each Tuesday, one for each business day of the previous week. This data is obtained through the Bloomberg.

5 Thursday is the day the LME's COTR is announced.

6 Other unit root tests such as the Phillips–Perron (PP) test and Kwiatkowski–Phillips–Schmidt–Shin (KPSS) test have similar results.

Harris 2011), was developed. A second hypothesis of Granger causality between LME metal price volatilities and position changes of money managers within the Irwin and Sanders (2012) framework was suggested. The idea is clear: if the investments of money managers drive metal prices, then price volatility may increase somewhat significantly. Hence, the hypotheses developed were as follows:

Hypothesis 1. *The position changes of only a money manager are associated with LME metal price changes.*

Hypothesis 2. *The position changes of only a money manager are associated with LME metal price volatilities.*

Pairs of variables were considered; the first member of each pair is an LME metal price movement, and the second is an investment flow of a specific group. As shown in Table 2, there are statistically significant unidirectional Granger causalities from metal price changes to net position changes of money managers. This finding is proof of positive feedback trading among money managers. Only aluminum, copper, and zinc exhibit bidirectional Granger causalities between metal price changes and net position changes of money managers. One of the probable reasons for this is liquidity, which means higher liquidity provides a better investment environment for money managers. Notice that the trading volumes of aluminum, copper, and zinc are relatively higher compared to other base metals in LME (see details in Park and Lim (2018)). This finding is strong and in line with the first hypothesis. The growth in hedge funds and commodity funds, such as major CTAs in the LME, has driven prices to be significantly higher. In addition, Park and Lim (2018) found that the LME market was inefficient, which could attract speculators. Buyuksahin et al. (2009) obtained a similar result in crude oil futures markets using Granger causality tests. Figure 1 depicts the trend of aluminum's net position for money managers and the LME aluminum price trend, which seem to be highly correlated with each other. Figures for other base metal prices and net positions of money managers are similar.

Table 2. Granger causality tests: First hypothesis.

Aluminum			Lead		
Causality Direction	Lags	*p*-Value	Causality Direction	Lags	*p*-Value
mm_al → r_al	3	0.045 **	mm_pb → r_pb	2	0.392
r_al → mm_al	3	0.000 ***	r_pb → mm_pb	2	0.000 ***
bd_al → r_al	3	0.074 *	bd_pb → r_pb	3	0.826
r_al → bd_al	3	0.697	r_pb → bd_pb	3	0.665
pm_al → r_al	3	0.700	pm_pb → r_pb	3	0.167
r_al → pm_al	3	0.000 ***	r_pb → pm_pb	3	0.245
Copper			**Tin**		
Causality Direction	Lags	*p*-Value	Causality Direction	Lags	*p*-Value
mm_cu → r_cu	3	0.003 ***	mm_sn → r_sn	2	0.321
r_cu → mm_cu	3	0.006 ***	r_sn → mm_sn	2	0.000 ***
bd_cu → r_cu	2	0.669	bd_sn → r_sn	2	0.032 **
r_cu → bd_cu	2	0.202	r_sn → bd_sn	2	0.467
pm_cu → r_cu	2	0.086 *	pm_sn → r_sn	2	0.315
r_cu → pm_cu	2	0.450	r_sn → pm_sn	2	0.416
Zinc			**Nickel**		
Causality Direction	Lags	*p*-Value	Causality Direction	Lags	*p*-Value
mm_zn → r_zn	2	0.048 **	mm_ni → r_ni	2	0.103
r_zn → mm_zn	2	0.042 **	r_ni → mm_ni	2	0.007 ***

Table 2. *Cont.*

bd_zn → r_zn	2	0.803	bd_ni → r_ni	2	0.404
r_zn → bd_zn	2	0.102	r_ni → bd_ni	2	0.411
pm_zn → r_zn	2	0.677	pm_ni → r_ni	2	0.444
r_zn → pm_zn	2	0.476	r_ni → pm_ni	2	0.579

Notes: The sample consists of 153 observations. Table 2 presents the Granger causality test results for metal prices and net position changes. The reported numbers represent p-values. ***, ** and * indicate the rejection of Granger non-causality at 1%, 5%, and 10% level of significance.

Figure 1. Plot of mm_al and price_al. Notes: The solid line is the price of aluminum on the LME over the period August 2014 to July 2017, while the bold dotted line is aluminum's net position trend for a money manager. The thin dotted line is aluminum's net position trend for a broker–dealer/index trader and the double line is aluminum's net position trend for a producer/merchant reveal with a somewhat different shape and indifferent from the price of aluminum.

Park and Lim (2018) evaluated the LME. First, the LME addresses daily rolling three-month futures contracts that are different from those in other commodity markets, which are based on monthly prompt dates. Second, the LME is traded electronically but is also traded through outcry, which is the oldest way of trading on the exchange. Park and Lim (2018) reported that these characteristics made markets inefficient and attracted speculators' investment money flows, which is in line with the result of this paper. Park (2019) concluded that the role of canceled warrants in the LME market intensifies the aluminum, zinc, tin, and nickel spot prices' direction. He argued that this evidence showed the financialization of the LME by speculative investors.

However, the tests for producer and index investors, similar to those employed for swap dealers, reject Granger causality. For the producer, the objective of investing in the LME futures market is purely hedging against price uncertainty. Figure 1 explains this result clearly. For the swap dealer front, Buyuksahin et al. (2009) note that they usually take positions using commodity index funds, which deliver returns based on the index and follow the herding mentality of unsophisticated traders, unlike active commodity funds. Therefore, the results for producers and index investors differ from those for money managers due to their own mandate characteristics. Indeed, the figures for base metal prices and net positions of producers and index investors reveal a somewhat different shape.

Table 3 examines the second hypothesis of Granger causality between metal price volatilities and net position changes of money managers within the research framework of Irwin and Sanders (2012). Notice that Irwin and Sanders (2012) used realized volatility and implied volatility within a similar empirical framework. The LME does not publish intra-day data or tick data. Hence, Figuerola-Ferretti and Gilbert (2008) argue that it is not possible to compute daily realized volatility measures for the LME market. This paper employs implied volatilities ATM (at-the-money) similarly to the work of Irwin and Sanders (2012) from Reuters as a measure of volatility. There is evidence of a link between money managers' net position changes and implied volatility in Table 3. Granger causality between the aluminum price volatility and position changes of money managers has been rejected. However, this causality has not been rejected for copper and zinc. It is found that copper and zinc are the only base metals that satisfy both hypotheses. In particular, a significant (p-value = 0.04) is found between money managers' net position changes and implied volatility in zinc, which implies a somewhat higher risk in zinc due to money managers' speculative investment changes. Irwin and Holt (2004) find a small positive relationship between the hedge fund trading volume and volatility in thirteen different futures markets.

Table 3. Granger causality tests: Second hypothesis.

Causality Direction	Lags	p-Value
	Aluminum	
mm_al → iv_al	2	0.166
iv_al → mm_al	2	0.379
	Copper	
mm_cu → iv_cu	2	0.084 *
iv_cu → mm_cu	2	0.161
	Zinc	
mm_zn → iv_zn	3	0.048 **
iv_zn → mm_zn	3	0.521

Notes: The sample consists of 153 observations. Table 3 presents the Granger causality test results for net position changes by money managers and implied volatilities. The volatilities variables (iv_al, iv_cu and iv_zn) follow I(0) processes. The reported numbers represent p-values. ** and * indicate the rejection of Granger non-causality at 5% and 10% levels of significance.

Given this result, the question arises of why zinc has the most robust result. As Otto (2011) argued, the possible reason for this may be liquidity. Zinc had the third largest liquidity in terms of trading volume in the LME market. Unlike other base metals, zinc has a dominant production company, Glencore. Its market share of the total global production is more than 50% (Park and Lim 2018). These reasons provide a possible answer to the above question.

Testing the first (Table 2) and second (Table 3) hypotheses, this paper concludes that a rise in investment flows of money managers increases aluminum, copper, and zinc prices, but increases price volatility for only copper and zinc. However, there is no evidence that producers' and swap deals' position changes have a Granger-cause on the LME futures prices.

5. Summary and Conclusions

Utilizing weekly trader positions, Granger causality tests were examined to determine the relationship between price changes and net position changes of various traders in the LME futures market. This paper establishes two hypotheses concerning whether money managers' investment flows impact base metal prices and implied volatility. This analysis identifies categories of traders to assess how speculators relate to price changes and volatility. Using three years of weekly data, this paper observes that money managers' speculative investment changes influence LME metal prices for aluminum, copper, and zinc, exhibiting unidirectional Granger causality. Price changes lead the net position changes of speculators for all six base metals, which imply procyclical trading. However, there is no evidence that producers' and swap deals' position changes have a Granger-cause on the LME futures prices. This is a somewhat strong result.

For the second hypothesis, there is a significant Granger causality relationship between net position changes of speculators and implied volatility of the prices of copper and zinc. However, Granger causality is rejected for aluminum price volatility and position changes of money managers.

The failure to reject Granger causality has important implications for the pricing of LME futures. Even though fundamentals remain the major driver of base metals prices over the long-term, commodity fund activity tends to raise price volatility in the short-term. Over the last decade, and even until now, growing activity in commodities futures markets by major financial institutions, such as hedge funds, commodity index funds, and pension funds, has been witnessed.

Funding: This article received no external funding.

Acknowledgments: Hyeon Sook Kim, my colleague, provided the data set and gave useful comments. The author would like to thank three anonymous referees for their valuable comments and suggestions which contributed to the quality of this paper.

Conflicts of Interest: The author declares no conflicts of interest. The author alone is responsible for the context and writing of the paper.

References

Arouri, Mohamed El Hedi, Fredj Jawadi, and Prosper Mouak. 2011. The Speculative Efficiency of the Aluminum Market: A Nonlinear Investigation. *International Economics* 126–27: 73–89. [CrossRef]

Brunetti, Celso, Bahattin Buyuksahin, and Jeffrey H. Harris. 2015. Speculators, Prices and Market Volatility. *Journal of Financial and Quantitative Analysis* 51: 1545–74. [CrossRef]

Brunetti, Celso, and Bahattin Buyuksahin. 2009. Is Speculation Destabilizing? Working Paper. US CFTC. Available online: https://papers.ssrn.com/sol3/papers.cfm?abstract_id=1393524 (accessed on 12 June 2019).

Buyuksahin, Bahattin, and Jeffrey H. Harris. 2011. Do Speculators Drive Crude Oil Futures Prices? *Energy Journal* 32: 167–202. [CrossRef]

Buyuksahin, Bahattin, Michael S. Haigh, Jeffrey H. Harris, James A. Overdahl, and Michel A. Robe. 2009. Fundamentals, Trader Activity and Derivative Pricing. Working Paper. US CFTC. Available online: https://papers.ssrn.com/sol3/papers.cfm?abstract_id=966692 (accessed on 12 June 2019).

Buyuksahin, Bahattin, and Michel A. Robe. 2009. Commodity Traders' Positions and Energy Prices: Evidence from the Recent Boom-Bust Cycle. Working Paper. US CFTC. Available online: https://www.aeaweb.org/conference/2010/retrieve.php?pdfid=355 (accessed on 12 June 2019).

Cheng, Ing-Haw, and Wei Xiong. 2014. Financialization of commodity markets. *Annual Review of Financial Economics* 6: 419–41. [CrossRef]

Figuerola-Ferretti, Isabel, and Christopher L. Gilbert. 2008. Commonality in the LME aluminum and copper volatility processes through a FIGARCH lens. *Journal of Futures Markets* 28: 935–62. [CrossRef]

Gilbert, C. 2010. How to understand high food prices. *Journal of Agricultural Economics* 61: 398–425. [CrossRef]

Irwin, S., and B. Holt. 2004. The impact of large hedge find and CTA trading on futures market volatility. In *Commodity Trading Advisors: Risk, Performance Analysis and Selection*. Hoboken: John Wiley and Sons, Inc., pp. 151–82.

Irwin, Scott H., and Dwight R. Sanders. 2012. Testing the Masters Hypothesis in commodity futures markets. *Energy Economics* 34: 256–69. [CrossRef]

Otto, S. 2011. A Speculative Efficiency Analysis of the London Metal Exchange in a Multi-Contract Framework. *International Journal of Economics and Finance* 3: 3–16. [CrossRef]

Park, J. 2018. Volatility Transmission between Oil and LME Futures. *Applied Economics and Finance* 5: 65–72. [CrossRef]

Park, J. 2019. The Role of Cancelled Warrants in the LME Market. *International Journal of Financial Studies* 7: 10. [CrossRef]

Park, Jaehwan, and Byungkwon Lim. 2018. Testing Efficiency of the London Metal Exchange: New Evidence. *International Journal of Financial Studies* 6: 32. [CrossRef]

Sanders, Dwight R., Scott H. Irwin, and Robert P. Merrin. 2010. The adequacy of speculation in agricultural futures markets: Too much of a good thing? *Applied Economic Perspectives and Policy* 32: 77–94. [CrossRef]

Singleton, Kenneth J. 2014. Investor Flows and the 2008 Boom/Bust in Oil Prices. *Management Science* 60: 300–18. [CrossRef]

Tang, Ke, and Wei Xiong. 2012. Index Investment and the Financialization of Commodities. *Financial Analysts Journal* 68: 54–74. [CrossRef]

US Senate Permanent Subcommittee on Investigations (USPSI). 2009. *Excessive Speculation in the Wheat Market*; Washington: USPSI, June 24.

8

Cross-Border Lending, Government Capital Injection, and Bank Performance

Jyh-Horng Lin [1], Pei-Chi Lii [2], Fu-Wei Huang [2,*] and Shi Chen [3]

[1] Department of International Business, Tamkang University, New Taipei City 25137, Taiwan; lin9015@mail.tku.edu.tw
[2] Department of Management Sciences, Tamkang University, New Taipei City 25137, Taiwan; 100679@mail.tku.edu.tw
[3] School of Economics, Southwestern University of Finance and Economics, Chengdu 611130, China; chenshi@swufe.edu.cn
* Correspondence: kwala.wei@mail.tku.edu.tw

Abstract: In this paper, we develop a contingent claim model to examine the optimal bank interest margin, i.e., the spread between the domestic loan rate and the deposit market rate of an international bank in distress. The framework is used to evaluate the cross-border lending efficiency for a bank that participates in a government capital injection program, a government intervention used in response to the 2008 financial crisis. This paper suggests that government capital injection is an appropriate way to recapitalize the distressed bank, enhancing the bank interest margin and survival probability. Nevertheless, the government capital injection lacks efficiency when the bank's cross-border lending is high. Stringent capital regulation, suggested to prevent future crises by literature, leads to superior lending efficiency when the government capital injection is low.

Keywords: cross-border lending; bank interest margin; government capital injection; barrier option

JEL Classification: G21; G28

1. Introduction

The 2007/2008 global financial crisis raises fundamental issues about the banking strategies of international loan portfolio diversification, especially from the standard of return/risk efficiency.[1] Figure 1 reports the overall cross-border claims on banks of BIS (Bank of International Settlements) reporting banks from 1998 to 2018. Clearly, these claims have cycled over time, with the home bias evident in the decline in the cross-border claims since the peak in 2007. The contrasting trends in cross-border lending reflect bank needs to deleverage because of changes in risk perceptions.[2] In addition, policy interventions having aimed at stabilizing domestic banking systems also provide incentives for banks to concentrate more on their economies.[3] Cross-border diversification in

[1] We are a bit informal here and use "international" and "cross-border" synonymously. The terms "efficiency" or "diversification efficiency" refer to "efficiency from international loan portfolio diversification".

[2] The decade since the onset of the global financial crisis has brought about significant structural changes in the banking sector. The Committee on the Global Financial System (2018) pointed out that, while many large advanced economy banks have moved away from trading and cross-border activities, there does not appear to be clear evidence of a systemic retrenchment from core credit provision. Bremus and Fratzscher (2014) found that total cross-border bank claims have significantly decreased in response to the global financial crisis and did not resume the pre-crisis upward trend since then. The authors analyzed the effects of changes to regulatory policy and to monetary policy on cross-border bank lending since the global financial crisis. We would like to thank an anonymous reviewer for pointing these effects out to us.

[3] Incentives, for example, include nationalizations, guarantees, or regulatory rules (see Rose and Wieladek 2011).

bank lending, however, is barely understood, as shown by the concern that it is not considered in recapitalization for distressed banks during the recent financial crisis. Particularly, distressed banks receive government bailout package of capital infusion during the financial crisis (Bayazitova and Shivdasani 2011), public outcries for more capital from banks tend to be greater after the financial crisis, and stringent capital regulation as a post-crisis reform proposal should adapt to prevent future crises (Kashyap et al. 2008). Our analysis of cross-border bank lending and recapitalization was motivated by the above observations. The aim of this paper is to investigate whether cross-border bank lending under capital regulation is an interest for bank equity holders when the bank in distress participates in a financial rescue program of government capital injections.

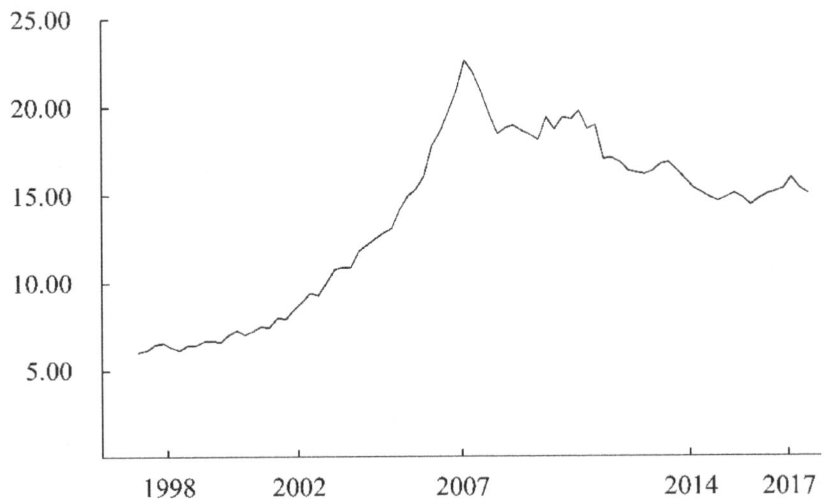

Figure 1. Cross-border bank lending, 1998Q1–2018Q3: Claims (in trillions of US dollars) on bank sector of banks in all reporting countries. Source: Locational statistics, International banking, BIS Statistics.

The effects of cross-border lending diversification on bank interest margin (commonly used to proxy lending-to-deposit rate spread), bank equity risk, and diversification efficiency are important issues that concern bank managers (e.g., Iskandar-Datta and McLaughlin 2007; de Blas and Russ 2013; Bremus 2015; Barrell and Nahhas 2019). The bank interest margin is crucial in strategic decisions made by banks because the interest margin is one of the principal elements of bank profitability and is often used as a proxy for the efficiency of financial intermediation (Saunders and Schumacher 2000). Bank equity risk in relation to bank survival is central not only in strategic decisions made by banks, but also in decisions made by the regulatory authority about banking stability (Berger and Bouwman 2013). Diversification efficiency/deficiency is an important evaluation for cross-border lending (Rossi et al. 2009; García-Herrero and Vázquez 2013), and banks often assess their performance to each other on this basis. Comprehending whether higher cross-border loan portfolio diversification has significant effects on the bank interest margin, the bank equity risk, and the diversification efficiency gain, and how these effects differ depending on the distressed bank's participation in a government capital injection program are important for the regulatory authority to achieve a desired level of banking stability. In the light of the recent financial crisis, this topic has become of uttermost important to the discussion of bank efficiency and stability.

To investigate diversification effects on bank interest margin and efficiency, we construct a contingent claim model along the line of Episcopos (2008) for the valuation of a bank's equity. According to Episcopos (2008), default can occur at any time before the maturity date that the risk of a premature default to the liability valuation is explicitly captured by a simple knock-out barrier option feature of different components of liabilities. However, the assumption of Episcopos' (2008) approach is not applicable to domestic loan markets since such markets are virtually always highly concentrated where cross-border banks set loan rates and face random loan levels (Claessens 2006).

We complement this by extending Episcopos' (2008) model to be able to capture the effects of the international loan portfolio diversification on the bank's interest margin, and then on the bank's equity risk and diversification efficiency. We do this by using a so-called firm-theoretic barrier option framework.

Our paper is also motivated by the observations of financial default events related to the 2007/2008 global financial crisis (Breitenfellner and Wagner 2010). The observations illustrate that, during a financial crisis, bank capital is depleted. A government capital injection program is expected to stabilize banks by providing a source of capital when public market alternatives are unavailable.[4] Further, as previously pointed out by Berger and Bouwman (2013), several post-crisis reform proposals tend to focus on how capital regulation should adapt to prevent future crises. Hence, from a policy standpoint, it is interesting to examine how government capital injections affect bank interest margin and cross-border lending efficiency at various levels of loan portfolio diversification, and how stringent capital regulation affects bank interest margin and cross-border lending efficiency at various levels of government capital injection.

Our results have distinct bank strategy and regulatory policy implications. Increasing international loan portfolio diversification by the bank increases not only the risk of foreign loan repayments due to additional exchange rate volatility and country risk (Rajan and Friedman 1997) but also the risk of domestic loan repayments due to the bank's more prone to loan risk-taking at a reduced margin, thereby increasing the bank's equity risk. Further, diversification efficiency increases after increasing the cross-border lending. As a result, a financially disadvantaged bank can use the cross-border lending strategy to benefit from the diversification efficiency gain. We also show that: (i) these augmented risk and efficiency are reduced when the government capital injection increases; and (ii) the augmented risk is decreased, and the augmented efficiency is increased when the capital regulation is increasingly stringent. Result (i) suggests that, from a safety viewpoint, a bank strategy of the cross-border loan portfolio diversification is encouraged when the bank participates in the bailout program of government capital injection although strategy itself is not efficient. Our result provides an explanation that the success of a financial rescue program of the government capital injection depends critically on the willingness of distressed banks to participate in it. Result (ii) suggests that a bank strategy of the cross-border loan portfolio diversification is also encouraged when the bank's capital requirement in the domestic market is increased. Our suggestion is consistent with the stability argument of Berger and Bouwman (2013). Overall, from a normative standpoint, our results sound a note to the adaption of government capital injection mechanism that reduces efficiency but contributes to stability, while the adaption of capital regulation mechanism after a financial crisis that increases efficiency and stability in the context of cross-border loan portfolio diversification.

The remainder of the paper is structured as follows. Section 2 briefly discusses related literature. Section 3 develops the basic structure of the model. Section 4 derives the solution of the model and comparative static analysis. The last section concludes the paper.

2. Related Literature

The following sketch is intended to provide broad motivation for our international lending theory. The first is the literature on bank interest margin including the recent studies of Saunders and Schumacher (2000), Kasman et al. (2010), de Blas and Russ (2010, 2013), and Bremus (2015). Saunders and Schumacher (2000) investigated the impact of the structure of bank competition and macro interest-rate volatility on interest margins in six selected European countries and the US over the 1988–1995 period. Their results suggest an important trade-off between assuring bank solvency (captured by high capital-to-asset ratios) and lowering the cost of consumer financial services

[4] A cornerstone of the Troubled Asset Relief Program (TARP) is the government's purchase of equity capital in financial institutions.

(measured by low net interest margins). Kasman et al. (2010) investigated the effects of the financial reforms on the determinants of bank net interest margin over the period 1995–2006 in the banking systems of the European countries. Their paper shows that increases in bank size and managerial efficiency significantly decrease the bank interest margins. Regulators also should promote merger and acquisition and market entry to increase the scale and efficiency of banks in the countries.

de Blas and Russ (2010) theoretically studied the implications of financial liberalization on bank net interest margins, and lending interest rates. They concluded that foreign-owned banks not only lead to superior efficiency to their host markets but also charge higher markups on borrowed funds than their domestically owned rivals when countries liberalize their financial sectors. de Blas and Russ (2013) studied both cross-border takeovers and cross-border lending on the structure of lending costs, bank profit, and interest rates charged to borrowers. They found that aggregate effects are more significant for cross-border lending than cross-border takeovers. Liberalization toward cross-border lending decreases net interest margins, and increases efficiency and competitive pressure (contestability), while liberalization toward cross-border takeovers increases net interest margins and do not lead to competitive pressure. Both the policies can increase aggregate out.

Bremus (2015) studied the role that international banking plays for market structures in the banking industry. The author suggested that bank foreign direct investment (FDI) is more stability-enhancing than cross-border lending. Further, an increase in bank interest margins in case of FDI increases the resistibility of banks against adverse shocks due to higher margins boosting bank profits. We add to the literature on bank interest margin by providing a theoretical illustration of how the cross-border lending can affect bank interest margin related to bank loan pricing behavior, bank equity risk, and efficiency gain from cross-border loan portfolio diversification for a bank in distress.

The second is the literature on international loan portfolio diversification versus focus. Conventional wisdom in the banking literature argues that banks should be as diversified as possible (Diamond 1984). Proponents of diversification suggest that diversified banks can benefit from leveraging managerial skills and abilities across products and geographic regions (Iskandar-Datta and McLaughlin 2007) and gaining economies of scope through spreading fixed costs over products and region (Drucker and Puri 2009). Diversified banks may also reduce the expected costs of financial distress or bankruptcy by lowering risks through spreading operations across different products or economic environment (Boot and Schmeits 2000). Rossi et al. (2009) found that diversification deteriorates cost efficiency, ameliorates profit efficiency, reduces bank' realized risk, and has a positive impact on banks' capitalization. Focusing on the anatomy of bank diversification, Elsas et al. (2010) investigated how revenue diversification affects bank value. They concluded that diversification does not reduce shareholder value but rather improves bank profitability and thereby bank value. Elsas et al. (2010) showed that diversification increases profitability and thus, indirectly, it also increases bank value.

On the other hand, some studies, for example, by Berger and Ofek (1996) and Denis et al. (1997) argue that the costs of diversification might outweigh the benefits. Proponents of focus argue that diversified banks can suffer from diluting the comparative advantage of management by going beyond their existing expertise (Klein and Saidenberg 1998), competition induced by diversification (Winton 1999), and increased agency costs resulting from value-decreasing activities of the managers who have lowered their personal risk (Laeven and Levine 2007). Diversification of banking activities across international boards can lead to increased political risk, and foreign exchange risk, which can destroy shareholder value (Deng and Elyasiani 2008). Tabak et al. (2011) found that loan portfolio concentration increases returns as well as reduces default risk; in particular, the impact of concentration on bank's return is decreasing on bank's risk; there are significant size effects; and foreign and state-owned banks seem to be less affected by the degree of diversification.

Cole and Obstfeld (1991) evaluated the social gains from international risk sharing in some simple general-equilibrium models with output uncertainty. They found that the direct welfare gains from cross-border portfolio diversification may be quite small as far as large industrialized economies are concerned. Cetorelli and Goldberg (2012a) provide some results to support the conjecture that banking globalization has a deep and pervasive impact on the consequences of domestic and international liquidity shocks. Cetorelli and Goldberg (2012b) contributed to further the understanding of global banking funding dynamics by taking a closer view from the perspective of a host country. Chakraborty et al. (2017) highlighted the benefits of financial integration that Europe enjoyed before the crisis and the costs of financial disintegration since then. They argued that, while financial separation is useful to limit contagion during a crisis, such ringfencing comes at certain costs borne by firms and consumers at other times. Barrell and Nahhas (2019) considered the cross-border lending stock from 19 advanced countries to European countries using quarterly data for 1999–2016. Their results suggest EU integration has had a large effect on cross-border lending, although this has been partly reversed after Euro debt crisis; this reversal probably arises more from the actions of home country bank regulators rather than from the rise in risk premia in host countries. While we also examine diversification, our focus on the bank spread management aspects of efficiency gain from international loan portfolio diversification takes our analysis in a different direction.

The third strand is the literature on bank equity capital during a financial crisis. Most theories (e.g., Acharya et al. 2011; Allen et al. 2011) predict that capital reduces bank equity risk and enhances bank survival probability. However, some theories (e.g., Koehn and Santomero 1980; Besanko and Kanatas 1996) suggest that increasing bank capital could be counterproductive because it perversely increases bank risk taking. Harris et al. (2013) examined the impact of the TARP capital injections on the operational efficiency of commercial banks. They showed a deteriorating pattern in the operating efficiency for banks that received the capital injection from TARP funds that is not evident in non-TARP banks. Lin and Li (2017) took a contingent claim approach to the market valuation of equity and default risk in a financial services holding company. They showed that an increase in bank capital requirement results in an increased default risk in the consolidated bank's equity return. This paper also examines the effect of capital, in particular capital regulation after government capital injection to a bank in distress. After establishing the effects of capital on bank performance, we turn our attention to understanding the efficiency gain from international loan portfolio diversification through which these effects work.

3. The Model Basics

This section mainly consists of two parts. In the first part, a few simplifying assumptions are made to get tractable solutions. The remaining part of this section focuses on the valuation of the international bank's equity and risk, and of the efficiency gain from international loan portfolio diversification.

3.1. The Framework and Assumptions

We consider an international bank whose planning horizon extends over a given time interval with two dates, 0 and 1, $t \in [0, 1]$. $t = 1$ can be considered as the time at which the bank subject to a comprehensive on-site audit by regulatory authorities, who assess the net worth of the bank and check that it is solvent. If assets are found to be less than liabilities at $t = 1$, the bank's assets are costlessly transferred to liability holders. Equity holders are residual claimants on the bank's assets after all other liabilities have been met. The book value of the bank's liabilities can be treated as the strike price in the contingent valuation. When the value of the bank's assets is less than the strike price, the equity value is zero. Several important assumptions of the framework are described as follows.

First, at time $t = 0$, the bank's balance sheet looks like what is shown in Table 1. For the sake of simplicity, the initial portfolio of assets is assumed to include domestic loans $(1 - \alpha)L$, foreign loans αM, and liquid asset B where $0 \leq \alpha < 1$ denotes the degree of international loan portfolio diversification. This is a decision variable of the bank. The cost structure of the bank at $t = 0$ includes deposits D, capital stock K, and government capital injection θK where $\theta > 0$ is a regulatory parameter. These variables are used in a later part when the model is developed.

Table 1. The bank's balance sheet at $t = 0$. [1]

Assets		Liabilities and Equity	
domestic loan	$(1-\alpha)L$	deposit	$D = (1+\theta)K/q$
foreign loan	αM	equity	$(1+\theta)K$
liquid asset	B		
Total	$(1-\alpha)L + \alpha M + B$	Total	$(1+\theta)K(1/q+1)$

[1] $0 \le \alpha < 1$, $\theta > 0$, and q = capital-to-deposits ratio.

Second, an international bank is assumed to diversify its loan portfolio across international regions including domestic and foreign markets. Our focus is on international loan portfolio diversification in the spirit of García-Herrero and Vázquez (2013): financial globalization since the mid-1990s has produced a massive expansion of bank activities overseas. We also follow Damanpour (1986) that the bank finds itself facing stiffer competition from banks in the foreign lending operation. This reflects an assumption in our model, relatively speaking, that the domestic loan market faced by the bank is imperfectly competitive and its foreign loan market is perfectly competitive. Except the domestic loan market faced by the bank, competitive markets are assumed for all financial assets. The bank is a rate-taker and, therefore, the interest rate it will have to pay on deposits is market determined.

Third, domestic loans, foreign loans, and liquid assets in the bank's earning-asset portfolio are assumed to be complete in the sense that any financial claim can be replicated in the market place by a combination of other financial assets. Therefore, the price of any asset is identical to the value of the replicating portfolio to avoid arbitrage opportunities (Crouhy and Galai 1991). This complete feature assumption allows the model to be silent on the separation of management from ownership, and to focus on market determined value for the financial claims on the bank's assets.

Fourth, government intervention in response to the subprime-related 2007/2008 financial crisis generally included three possible means: government guaranteed debt issuance programs, purchases of distressed assets by the government, and direct equity injections (Breitenfellner and Wagner 2010). The introduction of government capital injection in the model is understood because the bank in distress suddenly needs a source of new capital due to a liquidity shock event, as pointed out by Bayazitova and Shivdasani (2011). A government capital injection program assisting liquidity demand, in particular focusing on international loan portfolio diversification, can stabilize the bank by providing a source of capital when public market alternatives are unavailable.

3.2. Model Specifications

As shown in Table 1, the bank's liquidity constraint at $t = 0$ is given by the following balance sheet:

$$(1-\alpha)L + \alpha M + B = D + K + \theta K = (1+\theta)K(\frac{1}{q}+1). \tag{1}$$

In Equation (1), the demand for domestic loans faced by the bank is governed by a downward-sloping demand function $L(R_L)$ where R_L is the domestic loan rate chosen by the bank. The bank can also have foreign loans M normalizing exchange rate between domestic and foreign currencies to one on its balance sheet. The foreign loans earn the foreign market loan rate of R_M. In the earning-asset portfolio, the bank can also hold an amount B of liquid assets, for example, central bank reserves or Treasury bills, during the period horizon. These assets earn the security-market interest rate of R. The larger α is, the higher degree is the international diversification relative to the focus case. The total assets are financed partly by deposits. The supply of deposits faced by the bank is perfectly elastic at the deposit market rate of R_D. The bank's equity capital is tied by regulation to be a fixed proportion q of its deposits, $(1+\theta)K \ge qD$ where q is specified as a regulatory capital-to-deposits ratio (VanHoose 2007). The condition of $(1+\theta)K = qD$ can be motivated based on a binding argument that R is sufficiently larger than R_D (Wong 1997).

The bank's objective is to set R_L to maximize the value of a European down-and-out call (*DOC*) option function, subject to Equation (1). We now apply the *DOC* model and adapt it to evaluate bank claims. The market value of the bank's underlying assets follows a geometric Brownian motion of the form:

$$dV = \mu V dt + \sigma V dW, \tag{2}$$

where

$$V = V_L + V_M,\ V_L = (1-\alpha)(1+R_L)L,\ V_M = \alpha(1+R_M)M,$$
$$\sigma = (1-\alpha)\sigma_L + \alpha\sigma_M,$$

and where V is the value of the bank's total loan repayments including the domestic loan repayment V_L and the foreign loan repayments V_M, with an instantaneous drift μ, and an instantaneous weighted-average disaggregated volatility σ where σ_L is the domestic-loan volatility and σ_M is the foreign-loan volatility.[5] W is a standard Wiener process. In the model, the weighted-average parameter is denoted by country risk because the bank may expose itself to foreign country risk perhaps due to business cycles across countries not perfectly synchronized (García-Herrero and Vázquez 2013).

In this context, the value of the bank's equity is given by a *DOC* formula:

$$\underset{R_L}{\text{Max}}\ S = SC - (DIC_L + DIC_M), \tag{3}$$

where

$$SC = VN(d_1) - Ze^{-\delta}N(d_2),$$
$$Z = \frac{(1+R_D)(1+\theta)K}{q} - (1+R)[(1+\theta)K(\frac{1}{q}+1) - (1-\alpha)L - \alpha M],$$
$$\delta = R - R_D,$$
$$d_1 = \frac{1}{\sigma}(\ln\frac{V}{Z} + \delta + \frac{\sigma^2}{2}),\ d_2 = d_1 - \sigma,$$
$$DIC_L = V_L(\frac{H_L}{V_L})^{2\eta_L}N(c_1) - Z_L e^{-\delta}(\frac{H_L}{V_L})^{2\eta_L-2}N(c_2),$$
$$Z_L = \frac{V_L Z}{V},\ \eta_L = \frac{\delta}{[(1-\alpha)\sigma_L]^2} + \frac{1}{2},\ H_L = \varepsilon_L Z_L,$$
$$c_1 = \frac{1}{(1-\alpha)\sigma_L}(\ln\frac{H_L^2}{V_L Z_L} + \delta + \frac{[(1-\alpha)\sigma_L]^2}{2}),\ c_2 = c_1 - (1-\alpha)\sigma_L,$$
$$DIC_M = V_M(\frac{H_M}{V_M})^{2\eta_M}N(b_1) - Z_M e^{-\delta}(\frac{H_M}{V_M})^{2\eta_M-2}N(b_2),$$
$$Z_M = \frac{V_M Z}{V},\ \eta_M = \frac{\delta}{(\alpha\sigma_M)^2} + \frac{1}{2},\ H_M = \varepsilon_M Z_M,$$
$$b_1 = \frac{1}{\alpha\sigma_M}(\ln\frac{H_M^2}{V_M Z_M} + \delta + \frac{(\alpha\sigma_M)^2}{2}),\ b_2 = b_1 - \alpha\sigma_M.$$

The objective function S in Equation (3) is interpreted as follows. The first term SC is recognized as a standard call option on the underlying value of the bank's total loan repayments V where Z is the strike price of the call. Z is specified as the net-obligation payments, i.e., the difference between the

---

[5] Note that, in the standard context of the aggregated approach (e.g., Episcopos 2008), shareholders are indifferent among various asset compositions so long as the portfolio attains a specific level of overall portfolio risk instead of the used disaggregated approach and in our model.

payments to depositors and the repayments from the investment in the liquid-asset market. δ is the risk-free discounted rate. $N(\cdot)$ is the cumulative density function of the standard normal distribution. The second term DIC_L is interpreted as the net value between the expected domestic-loan repayment value and the present value of the weighted-average (V_L/V) net-obligation payments using the down-and-in call option view of the bank. The H_L is explained as the value of domestic loans which creditors cannot force dissolution. We assume that H_L is proportional to Z_L by a barrier-to-debt ratio ε_L, $H_L = \varepsilon_L Z_L$ where $0 \leq \varepsilon_L < 1$. Similarly, the third term DIC_M is the down-and-in call on the bank's foreign-loan repayments V_M with the strike price of the weighted-average (V_M/V) net-obligation payments Z_M. The barrier H_M is proportional to Z_X by a barrier-to-debt ratio ε_M where $0 \leq \varepsilon_M < 1$. It is seen easily that the barrier option is a wider class than the standard call option because as H_L and H_M approach zero in Equation (3), DIC_L and DIC_H vanish, and we arrive at the usual Merton (1974) call option price that captures the bank's equity.

With the equity function well described, one can now move on to considering the equity risk of the bank. The equity risk is used below when the efficiency gain from international loan portfolio diversification is measured. For this purpose, we define the variance of the return on S in Equation (3) in the spirit of Ronn and Verma (1986) as follows:

$$\sigma_S^2 = [\sigma_{SC} - (\sigma_{DL} + \sigma_{DM})]^2, \tag{4}$$

where

$$\sigma_{SC} = \frac{V}{S}\frac{\partial S}{\partial V}\sigma = \frac{V}{S}N(d_1)\sigma,$$

$$\sigma_{DL} = \frac{V_L}{S}\frac{\partial S}{\partial V_L}(1-\alpha)\sigma_L = \frac{V_L}{S}(\frac{H_L}{V_L})^{2\eta_L}N(c_1)(1-\alpha)\sigma_L,$$

$$\sigma_{DM} = \frac{V_M}{S}\frac{\partial S}{\partial V_M}\alpha\sigma_M = \frac{V_M}{S}(\frac{H_M}{V_M})^{2\eta_M}N(b_1)\alpha\sigma_M,$$

The first term on the right-hand side of Equation (4), σ_{SC}, can be interpreted as the call-based equity deviation with a corresponding underlying value of the bank's total loan repayments. The second term, σ_{DL}, can be interpreted as the knock-out value deviation with a corresponding underlying value of the domestic loan repayments. The third term, σ_{DM}, can be interpreted as that of the foreign loan repayments.

Given the preceding settings, it is interesting to compare the equity risk/return efficiency of the international loan portfolio with that of the domestic loan portfolio and determine the efficiency gains if existent from international diversification, from the viewpoint of shareholder investment. Toward that end, let $SHP(IP)$ denote the ratio excess equity return to equity volatility when $0 < \alpha < 1$ for the international loan portfolio and $SHP(DP)$ the same ratio when $\alpha = 0$ for the domestic loan portfolio. In other words,

$$SHP(IP) = \frac{S-(1+R)(1+\theta)K}{\sigma_S^2} \text{ when } 0 < \alpha < 1, \tag{5}$$

and

$$SHP(DP) = \frac{(SC-DIC_L)-(1+R)(1+\theta)K}{(\sigma_{SC}-\sigma_{DL})^2} \text{ when } \alpha = 0, \tag{6}$$

where $(1+R)(1+\theta)K$ is the risk-free equity return, implying the opportunity cost of the shareholder investment including government capital injection. Then, the efficiency gains from international loan portfolio diversification can be measured by the SHP differential:

$$\Delta SHP = SHP(IP) - SHP(DP). \tag{7}$$

ΔSHP measures the equity return differential, per unit of equity risk, that accrues from holding the international loan portfolio in lieu of the domestic loan portfolio. Note that $SHP(DP)$ in our model is treated as the benchmark of the equity risk/return efficiency that is assumed to be positive in sign. $\Delta SHP > 0$ yields the efficiency gain from the international loan portfolio diversification, whereas $\Delta SHP < 0$ yields the efficiency loss.

4. Solution and Results

In this section, we first discuss the theoretic modeling of solution and comparative static results. Then, several numerical examples are employed to explain the comparative static results derived from the theoretical model.

4.1. Optimum and Comparative Static Analysis

With all assumptions in place, we are ready to solve for the bank's optimal choice of domestic loan rate. Partially differentiating Equation (3) with respect to R_L, the first-order condition is given by:

$$\frac{\partial S}{\partial R_L} = \frac{\partial SC}{\partial R_L} - \left(\frac{\partial DIC_L}{\partial R_L} + \frac{\partial DIC_M}{\partial R_L}\right) = 0. \tag{8}$$

We require that the second-order condition be satisfied, $\partial^2 S/\partial R_L^2 < 0$. The optimal domestic loan rate can be chosen based on Equation (8) where the marginal SC value of R_L equals to the marginal total knock-out values of R_L. We can further substitute the optimal domestic loan rate to obtain ΔSHP in Equation (7) remaining on the optimization.

Consider next the impact on the SHP differential from changes in international loan portfolio diversification degree, government capital injection, and capital regulation. Differentiation of Equation (7) evaluated at the optimal domestic loan rate with respect to parameter m (where $m = \alpha, \theta$, and q) yields:

$$\frac{d\Delta SHP}{dm} = \frac{\partial \Delta SHP}{\partial m} + \frac{\partial \Delta SHP}{\partial R_L}\frac{\partial R_L}{\partial m}, \tag{9}$$

where

$$\frac{\partial \Delta SHP}{\partial m} = \frac{\partial SHP(IP)}{\partial m} - \frac{\partial SHP(DP)}{\partial m},$$

$$\frac{\partial \Delta SHP}{\partial R_L} = \frac{\partial SHP(IP)}{\partial R_L} - \frac{\partial SHP(DP)}{\partial R_L},$$

$$\frac{d\sigma_S^2}{dm} = \frac{\partial \sigma_S^2}{\partial m} + \frac{\partial \sigma_S^2}{\partial R_L}\frac{\partial R_L}{\partial m},$$

$$\frac{\partial R_L}{\partial m} = -\frac{\partial^2 S}{\partial R_L \partial m} / \frac{\partial^2 S}{\partial R_L^2}.$$

The first term on the right-hand side of Equation (9) can be identified as the direct effect, while the second term can be identified as the indirect effect. The direct effect captures the change in ΔSHP due to an increase in parameter m, holding the optimal domestic loan rate constant. The indirect effect arises because an increase in m changes the bank's profits by $L(R_L)$ in every possible state. In general, the added complexity of path dependent options in Equation (9) does not always lead to clear-cut results, but we can certainly speak of tendencies for reasonable parameter levels corresponding roughly to a hypothetical bank. A numerical exercise is designed to investigate the comparative static results of Equation (9) in the following subsection.

4.2. Parameter Basics

The formulas for the values of the equity claim, the equity risk, the efficiency measure, and the comparative static results of Equation (9) presented above are truly closed formulas that can be readily implemented once the relevant parameters are given. In the following, we assume that the case parameter levels, unless otherwise indicated, are as follows: $R = 3.5\%$, $R_D = 2.5\%$, $R_M = 4.7\%$,

$M = 347$, $K = 25$, $q = 8.3\%$, $\sigma_L = 0.5$, $\sigma_M = 0.6$, $\varepsilon_L = 0.6$, $\varepsilon_M = 0.7$, and $\theta = 0.2$. Let (R_L, L) change from $(4.5, 350)$ to $(5.1, 329)$ due to $\partial L/\partial R_L < 0$. These parameter levels used for simulation exercises are interpreted as follows.

(i) The conditions of $R_L > R = 3.5\%$ and $R_M = 4.7\% > R$ indicate the scope of earning-asset portfolio substitution (Kashyap et al. 2002). $R > R_D = 2.5\%$ captures the binding condition of the capital constraint (Wong 1997). $R_L > R_D$ demonstrates the bank interest margin as an element of after-tax earnings (Saunders and Schumacher 2000).

(ii) The specification of capital adequacy requirement is set by the capital-to-deposits ratio $q = (1+\theta)K/D = 8.3\%$ (VanHoose 2007). In the case, without government capital injection where $\theta = 0$, the capital-to-asset ratio at $t = 0$ is $25/348.2 = 7.18\%$, where $L = 350$, $M = 347$, and $\alpha = 0.6$, which does not meet the capital adequacy requirement of 8.00%. This indicates a situation of the bank's depleted capital. This possible case is supportive to an argument of Bayazitova and Shivdasani (2011): the government capital injection is anticipated by the distressed bank when raising new capital in public markets by the bank is difficult.

(iii) The condition of $\sigma_L = 0.5 < \sigma_M = 0.6$ indicates that the standard deviation of domestic loan repayments is less than the standard deviation of foreign loan repayments. This can be understood that international portfolio investment involves, at the very least, two additional sources of risk, exchange rate volatility and country risk (Rajan and Friedman 1997). Accordingly, we further assume the condition of $\varepsilon_L = 0.6 < \varepsilon_M = 0.7$, implying that the bank with high asset volatility are more likely to exhibit a higher probability of hitting the barrier before the expiration date than the bank without such the characteristic.

4.3. International Loan Portfolio Diversification Effect

In this subsection, three sets of comparative statics are computed and used to assess the effects of the increased international loan portfolio diversification degree of the bank on its domestic loan rate, equity risk, and diversification efficiency at various levels of capital (increased government capital injection or stringent capital regulation).

Equation (9) with $m = \alpha$ captures the response of the diversification efficiency to a change in international loan portfolio diversification degree. The findings are shown in Table 2. First, we have the result of $S > 0$ with an approximate optimal domestic loan rate of 4.6% in the shaded area according to the equilibrium condition of Equation (8). The result of $\partial R_L/\partial\alpha < 0$ demonstrates that an increase in the international loan portfolio diversification degree decreases the bank's domestic loan rate (and thus on the bank's interest margin since the foreign market loan rate and the deposit market rate are not choice variables of the bank). As the bank increases its international loan portfolio diversification, it must now provide a return to a larger foreign loan base. One way the bank may attempt to augment its total returns is by shifting its investments to its domestic loan portfolio and away from the liquid-asset market. If domestic loan demand is relatively rate-elastic, a larger loan portfolio is possible at a reduced margin. de Blas and Russ (2013) found that cross-border lending decreases bank interest margins. Thus, their finding lends support to our result.

Second, the effect of international diversification on bank equity risk is reported in the third panel of Table 2. The direct effect captures the change in σ_S^2 due to an increase in α, holding the optimal bank interest margin constant. It is unambiguously positive because an increase in the extent of diversification makes the loan portfolio riskier to grant due to an increase in high-risk foreign loans with a decrease in low-risk domestic loans in the down-and-in call options. The indirect effect arises because an increase in α changes the equity volatility by $L(R_L)$ in every possible state. An increase in α increases domestic loan risk-taking at a reduced optimal margin; consequently, increasing the bank's equity volatility. Since the indirect effect reinforces the direct effect to give an overall positive response of σ_S^2 to an increase in α, we conclude that loan portfolio diversification increases bank equity volatility. Our result is consistent with a theory (e.g., Denis et al. 1997; Deng and Elyasiani 2008) that predicts a deterioration in the effectiveness of international loan portfolio diversification on the bank's equity risk.

Table 2. Effects of international loan portfolio diversification degree on domestic loan rate, equity risk, and diversification efficiency. [1]

	$(R_L(\%), L)$						
α	(4.5, 350)	(4.6, 349)	(4.7, 347)	(4.8, 344)	(4.9, 340)	(5.0, 335)	(5.1, 329)
				S			
0.20	93.2192	93.2374	93.0793	92.7432	92.2279	91.5320	90.6542
0.25	93.8960	93.9113	93.7594	93.4391	92.9490	92.2877	91.4542
0.30	94.5521	94.5648	94.4200	94.1164	93.6527	93.0278	92.2405
0.35	95.1957	95.2062	95.0690	94.7829	94.3469	93.7597	93.0202
0.40	95.8309	95.8394	95.7103	95.4426	95.0352	94.4870	93.7969
				$\partial R_L/\partial\alpha$ (%)			
0.20→0.25	-	−3.3956	7.1035	17.5259	27.8752	38.1549	-
0.25→0.30	-	−3.0997	8.3386	19.6909	30.9609	42.1522	-
0.30→0.35	-	−2.8738	9.5909	21.9600	34.2373	46.4267	-
0.35→0.40	-	−2.6778	10.9402	24.4524	37.8628	51.1755	-
				$d\sigma_S^2/d\alpha$ (%)			
0.20→0.25	-	26.9056	26.9813	27.0038	26.9757	26.8981	-
0.25→0.30	-	24.5969	24.6820	24.7147	24.6976	24.6317	-
0.30→0.35	-	23.0997	23.1893	23.2266	23.2144	23.1539	-
0.35→0.40	-	22.0011	22.0925	22.1315	22.1206	22.0613	-
				$d\Delta SHP/d\alpha$: total effect (10^{-4})			
0.20→0.25	-	0.0186	0.0178	0.0169	0.0158	0.0147	-
0.25→0.30	-	3.1350	3.0477	2.9435	2.8237	2.6897	-
0.30→0.35	-	74.9129	73.5032	71.7871	69.7776	67.4876	-
0.35→0.40	-	603.8547	596.0278	586.3013	574.7190	561.3216	-

[1] Parameter values, unless stated otherwise: $R = 3.5\%$, $R_D = 2.5\%$, $R_M = 4.7\%$, $M = 347$, $K = 25$, $\theta = 0.20$, $q = 8.3\%$, $\sigma_L = 0.5$, $\sigma_M = 0.6$, $\varepsilon_L = 0.6$, and $\varepsilon_M = 0.7$. The values in the shaded areas are computed with a corresponding optimal domestic loan rate of 4.6%. $\partial^2 S/\partial R_L^2 < 0$ meets the required second-order condition. The direct effect of $\partial\sigma_S^2/\partial\alpha$ is positive. The indirect effect of $(\partial\sigma_S^2/\partial R_L)(\partial R_L/\partial\alpha)$ is positive. The direct effect of $\partial\Delta SHP/\partial\alpha$ is positive. The indirect effect of $(\partial\Delta SHP/\partial R_L)(\partial R_L/\partial\alpha)$ is positive.

Third, as indicated in the fourth panel of Table 2, the efficiency gain from international loan portfolio diversification at various levels of diversification degree is positive in sign. This effect simply reflects an efficiency gain required by the bank for the international diversification. Further, the last panel demonstrates both the direct effect and the indirect effect evaluated at the optimal domestic loan rate are positive. The positive direct effect reflects an increasing gain required by the bank for the increasing diversification decision it makes. The indirect effect is therefore positive and reinforces the direct effect. The result is understood because the bank with broad global exposure should be better positioned to diversify away country-specific risks since business cycles across countries are not perfectly synchronized. Our result is consistent with Rossi et al. (2009): the benefits of international diversification in loan portfolio could be potentially existent.

The computed comparative static results are listed in Table 3. The negative effect of the international loan portfolio diversification on the bank's interest margin is increased as the government capital injection increases. This result suggests a positive relation between capital and domestic loan market share in the domestic loan market. This is understood that a high-capital international bank is able to compete more effectively for its domestic loans (Calomiris and Wilson 2004), providing some support. We also show that the positive effect on international loan portfolio diversification on the bank's equity risk is decreased as the government capital injection increases. This result suggests that a negative relation between capital and equity risk. Thus, we argue that higher capital helps bank safety because the higher-capital bank engages in more monitoring investment, thereby reducing the bank's equity risk, and implicitly reducing the probability of default of the bank. Our argument is largely supported by Holmstrom and Tirole (1997). Overall, the international bank views a relatively large amount of government capital injection to be beneficial when the bank's international loan portfolio diversification is efficient and increased.

Table 3. Effects of international loan portfolio diversification degree on diversification efficiency at various levels of government capital injection. [1]

			θ		
α	0.20	0.25	0.30	0.35	0.40
			S		
0.20	93.2374	93.9430	94.6534	95.3686	96.0887
0.25	93.9113	94.6128	95.3191	96.0302	96.7462
0.30	94.5648	95.2629	95.9657	96.6734	97.3859
0.35	95.2062	95.9013	96.6011	97.3057	98.0151
0.40	95.8394	96.5319	97.2291	97.9311	98.6377
			$\partial R_L/\partial\alpha$ (%)		
0.20→0.25	−3.3956	−3.4785	−3.5631	−3.6494	−3.7374
0.25→0.30	−3.0997	−3.1896	−3.2812	−3.3744	−3.4694
0.30→0.35	−2.8738	−2.9709	−3.0697	−3.1702	−3.2724
0.35→0.40	−2.6778	−2.7833	−2.8904	−2.9991	−3.1095
			$d\sigma_S^2/d\alpha$ (%)		
0.20→0.25	26.9056	26.8632	26.8252	26.8252	26.7614
0.25→0.30	24.5969	24.6292	24.6638	24.6638	24.7400
0.30→0.35	23.0997	23.1883	23.2773	23.2773	23.4568
0.35→0.40	22.0011	22.1420	22.2811	22.2811	22.5538
			$d\Delta SHP/d\alpha$: total effect (10^{-4})		
0.20→0.25	0.0186	0.0155	0.0129	0.0107	0.0089
0.25→0.30	3.1350	2.7478	2.4057	2.1037	1.8375
0.30→0.35	74.9129	67.7320	61.1863	55.2250	49.8004
0.35→0.40	603.8547	557.3680	514.1072	473.8757	436.4872

[1] Parameter values, unless stated otherwise: $R = 3.5\%$, $R_D = 2.5\%$, $R_M = 4.7\%$, $M = 347$, $K = 25$, $q = 8.3\%$, $\sigma_L = 0.5$, $\sigma_M = 0.6$, $\varepsilon_L = 0.6$, and $\varepsilon_M = 0.7$. All results are valued at the optimal loan rate of 4.6%.

There are interesting results obtained, as shown in Table 4. First, the negative effect of international loan portfolio diversification on the bank's interest margin is decreased as the capital-to-deposits ratio increases. This result suggests that a lower-capital international bank due to stringent capital requirements is less likely to compete more effectively for domestic loans when its cross-border lending is increased. Our theory demonstrates a positive relation between capital and market share in the domestic loan market. Second, when the international loan portfolio diversification is high, the positive effect of international loan portfolio diversification on the bank's equity risk is decreased as the capital requirement is increased. We argue that capital regulation helps from the standpoint of bank survival, consistent with Holmstrom and Tirole (1997). Third, the positive effect of the international diversification on the diversification efficiency is increased as the capital requirement is increased. This suggests that the bank views a relatively high capital regulation to be beneficial when the bank's international loan portfolio diversification is increased. Our result is largely supported by the argument of Berger and Bouwman (2013): post-crisis reform proposals tend to focus on how capital regulation should adapt to prevent future crises.

Table 4. Effects of international loan portfolio diversification degree on diversification efficiency at various levels of capital-to-deposits ratio. [1]

			q (%)		
α	8.3	8.5	8.7	8.9	9.1
			S		
0.20	93.2374	93.1960	93.1566	93.1189	93.0828
0.25	93.9113	93.8701	93.8309	93.7934	93.7576
0.30	94.5648	94.5238	94.4848	94.4475	94.4118
0.35	95.2062	95.1654	95.1265	95.0894	95.0539
0.40	95.8394	95.7987	95.7600	95.7230	95.6876
			$\partial R_L/\partial\alpha$ (%)		
0.20→0.25	−3.3956	−3.3907	−3.3861	−3.3817	−3.3775
0.25→0.30	−3.0997	−3.0944	−3.0894	−3.0847	−3.0801
0.30→0.35	−2.8738	−2.8681	−2.8627	−2.8576	−2.8526
0.35→0.40	−2.6778	−2.6717	−2.6658	−2.6602	−2.6548
			$d\sigma_S^2/d\alpha$ (%)		
0.20→0.25	26.9056	26.9082	26.9107	26.9131	26.9155
0.25→0.30	24.5969	24.5951	24.5934	24.5917	24.5902
0.30→0.35	23.0997	23.0945	23.0896	23.0848	23.0803
0.35→0.40	22.0011	21.9927	21.9847	21.9771	21.9698
			$d\Delta SHP/d\alpha$: total effect (10^{-4})		
0.20→0.25	0.0186	0.0188	0.0189	0.0191	0.0192
0.25→0.30	3.1350	3.1546	3.1733	3.1913	3.2086
0.30→0.35	74.9129	75.2395	75.5521	75.8517	76.1390
0.35→0.40	603.8547	605.7287	607.5206	609.2355	610.8784

[1] Parameter values, unless stated otherwise: $R = 3.5\%$, $R_D = 2.5\%$, $R_M = 4.7\%$, $M = 347$, $K = 25$, $\theta = 0.20$, $\sigma_L = 0.5$, $\sigma_M = 0.6$, $\varepsilon_L = 0.6$, and $\varepsilon_M = 0.7$. All results are valued at the optimal loan rate of 4.6%.

4.4. Government Capital Injection Effect

In this subsection, we compute the effects of government capital injection on bank interest margin, equity risk, and diversification efficiency at various levels of cross-border lending diversification.

To study the overall effect of government capital injections, we report the findings in Table 5. We show that government capital injection produces an increase in bank interest margin and a decrease in bank equity risk. As can be seen from the last panel, however, an increase in the government capital injection decreases the efficiency gain from the international loan portfolio diversification. The result is understood because the positive impact on the bank's interest margin from increases in the government's capital injection, making the bank less prone to risk-taking, is less likely to vanish and the negative impact on the bank's equity risk is less likely to come into effect. From a normative standpoint, our results sound a cautionary note to the adoption of increasing government capital injections that discourage international loan portfolio diversification although government capital injection is an efficient way to stabilize the bank. Our results complement the analysis of the efficiency gain from international diversification as proposed in Rossi et al. (2009).

Table 5. Effects of government capital injection on domestic loan rate, equity risk, and diversification efficiency. [1]

	$(R_L(\%), L)$						
θ	(4.5, 350)	(4.6, 349)	(4.7, 347)	(4.8, 344)	(4.9, 340)	(5.0, 335)	(5.1, 329)
				S			
0.10	91.8244	91.8405	91.6797	91.3405	90.8215	90.1213	89.2386
0.15	92.5194	92.5366	92.3771	92.0395	91.5223	90.8242	89.9439
0.20	93.2192	93.2374	93.0793	92.7432	92.2279	91.5320	90.6542
0.25	93.9237	93.9430	93.7862	93.4518	92.9385	92.2448	91.3695
0.30	94.6330	94.6534	94.4980	94.1653	93.6539	92.9625	92.0898
0.35	95.3471	95.3686	95.2146	94.8836	94.3742	93.6852	92.8152
0.40	96.0660	96.0887	95.9361	95.6068	95.0995	94.4129	93.5457
				$\partial R_L/\partial\theta$ (%)			
0.10→0.15	-	1.2036	1.4671	1.7333	2.0066	2.2918	-
0.15→0.20	-	1.2200	1.4976	1.7782	2.0665	2.3675	-
0.20→0.25	-	1.2365	1.5285	1.8237	2.1272	2.4441	-
0.25→0.30	-	1.2532	1.5597	1.8698	2.1886	2.5218	-
0.30→0.35	-	1.2700	1.5913	1.9164	2.2507	2.6004	-
0.35→0.40	-	1.2870	1.6233	1.9635	2.3137	2.6800	-
				$d\sigma_S^2/d\theta$ (%)			
0.10→0.15	-	−24.3328	−24.4345	−24.5960	−24.8199	−25.1100	-
0.15→0.20	-	−24.3034	−24.4056	−24.5678	−24.7925	−25.0837	-
0.20→0.25	-	−24.2731	−24.3759	−24.5387	−24.7643	−25.0566	-
0.25→0.30	-	−24.2419	−24.3452	−24.5087	−24.7353	−25.0287	-
0.30→0.35	-	−24.2097	−24.3136	−24.4779	−24.7054	−25.0001	-
0.35→0.40	-	−24.1766	−24.2810	−24.4461	−24.6746	−24.9706	-
				$d\Delta SHP/d\theta$ (10^{-11})			
0.10→0.15	-	−8.0267	−7.5342	−6.9854	−6.4009	−5.7878	-
0.15→0.20	-	−6.1554	−5.7757	−5.3326	−4.8821	−4.4244	-
0.20→0.25	-	−4.7536	−4.4444	−4.1140	−3.7269	−3.3325	-
0.25→0.30	-	−3.6153	−3.3763	−3.1093	−2.8562	−2.5679	-
0.30→0.35	-	−2.7754	−2.5717	−2.3823	−2.1077	−1.8754	-
0.35→0.40	-	−2.1137	−1.9946	−1.7980	−1.6359	−1.4463	-

[1] Parameter values, unless stated otherwise: $R = 3.5\%$, $R_D = 2.5\%$, $R_M = 4.7\%$, $M = 347$, $K = 25$, $\alpha = 0.20$, $q = 8.3\%$, $\sigma_L = 0.5$, $\sigma_M = 0.6$, $\varepsilon_L = 0.6$, and $\varepsilon_M = 0.7$. The values in the shaded area are computed with a corresponding optimal domestic loan rate of 4.6%. $\partial^2 S/\partial R_L^2 < 0$ meets the required second-order condition.

Table 6 depicts the effect of government capital injection on bank interest margin, equity risk, and international diversification efficiency at various levels of international loan portfolio diversification. We show that the positive effect on the bank's interest margin and the negative effect on the bank's equity risk are decreased as the degree of international loan portfolio diversification increases. These results indicate that capital significantly enhances the bank's interest margin (and thus the bank's profit) and survival probability in particular when the international loan portfolio diversification status is not high. Moreover, the negative effect on diversification efficiency is increased as the degree of international loan portfolio diversification increases. This result demonstrates that capital significantly deteriorates fficiency in particular when the international loan portfolio diversification is high. Complementing Bayazitova and Shivdasani (2011), we suggest that a government capital injection program can stabilize a distressed bank when the bank does not take an active part in cross-border lending.

Table 6. Effects of government capital injection on diversification efficiency at various levels of international loan portfolio diversification. [1]

	α				
θ	0.20	0.25	0.30	0.35	0.40
			S		
0.10	91.8405	92.5224	93.1828	93.8300	94.4683
0.15	92.5366	93.2145	93.8714	94.5157	95.1515
0.20	93.2374	93.9113	94.5648	95.2062	95.8394
0.25	93.9430	94.6128	95.2629	95.9013	96.5319
0.30	94.6534	95.3191	95.9657	96.6011	97.2291
0.35	95.3686	96.0302	96.6734	97.3057	97.9311
0.40	96.0887	96.7462	97.3859	98.0151	98.6377
			$\partial R_L/\partial\theta$ (%)		
0.10→0.15	1.2036	1.1914	1.1765	1.1591	1.1382
0.15→0.20	1.2200	1.2073	1.1921	1.1743	1.1532
0.20→0.25	1.2365	1.2234	1.2078	1.1896	1.1683
0.25→0.30	1.2532	1.2397	1.2236	1.2052	1.1836
0.30→0.35	1.2700	1.2561	1.2397	1.2209	1.1991
0.35→0.40	1.2870	1.2727	1.2559	1.2368	1.2147
			$d\sigma_S^2/d\theta$ (%)		
0.10→0.15	−24.3328	−24.3846	−24.3579	−24.2708	−24.1261
0.15→0.20	−24.3034	−24.3507	−24.3212	−24.2334	−24.0907
0.20→0.25	−24.2731	−24.3159	−24.2839	−24.1955	−24.0546
0.25→0.30	−24.2419	−24.2803	−24.2459	−24.1570	−24.0180
0.30→0.35	−24.2097	−24.2440	−24.2073	−24.1179	−23.9807
0.35→0.40	−24.1766	−24.2069	−24.1680	−24.0782	−23.9429
			$d\Delta SHP/d\theta$: total effect		
	$(10^{-11}55)$	$(10^{-7}55)$	$(10^{-5}55)$	$(10^{-4}55)$	$(10^{-3}55)$
0.10→0.15	−8.0267	−4.3761	−4.9923	−9.1272	−6.2734
0.15→0.20	−6.1554	−3.6880	−4.4191	−8.3200	−5.8274
0.20→0.25	−4.7536	−3.1032	−3.9074	−7.5781	−5.4098
0.25→0.30	−3.6153	−2.6070	−3.4512	−6.8967	−5.0189
0.30→0.35	−2.7754	−2.1867	−3.0448	−6.2714	−4.6533
0.35→0.40	−2.1137	−1.8311	−2.6833	−5.6980	−4.3115

[1] Parameter values, unless stated otherwise: $R = 3.5\%$, $R_D = 2.5\%$, $R_M = 4.7\%$, $M = 347$, $K = 25$, $q = 8.3\%$, $\sigma_L = 0.5$, $\sigma_M = 0.6$, $\varepsilon_L = 0.6$, and $\varepsilon_M = 0.7$. All results are valued at the optimal loan rate of 4.6%.

4.5. Capital Regulation Effect

It is necessary to elaborate on the capital regulation issue based on Equation (9) where $m = q$. The findings are summarized in Table 7. It is interesting that, as the capital-to-deposits ratio increases, a larger domestic loan portfolio is possible at a reduced interest margin, resulting in increasing risk-taking. In the problem at hand, increases in the capital-to-deposits ratio have a positive effect on bank equity risk. However, the efficiency gain from the international loan portfolio diversification is robust to a wide range of capital regulation. We conclude that increased capital regulation is likely to deteriorate the international bank's equity risk, but ameliorate the international bank's efficiency gain. The former can be motivated based on an argument about the presence of market power in the domestic loan market, and the latter can be motivated based on an argument about the importance of international loan portfolio diversification when the justification of capital regulation is focused.

Table 7. Effects of capital-to-deposits ratio on domestic loan rate, equity risk, and diversification efficiency. [1]

	$(R_L(\%), L)$						
q (%)	(4.5, 350)	(4.6, 349)	(4.7, 347)	(4.8, 344)	(4.9, 340)	(5.0, 335)	(5.1, 329)
				S			
8.1	93.2626	93.2809	93.1228	92.7869	92.2717	91.5759	90.6982
8.3	93.2192	93.2374	93.0793	92.7432	92.2279	91.5320	90.6542
8.5	93.1778	93.1960	93.0378	92.7017	92.1863	91.4902	90.6122
8.7	93.1384	93.1566	92.9982	92.6620	92.1465	91.4503	90.5722
8.9	93.1008	93.1189	92.9605	92.6242	92.1085	91.4123	90.5340
9.1	93.0648	93.0828	92.9244	92.5880	92.0723	91.3759	90.4975
9.3	93.0304	93.0484	92.8899	92.5534	92.0376	91.3411	90.4626
				$\partial R_L/\partial q$ (10^{-4})			
8.1→8.3	-	−1.8995	−2.3405	−2.7864	−3.2446	−3.7232	-
8.3→8.5	-	−1.8087	−2.2276	−2.6512	−3.0865	−3.5411	-
8.5→8.7	-	−1.7242	−2.1227	−2.5256	−2.9396	−3.3721	-
8.7→8.9	-	−1.6454	−2.0250	−2.4087	−2.8030	−3.2149	-
8.9→9.1	-	−1.5720	−1.9339	−2.2998	−2.6758	−3.0684	-
9.1→9.3	-	−1.5034	−1.8488	−2.1981	−2.5569	−2.9317	-
				$d\sigma_S^2/dq$ (‰)			
8.1→8.3	-	3.7518	3.7677	3.7928	3.8277	3.8729	-
8.3→8.5	-	3.5755	3.5906	3.6146	3.6478	3.6908	-
8.5→8.7	-	3.4114	3.4258	3.4486	3.4803	3.5214	-
8.7→8.9	-	3.2583	3.2720	3.2939	3.3241	3.3633	-
8.9→9.1	-	3.1153	3.1284	3.1493	3.1782	3.2156	-
9.1→9.3	-	2.9814	2.9940	3.0140	3.0417	3.0775	-
				$d\Delta SHP/dq$ (10^{-13})			
8.1→8.3	-	7.8270	7.2990	6.9492	5.5330	5.3615	-
8.3→8.5	-	6.9383	6.5880	5.7049	5.3549	5.3600	-
8.5→8.7	-	7.2932	6.2321	6.0596	6.2421	5.0033	-
8.7→8.9	-	6.9376	7.1200	6.2364	4.6421	5.1803	-
8.9→9.1	-	6.4044	5.6982	6.0583	5.3525	4.6458	-
9.1→9.3	-	6.0489	6.4084	5.1692	5.3518	4.6450	-

[1] Parameter values, unless stated otherwise: $R = 3.5\%$, $R_D = 2.5\%$, $R_M = 4.7\%$, $M = 347$, $K = 25$, $\theta = 0.20$, $\alpha = 0.20$, $\sigma_L = 0.5$, $\sigma_M = 0.6$, $\varepsilon_L = 0.6$, and $\varepsilon_M = 0.7$. The values in the shaded area are computed with a corresponding optimal domestic loan rate of 4.6%. $\partial^2 S/\partial R_L^2 < 0$ meets the required second-order condition.

As shown in Table 8, the negative impact on the bank's interest margin is increased and the positive impact on the bank's equity risk is increased as well when the total amount of the government's capital injections is increased. The government's capital injection effect reinforces the capital regulation effect to give an overall positive response of the bank's equity risk. Relying on a comprehensive framework for bank equity risk measurement, we find evidence against strategic substitutes between capital regulation and government capital injection, unlike studies concerned with government intervention packages. However, the positive effect of capital regulation on the bank's international loan portfolio diversification efficiency is weakened when the government's capital injection is increased. We suggest that bank diversification efficiency is from capital regulation, not from government capital injection.

Table 8. Effects of capital-to-deposits ratio on diversification efficiency at various levels of government capital injection. [1]

	θ				
q (%)	0.20	0.25	0.30	0.35	0.40
			S		
8.1	93.2809	93.9886	94.7012	95.4185	96.1408
8.3	93.2374	93.9430	94.6534	95.3686	96.0887
8.5	93.1960	93.8996	94.6080	95.3211	96.0390
8.7	93.1566	93.8582	94.5646	95.2758	95.9917
8.9	93.1189	93.8187	94.5232	95.2325	95.9466
9.1	93.0828	93.7809	94.4837	95.1912	95.9034
9.3	93.0484	93.7448	94.4459	95.1516	95.8621
			$\partial R_L/\partial q$ (10^{-4})		
8.1→8.3	−1.8995	−2.0055	−2.1140	−2.2249	−2.3383
8.3→8.5	−1.8087	−1.9095	−2.0127	−2.1182	−2.2262
8.5→8.7	−1.7242	−1.8203	−1.9186	−2.0191	−2.1219
8.7→8.9	−1.6454	−1.7371	−1.8309	−1.9268	−2.0248
8.9→9.1	−1.5720	−1.6595	−1.7491	−1.8406	−1.9342
9.1→9.3	−1.5034	−1.5870	−1.6726	−1.7601	−1.8496
			$d\sigma_S^2/dq$ (‰)		
8.1→8.3	3.7518	3.9032	4.0540	4.2042	4.3539
8.3→8.5	3.5755	3.7198	3.8635	4.0067	4.1494
8.5→8.7	3.4114	3.5490	3.6862	3.8229	3.9590
8.7→8.9	3.2583	3.3898	3.5208	3.6514	3.7814
8.9→9.1	3.1153	3.2410	3.3663	3.4911	3.6155
9.1→9.3	2.9814	3.1018	3.2217	3.3412	3.4603
			$d\Delta SHP/dq$: total effect (10^{-13})		
8.1→8.3	7.8270	6.0484	4.4478	3.9137	3.0249
8.3→8.5	6.9383	6.5812	4.2701	3.3807	2.6693
8.5→8.7	7.2932	4.6264	4.8030	4.0913	3.0243
8.7→8.9	6.9376	6.0479	4.2698	3.0251	2.4911
8.9→9.1	6.4044	4.9818	4.2695	3.7356	2.8464
9.1→9.3	6.0489	4.9813	3.3811	3.3799	2.6687

[1] Parameter values, unless stated otherwise: $R = 3.5\%$, $R_D = 2.5\%$, $R_M = 4.7\%$, $M = 347$, $K = 25$, $\alpha = 0.20$, $\sigma_L = 0.5$, $\sigma_M = 0.6$, $\varepsilon_L = 0.6$, and $\varepsilon_M = 0.7$. All results are valued at the optimal loan rate of 4.6%.

5. Conclusions

Recently, international lending dropped significantly and has remained at a comparatively low level since the 2007/2008 global financial crisis. This trend occurs at a time where an unprecedented tide of financial internationalization has raised growing concerns among investors, claimholders, and regulators. By relying on a barrier option valuation framework, the model presented in this paper tries to study international loan portfolio diversification efficiency, particularly concerning an international bank in distress. International loan portfolio diversification status, government capital injection, and capital regulation are considered. Their respective effects on the distressed bank has been assessed.

First, we suggest that, from an efficiency viewpoint, international loan portfolio diversification conducted by the distressed bank be encouraged although diversification produces higher domestic lending and equity risk for the bank. The effect of the diversification encouragement is relatively low when the government capital injection is at a high level. Second, we show that an increase in the government capital injection significantly decreases the bank's international loan portfolio diversification efficiency when the bank's diversification degree is high. Third, we find that an increase in the capital regulation significantly increases diversification efficiency when the bank helped by the government capital injection is low. Three insights on regulation have been given in banking diversification.

The valuation framework presented here is fairly general and should open at least one further avenues of research. One issue that has not been addressed is the efficiency gain from international loan portfolio diversification with credit swaps of domestic loan portfolio. Credit swaps as such may make the distressed bank shift the focus on local geographic diversification instead of international geographic diversification. Such concerns are beyond the scope of this paper and thus are not addressed here. What this paper does demonstrate, however, is the important role played by efficiency gains from international loan portfolio diversification related to bank performance and safety and thereby the stability of the banking system during a financial crisis.

Author Contributions: Conceptualization, J.-H.L.; Formal analysis, S.C.; Funding acquisition, F.-W.H.; Investigation, F.-W.H.; Methodology, J.-H.L.; Project administration, J.-H.L.; Resources, P.-C.L.; Software, S.C.; Validation, P.-C.L.; Visualization, P.-C.L.; Writing—original draft, F.-W.H.; and Writing—review and editing, F.-W.H.

Funding: This research was funded by National Natural Science Foundation of China, grant number 71603217.

Acknowledgments: We would like to thank Mila Marinkovic (assistant editor), two anonymous referees, and the English editor for their helpful comments and suggestions. The usual disclaimer applies.

Conflicts of Interest: The authors declare no conflict of interest.

References

Acharya, Viral V., Hamid Mehran, Til Schuermann, and Anjan V. Thakor. 2011. Robust capital regulation. Staff Report no. 490, Federal Reserve Bank of New York, New York, NY. Available online: https://www.newyorkfed.org/medialibrary/media/research/staff_reports/sr490.pdf (accessed on 31 January 2019).

Allen, Franklin, Elena Carletti, and Robert Marquez. 2011. Credit market competition and capital regulation. *Review of Financial Studies* 24: 983–1018. [CrossRef]

Barrell, Ray, and Abdulkader Nahhas. 2019. The role of lender country factors in cross border bank lending. *International Review of Financial Analysis*. in press. [CrossRef]

Bayazitova, Dinara, and Anil Shivdasani. 2011. Assessing TARP. *Review of Financial Studies* 25: 377–407. [CrossRef]

Berger, Allen N., and Christa H. S. Bouwman. 2013. How does capital affect bank performance during financial crises? *Journal of Financial Economics* 109: 146–76. [CrossRef]

Berger, Philip G., and Eli Ofek. 1996. Bustup takeovers of value-destroying diversified firms. *Journal of Finance* 51: 1175–200. [CrossRef]

Besanko, David, and George Kanatas. 1996. The regulation of bank capital: Do capital standards promote bank safety? *Journal of Financial Intermediation* 5: 160–83. [CrossRef]

Boot, Arnoud W. A., and Anjolein Schmeits. 2000. Market discipline and incentive problems in conglomerate firms with applications to banking. *Journal of Financial Intermediation* 9: 240–73. [CrossRef]

Breitenfellner, Bastian, and Niklas Wagner. 2010. Government intervention in response to the subprime financial crisis: The good into the pot, the bad into the crop. *International Review of Financial Analysis* 19: 289–97. [CrossRef]

Bremus, Franziska M. 2015. Cross-border banking, bank market structures and market power: Theory and cross-country evidence. *Journal of Banking & Finance* 50: 242–59. [CrossRef]

Bremus, Franziska, and Marcel Fratzscher. 2014. *Drivers of Structural Change in Cross-Border Banking Since the Global Financial Crisis*. DIW Berlin Discussion Paper No. 1411. Berlin: German Institute for Economic Research. [CrossRef]

Calomiris, Charles W., and Berry Wilson. 2004. Bank capital and portfolio management: The 1930s "capital crunch" and the scramble to shed risk. *Journal of Business* 77: 421–55. [CrossRef]

Cetorelli, Nicola, and Linda S. Goldberg. 2012a. Banking globalization and monetary transmission. *Journal of Finance* 67: 1811–43. [CrossRef]

Cetorelli, Nicola, and Linda S. Goldberg. 2012b. Follow the money: Quantifying domestic effects of foreign bank shocks in the great recession. *American Economic Review* 102: 213–18. [CrossRef]

Chakraborty, Indraneel, Rong Hai, Hans A. Holter, and Serhiy Stepanchuk. 2017. The real effects of financial (dis)integration: A multi-country equilibrium analysis of Europe. *Journal of Monetary Economics* 85: 28–45. [CrossRef]

Claessens, Stijn. 2006. *Competitive Implications of Cross-Border Banking*. Policy Research Working Paper 3854. Washington: World Bank. [CrossRef]

Cole, Harold L., and Maurice Obstfeld. 1991. Commodity trade and international risk sharing: How much do financial markets matter? *Journal of Monetary Economics* 28: 3–24. [CrossRef]

Committee on the Global Financial System. 2018. Structural Changes in Banking after the Crisis. CGFS Papers No 60, Bank for International Settlements. Available online: https://www.bis.org/publ/cgfs60.pdf (accessed on 3 April 2019).

Crouhy, Michel, and Dan Galai. 1991. A contingent claim analysis of a regulated depository institution. *Journal of Banking & Finance* 15: 73–90. [CrossRef]

Damanpour, Faramarz. 1986. A survey of market structure and activities of foreign banking in the US. *Columbia Journal of World Business* 21: 35–46.

de Blas, Beatriz, and Katheryn Niles Russ. 2010. FDI in the Banking Sector. Working Paper No. 10–8, University of California, Davis, Department of Economics, Davis, CA. Available online: https://ssrn.com/abstract=1647347 (accessed on 31 January 2019).

de Blas, Beatriz, and Katheryn Niles Russ. 2013. All Banks Great, Small, and Global: Loan Pricing and Foreign Competition. *International Review of Economics & Finance* 26: 4–24. [CrossRef]

Deng, Saiying, and Elyas Elyasiani. 2008. Geographic diversification, bank holding company value, and risk. *Journal of Money, Credit and Banking* 40: 1217–38. [CrossRef]

Denis, David J., Diane K. Denis, and Atulya Sarin. 1997. Agency problems, equity ownership, and corporate diversification. *Journal of Finance* 52: 135–60. [CrossRef]

Diamond, Douglas W. 1984. Financial intermediation and delegated monitoring. *Review of Economic Studies* 51: 393–414. [CrossRef]

Drucker, Steven, and Manju Puri. 2009. On loan sales, loan contracting, and lending relationships. *Review of Financial Studies* 22: 2835–72. [CrossRef]

Elsas, Ralf, Andreas Hackethal, and Markus Holzhäuser. 2010. The anatomy of bank diversification. *Journal of Banking & Finance* 34: 1274–87. [CrossRef]

Episcopos, Athanasios. 2008. Bank capital regulation in a barrier option framework. *Journal of Banking & Finance* 32: 1677–86. [CrossRef]

García-Herrero, Alicia, and Francisco Vázquez. 2013. International diversification gains and home bias in banking. *Journal of Banking & Finance* 37: 2560–71. [CrossRef]

Harris, Oneil, Daniel Huerta, and Thanh Ngo. 2013. The impact of TARP on bank efficiency. *Journal of International Financial Markets, Institutions & Money* 24: 85–104. [CrossRef]

Holmstrom, Bengt, and Jean Tirole. 1997. Financial intermediation, loanable funds, and the real sector. *Quarterly Journal of Economics* 112: 663–91. [CrossRef]

Iskandar-Datta, Mai, and Robyn McLaughlin. 2007. Global diversification: New evidence from corporate operating performance. *Corporate Ownership and Control* 4: 228–50. Available online: http://www.virtusinterpress.org/IMG/pdf/COC__Volume_4_Issue_4_Summer_2007_Continued_.pdf#page=68 (accessed on 31 January 2019). [CrossRef]

Kashyap, Anil K., Raghuram G. Rajan, and Jeremy C. Stein. 2002. Banks as liquidity providers: An explanation for the coexistence of lending and deposit-taking. *Journal of Finance* 57: 33–73. [CrossRef]

Kashyap, Anil K., Raghuram G. Rajan, and Jeremy C. Stein. 2008. Rethinking capital regulation. In *Maintaining Stability in a Changing Financial System*. Kansas City: Federal Reserve Bank of Kansas City, pp. 431–71.

Kasman, Adnan, Gokce Tunc, Gulin Vardar, and Berna Okan. 2010. Consolidation and commercial bank net interest margins: Evidence from the old and new European Union members and candidate countries. *Economic Modelling* 27: 648–55. [CrossRef]

Klein, Peter G., and Marc R. Saidenberg. 1998. Diversification, Organization, and Efficiency: Evidence from Bank Holding Companies. Working Paper, Federal Reserve Bank of New York, New York, NY. Available online: https://ssrn.com/abstract=98653 (accessed on 31 January 2019).

Koehn, Michael, and Anthony M. Santomero. 1980. Regulation of bank capital and portfolio risk. *Journal of Finance* 35: 1235–44. [CrossRef]

Laeven, Luc, and Ross Levine. 2007. Is there a diversification discount in financial conglomerates? *Journal of Financial Economics* 85: 331–67. [CrossRef]

Lin, Jyh-Horng, and Xuelian Li. 2017. Regulatory policies on Gramm-Leach-Bliley consolidation of commercial banking, shadow banking, and life insurance. *Journal of International Financial Markets, Institutions & Money* 50: 69–84. [CrossRef]

Merton, Robert C. 1974. On the pricing of corporate debt: The risk structure of interest rates. *Journal of Finance* 29: 449–70. [CrossRef]

Rajan, Murli, and Joseph Friedman. 1997. An examination of the impact of country risk on the international portfolio selection decision. *Global Finance Journal* 8: 55–70. [CrossRef]

Ronn, Ehud I., and Avinash K. Verma. 1986. Pricing risk-adjusted deposit insurance: An option-based model. *Journal of Finance* 41: 871–95. [CrossRef]

Rose, Andrew K., and Tomasz Wieladek. 2011. Financial Protectionism: The First Tests. NBER Working Paper No. 17073, National Bureau of Economic Research, Cambridge, MA. Available online: https://www.nber.org/papers/w17073.pdf (accessed on 31 January 2019).

Rossi, Stefania P.S., Markus S. Schwaiger, and Gerhard Winkler. 2009. How loan portfolio diversification affects risk, efficiency and capitalization: A managerial behavior model for Austrian banks. *Journal of Banking & Finance* 33: 2218–26. [CrossRef]

Saunders, Anthony, and Liliana Schumacher. 2000. The determinants of bank interest rate margins: An international study. *Journal of International Money and Finance* 19: 813–32. [CrossRef]

Tabak, Benjamin M., Dimas M. Fazio, and Daniel O. Cajueiro. 2011. The effects of loan portfolio concentration on Brazilian banks' return and risk. *Journal of Banking & Finance* 35: 3065–76. [CrossRef]

VanHoose, David. 2007. Theories of bank behavior under capital regulation. *Journal of Banking & Finance* 31: 3680–97. [CrossRef]

Winton, Andrew. 1999. Don't Put All Your Eggs in One Basket? Diversification and Specialization in Lending. Working Paper, University of Minnesota, Minneapolis, MN. Available online: https://ssrn.com/abstract=173615 (accessed on 31 January 2019).

Wong, Kit Pong. 1997. On the determinants of bank interest margins under credit and interest rate risks. *Journal of Banking & Finance* 21: 251–71. [CrossRef]

9

Selectivity and Market Timing Ability of Fund Managers: Comparative Analysis of Islamic and Conventional HSBC Saudi Mutual Funds

Marwa Zouaoui [1,2]

[1] Department of Finance, Northern Border University, Arar 91431, Saudi Arabia; marwazoua@gmail.com

[2] Department of Finance, ISG Tunisia, University of Tunis, Tunis 20000, Tunisia

Abstract: This paper empirically compares the market timing, the stock selection and the performance persistence of Islamic and conventional HSBC Saudi mutual funds by using monthly returns from April 2011 to December 2018. The data was grouped into five portfolios based on geographical investment basis (locally, Arab, internationally) and Sharia compliance (Islamic and conventional). The empirical results indicate that Islamic funds underperformed conventional funds internationally but not locally. Findings suggest that the market selectivity skills of managers in the Islamic funds are better than the conventional funds. In addition, only the managers of Saudi conventional funds investing internationally have a good market timing skills, thus, they are able to beat the market index by predicting its movements and buying and selling accordingly. Furthermore, this study gives a brief idea about the performance persistence of HSBC Saudi funds. The results confirm existence of the persistence performance when the funds do not apply Sharia law and when they are instead focused internationally.

Keywords: Islamic mutual funds; performance analysis; performance persistence; market timing; selectivity skills; GARCH modeling

JEL Classification: G23; G11; G12; G10; C52

---

1. Introduction

Analyzing the performance is extremely important to understand investment funds operation, but knowing if this performance could persist in the future is even more attracting. The study of performance persistence is crucial in explaining how investors should choose funds and develop their investment strategies.

The performance persistence of mutual funds is appreciated as a means of selecting funds that can beat the market. Many previous studies established that the persistent performance of investment funds managers is the result of two skills: market and timing selection ability. Some authors argued that the persistent or superior performance can be achieved if managers develop both selectivity and market anticipation strategies (Oliveira et al. 2019)

The ability of fund managers to outperform the benchmark has been well documented in the literature. However, the empirical findings are mixed. Academics and researchers present two opposite points of view. The first group have argued that the conventional funds outperform stock market (Bialkowski and Otten 2011; Kiymaz 2015). The second group have showed that the mutual funds cannot outperform their benchmark over long periods without this being attributed to the luck (Ramesh and Dhume 2014). The conclusions differ depending the data selected or country selected and the time horizon used, long or short term horizon. Additionally, many researchers found a significant difference between the performance persistence of conventional funds and religious mutual funds (Islamic, Jewish or Christian), ethical funds whether based on social responsibility principles; environmental considerations, good corporate governance. That is what caught our attention for investigating about non-conventional funds.

Over the last couple of years, investing in religious funds as well as the Islamic mutual funds have grown considerably around the world. The Islamic mutual funds can be seen as an alternative for investors used to invest in conventional funds. Islamic funds differ from traditional funds because they do not invest in companies whose operations, products or capital structure are contrary to Islamic law, as well as banking activity associated with conventional banking and all services for gambling, alcoholic beverages. Any investor, both Muslim and non-Muslim, are able to invest in Islamic mutual funds. Some investors have religious reasons and some others may regard these funds as socially responsible products. Other investors may invest in Islamic funds for diversification goals.

The increasingly growth of Islamic mutual funds attracted attention from academicians. Girard and Hassan (2008), Ashraf (2013), Mohamad and Ashraf (2015) and Omri et al. (2018) has focused on the performance of Islamic funds, and has compared these funds with their conventional counterparts across different countries. Mansor and Bhatti (2011) and Omri et al. (2018) showed that the Islamic funds are able to perform better than the conventional funds in the long term due to lower market risk globally, inferior cash outflows, lower volatility and investors' commitment to the funds.

Hayat and Kraeussl (2011) found that Islamic funds underperformed compared to the conventional funds in either bullish or bearish periods. These authors suggested that the worst performance of Islamic funds is due to poor management capacities of Islamic funds managers (as well as the market timing and stock selection abilities). However, many empirical studies (Hussein 2005; Girard and Hassan 2008) showed no difference in performance between the Islamic funds and their conventional counterparts.

The most empirical research that investigated about Islamic mutual funds still do not provide a definite answer to this most critical question: are the management ability of manager in Islamic mutual funds different from the conventional fund?

Globally, this insufficiency motivated us to compare the performance persistence and management capacities of Islamic mutual fund and conventional funds in Saudi Arabia. We are motivated to study Islamic funds in Saudi Arabia for several reasons. First, Saudi Arabia remains the key home country contributing to the biggest market share of the largest Islamic funds industry. Moreover, Saudi Islamic and other non-Islamic mutual funds have grown considerably. We are going to make a comparative study between this two funds category. Given the lack of information on the period studied for most data from Saudi funds, we had to choose a fund and how to present complete information spanning from 2011 to 2018. For this reason, in the present study, we selected the funds managed by HSBC Saudi Arabia. HSBC is a very experienced financial institution and has a good reputation managing funds in the world. Moreover, HSBC funds are well balanced and they can be divided into many sub-groups, namely, Local, International, Islamic and Conventional, consisting of the specific aim of the our study. The funds managed by HSBC are diversified in terms of investment goal classification, geographical focus and security type, thus, these different category funds give us a general view of some Saudi funds operating during 2008–2018.

This studies add to the existing literature by discussing the interaction between selectivity and market timing abilities of HSBC Saudi Islamic and conventional mutual funds. To contribute in the empirical work, we used the measure detailed by Ferson and Schadt (1996) and applied different information variables. To our knowledge, no studies have thus far used this method to assess Saudi mutual funds. An additional contribution to the existing literature is the analysis of the persistence of fund returns enables to help investor to draw conclusions about performance stability, the active managers' skill and help to choose the best funds that will outperform the market index.

The rest of the paper is organized as follows. Section 2 provides a review of the previous study focused on conventional and Islamic mutual funds. Section 3 explains empirical methodology and data choice. Section 4 provides empirical findings on market timing and selection ability of conventional and Islamic fund managers and discusses the results. Finally, Section 5 concludes.

2. Literature Revue

2.1. Active Management Strategies

Active management seeks to take advantage of potential market inefficiencies, with the aim of maximizing returns and minimizing risk, through different strategies such as Stock Picking (Selectivity of Securities) and Market Timing (Market Anticipation). This active management strategies aims to outperform the market, by taking active positions against a benchmark.

Several studies as well as Sharpe (1966) and Wermers (1999) have showed that the performance of the mutual funds is not greater than the normal average performance, and they have suggested that the mutual funds cannot beat the market, and they did not select the winning stocks and anticipated the tendency of the market.

In the same way, Treynor and Mazuy (1966) proposed a quadratic regression analysis method to measure timing ability of the 57 fund managers over the period 1983 to 1995. They showed only one fund, which had statistically significant market timing ability. The 56 other funds have no significant evidence of timing ability. These authors did not find evidence that fund managers can outperform the market. The work of Treynor and Mazuy (1966) made significant contributions to the literature on performance-based portfolio risk-return evaluation, which distinguishes a manager's abilities to act to information and the abilities to predict systematic risk premiums and adjust the portfolio. Their study has generated much more other literature.

Using the model proposed by Treynor and Mazuy (1966), Bollen and Busse (2001) measured the performance of 230 mutual funds. In this work, the authors used both the monthly and daily data. Bollen and Busse (2001) found that in shorter periods of analysis mutual funds present a higher market timing abilities. The conclusions of this research consisted of drawing attention to an important point of view. The high funds returns generate a cash inflow that could pose a challenge in terms of investment to achieve similar rates of return. This indicates that investor cash flow dynamics can negatively impact mutual fund performance. Thereafter, Bollen and Busse (2001) explained that data frequency can play an important role in detecting managers' abilities. The authors revealed that when they use the daily data, the results showed more funds exhibit timing ability than monthly data results. This finding may be due to market exposure decisions are probably taken shorter term for many funds. Apart from pioneering studies on the active management strategies, more recent literature Ramesh and Dhume (2014) confirmed the conclusion of Sharpe (1966), which suggests that the mutual funds cannot beat the market index. Conversely, Kiymaz (2015) and Rao et al. (2017) evaluated the performance of fund managers and found a significant ability to anticipate the market. Kiymaz (2015) showed that a manager who correctly forecasts the difference between the expected return of a diversified portfolio and the risk-free rate each year tends to outperform a naïve holder. Kiymaz (2015) showed that funds that invest in risky assets, with profitability above the risk-free rate, record a positive annual gap in favor of a perfect Market Timing. Rao et al. (2017) reported that Chinese funds can successfully outperform the market index and that fund managers have a positive market timing ability. They also found that unlike developed markets, Chinese funds do not have a persistence performance.

Apart from timing skills, the performance of fund managers also depends on the stock picking skills. The approach by Ferson and Schadt (1996) has incorporated publicly available information, and has attracted the attention of academics and researchers. This approach modifies traditional performance measures (timing and stock selection capacity) using the information variables such as interest rate and market dividend yield. Ferson and Schadt (1996) incorporated conditional models into the investigation of mutual fund performance selection and timing ability for 67 mutual funds. They found that the public information contained in this model control the biases that existed in traditional models, regarding market timing and stock picking ability.

Silva et al. (2003) used the conditional measure of Ferson and Schadt (1996) on European mutual funds. They provided that using conditional measures gives clearer results than unconditional measures. According to these researchers, the European funds are generally unable to beat their benchmark. Elton et al. (2012), using the same model, found a slight presence of market timing. Clare et al. (2016) measured the performance and management capabilities of US, UK and Canadian fund managers using the same measure as Ferson and Schadt (1996). Overall, whether they applied a yield-based method or a farm-based test method, their results showed a lower capacity of funds to outperform the benchmark and to anticipate market change.

Christopherson et al. (1999) chose two information variables, the dividend yield (dividend/price), and the lagged level of short-term treasury bill (TB) yields. These authors suggest that each variable is evaluated by its expected (average) value. These measurements can be applied to single-factor models, such as the Capital Asset Pricing Model (CAPMF), or multi-factor models or to Market Timing (Treynor-Mazuy) measures. The authors suggested that investors should evaluate the manager's return series using public information.

Coggins et al. (2009) measured the performance of mutual funds using a daily data with a bivariate GARCH framework, which in particular makes it possible to condition the beta and the specific risk of mutual funds. They found similar results to those of Ferson and Schadt (1996). The conditional alpha and global performances with GARCH are considerably better than those estimated with other parameters and they persist over time. The results will be justified by the existence of a negative relation between the conditional beta of mutual funds and the market premium. Ferson and Warther (1996) provided two explanations for this negative relationship (Marhfor 2016). Firstly, this correlation can be explained by the emergence of new players, and therefore, new cash flows that are likely to change the composition of mutual funds and consequently to modify their exposure to risk. Secondly, the negative relationship may be related to the impact of transformation in the risk measures of the securities that make up the funds.

Other researchers used different measures to evaluate performance and detected the management abilities. To estimate the performance of South African equity funds and to determine the relationship between the independent and dependent variables, Tan (2015) used a multiple regression analysis (Sharpe ratio (Sharpe 1966), Treynor ratio (Treynor 1965), Jensen's alpha (Jensen 1967) methods, Treynor and Mazuy (1966) and Henriksson and Merton (1981)). The author suggested that South African fund managers could not display a good performance both in market timing abilities and selection skills.

For examining the risk-adjusted performance and selectivity skills of Indian mutual funds, Sharma and Verma (2018) used divers models as well as Sharpe Ratio, Treynor Ratio, Jensen Measure and Fama Measures. They found that only the Fama measures indicated the positive selectivity performance of Indian mutual funds over a period of 2008 to 2018.

For investigating the effects of information asymmetry on market timing in the mutual fund industry, Tchamyou et al. (Tchamyou et al. 2018) used a panel of 1488 active mutual funds for during the period of 2004–2013, and based on endogeneity-robust Difference and System Generalized Method of Moments. The dataset is decomposed into five market fundamentals (i) equity, (ii) fixed income, (iii) allocation, (iv) alternative and (v) tax preferred mutual funds. They made several conclusions. The authors documented that funds with low-grade risk exposure can outperform their benchmarks with superior exposure to fluctuation in market conditions. Agarwal and Pradhan (2018) examined the existence of superior performance of Indian mutual funds in India with several models, using unconditional models of Treynor and Mazuy (1966) and Henriksson and Merton (1981). They extended these models by incorporating Fama–French–Carhart-factors-based models. They showed evidence of selectivity and timing abilities in Indian open-ended fund managers. According to these authors the explanation of their results is that the selection of titles takes place much more frequently than at monthly intervals. The absolute superior returns are lower for multifactor models. Pilbeam and Preston (2019) studied the performance of 355 actively managed Japanese Mutual Funds between 2011 and 2016. Using Jensen's alpha measures, the authors found that the Japanese Mutual Funds underperformed the benchmark. When the Treynor and Mazuy measure were used, the results showed that only 33 funds have significant positive market timing ability which was largely offset by 31 funds with significant negative timing ability.

2.2. Persistent Performance

The evaluation of active management takes into account of the persistence of funds' abnormal returns relative to their benchmarks; if there is low persistence, the abnormal performance are probably motivated by luck rather than skill.

Before the work of Carhart (1997) the majority of studies had reported that past performance can weakly predict future performance. However, Carhart (1997) found evidence of persistence performance in American mutual funds. Carhart (1997) included the 'Momentum' variable, which refers to the risk premium on the past performance. This factor represents the difference between the returns of the portfolios with a high historical return and the returns of the portfolios with a low historical return. Indeed, Carhart (1997) indicated that there managers are not able to maintain a good performance without taking more risk. This study further suggested that underperforming stocks and those that perform very well over the last six months retain the same trends in the future. Carhart (1997) showed that funds with the worst recent performance continued to offer terrible returns, which momentum and expenses could not fully explain. Differences in style, luck, skill and cost orientation determine the relative performance of the funds. Therefore, the performance gives an idea about managerial skills. However, there is no good skill in creating long-term performance persistence, as differences in style and expense may also create this effect. Funds with long-term positive past experience tend to have lower fees than losers, and these cost differences are likely to persist.

Working on 18 stock markets in Asia, Latin America and Eastern Europe, Cakici et al. (2013) used Carhart (1997) four-factor model to evaluate persistence performance of mutual funds. They concluded that persistence is more significant in smaller companies.

Since the work by Carhart (1997), several studies has been done on persistence in the performance of mutual funds, but the finding is mixed. Bollen and Busse (2001) documented that the Mutual funds with a past higher (lower) performance tend to offer higher (lower) performance in the future. However, Bialkowski and Otten (2011), Brown and Goetzmann (1995) found evidence of predictability in the performance of mutual funds over short time horizons. Whereas, Grinblatt and Titman (1992) showed that the performance of mutual fund persist only in the long term. Brown and Goetzmann (1995) confirmed that the persistence of performance depends on the period under study.

However, Carhart (1997) provide evidence that the effect of "hot hands" is due to the persistence of expenditure ratios and the adoption of stability strategies. Papadamou and Siriopoulos (2004) showed that the performance of US funds investing in Europe is lower than the benchmark (Eurostoxx), and in the most case, the phenomenon of "hot hands" does not persist. Mutual funds that have performed well over the past five months will continue to outperform over the next four months.

Papadamou et al. (2017) investigated how mutual funds performed in Japan before and after the 2008 outburst of the global financial crisis. The authors showed that active management over the two periods does not add significant value to the mutual fund performance. Thus, no funds could outperform the market index.

More recently, Mateus et al. (2019) performed research using the 817 active UK long-only equity mutual funds during the period 1992–2016. They documented that the funds is with the most significant positive alpha that was already recorded a good performance in the previous year. In terms of parametric and non-parametric measurements, these funds showed a persistence of performance.

By contrast, several authors did not find persistence in the performance of mutual funds over time (see Christensen 2005; Huang and Mahieu 2012; Rao et al. 2016, 2017). Using parametric and non-parametric methodologies, Christensen (2005), evaluated performance persistence of 47 Danish mutual funds. They concluded that in general Danish mutual funds perform neutrally, returns are non-persistent and funds don't have the timing and selectivity skills.

Rao et al. (2017) evaluated the equity funds in China. Appling the capital asset pricing model (CAPM) and the Carhart four-factor model, the authors showed that the equity funds outperform their benchmark but they do not find any evidence of persistence in fund performance.

2.3. Previous Literature on Islamic Mutual Funds

Islamic funds are in full compliance with Sharia, which formally prohibits investing in companies engaged in noncompliant operations. In order to fulfill with the needs of investors who wish to comply with the Sharia rules, the specialists have relaxed the ideal form of Sharia investments and formulated a relatively more balanced investment criterion, known as Sharia-compliant equity investment guidelines.

The diversity of Sharia selection criteria extends the selection choices of Sharia candidates. However, there are several problems with the investor who prefers Islamic investment. First, the Sharia investor always has specific criteria with the constraint of the opportunity cost. Secondly, there is currently no mutual agreement on the use of financial screens.

Mansor and Bhatti (2016) argued that the goal of the Islamic mutual funds is to meet ethical and religious objectives without harming the conventional needs in terms of liquidity, diversification and return. Conversely, according to other authors (Boo et al. 2017), Islamic mutual funds are a means of hedging against financial crises, because they invest in higher liquid and low-leverage stocks, likely to outperform the conventional benchmarks.

The most research in Islamic finance have always been interested in investigating the question whether the strategies pursued by Islamic funds help them to beat the market index and to perform better their conventional counterparts in terms of performance and active management strategies.

Recently, research on Islamic Mutual Funds has grown considerably and gained momentum in the global market. Several studies concentrated on risk and return behavior comparisons between conventional and Islamic mutual funds and found quiet mixed results. Some of them did not find any significant difference between performance Islamic fund and the performance of their counterparts. Others studies have shown that these funds record performances and totally different management styles. As a whole, we can say that the empirical literature on Islamic mutual funds performance analysis is still in its infancy. Girard and Hassan (2008) used different performance measures for compare five FTSE (Financial Times Stock Exchange) Islamic indices and five conventional benchmarks (MSCI) (Morgan Stanley Capital International). They did not find a significant performance differential or managerial capabilities between Islamic and conventional funds (Dow Jones Islamic indices and Morgan and Stanley conventional indices). Consistent with other studies, the study of Hassan and Girard (2010) produced similar evidence to that of Girard and Hassan (2008). They concluded that there was no difference in performance between Islamic and traditional funds in Malaysia. Al Rahahleh and Bhatti (2017) compared Islamic and conventional funds in Saudi Arabia and they found that Sharia compliant funds did not outperform or underperform their benchmark (the S&P Saudi Arabia Domestic Sharia Index).

On the other hand, other studies such as Hussein (2005) have shown that compliance with Sharia law has a negative impact on fund performance during downturns. Other researchers explain this underperformance of Islamic funds compared to traditional funds. They suggested that this underperformance is due to the many restrictions imposed by Sharia. Merdad et al. (2010) studied the performance of Saudi funds managed by HSBC. They found that Islamic funds underperformed conventional funds during overall and bullish periods, but outperformed during periods of economic downturn and financial crisis. In addition, they found that Islamic HSBC funds managers have a good ability of market timing and selectivity skills only during the downturn and the conventional funds have a significant ability of market timing and selectivity skills only during the bullish period. Hayat and Kraeussl (2011) found that Islamic funds have performed worst in either economic scenario, bullish or bearish period. They further suggested that managers of Islamic funds exhibit poor stock selection and market timing abilities. Rana and Akther (2015), by using different performance measures

(Sharp ratio, Jensen alpha, Treynor ratio), investigated the Pakistani Islamic and conventional funds. They employ The GARCH-M framework to investigate about risk-return trade-off in the context of both Islamic and conventional stock indices. They found that the Islamic stock index underperform their conventional counterparts due to availability of a smaller investment universe, increased monitoring costs and limited diversification. On the other hand, other researchers believe that Islamic investment offers a good economic and social sense to evaluate potential investments. Islamic ethical investors can side with their potential investments and their religious and ethical beliefs, which will not only give them peace of mind, but also a legal monetary reward (Rana and Akther 2015). Mansor and Bhatti (2016) found that IMF and CMF funds are able to outperform market performance throughout the overall study period. However, they showed that during financial crises and pre-crisis periods; Islamic funds did not outperform or underperform conventional funds. This study concluded that the performance of ethical funds is more persistent, especially during and after the crisis period. Elfakhani et al. (2007) argued that the ability to outperformance or underperformance the market depends on the measure and benchmark used for the performance evaluation.

According to the empirical literature the excess performance of investment funds had been attributed to management skills and to selection criteria if an ability inherent in selecting the right securities (selection) and choosing the best timing. The existing literature focuses primarily on determining abnormal performance (stock selection and market anticipation) using models such as Treynor and Mazuy (1966) and Jensen (1967). Mohamad and Ashraf (2015) suggested that the stock selection and rebalancing of funds to comply with Islamic laws may result in superior returns for the investing public. The results between the Islamic funds from developed markets (North America and Europe) and those from emerging markets are totally different. Mohamad and Ashraf (2015) suggested that Sharia law helps the Islamic funds to select the ideal stocks for example, the stocks of firm who are not financially distressed, are growth oriented and are exhibiting a positive momentum. However, with using both parametric and non-parametric based tests, their results indicated that the Islamic funds showed a negative significant market timing ability. The authors argued that Islamic indices do not necessarily have a higher risk or a lower diversification than conventional indices. The difference in performance is most pronounced in developed regions where leverage plays a key role in companies' capital structure. In addition, the importance of growth and momentum factors is more evident among the S&P Dow Jones Islamic index that use the market value of stocks as a denominator in the calculation of financial filter ratios. There is not a big difference between emerging market Islamic index returns and conventional indices.

Abdullah et al. (2007) studied the performance of Islamic and conventional unit trust funds in Malaysia. They used the Treynor and Mazuy (1966) model and found that Islamic funds performed better than conventional funds only during bearish period. However, during the bullish period, conventional funds outperformed the Islamic funds. They concluded that there was little evidence of market timing and stock picking ability in Malaysian mutual funds.

Ashraf (2013) found that Saudi IMFs perform better than conventional funds from 2007 to 2011. Managers of Islamic mutual funds have a better selection ability than managers of conventional funds. However, in Islamic mutual funds, the managers do not have superior market timing capabilities. In contrast, managers of conventional funds not only exhibit a poor stock selection ability but also exhibit significant negative market timing ability. The combination of superior stock selection ability of Islamic mutual funds and the negative market timing ability of conventional funds suggests that Islamic mutual funds offer better hedging opportunity to investors during periods of economic downturn.

Concentrated on only after financial crisis, Omri et al. (2018) compared the risk-adjusted performance and investment style of Islamic mutual funds and conventional funds. They applied models of absolute and relative risk-adjusted measures with single factor (Jensen) and multifactor (Carhart). To obtain diverse portfolios, they used geographical and religious diversification of the sample. Their results showed that the Islamic portfolios were able to outperform the conventional portfolios given similar risk exposure, and produced comparable results under lower market risk globally. Omri et al. (2018) concluded that respect for Sharia did not have a negative impact on the performance of Islamic funds and did not entail any additional risk for holding such investments. This suggests that Islamic funds in Saudi Arabia are very competitive, they take reasonable risks and generate respectable returns.

Using the performance measurement approaches of Carhart (1997) and Ferson and Schadt (1996), Bauer et al. (2007) provide evidence that risk-adjusted returns between conventional and ethical Canadian mutual funds do not differ. Moreover, Chau et al. (2003) found that management skills do not extremely matter, and they showed no significant differences between styles.

2.4. A Contextual Overview of the Saudian Mutual Fund Industry

This paper focuses the critical investigation of Islamic Saudi mutual funds. Saudi Arabia is an interesting context for further investigating the performance and active management for several reasons. Firstly, Saudi Arabia is still the biggest market for mutual funds in GCC countries and accounts for more than 80% of the total funds market in GCC region (Ernst and Young 2015). In 2017 in Saudi Arabia, there exist more than 275 mutual funds managed by more than 40 fund managers. Secondly, it is considered one of the few countries that strictly adhere to Sharia rules and follow regulations derived from Islamic law. Moreover, more than 70% of the mutual funds operating in Saudi Arabia are Sharia compliant, compared with just 21% in the rest of the GCC region (Ernst and Young 2015). This means that the performance and management of these funds can be different from their conventional counterparts and depends essentially on fund geographical focus. Thirdly, the Saudi mutual fund industry has been growing considerably in the last couple of years. According to the official web of Saudi stock market TADAWUL, in 2015 Saudi equity mutual funds based on geographical location present 46% of locally mutual funds, 34% internationally focused and 20% are invested in the Arab or GCC countries. According to Saudi Arabian Monetary Authority (SAMA), the total value of assets under management (AUM) of Saudi funds augmented by 25.5 percent year-on-year (YoY) by the end of 2017. The Saudi market is intensively participates in activities aimed at strengthening financial liberalization. This market continually attempts to improve the efficiency of the market and the corporate governance of companies; however, it suffers from some limitations existing in emerging markets, such as lack of complete and free information, transaction costs and illiquidity of stocks (El-Masry and El-Mosallamy 2016). To the best of our knowledge, some research on Saudi Arabia based IMFs performances is available, but little work has been done to provide a comprehensive managers ability to beat a market and to have a good and persistent performance and analysis of both IMFs and conventional funds offered in Saudi Arabia.

3. Data and Estimation Methodology

3.1. Sample and Data

The objective of the present study is to following and to expanding the work of Merdad et al. (2010). The previous study of Merdad et al. (2010) investigated the impact of Sharia screening on the performance of HSBC mutual funds. However, this paper expanded their results by examining the selectivity and market timing abilities among Islamic and conventional HSBC funds.

For this study, our data consist of 15 mutual funds managed by HSBC spanning from 2011 to 2018. Taking into account the survivor bias, we excluded those portfolios that did not have a complete historical data from April 2011 until December 2018. We also considered in our study the population that includes only the surviving funds on our study period and excludes from our sample those who were present at the beginning of sample period, but who did not remain until the end. We then eliminated from the total HSBC-managed funds those that were closed before 2018 and those created after 2011, hence, obtaining the 15 funds.

We calculated the monthly returns of Saudi mutual funds from their net asset value that have been provided by the official site of the Saudi Stock Exchange (Tadawul) (www.tadawul.com.sa), the official site of HSBC Saudi Arabia Limited (www.hsbcsaudi.com) and the Zawya database. Moreover, the funds management by HSBC can be divided into five sub-groups, Local, Arab, Global, Islamic and Conventional, consisting of the particular aims of this study. Based on their type and geographical focus, these 15 Saudi mutual funds are grouped into equally balanced portfolios and divided into five subgroups based on geographical focused and Sharia compliance: Local/Islamic, local/conventional, global/Islamic and global/conventional, and Arabic Islamic. We did not find any Arab conventional fund managed by HSBC between 2011 and 2018. All these portfolios are denominated in Saudi currency (RAS) and USD converted into a single currency, USD.

For more correct and unbiased results, each portfolio was compared to the conventional and Islamic indices that have the same geographical focus as the examined portfolio. The selected funds and the used benchmarks are given in Table 1. We employed six different market indices. These indices diversified under two main classifications. The first classification is the Islamic indices: (1) S&P Quality Saudi Arabia Sharia Index, (2) S&P Pan Arab Composite Sharia, (3) S&P Global BMI Sharia. The second classification is the conventional indices: (1) S&P Pan Arab Composite S&P Saudi, (2) Arabia total return index and (3) S&P GLOBAL 1200.

Table 1. Descriptive portfolios and benchmarks.

Portfolios	Funds Benchmarks
LS: Local Sharia	LSBM: S&P Quality Saudi Arabia Sharia Index
LC: Local Conventional	LCBM: S&P Saudi Arabia Total Return Index:
AS: Arab Sharia	ASBM: S&P Pan Arab Composite Sharia:
IC: International Conventional	ACBM: S &P Pan Arab Composite:
IS: International Sharia	INSBM: S&P GLOBAL 1200:
	INCBM: S&P Global BMI Sharia:

Note: The table presents different five open-ended mutual fund portfolios managed by HSBC over the period April 2011 to December 2018. We are divide the funds managed by HSBC into three geographical focus (Arab-local-international) and Sharia compliance focus (Islamic–conventional).

3.2. Methodology

In order to evaluate the performance of the 15 HSBC funds and to assess the ability of their managers to outperform the market through selectivity and market anticipation, we used the model of Ferson and Schadt (1996). Each portfolio was initially examined against two market indices, the Islamic and the conventional indices.

We chose the model proposed by Ferson and Schadt (1996) for several reasons. Firstly, this model takes into account the manager's ability to select and anticipate both the best stocks. Secondly, the method is able to estimate the persistence of the performance of these funds over time.

The finding of Ferson and Schadt (1996) are very relevant to our research. First, they found that the level of risk to which funds are exposed varies in response to public information. Second, they observed a significant difference between conditionally measured and traditionally measured performance.

Based on a daily publication of the Saudi stock exchange market, we have monthly adjusted the net asset value (NAV) that will help us to calculate the $R_{p,t}$:

$$R_{p,t} = \frac{(NAV_{it} - NAV_{it-1}) + D_t}{NAV_{it-1}} R_{it} \tag{1}$$

where:

$R_{i,t}$: The return of the funds i in the month t.
NAV_{it} and NAV_{it-1}: Net asset values of the fund i, respectively, at the end of the month t and $t-1$.
D_t: Dividend paid out for Fund i at month t.

$$R_{it} = 1/n \sum_{i-1}^{n} R_{\mathrm{i},t} \tag{2}$$

R_{it} : averege return of the portfolio p during the month t.

Therefore, the model by Ferson and Schadt (1996) was constructed as follows:

$$R_{p,t} = \alpha_p + \beta_1 R_{m,t} + \beta_2 R^2_{m,t} + \beta_3 (Zt_{-1} R_{m,t}) + \varepsilon_{p,t} \quad (3)$$

where:

$R_{P,t}$ represents the average rate of return on portfolio "p" in month t. $R_{m,t}$ is the average market Benchmark.

α_p and β_1 are the coefficient indicate the stock selection, and the systematic risk. If the α is positive, the fund manager has an ability to forecast security prices. On the other hand, if the α is negative, the manager of the mutual funds is not doing well in funds selection.

β_2 is the market timing ability. If $\beta_2 > 0$ and is significant, the fund manager has an ability to beat the market. β_3 captures the response of the fund's managers to public information (Z_{t-1}).

$\beta_3(Z_{t-1} R_{m,t})$ controls the public information effects.

$\varepsilon_{p,t}$ The residual excess return of the portfolio p.

Our model is different from that of Ferson and Schadt (1996) because validation will focus only on two information variables, while Ferson and Schadt (1996) introduced four information variables.

Indeed, the main difficulty when using this model will be to determine the information vector that will be used. We chose the variable Ramadan effect and the variable treasury bills at three months, as an information variable. Regarding our choice the information variable, first, the value of the lagged level of short-term treasury bill (TB) yields is similar to the study for Christopherson et al. (1999) and Ferson and Schadt (1996). Second, the choice of Ramadan effect as well as a dummy variable is motivated by the fact that this event could have an influence on the performance, behavior and abilities of the agent who manage the funds in a Muslim country.

Ferson and Schadt (1996) have shown that the model estimated by OLS is equivalent to an estimate by the method of Hansen (1982). For our case we will estimate the model of Ferson and Schadt (1996) by following the GARCH (1.1) process for each portfolio. In order to assess the Saudi manager market capacity we use:

$$R_{p,t} = \alpha_p + \beta_1 R_{m,t} + \beta_2 R^2_{m,t} + \beta_3 (T_{Bt-52} R_{m,t}) + \beta_4 (D_{ramadan} R_{m,t}) + \varepsilon_{p,t} \quad (4)$$

If $\beta_2 > 0$ and significant then the fund manager has a capacity to beat the market.

β_3 and β_4 indicating the response of the fund's managers to public information.

T_{Bt-52} is the return of three month treasury bills for the previous years.

$D_{ramadan}$ is a dummy variable captures the Ramadan effect on return. where $D_{ramadan} = 1$ if it is Ramadan month or zero otherwise.

3.3. Hypothesis

The aims of this study were twofold. Firstly, identify the investment strategy of Islamic and conventional mutual funds managed by HSBC and the ability of Islamic portfolio and conventional portfolios managers to anticipate market movements and select the best stocks at the right time. Secondly, this research addresses the persistence of the different portfolios. Based on the reviewed theoretical and empirical literature on Saudi Arabia and Mutual funds, we investigate the following hypothesis.

Hypothesis 1. *Both Islamic and conventional portfolios reveal similar market timing and selectivity skills on the local and global and Arabic basis.*

Hypothesis 2. *The market ability (selectivity and timing) of Islamic portfolios manager are more sensitive to Ramadan effect than conventional portfolios, on locally, globally and Arabic bases.*

Hypothesis 3. *Both Islamic and convention portfolios perform persistently.*

3.4. Descriptive Statistics

Table 2 presents the summary statistics on HSBC Islamic and Conventional mutual funds and the associated benchmarks based on the monthly aggregated return funds from April 2011 to December 2018. The Islamic and Conventional fund returns are calculated based on an equally weighted portfolio of all funds belong to each of the portfolios. Panel A reports the descriptive statistic for five portfolio divided into sub-groups, Local, Arab and Global; each group was also divided into both Islamic and non-Islamic portfolio. Panel B reports the same descriptive statistic for six market indices: S&P Quality Saudi Arabia Sharia Index (locally focused on Islamic index), S&P Saudi Arabia total return index (locally focused on conventional index), S&P Pan Arab Composite Sharia (Arab focused on Islamic index), S&P Pan Arab Composite (Arab focused on conventional index), S&P GLOBAL 1200 (international focused on conventional index) and S&P Global BMI Sharia 1200 (international focused on Sharia index).

Table 2. Summary statistics on return performance on Islamic and conventional HSBC funds.

Portfolio	MEAN	STDV	MIN	MAX	MEDIAN
Local Sharia (LS)	0.0333	5.52	−34.9850	22.107	0.1063
Local Conventional(LC)	0.3143	6.1713	−20.7901	13.314	0.4755
Arab Sharia (AS)	−0.0361	1.4028	−8.8396	8.8043	−0.0114
Inter Sharia (IS)	0.2084	2.9184	−9.2039	5.5153	0.6625
Inter Conventional (IC)	0.05897	0.16482	−0.4185	0.6269	0.0054
BENCHMARK	**MEAN**	**STDV**	**MIN**	**MAX**	**MEDIAN**
S&P Quality Saudi Arabia Sharia Index (ISBM)	0.6847	5.1955	−18.6807	16.4436	0.6525
S&P Saudi Arabia Total Return Index (LCBM)	0.4968	5.9591	−18.7462	18.6326	1.1004
S&P Pan Arab Composite Sharia (ASBM)	0.2582	4.6255	−18.6213	18.9324	0.2855
S &P Pan Arab Composite (ACBM)	0.1511	3.4526	−11.1467	8.2988	0.4434
S&P GLOBAL 1200 (ISBM)	0.4958	3.6368	−10.8828	10.3697	1.1637
S&P Global BMI Sharia (ICBM)	0.5672	3.4808	−9.0738	10.0082	1.2564

Note: This table provides the descriptive statistics on the sample of the five equally weighted portfolios managed by HSBC funds. These portfolios are formed based on the following characteristics of the funds geographical focus (local, Arab and conventional) funds and Sharia compliancy (Islamic and conventional). The model is significant at 10%, 5% and 1%, respectively.

According to this table, we can show some preliminary findings. First, the monthly returns of the portfolios managed by HSBC over a period of eight years are significant. We note that all portfolios have a positive average return with the exception of the Arab Sharia portfolio. It is clear that the portfolios studied achieve significantly lower averages than corresponding benchmarks. However, those who achieved the highest average returns over the period of analysis are local portfolios, either Islamic or conventional portfolios. Indeed, these two categories base the exception and record a higher standard deviation than their benchmarks. Table 2 also documents the local conventional funds have higher performance with a higher risk that local Sharia portfolio. However, the international Sharia portfolio has higher performance with a higher risk that international conventional portfolio. The benchmarks showed a similar pattern. All international, local and Arab portfolios underperformed their corresponding benchmarks with a smaller mean.

Our results seem to contradict those of Omri et al. (2018), according to whom the Islamic funds outperformed their conventional counterparts. However, our results agree with Merdad et al. (2010), who found that during the full analysis period the Saudi Islamic mutual funds managed by HSBC unperformed than their conventional counterparts.

Following Merdad et al. (2010) and Omri et al. (2018), as a second step, we calculated the absolute performance difference between Islamic and conventional portfolios and their index. We found that the differences mean between portfolios and different benchmarks are not statistically significant (Table 3).

Table 3. Mean difference.

		MEAN DIFF	T-STAT	F-TRST	P-VALUE
LS	LC	−0.2843	0.6330	0.0350	0.5509
LS	ISBM	−0.6515	0.4602	0.0983	0.4597
LS	LCBM	−0.4660	0.5968	0.0000	0.6198
LC	ISBM	−0.3657	0.6689	0.6461	0.9096
LC	LCBM	−0.1820	0.8441	0.0000	0.2470
ISBM	LCBM	0.1840	0.8110	0.0000	0.1689
AS	ASBM	−0.2480	0.5875	0.0000	0.5583
AS	ACBM	−0.0990	0.4855	0.0000	0.6285
ASBM	ACBM	0.2660	0.1791	0.0054	0.8583
IS	IC	0.2211	0.4979	0.0000	0.6198
IC	ISBM	−0.4361	1.1688	0.0000	0.2455
IC	ICBM	−0.5081	1.3867	0.0000	0.1689
IS	ISBM	−0.2870	0.5986	0.0350	0.5509
IS	ICBM	−0.3590	0.7424	0.0983	0.4597
ISBM	ICBM	−0.0720	0.1139	0.6461	0.9096

In order to check the dependence between the different portfolios as well as the portfolio and their benchmarks, at the same time, we did a correlation analysis. According to Table 4, we found that most Islamic and conventional and their benchmarks have statistically significant positive relationships overall. These results confirmed the findings of Mansor and Bhatti (2011) and Omri et al. (2018). However, the International Islamic benchmarks (ISBM) and the International conventional benchmarks (ICBM) were strongly positively correlated with each other. We can conclude that this combination is almost a perfect correlation.

Table 4. Person correlation.

		Panel 1		
		Local		
Portfolio	**LS**	**LC**	**LSBM**	**LCBM**
LS	1.00			
LC	0.54	1.00		
LSBM	−0.092	−0.26	1.00	
LCBM	−0.027	−0.09	0.08	1.00
		Panel 2		
		International		
Portfolio	**IS**	**IC**	**ISBM**	**ICBM**
IS	1			
IC	−0.043	1		
ISBM	0.555	−0.026	1	
ICBM	0.503	0.0438	0.927	1

Note: The model is significant at 10%, 5% and 1%, respectively.

4. Results and Discussion

4.1. *The Market Timing and the Selection Skills of Islamic and Conventional Funds*

Table 5 reports the result for the five portfolios benchmarked each time against two different market indices. Following Omri et al. (2018) the performance of each funds is regressed against the relevant benchmark. Focusing on Table 5, results indicate that 70% of funds operated by HSBC have significant statistics market selection.

Table 5. Regression analysis on market timing and selectivity.

Portfolio	LS		LC		AS		IC		IS	
Benchmark	LIBM	LCBM	LCBM	LSBM	ASBM	ACBM	INCBM	INSBM	INSBM	INCBM
α	1.1480 **	1.0053 *	0.9791	0.9773	−0.2200 ***	−0.3070 ***	0.001 ***	0.0070 ***	0.2280	0.4180 ***
t(α)	2.0733	1.8146	1.4659	1.5492	−3.4122	−4.4068	20.93	26.69	1.0802	6.635
β1	−0.0260	0.06140	0.2070	0.4160	−0.0330	0.1310 ***	0.000 ***	−5.780	1.0870 ***	1.1410 ***
t (β1)	−0.090	0.3283	0.6424	1.1994	−2.2475	3.222	8.879	−0.30485	172.68	9.738
β2	−0.012	−0.007	−0.013	−0.006	0.003	0.002	0.000 ***	0.000 ***	-0.023 ***	−0.029 ***
t (β2)	−0.560	−0.7294	−1.1297	−0.3194	0.7293	0.4462	32.767	−6.5763	−2.5502	−3.7936
β3	−0.124	−0.155	−0.361	−0.640 **	−0.002	−0.096 ***	0.001 ***	−0.003 ***	−0.512 ***	−0.644 ***
t (β3)	−0.451	−1.0545	−1.471893	−1.852392	−1.0153	−2.7967	8.839	−9.2097	−7.1719	−8.1524
β4	−0.456	−0.057	0.041	−0.496	0.026	0.015	0.000 **	0.000	−0.108	0.095
t (β4)	−0.513	−0.1260	0.1199	−0.7694	0.4929	0.2940	−2.0016	−0.8922	−0.5304	0.5549
α 0	19.083 ***	16.809 ***	2.804	1.246	0.192	0.221 ***	0.000	0.000	0.053	3.376 ***
t (α0)	2.3118	3.2372	0.5877	0.3514	1.4568	2.773	−0.0032	−0.3798	1.0698	2.686
α'1	0.242 *	0.329 ***	0.054	0.075	3.601 ***	3.459 ***	51.024 ***	16.575 ***	−0.086 ***	0.650 **
t (α'1)	1.6785	3.2033	0.5977	0.8979	3.780	4.084	9.388	6.3847	−4.4875	2.0854
β'	−0.125	−0.063	0.867 ***	0.903 ***	0.000	−0.002	0.000	0.014 **	1.082 ***	−0.108
t (β')	−0.300	−0.2617	4.1257	5.5738	−0.0030	−0.0851	−0.1107	2.0492	29.796	−0.9283
R2	0.119	0.017	0.117	0.646	0.002	0.006	0.113	0.104	0.231	0.127

Note: this table presents the performance of the 15 portfolios managed by HSBC from April 2011 to December 2018. This table displays the results of the Ferson and Schadt (1996) model, where the α coefficient indicate the selectivity skills and the β2 coefficient indicate the market timing ability. The model is significant at * 10%, ** 5% and *** 1%.

The regression results show that the local Islamic portfolio (LS) have a statistically positive significant α. These results report the selectivity skills for local Sharia portfolio (LS) are lower when the portfolio is benchmarked against the S&P Saudi Arabia total return index (LCBM). Therefore, when benchmarked this portfolio with the S&P Quality Saudi Arabia Sharia Index (LSBM), we showed that the local Islamic portfolio have a significant and higher selectivity skills. This conclusion holds for the two different market benchmarks. On the other hand, local conventional portfolios (LC) generally do not reflect any evidence for a managers selectivity skills even when using two different market indices.

This finding indicates that market selection skills of local Islamic portfolio (LS) are stronger than the local conventional portfolio (LC). The managers of Saudi Islamic portfolios (LS) are able to take advantage of earnings anomalies, and thus, they make the right choice among stocks and sectors of activity. Our results specify that local Islamic funds are highly competitive and generate good returns with reasonable risk. The result may indicates the presence of home bias towards Islamic assets, due to the fact that manager or investor prefer invest in Saudi Islamic companies how prohibit alcohol, pork products, Gambling and any other forms whose activities the Sharia Board feels are prejudicial to the interests of Islam or Muslims.

We observed that the HSBC managers invested locally performed better in stock selectivity skill. The Islamic funds can able to select the ideal stocks for example, the stocks of firm who are not financially distressed, are growth oriented and are exhibiting a positive momentum.

Using two different benchmarks, S&P GLOBAL 1200 (INSBM) and S&P Global BMI Sharia (INCBM), we found that the international conventional portfolio (IC) have a good capacities to forecast security prices. This same table reports that if the Arab Islamic portfolios present negative and statistically significant α, then these managers are not doing well in funds selection.

Nevertheless, when the S&P Global benchmark Sharia or S&P GLOBAL 1200 (INSBM) are used as international market index, the results indicate that international Islamic portfolios (IS) have a higher statistically positive significant α than the international conventional portfolio (IC). The results also provide evidence of better performance in stock selectivity skill of Islamic portfolios (IS) comparing to the international conventional portfolios (IC).

An overall sample reveals a significant stock selectivity of the HSBC funds' performance over the period of 2011 through 2018. Finally, 50% of the managers of these funds are able to take advantage of compensation anomalies and so they know how to make the right choice in the selection of securities and business sectors. These portfolios are able to generate higher excess returns than all the portfolios in the study.

The results of significant stock selectivity in Saudi Islamic portfolio are inconsistent with the finding of Hayat and Kraeussl (2011). The contrasting finding can be due to the shorter duration of the study period and the limited sample of Saudi mutual funds. However, the evidence of positive market selectivity of the fund managers supports the previous study by Omri et al. (2018), as they denoted that the Islamic funds are able to obtain superior return by investing in large, well-diversified corporations while applying the purification process through profits distribution.

In keeping with the approach of Ferson and Schadt (1996), positive and statistically significant β2 value indicate evidence of timing ability of the associated mutual funds. Negative significant β2 values may be interpreted as negative market timing. Table 5 reports a significant market timing ability coefficient for only 40% HSBC portfolios (as well as international funds; IC and IS).

When the international-focused conventional portfolio (IC) is benchmarked against two different Index, the results report a positive and statistically significant coefficient of timing skills at 1 percent. We conclude that on average the managers of HSBC conventional funds investing internationally have little market timing ability and selection skills. In addition, the managers of this portfolio have little capacity to beat the market index by predicting its movements and buying and selling accordingly.

However, the results show that there are differences in market timing between the Islamic and the conventional internationally-focused portfolios. We showed that Islamic internationally-focused portfolios (IS) present negative and statistically significant coefficient regardless of the choice of the benchmark portfolio. This negative value may be interpreted as the incapacity of (IS) fund manager to beat the market. Moreover, the (IS) fund managers tend to augment (reduce) their exposures to the market in question at a time when the market is declining (rising). This evidence about the poor market timing is consistent with research conducted by Fauziah et al. (2002), who failed to capture the contribution of a manager's timing activities to fund returns.

Furthermore, the results indicate evidence of differences in market timing skills between the Islamic and the conventional internationally-focused fund portfolios. The paper also provides evidence that the Conventional fund managers performing better in market timing ability (significant at 10%) in relation to the market performance. These results are consistent with the findings of research conducted by Hoepner et al. (2011) and Hayat and Kraeussl (2011). According to these authors, this insignificance of market timing can be recognized like the fact that the flow of Islamic funds is more stable than conventional funds, because on average the manager of Islamic funds select stock with long term perspectives and lower market risk.

Globally, the performance of the (IS) funds in stock selectivity skill is higher, and in market timing ability is slightly lower than its (IC) funds peers, with both statistically significant at 10%. Finally, it is evident that the investors are better off investing in international-focused conventional funds (IC) than international-focused Sharia funds (IS). This finding is due to the Sharia selection process and the way in which low-leverage firms are part of Islamic funds. This finding are inconsistent with the results of Treynor and Mazuy (1966) and Girard and Hassan (2008), who suggested that there are no differences in market timing skills between the Islamic and the conventional internationally-focused fund portfolios.

The inability to timing skills of the 60% other HSBC portfolios (LS; LC and AS) can be endorsed to the fact that the flow of local and Arab funds is more constant and persistent than HSBC international portfolios. Because investors in domestic and Arab funds are less sensitive to volatility of market returns, the manager chooses to invest in the long-term stocks.

Thus, regarding the first hypothesis, the results reveal that both Islamic and conventional portfolios have similar market timing and selectivity skills on the local and global and Arabic basis. Thus, the first hypothesis can be rejected, implying there is a statistically significant difference in terms of performance and strategy management between Islamic and conventional portfolios.

After that, we found strong evidence that the holy month of Ramadan has no affect on the market ability of HSBC portfolios, except on the international-focused conventional funds. The coefficient $\beta 4$, which reflects the response of the portfolio manager's beta to Ramadan effect is not statistically significant for 90% HSBC portfolios. According to these finding, no evidence was found to support the effect of Ramadan on the performance of the Islamic and conventional HSBC Saudi Fund.

For this reason, we can reject the second hypothesis, which was concerned with that the selectivity and market timing of HSBC Islamic portfolios are more sensitive to Ramadan effect than HSBC conventional portfolios. These results are inconsistent with the work of Mitchell et al. (2014), who suggested evidence for a significant Ramadan effect within Muslim majority countries and regions.

To take an account for Heteroscedasticity in the error term, we used the GARCH model. According to Panel 2, we find that the parameters α' and β' of ARCH and GARCH are statistically significant and all most case, that indicate volatility clustering effect. Furthermore the sum of GARCH and ARCH parameter are near of one indicating volatility persistence.

4.2. Persistence of Performance

In order, to clarify the phenomenon of persistence of performance of HSBC portfolio, we have applied a measurement model, which inspired by Grinblatt and Titman (1992). This regression is basically used to find out if past performance is a good predictor of future performance. This regression is presented as follows:

$$R_{p(t+1)} = \alpha''_p + \beta''_p R_{p(t)} + \varepsilon_p \quad (5)$$

where $R_{p(t+1)}$ *et* $R_{p(t)}$ represent the performance of each portfolio p in the periods $t + 1$ and t, respectively. The hypotheses tested were:

H'0: $\beta''_p = 0$

H'1: $\beta''_p \neq 0$

Thus, if we accept the null hypothesis, there is no relationship between performance ($t + 1$) and performance (t).

Alternatively, if we reject hypothesis H'0, there is a relationship between the performance ($t + 1$) and the performance (t).

Table 6 shows the performance persistence of 15 HSBC portfolios funds over a period from 2011 to 2018, measured through the simple regression presented previously in Equation (4). By looking at the coefficient β''_p we can conclude the performance of next month, as well as the persistence of performance.

Table 6. Performance persistence.

Portfolios	α''	t(α'')	β''	t (β'')	R2
LC	0.3165	0.4737	0.0182	0.1678	0.0003
LS	0.0226	0.0440	−0.1887 ***	−4.0294	0.0358
AS	−0.0316	−0.3010	−0.4484 ***	−15.4669	0.2034
IC	0.0604 **	1.7430	0.3017 ***	4.5690	0.0832
IS	0.1964	0.4757	0.1638	1.4494	0.0268

Note: this table estimates the persistence performance of the 5 portfolios through the coefficients β'' and α''. We used a simple regression: $R_{p(t+1)} = \alpha''_p + \beta''_p R_{p(t)} + \varepsilon_p$. The model is significant at * 10%, ** 5% and *** 1%.

According to the table below, we note that all portfolios managed by HSBC Saudi mutual funds present a coefficient β''_p different than zero; for this reason, we are able to reject hypothesis H'0 that implies that, there is a relationship between the performance ($t + 1$) and the performance (t). In spite of that this relationship does not give an answer about the existence of persistence.

From Table 6 we can show that 50% of portfolios have a significant β''_p coefficient at the 10 per cent level, as well as: international-focused conventional portfolio (IC), Arab sharia (AS) and Local Sharia (LS). Despite that, the international-focused conventional portfolio (IC) is the unique portfolio that has positive significant coefficients this means that, IC portfolio present a persistent performance during eight years. The managers of these portfolios have a certain degree of predictability of future performance, so they are able to maintain a certain stability in their performance. Moreover, the existence of performance persistence of (IC) confirms that the managers of this portfolio are encouraged to make their investment choices based on the historical performance. The performance persistence finding is considered as a test of manager's market ability to underperform the market index. Finally, our empirical results reported in Table 6 provide empirical evidence to reject hypothesis H3, because only a special case of conventional portfolios (as well as the IC portfolio) are able to present a stable performance and all Islamic portfolios are not able to perform significantly.

5. Conclusions

The main objective of this paper is to compare investment strategies and financial performance persistence of Islamic and conventional Saudi funds managed by HSBC Saudi Arabia limited for the period 2011–2018.

The study used a portfolios approach to help diversify away funds specific risks. The Saudi HSBC mutual funds are grouped into equally balanced portfolios and divided into five subgroups based on geographical focused and Sharia compliance: Local/Islamic, local/conventional, global/Islamic and global/conventional and Arabic Islamic.

The preliminary empirical findings of this work show that all international, local and Arab portfolios underperformed their corresponding benchmarks with a smaller mean. We showed that Saudi Islamic mutual funds managed by HSBC underperformed their conventional counterparts. However, to conclude about active management strategy we have using a qualitative method through a model based on Ferson and Schadt (1996) model, with different informational variables as well as a Ramadan effect and treasury bills.

We found that the selectivity skills of manager in the Islamic Saudi HSBC portfolios are stronger and they have better selectivity skills than the conventional Saudi HSBC portfolios. The local Islamic portfolios are highly competitive and generate good returns with reasonable risk. The manager of HSBC Islamic portfolio (LS) is able to take advantage of earnings anomalies, and thus, they make the right choice in the selection of securities. These portfolios are able to generate higher excess returns than conventional Saudi HSBC portfolios.

In terms of market timing ability, the finding from this article showed that local Islamic and conventional HSBC portfolios did not exhibit a market timing ability when using different market benchmarks. However, the international-focused conventional HSBC portfolios possess significant and modest market timing ability; thus, they are able to beat the market index by predicting its movements and buying and selling accordingly. The other international HSBC portfolios have a negative market timing, which can be interpreted as a failure of the fund manager to beat the market and their ability to do the opposite of the market. The international HSBC portfolios focused Sharia increase (decrease) their market exposure in question at a time when the market is down (up).

According to this study, we can note that 20% of HSBC portfolios present a performance persistent over eight years. The managers of these portfolios have a certain degree of predictability of future performance, thus, they are able to maintain a certain stability in their performance.

The choice of benchmark in this paper might not be ideal. Dellva et al. (2001) found quite different results through analysis of the selectivity and market timing estimates with respect to three distinct benchmarks, which can show that the user market index has the ability to incorporate biases in estimates. Hence, in the future work, it will be interesting to use other benchmarks. In summary, in future empirical works, we can use longer data, a larger sample of Saudi mutual funds and we can also incorporate new variables that allows to understand to what extent Islamic law affects mutual funds active management strategies and the performance.

Funding: The author gratefully acknowledge the approval and the support of this research study by the grant from the Deanship of Scientific Research at Northern Border University, Arar, K.S.A.

Conflicts of Interest: The author declares no conflict of interest. The views expressed in the paper are attributed entirely to the author and do not necessarily reflect the views of the places at which they work.

References

Abdullah, Fikriyah, Taufiq Hassan, and Shamsher Mohamad. 2007. Investigation of Performance of Malaysian Islamic Unit Trust Funds Comparison with Conventional Unit Trust Funds. *Managerial Finance* 2: 142–53. [CrossRef]

Agarwal, Pankaj K., and Sitangshu Khatua Pradhan. 2018. Mutual Fund Performance Using Unconditional Multifactor Models: Evidence from India. *Journal of Emerging Market Finance* 17: 157–84. [CrossRef]

Al Rahahleh, Naseem, and Muhammad Bhatti. 2017. Co-movement measure of information transmission on international equity markets. *Statistical Mechanics and Its Applications* 470: 119–31. [CrossRef]

Ashraf, Dawood. 2013. Performance Evaluation of Islamic Mutual Funds Relative to Conventional Funds Empirical Evidence from Saudi Arabia. *International Journal of Islamic and Middle Eastern Finance and Management* 6: 105–21. [CrossRef]

Bauer, Rob, Joreon Derwall, and Roger Otten. 2007. The Ethical Mutual Fund Performance Debate: New Evidence from Canada. *Journal of Business Ethics* 70: 111–24. [CrossRef]

Bialkowski, Jedrzej, and Rodger Otten. 2011. Emerging market mutual fund performance: Evidence for Poland. *North American Journal of Economics and Finance* 22: 118–30. [CrossRef]

Bollen, Nicolas P. B., and Jeffrey A. Busse. 2001. On the timing ability of mutual fund managers. *The Journal of Finance* 3: 1075–94. [CrossRef]

Boo, Yee Ling, Mong Shan Ee, Li Bob, and Mamunur Rashid. 2017. Islamic or conventional mutual funds: Who has the upper hand? Evidence from Malaysia. *Pacific-Basin Finance Journal* 42: 183–92. [CrossRef]

Brown, Stephen, and William Goetzmann. 1995. Performance persistence. *The Journal of Finance* 50: 679–98. [CrossRef]

Cakici, Nusret, Frank J. Fabozzi, and Tan Sinan. 2013. Size, value, and momentum in emerging market stock returns. *Emerging Markets Review* 16: 46–65. [CrossRef]

Carhart, Mark M. 1997. On Persistence in Mutual Fund Performance. *Journal of Finance* 52: 57–82. [CrossRef]

Chau, Kwong, Siu Kei Wong Wing, and Graeme Newell. 2003. Performance of property companies in Hong Kong: A style analysis approach. *Journal of Real Estate Portfolio Management* 9: 29–44.

Christensen, Michael. 2005. *Danish Mutual Fund Performance—Selectivity, Market Timing and Persistence*. Finance Research Group Working Paper No. F-2005-1. Aarhus: Aarhus School of Business.

Christopherson, Jon, Wayne Ferson, and Andrew Turner. 1999. Performance Evaluation using Conditional Alphas and Betas. *Journal of Portfolio Management* 26: 59–72. [CrossRef]

Clare, Andrew, Meadhbh Sherman, and Stephane Thomas. 2016. Multi-asset class mutual funds: Can they time the market? Evidence from the US, UK and Canada. *Research in International Business and Finance* 36: 212–21. [CrossRef]

Coggins, Frank, Marie Claude Beaulieu, and Michel Gendron. 2009. Mutual Fund Daily Conditional Performance Evaluation. *Journal of Financial Research* 32: 95–122. [CrossRef]

Dellva, Wilfred, Andrea DeMaskey, and Collen Smith. 2001. Selectivity and Market Timing Performance of Fidelity Sector Mutual Funds. *The Financial Review* 36: 39–54. [CrossRef]

Elfakhani, Saied, M. Kabir Hassan, and Sidani Yusuf. 2007. Islamic Mutual funds. In *Handbook of Islamic Banking*. Cheltenham: Edward Elgar, pp. 256–73.

El-Masry, Ahmad, and Dalia A. El-Mosallamy. 2016. A comparative study of the performance of Saudi mutual funds. *Corporate Ownership & Control* 13: 89–101.

Elton, Edwin J., Martin J. Gruber, and Christopher R. Blake. 2012. An Examination of Mutual Fund Timing Ability Using Monthly Holdings Data. *Review of Finance* 16: 619–45. [CrossRef]

Ernst and Young. 2015. Fast Growth, Divergent Paths—The EY GCC Wealth and Asset Management Report 2015. Available online: https://www.ey.com (accessed on 3 September 2019).

Fauziah, Md. Taib., Shahnon Suhaimi, and H. Ling Lee. 2002. Malaysian Unit Trust Fund Performance. Paper presented at the Fourth Annual Malaysian Finance Association Symposium, Penang, Malaysia, May 31–June 1; pp. 451–74.

Ferson, Wayne E., and Rudi W. Schadt. 1996. Measuring fund stategy and performance in changing economic conditions. *Journal of Finance* 2: 425–61. [CrossRef]

Ferson, Wayne E., and Vincent A. Warther. 1996. Evaluating Fund Performance in a Dynamic Market. *Financial Analysts Journal* 52: 20–28. [CrossRef]

Girard, Eric, and M. Kabir Hassan. 2008. Is there a cost to faith-based investing: Evidence from FTSE Islamic indices. *Journal of Investing* 17: 112–21. [CrossRef]

Grinblatt, Mark, and Sheridan Titman. 1992. The Persistence of Mutual Fund Performance. *Journal of Finance* 47: 1977–84. [CrossRef]

Hansen, Lars Peter. 1982. Large Sample Properties of Generalized Method of Moments Estimators. *Econometrica* 50: 1029–54. [CrossRef]

Hassan, M. Kabir, and Eric Girard. 2010. Faith-Based Ethical Investing: The Case of Dow Jones Islamic Indexes. *Economic Studies* 17: 1–31. [CrossRef]

Hayat, Raphie, and Roman Kraeussl. 2011. Risk and Return Characteristics of Islamic Equity Funds. *Emerging Markets Review* 12: 189–203. [CrossRef]

Henriksson, Roy, and Robert C. Merton. 1981. On Market Timing and Investment Performance II: Statistical Procedures for Evaluating Forecasting Skills. *Journal of Business* 54: 513–33. [CrossRef]

Hoepner, Andrea G., Hussain G. Rammal, and Michael Rezec. 2011. Islamic mutual funds financial performance and international investment style: Evidence from 20 countries. *European Journal of Finance* 17: 829–50. [CrossRef]

Huang, Xiaohong, and Ronald J. Mahieu. 2012. Performance persistence of Dutch pension funds. *De Economist* 160: 17–34. [CrossRef]

Hussein, Khaled. 2005. Islamic Investment: Evidence from Dow Jones and FTSE Indices. Paper presented at the 6th International Conference on Islamic Banking and Finance, Jakarta, Indonesia, September 18–19.

Jensen, Michael C. 1967. The Performance of Mutual Funds in the Period 1945–1964. *Journal of Finance* 23: 389–416. [CrossRef]

Kiymaz, Halil. 2015. A performance evaluation of Chinese mutual funds. *International Journal of Emerging Markets* 10: 820–36. [CrossRef]

Mansor, Fadillah, and M. Isaq Bhatti. 2011. The Islamic mutual fund performance: New evidence on market timing and stock selectivity. Paper presented at the 2011 International Conference on Economics and Finance Research (ICEFR 2011), Singapore, February 26–28.

Mansor, Fadillah, and M. Ishaq Bhatti. 2016. Evidence of Risk and Return Performance of Islamic Mutual Funds: The Case of Malaysia: An Asian Perspective. *Advances in Islamic Finance, Marketing, and Management* 6: 81–101.

Marhfor, Ahmed. 2016. Portfolio Performance Measurement: Review of Literature and Avenues of Future Research. *American Journal of Industrial and Business Management* 6: 432–38. [CrossRef]

Mateus, Irena, Cesario Mateus, and Natasa Todorovic. 2019. Use of Active Peer Benchmarks in assessing UK mutual fund performance and performance persistence. *The European Journal of Finance* 12: 1–39. [CrossRef]

Mitchell, Matthew C., Mohd Rafi, Muhamad Iqbal, and Sean Severe. 2014. Conventional Vs. Islamic Finance: The Impact of Ramadan upon Sharia-Compliant Markets. *Organizations and Markets in Emerging Economies* 5: 105–24.

Merdad, Hesham, Hassan M. Kabir, and Yasser Alhenawi. 2010. Islamic versus Conventional Mutual Funds Performance in Saudi Arabia: A Case Study. *Journal of King Abdulaziz University: Islamic Economic* 23: 161–98.

Mohamad, Noureddine, and Dawood Ashraf. 2015. The market timing ability and return performance of Islamic equities: An empirical study. *Pacific-Basin Finance Journal* 34: 169–83. [CrossRef]

Oliveira, Luís, Tomás Salen, José Curto, and Nuno Ferreira. 2019. Market Timing and Selectivity: An Empirical Investigation of European Mutual Fund Performance. *International Journal of Economics and Finance* 11: 1–16. [CrossRef]

Omri, Abdelwahed, Karim Sassou, and Nadia Ben Sedrine Goucha. 2018. On the post-financial crisis performance of Islamic mutual funds: the case of Riyad funds. *Applied Economics* 51: 1929–46. [CrossRef]

Papadamou, Stephanos, and Costals Siriopoulos. 2004. American equity mutual funds in European markets: Hot hands phenomenon and style analysis. *International Journal of Finance & Economics* 9: 85–97.

Papadamou, Stephanos, Nikolaos A. Kyriazis, and Lydia L. Mermigka. 2017. Japanese mutual funds before and after the crisis outburst: A style-and performance-analysis. *International Journal of Financial Studies* 5: 9. [CrossRef]

Pilbeam, Keith, and Hamish Preston. 2019. An Empirical Investigation of the Performance of Japanese Mutual Funds: Skill or Luck? *International Journal of Financial Studies* 7: 6. [CrossRef]

Ramesh, Brames, and Pournima Shenvi Dhume. 2014. Market timing ability of fund managers-Indian Experience. *The Indian Journal of Commerce* 67: 1–15.

Rana, Md Ejaz, and Waheed Akther. 2015. Performance of Islamic and conventional stock indices: Empirical evidence from an emerging economy. *Financial Innovation* 1: 1–15. [CrossRef]

Rao, Zia-ur-Rehma, Muhammad Zubair Tauni, and Ajid ur Rehman. 2016. Asymmetric Flow-performance Relationship: Case of Chinese Equity Funds. *International Journal of Economics and Financial* 6: 492–96.

Rao, Zia-ur-Rehman, Muhammad Zubair Tauni, and Amjad Iqbal. 2017. Emerging market mutual fund performance: Evidence for China. *Journal of Asia Business Studies* 11: 167–87. [CrossRef]

Sharma, Dhanraj, and Ruchita Verma. 2018. Performance Evaluation of Selectivity Skills of Fund Managers in India: An Analysis of Index Funds. *International Journal of Engineering Technology Science and Research* 5: 2394–3386.

Sharpe, William F. 1966. Mutual Fund Performance. *The Journal of Business* 39: 119–38. [CrossRef]

Silva, Florinda, Maria do Céu Cortez, and Manuel Rocha Armada. 2003. Conditioning Information and European Bond Fund Performance. *European Financial Management* 9: 201–30. [CrossRef]

Tan, Ömar Farouk. 2015. Mutual Fund Performance: Evidence from South Africa. *Emerging Markets Journal* 5: 49. [CrossRef]

Tchamyou, Venessa, Simplice A. Asongu, and Jacinta C. Nwachukwu. 2018. Effects of asymmetric information on market timing in the mutual fund industry. *International Journal of Managerial Finance* 14: 542–57. [CrossRef]

Treynor, Jack L. 1965. How to rate mutual fund performance. *Harvard Business Review* 43: 63–75.

Treynor, Jack, and Kay Mazuy. 1966. Can mutual funds outguess the market? *Harvard Business Review* 44: 131–36.

Wermers, Russ. 1999. Mutual fund herding and the impact of stock prices. *Journal of Finance* 54: 581–622. [CrossRef]

10

Explanatory Power of Pre-Issue Financial Strength for Long-Term Market Performance: Evidence from Initial Equity Offerings on an Emerging Market

Leszek Czapiewski and **Joanna Lizińska** *

Department of Corporate Finance, Poznań University of Economics and Business, 61-875 Poznań, Poland; leszek.czapiewski@ue.poznan.pl

* Correspondence: joanna.lizinska@ue.poznan.pl

Abstract: This study tests possible sources of long-term risk-adjusted returns on initial public offerings (IPO) in Poland under the calendar-time portfolio (CTP) approach. The moment of going public still remains a puzzle in many areas. Poland's status as an emerging market has been indisputable for many years, though improvements in capital market infrastructure have led to its recent reclassification as a developed country. It is an important European equity market. Thus, research on IPO pricing explanation for Poland is important for both investors and academics. In this study, we estimate risk premiums and run regressions on four asset pricing models, including the latest innovation, which is the Fama-French 5-factor model. We also check the robustness. The research documents the existence of the long-run underperformance for Polish IPOs independently of the specification of the calendar-time portfolio approach as alphas range from −9.6% to −13.2% annually. We show that the underperformance is mainly driven by IPOs in a position of weak pre-issue financial health. More profitable IPOs experience less negative long-term returns and the underperformance is even absent in some specifications.

Keywords: initial public offering; equity issue; calendar-time portfolio approach; asset pricing model; risk premium; profitability

JEL Classification: G14; G32; O16

---

1. Introduction

This research focuses on possible sources of long-term returns of initial public offerings of equities (IPO). More precisely, we explore the relationship between pre-issue financial health and subsequent long-term equity returns in Poland, which was an example of an emerging market during the research period. Our paper contributes to the existing research in several ways. First, we offer some new international evidence on the long-term returns observed after going public in an emerging market. This paper investigates the long-term performance of initial public offerings listed in Poland with the calendar-time portfolio approach, including the Capital Asset Pricing Model (Sharpe 1964; Lintner 1969); the Fama French 3-factor model (Fama and French 1993); the Carhart four 4-factor model (Carhart 1997); and the latest innovations in capital asset pricing models, such as the Fama-French 5-factor model (Fama and French 2015, 2016). Second, we check the link between pre-issue accounting performance and long-term market abnormal returns. We test the divergence of opinion as a theory explaining the IPO long-term underperformance. Providing empirical conclusions in these areas is important for both investors and academics. Our study also provides additional insights into market efficiency for an emerging market, especially in the area connected with IPO anomalies and asset pricing models. Third, we investigate the robustness of both the long-run underperformance of initial public offerings and the relation between pre-issue financial health and long-term returns for equity issuers.

Exploring the long-term predictive power of indicators of divergence of opinion, we apply accounting performance measures connected with earnings, as well as cash flow. We check whether uncertainty about the real value of IPO firms experiencing good pre-issue financial health is less pronounced. If this is the case, the long-term performance of such firms should be better. At the same time, the long-term underperformance for less profitable IPOs would be stronger. However, if a better profitability is a result of earnings management, the long-term consequences may not be so obvious.

The methodology for measuring long-term market performance after important company events has been much debated in the literature. This question is probably going to remain an unresolved practical and theoretical issue (Kothari and Warner 2007). Beginning with the milestone of the event study by Ritter (1991), an extensively used measure of long-term IPO performance is a buy-and-hold abnormal return (BHAR). Other early studies on the long-term performance of US IPOs reveal negative abnormal returns (Ibbotson 1975; Loughran and Ritter 1995; Rajan and Servaes 1997). The first studies on IPOs in Poland were also based on the buy-and-hold approach (Aussenegg 2000; Jelic and Briston 2003; Lyn and Zychowicz 2003; Jewartowski and Lizińska 2012). However, the literature points to the many misspecifications of the buy-and-hold approach, such as violations in cross-sectional independence, re-balancing, and skewness bias (Barber and Lyon 1997; Lyon et al. 1999; Jegadeesh and Karceski 2009).

Fama (1998) advocates the application of the calendar-time portfolio approach (CTP), arguing that it alleviates most of the systematic errors that may arise in measuring long-term wealth effects of events. Mitchell and Stafford (2000) and Lyon et al. (1999) also advocate this methodology as robust to the most critical statistical problems in empirical corporate finance. This approach is quite well-known in studies on the long-term effects of US equity issues (Loughran and Ritter 1995; Brav and Gompers 1997; Brav et al. 2000), though there is an indisputably smaller body of evidence for less developed markets. This research applies this method for long-term IPO abnormal performance estimation. Empirically, we use the calendar-time portfolio approach and four factor models. The sample is divided into quantiles, depending on the financial health before going public. The results document significant underperformance following initial public offerings in Poland. The intercepts are negative and robust to methodology specifications. We report that IPO underperformance was mainly driven by issues with a low pre-issue accounting performance. A higher level of divergence of opinion about the future prospects of companies approximated with a worse pre-issue accounting performance resulted in a more severe underperformance. The findings on the explanatory power of pre-issue financial health for IPO long-term performance are robust to different methodology specifications.

The paper is organized as follows. Section 2 discusses the previous literature. In Section 3, we describe the data and explain the methodology. Section 4.1 reports the post-issue long-term IPO performance according to the calendar time-portfolio approach. Sections 4.2–4.4 provide evidence for abnormal risk-adjusted returns in performance groups using alternative measures of financial health. Section 5 provides a discussion of the robustness checks of empirical results. The last section concludes the research and discusses future research.

2. Related Literature

This section starts by providing a brief review of studies on the abnormal long-term market performance of IPOs. This has been discussed most extensively for US stock exchanges. The evidence is less comprehensive for other markets. The research applies the event study tools proposed by, e.g., Fama et al. (1969) and their followers, for testing market efficiency. These procedures apply to events such as equity offerings, mergers, splits etc. This way of testing the long-term effects has evoked many discussions and resulted in many proposals. The fact is that proper estimators of long-term performance, as well as ways of testing its statistical significance, are still much debated in the literature. Two main approaches have appeared. First, the buy-and-hold abnormal return

(BHAR) applied by Ritter (1991). The second approach is advocated by Fama (1998) and is based on calendar-time portfolios (CTP) and asset pricing models.

Some academics argue that the buy-and-hold approach is appropriate for measuring an investor's wealth changes as it resembles the real investment situation. In practice, it is an average long-term return earned on a strategy of investing in all IPO firms on the event date, and selling the portfolio at the end of a specified holding period compared with the gains from implementing a comparable strategy for a benchmark (Mitchell and Stafford 2000). Some studies have shown that a buy-and-hold return suffers from several biases. Jegadeesh and Jegadeesh and Karceski (2009) argue that the event-time approach connected with the estimation of buy-and-hold returns assumes the cross-sectional independence of returns. Event samples are not random and IPO returns are correlated. Barber and Lyon (1997) use simulations to show new listing, re-balancing, and skewness biases in the BHAR approach and discuss the reference portfolio choice. The buy-and-hold approach was also criticized for magnifying the long-run underperformance (Brav et al. 2000).

Fama (1998) recommends the use of the calendar-time portfolio approach and points out that monthly returns better address the bad model problem, the cross-correlation problem, and the skewness bias. We follow the proposal of Fama (1998) and investigate the long-term performance of initial public offerings in Poland with calendar-time portfolios. The idea of this approach is as follows. First, portfolios consisting of IPO firms are formed for each calendar month in a sample period. These portfolios consist of all IPO companies that went public within a specified period of time. For each calendar month, calendar portfolios are rebalanced as new IPO companies enter and some firms drop out. Then, a mean monthly portfolio abnormal return is estimated by regressing excess returns using models such as CAPM or multifactor models. The intercept proxies for the abnormal monthly return.

Calendar-time portfolios have mainly been implemented for IPOs listed in the United States. The first research with empirical testing of long-term abnormal IPO market performance was published by Loughran and Ritter (1995). With a sample of both initial and seasoned US equity offerings, they reported negative intercepts. Negative returns were also found by Brav et al. (2000) for the equal weights and for the smallest tercile. However, alphas for value weighted and large portfolios were statistically insignificant. Brav and Gompers (1997) found significant and negative intercepts for non-venture backed initial equity offerings. The results for venture backed IPOs were not significant. They also drew the conclusion that the long-term underperformance of IPOs was driven by non-venture backed IPOs in the smallest decile of firms. Mitchell and Stafford (2000) also reported a significant negative abnormal performance for US IPO portfolios. The calendar-time portfolio approach was also applied to non-US markets in countries such as Canada (Kooli et al. 2006), Spain (Alvarez and González 2001), and China (Shen et al. 2015).

The performance of initial public offerings listed in Poland has been discussed using the buy-and-hold approach. The first studies mainly focused on the privatization issues (Aussenegg 2000; Jelic and Briston 2003; Lyn and Zychowicz 2003). More recently, long-term underperformance was found with the buy-and-hold approach, according to different benchmarks (Jewartowski and Lizińska 2012; Lizińska and Czapiewski 2016; Brycz et al. 2017).

There are several theories explaining why initial public offerings underperform in the long-run. One of them is the divergence of opinion hypothesis and the optimistic investor theory. Under the divergence of opinion hypothesis (Miller 1977), the higher the level of divergence of opinion, the worse the subsequent long-term returns. Some optimistic investors may perceive the situation around equity offerings to be much better than others and offer higher prices. The level of information asymmetry is relatively high around the time of going public as usually little is known about market newcomers. The higher the asymmetry of an IPO and the higher the uncertainty, the worse the level of the long-term performance (Levis 1993; Brav and Gompers 1997). One cannot measure the level of divergence of opinion directly. The proxies can be based on both accounting and market data. There have been several measures of the divergence of opinion proposed in previous empirical research. Diether et al. (2002) used analyst forecast dispersion and Gao et al. (2006) applied early-market return volatility. We proxy for the divergence of opinion with accounting measures of financial health. We use ratios based on financial statements as such reports seem to be a very important source of information about market newcomers.

Relating the market performance of Polish IPOs to around-the-issue accounting performance is not a new idea. Lyn and Zychowicz (2003) found no significant relationship between profitability and short-term IPO underpricing. Lizińska and Czapiewski (2014) observed that short-term IPO returns in Poland were much higher for more profitable firms. However, the relationship between around-the-IPO profitability was not so evident for long-term abnormal performance measured with BHARs as it was not robust to alternative methods. Brycz et al. (2017) found that short-term IPO success is strongly determined by pre-IPO profitability, with no significant results for the long-term buy-and-hold returns. We propose to test the relationship for Polish IPOs using the improved estimation method of long-term performance.

3. Empirical Modelling

The research sample consists of non-financial initial public offerings (IPOs) listed on the Warsaw Stock Exchange (WSE), which is the main equity market in Poland. The research only includes issues with a new common stock issuance, and those without a prior trading history on alternative markets. The data sources include Notoria Serwis, the official site of the WSE and InfoStrefa.com. The database also covers delisted firms. We use equity close prices with the necessary adjustments (such as dividends, splits, and pre-emptive rights) to calculate returns. The sample period ranges from January 2002 to December 2014. However, the timespan of market data for returns and other financial items for asset pricing models is longer because it also covers the succeeding years as it was necessary to observe the long-term performance of equity offerings.

There are two main groups of methods for assessing the long-term performance of post-event firms. The risk adjusted performance can be analysed using benchmarks together with the buy-and-hold approach, or the calendar-time portfolio approach (Fama 1998; Eckbo et al. 2000; Mitchell and Stafford 2000). Fama (1998) proposes using the rolling calendar-month portfolio approach to reduce some of the drawbacks of buy-and-hold returns. We apply the calendar-time portfolio approach to measure abnormal return with the application of four asset pricing models. The monthly abnormal returns are intercepts in regressions.

The idea for the empirical research encompasses three steps. First, we test the long-term abnormal performance of initial public offerings with the calendar-time portfolio approach. Hence, we estimate risk premiums for asset pricing models and construct calendar IPO portfolios to regress the monthly excess return for each of these portfolios on factor models. Second, we assess the long-term performance of quantiles of IPOs according to the around-the-issue accounting performance. Here, we start by selecting a measure and we repeat the procedure of the calendar-time portfolio approach in performance quantiles. Third, we check the robustness of empirical results.

The relationship between average return and market beta was first described in the Sharp-Lintner Capital Asset Pricing Model (CAPM) (Sharpe 1964; Lintner 1969). Fama and French (1993) shed new light on the explanation of the cross-section of average returns in their 3-factor model with size and price ratios (3FF, hereafter). Carhart (1997) proposed a 4-factor model (4C, hereafter) capturing the momentum factor as this anomaly was proposed by Jegadeesh and Titman (1993). Fama and French (2015) and Fama and French (2016) proposed a 5-factor model (5FF, hereafter) that captured the size, value, profitability, and investment patterns in average stock returns. Factor models have a very broad application in research in the area of finance and capital markets and are not the only constraint to measuring effects of equity offerings. Their use in studies of US capital markets has a long history. Recently, they have started becoming popular in studies for emerging markets (Ewen 2018; Fu 2018; Ali et al. 2018).

First, risk premiums for portfolios are estimated according to each of the asset pricing models. The portfolios include all stocks listed on the main market of the Warsaw Stock Exchange, also including delisted companies. The method of portfolio formation for the risk-premium estimation according to the Fama-French 3-factor model, the Carhart 4-factor model, and the Fama-French 5-factor model is illustrated in Figures 1–3.

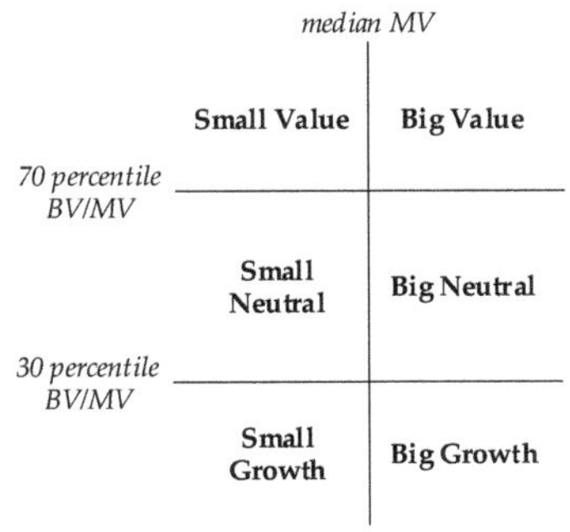

Figure 1. Construction of portfolios for the Fama-French 3-factor model.

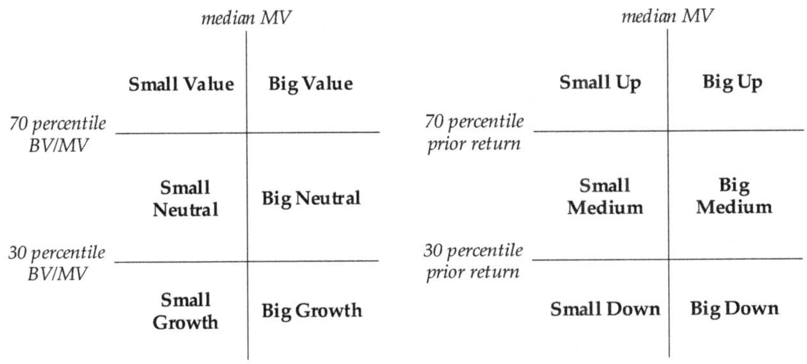

Figure 2. Construction of portfolios for the Carhart 4-factor model.

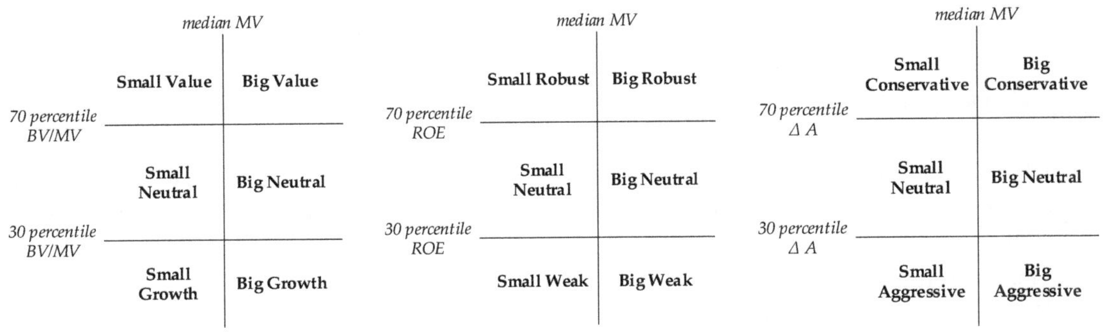

Figure 3. Construction of portfolios for the Fama-French 5-factor model.

Risk premiums for the Fama-French 3-factor model are estimated according to formulas:

$$SMB_t = \frac{Small\ Value_t + Small\ Neutral_t + Small\ Growth_t}{3} - \frac{Big\ Value_t + Big\ Neutral_t + Big\ Growth_t}{3} \tag{1}$$

$$HML_t = \frac{Small\ Value_t + Big\ Value_t}{2} - \frac{Small\ Growth_t + Big\ Growth_t}{2}, \tag{2}$$

Risk premiums for the Carhart 4-factor model are estimated as:

$$SMB_t = \frac{SMB_t^{BM/MV} + SMB_t^{PR}}{2}, \tag{3}$$

$$SMB_t^{BM/MV} = \left(\frac{Small\ Value_t + Small\ Neutral_t + Small\ Growth_t}{3} - \frac{Big\ Value_t + Big\ Neutral_t + Big\ Growth_t}{3} \right), \tag{4}$$

$$SMB_t^{PR} = \left(\frac{Small\ Value_t + Small\ Medium_t + Small\ Growth_t}{3} - \frac{Big\ Value_t + Big\ Medium_t + Big\ Growth_t}{3} \right), \tag{5}$$

$$HML_t = \frac{Small\ Value_t + Big\ Value_t}{2} - \frac{Small\ Growth_t + Big\ Growth_t}{2}, \tag{6}$$

$$WML_t = \frac{Small\ Up_t + Big\ Up_t}{2} - \frac{Small\ Down_t + Big\ Down_t}{2}, \tag{7}$$

Risk premiums for the Fama-French 5-factor model are as follows:

$$SMB_t = \frac{SMB_t^{BM/MV} + SMB_t^{ROE} + SMB_t^{\Delta A}}{3}, \tag{8}$$

$$SMB_t^{BM/MV} = \left(\frac{Small\ Value_t + Small\ Neutral_t + Small\ Growth_t}{3} - \frac{Big\ Value_t + Big\ Neutral_t + Big\ Growth_t}{3} \right), \tag{9}$$

$$SMB_t^{ROE} = \left(\frac{Small\ Robust_t + Small\ Neutral_t + Small\ Weak_t}{3} - \frac{Big\ Robust_t + Big\ Neutral_t + Big\ Weak_t}{3} \right), \tag{10}$$

$$SMB_t^{\Delta A} = \left(\frac{Small\ Conservative_t + Small\ Neutral_t + Small\ Aggressive_t}{3} - \frac{Big\ Conservative_t + Big\ Neutral_t + Big\ Aggressive_t}{3} \right), \tag{11}$$

$$HML_t = \frac{Small\ Value_t + Big\ Value_t}{2} - \frac{Small\ Growth_t + Big\ Growth_t}{2}, \tag{12}$$

$$RMW_t = \frac{Small\ Robust_t + Big\ Robust_t}{2} - \frac{Small\ Weak_t + Big\ Weak_t}{2}, \tag{13}$$

$$CMA_t = \frac{Small\ Conservative_t + Big\ Conservative_t}{2} - \frac{Small\ Aggressive_t + Big\ Aggressive_t}{2}, \tag{14}$$

Starting with January 2002, each calendar month, we construct a portfolio of firms that went public in the past 36 months. Portfolios based on 24-month periods are also included for a robustness check. The portfolios are rebalanced each month as some IPO companies exit and enter. Next, we regress the monthly excess returns, on the monthly factors of the CAPM, 3FF, 4C, and 5FF models. We start with the CAPM model, where the monthly returns, adjusted by the risk-free rate, are regressed as follows:

$$R_t^P - R_t^F = \alpha + \beta\left(R_t^M - R_t^F\right) + \varepsilon_t^P, \tag{15}$$

where the calendar time portfolio return is given as R_t^P, the risk-free rate R_t^F is calculated with WIBOR, the monthly market return R_t^M is approximated using the main Polish stock index (Warsaw Stock Index, WIG), market risk premium is expressed as $(R_t^M - R_t^F)$, α is an average monthly abnormal return on a portfolio of IPO firms, β is the OLS regression parameter specific to the portfolio, and ε_t^P is the error term.

The regressions on the Fama-French 3-factor model proceed as follows:

$$R_t^P - R_t^F = \alpha + \beta_M\left(R_t^M - R_t^F\right) + \beta_{SMB} SMB_t + \beta_{HML} HML_t + \varepsilon_t^P, \tag{16}$$

where SMB_t is the difference in returns between the portfolios of small and big firms, and HML_t is the average return on the two value portfolios minus the average return on the two growth portfolios.

The regression on the Carhart model proceeds as follows:

$$R_t^P - R_t^F = \alpha + \beta_{RM}\left(R_t^M - R_t^F\right) + \beta_{SMB}SMB_t + \beta_{HML}HML_t + \beta_{WML}WML_t, \quad (17)$$

where WML_t is the average return on the two high prior return portfolios minus the average return on the two low prior return portfolios.

The regression on the Fama-French 5-factor model is:

$$R_t^P - R_t^F = (\alpha + \beta_{RM}(R_t^M - R_t^F) + \beta_{SMB}SMB_t + \beta_{HML}HML_t + \beta_{RMW}RMW_t + \beta_{CMA}CMA_t), \quad (18)$$

where RMW_t is the average return on the two robust operating profitability portfolios minus the average return on the two weak operating profitability portfolios, and CMA_t is the average return on the two conservative investment portfolios minus the average return on the two aggressive investment portfolios.

Next, we run quantile regressions based on the pre-issue accounting performance of IPOs. Three measures of financial results are applied: net income, operating income, and operating cash flow. In the basic research design, they are all scaled by sales. IPO firms are divided according to the accounting performance into two groups, below (L) and above the median (H). Finally, we again estimate regressions according to the CAPM, FF3, C4, and FF5 models to assess the long-term abnormal market performance of initial public offerings in performance groups.

We check the robustness of empirical results and we employ additional measures of accounting performance. We expand proxies by adding another scaling factor, namely the size of a company according to its pre-issue assets. Taken together, it gives us six measures of pre-issue accounting performance: net profitability of sales (net income to sales, ROS), net profitability of assets (net income to assets, ROA), operating profitability of sales (operating income to sales, OROS), operating profitability of assets (operating income to assets, OROA), operating cash flow to sales (OCFS), and operating cash flow to assets (OCFA). Factor regressions are run independently in all of the previously described specifications. Summing up, we repeat factor-regressions 48 times under the calendar-time portfolio approach (four asset pricing models, two portfolio periods, and six performance measurements). Alphas are tested in quantiles under 96 specifications in the basic approach and in the robustness check.

4. Empirical Results

4.1. Long-Term IPO Performance According to the Calendar-Time Portfolio Approach for All Issuers

We investigate long-term abnormal IPO market performance with the calendar-time portfolio approach and estimate alpha in factor regressions. The results are detailed in Table 1. We use the CAPM model, the Fama-French 3-factor model, the Carhart 4-factor model, and the Fama-French 5-factor model (CAPM, 3FF, 4C, and 5FF, respectively). The dependent variables in regressions are the IPO portfolio returns in excess of the risk-free rate. The portfolios are formed from all initial public offerings that have gone public within the previous 36 or 24 months (Panel A and Panel B, respectively of Table 1).

Table 1 reports strong evidence of underperformance following the initial public offering in Poland for all specifications of methodology. The intercept is the lowest in regressions for the CAPM and equals −9.6% annually for portfolios built both on 36- and 24-month samples. For multifactor models, similar results were obtained. The alphas from the 3FF, 4C, and 5FF regressions were also negative and statistically significant. If we look at 36-month portfolios in Panel A, the post-issue underperformance of IPOs measured with the annualized intercepts from the 3FF, 4C, and 5FF regressions is equal to −12.0%, −9.6%, and −13.2% annually, respectively. It is also negative and economically important for 24-month portfolios as it respectively equals −9.6%, −12%, and −9.6% annually, as reported in Panel

B. The research documents the existence of long-run underperformance for Polish IPOs independently of the specification of the calendar-time portfolio approach.

Table 1. Results of calendar-time portfolio regressions for IPO firms.

	CAPM	3FF	4C	5FF
		Panel A: 36-month portoflio		
α	−0.008 **	−0.010 ***	−0.008 **	−0.011 ***
	(−2.503)	(−3.308)	(−2.570)	(−3.977)
RMP	0.864 ***	0.823 ***	0.811 ***	0.763 ***
	(16.648)	(17.112)	(16.457)	(16.795)
SBM		0.491 ***	0.511 ***	0.649 ***
		(5.312)	(5.367)	(7.005)
HML		0.326 ***	0.264 **	0.496 ***
		(2.724)	(2.176)	(4.136)
WML			−0.100 *	
			(−1.689)	
RMW				0.067
				(0.711)
CMA				−0.575 ***
				(−4.785)
p-value for F	0.000	0.000	0.000	0.000
adj. R^2	0.699	0.759	0.761	0.800
		Panel B: 24-month portfolio		
α	−0.008 **	−0.010 ***	−0.008 **	−0.010 ***
	(−2.372)	(−2.958)	(−2.339)	(−3.050)
RMP	0.867 ***	0.834 ***	0.826 ***	0.786 ***
	(15.680)	(15.347)	(14.723)	(15.063)
SBM		0.365 ***	0.376 ***	0.528 ***
		(3.856)	(3.855)	(5.381)
HML		0.175	0.125	0.239 **
		(1.498)	(1.080)	(2.131)
WML			−0.070	
			(−1.038)	
RMW				0.007
				(0.072)
CMA				−0.543 ***
				(−4.233)
p-value for F	0.000	0.000	0.000	0.000
adj. R^2	0.651	0.683	0.682	0.721

Note: The t-statistic is in parentheses. *, **, and *** indicate significance at the 10, 5, and 1 percent levels, respectively.

4.2. Net Profitability and Long-Term IPO Performance

Having established the robustness of the findings about the long-term IPO underperformance with the calendar-time portfolio approach, we next explore the relationship between pre-issue financial health and the long-term performance of initial public offerings in Poland. We proxy for the financial health with a set of measures. First, we use net return on sales (ROS), defined as net income to sales. IPOs are partitioned using the median value of net profitability of sales before going public as a breakeven point. The first quantile encompasses low-profitable IPOs (L), and the second quantile includes high-profitable issues (H). In the next step, we follow the methodology applied in the previous section and re-estimate factor regressions on profitability quantiles. We again use the CAPM model, the Fama-French 3-factor model, the Carhart 4-factor model, and the Fama-French 5-factor model (CAPM, 3FF, 4C, and 5FF, respectively). The dependent variables in regressions are the IPO portfolio returns in excess of the risk-free rate and portfolios are formed from all IPOs that have gone public within the previous 36 months. The results are detailed in Table 2.

Table 2. Results of calendar-time portfolio regressions in quantiles based on net profitability of sales of IPO firms.

	CAPM (L)	CAPM (H)	3FF (L)	3FF (H)	4C (L)	4C (H)	5FF (L)	5FF (H)
α	−0.012 ***	−0.005	−0.014 ***	−0.006 *	−0.011 ***	−0.006 *	−0.015 ***	−0.008 ***
	(−2.793)	(−1.593)	(−3.675)	(−1.961)	(−2.643)	(−1.856)	(−3.906)	(−2.748)
RMP	0.922 ***	0.809 ***	0.867 ***	0.782 ***	0.841 ***	0.786 ***	0.804 ***	0.729 ***
	(13.458)	(16.163)	(13.831)	(15.643)	(13.192)	(15.224)	(13.067)	(15.178)
SBM			0.682 ***	0.291 ***	0.703 ***	0.311 ***	0.821 ***	0.468 ***
			(5.662)	(3.031)	(5.704)	(3.122)	(6.548)	(4.780)
HML			0.429 ***	0.209 *	0.320 **	0.196	0.553 ***	0.421 ***
			(2.747)	(1.677)	(2.037)	(1.541)	(3.400)	(3.318)
WML					−0.187 **	−0.009		
					(−2.439)	(−0.148)		
RMW							−0.043	0.186 *
							(−0.332)	(1.856)
CMA							−0.616 ***	−0.503 ***
							(−3.787)	(−3.961)
p-value for F	0.000	0.000	0.000	0.000	0.000	0.000	0.000	0.000
adj. R^2	0.602	0.686	0.689	0.707	0.697	0.706	0.722	0.749
α(H)−α(L)		0.086 **		0.099 **		0.058		0.081 **

Note: The difference α(H)−α(L) is annualized. The t-statistic is in parentheses. *, **, and *** indicate significance at the 10, 5, and 1 percent levels, respectively.

Alphas are statistically and economically significant for all low-profitability IPO quantiles. We find that the levels of monthly abnormal returns vary across models, but they are negative in all specifications. The intercepts are less negative for the high-profitability quantiles, where they are significant in most of the cases. Annual returns for the low-profitability quantile range from −13.4% up to −18.0%, whereas for the high-profitability IPOs, they range from −6.1% to −9.9% annually. IPO firms with lower pre-issue net profitability of sales experience stronger long-term market underperformance. The difference in annual returns between quantiles is quite substantial, no matter the regression specification. The average equals almost nine percentage points annually. The differences between more and less profitable portfolios are economically significant and they are statistically significant in most of the specifications.

We show that less-profitable firms drive the IPO long-term underperformance. For less-profitable firms, the effect of negative returns is much more severe and significant under all specifications. The evidence on negative alphas for IPOs with a lower level of divergence of opinion proxied with high profitability is generally mixed as the negative returns are either much less negative or they are not statistically significant.

4.3. Operating Profitability and Long-Term IPO Performance

Net income is an important item of a company's financial statement for its stakeholders. It gives an overall idea of the firm's financial health. It also helps to assess the prospects for the future. Reported earnings seem to be especially important for potential investors in IPO companies as relatively little is known about companies that are going public. A change to a company's status from a private to public one attracts a lot of attention from market participants. This is one of the arguments for suspecting that the moment of going public is especially susceptible to earnings management practices (Teoh et al. 1998). It is not easy to manipulate each income level. This was a motivation for testing whether operating earnings explain the long-term IPO performance in the same way as in the case of net profitability.

In this section, we continue the investigation of the relationship between pre-issue financial profitability and the long-term performance of IPOs listed on the WSE in Poland. We change the measure of profitability into the operating return on sales, which is defined as operating income to sales (OROS). As proceeded in the adjacent anteceding section, IPOs are partitioned into new quantiles. In this research step, we use the median value of operating profitability of sales before going public as a breakeven point. The first quantile encompasses low-profitable IPOs (L), and the second quantile includes high-profitable issues (H), both in terms of operating profitability of sales. We repeat the calendar-time portfolio estimation based on the CAPM model, the Fama-French 3-factor model, the Carhart 4-factor model, and the Fama-French 5-factor model (CAPM, 3FF, 4C, and 5FF, respectively) and we re-estimate factor regressions on two quantiles. The dependent variables in regressions are the IPO portfolio returns in excess of the risk-free rate and portfolios are formed from all IPOs that have gone public within the previous 36 months. The results are detailed in Table 3.

Table 3. Results of calendar-time portfolio regressions in quantiles based on operating profitability of sales of IPO firms.

	CAPM (L)	CAPM (H)	3FF (L)	3FF (H)	4C (L)	4C (H)	5FF (L)	5FF (H)
α	−0.012 ***	−0.006 *	−0.014 ***	−0.007 **	−0.011 ***	−0.006 *	−0.014 ***	−0.009 ***
	(−2.790)	(−1.668)	(−3.676)	(−2.091)	(−2.811)	(−1.700)	(−3.923)	(−2.791)
RMP	0.924 ***	0.804 ***	0.871 ***	0.774 ***	0.854 ***	0.769 ***	0.810 ***	0.720 ***
	(14.154)	(15.377)	(14.581)	(14.992)	(13.938)	(14.453)	(13.846)	(14.424)
SBM			0.648 ***	0.346 ***	0.668 ***	0.366 ***	0.783 ***	0.516 ***
			(5.644)	(3.481)	(5.640)	(3.561)	(6.571)	(5.079)
HML			0.413 ***	0.235 *	0.324 **	0.199	0.536 ***	0.436 ***
			(2.776)	(1.826)	(2.152)	(1.517)	(3.471)	(3.309)
WML					−0.144 *	−0.056		
					(−1.951)	(−0.878)		
RMW							−0.040	0.162
							(−0.330)	(1.551)
CMA							−0.603 ***	−0.515 ***
							(−3.901)	(−3.901)
p-value for F	0.000	0.000	0.000	0.000	0.000	0.000	0.000	0.000
adj. R^2	0.626	0.664	0.708	0.694	0.711	0.694	0.740	0.735
α(H)–α(L)		0.073 **		0.084 **		0.065 *		0.068 *

Note: The difference α(H)–α(L) is annualized. The t-statistic is in parentheses. *, **, and *** indicate significance at the 10, 5, and 1 percent levels, respectively.

Alphas are statistically significant for all of the low- and high-profitability quantiles. The level of monthly abnormal returns varies across models, but it is negative in all specifications for the low- and high-profitability quantiles. Annual returns for the low-profitability quantile are quite substantial and range from −13.7% up to −17.2%. IPO firms with a higher level of divergence of opinion proxied with a lower pre-issue operating profitability of sales experienced strong underperformance measured with alpha. Alphas for the high-profitability IPOs seem to be less negative as they range from −6.7% to −10.5% annually. The conclusions about substantial differences in intercepts between the low- and high-profitability portfolios remain unchanged, no matter the regression specification. They are also statistically significant. The most pronounced difference is reported for the Fama-French 3-factor model, where the difference between the profitability quantiles equals 8.4 percentage points annually. The empirical results for operating profitability mostly confirm the conclusions based on net profitability.

4.4. *Cash-Flow Efficiency and Long-Term IPO Performance*

Market participants usually react strongly to any kind of information connected with earnings. Income is the item from financial statements that attracts a lot of stakeholders' attention. Hence, insiders sometimes try to increase earnings and manage it. Teoh et al. (1998) suggest that IPO companies can boost their earnings with accrual adjustments. Investor over-optimism around going public might be at least partly induced by equity issuers. If this is the case for the IPO firms in our sample, then two previous measures of profitability may give a misleading picture of the financial health of a company. It is much more difficult to manipulate cash flow. Hence, we continue the investigation of the relationship between pre-issue financial health and the long-term performance of Polish IPOs with cash flow ratios defined as operating cash flow to sales (OCFS). IPOs are again partitioned into two quantiles with the median value. So, the first quantile includes IPOs with a low cash flow efficiency (L), and the second encompasses issuers in better financial health (H). We repeat the calendar-time portfolio estimation based on the CAPM model, the Fama-French 3-factor model, the Carhart 4-factor model, and the Fama-French 5-factor model (CAPM, 3FF, 4C, and 5FF, respectively) and re-estimate factor regressions. The dependent variables in regressions are the IPO portfolio returns in excess of the risk-free rate and portfolios are formed from all IPOs that have gone public within the previous 36 months. The results are detailed in Table 4.

Table 4. Results of calendar-time portfolio regressions in quantiles based on the operating cash flow to sales of IPO firms.

	CAPM (L)	CAPM (H)	3FF (L)	3FF (H)	4C (L)	4C (H)	5FF (L)	5FF (H)
α	−0.011 ***	−0.006 *	−0.013 ***	−0.007 **	−0.012 ***	−0.005	−0.014 ***	−0.009 ***
	(−2.641)	(−1.741)	(−3.222)	(−2.436)	(−2.700)	(−1.597)	(−3.795)	(−2.898)
RMP	0.915 ***	0.817 ***	0.874 ***	0.775 ***	0.869 ***	0.756 ***	0.795 ***	0.738 ***
	(13.746)	(15.983)	(13.751)	(15.972)	(13.170)	(15.420)	(13.178)	(15.233)
SBM			0.565 ***	0.417 ***	0.567 ***	0.454 ***	0.754 ***	0.550 ***
			(4.623)	(4.478)	(4.447)	(4.792)	(6.132)	(5.567)
HML			0.305 *	0.347 ***	0.246	0.279 **	0.526 ***	0.469 ***
			(1.925)	(2.869)	(1.515)	(2.309)	(3.300)	(3.664)
WML					−0.077	−0.128 **		
					(−0.969)	(−2.165)		
RMW							0.056	0.106
							(0.448)	(1.044)
CMA							−0.777 ***	−0.344 ***
							(−4.872)	(−2.682)
p-value for F	0.000	0.000	0.000	0.000	0.000	0.000	0.000	0.000
adj. R^2	0.612	0.681	0.670	0.732	0.665	0.742	0.724	0.752
α(H)−α(L)		0.067 *		0.065 *		0.080 *		0.066 *

Note: The difference α(H)−α(L) is annualized. The t-statistic is in parentheses. *, **, and *** indicate significance at the 10, 5, and 1 percent levels, respectively.

The differences for portfolios based on cash flow according to different specifications are a little bit less economically pronounced compared to results based on profitability, but they are still statistically significant. The regression results for the IPO grouping based on pre-issue cash flow efficiency may be interpreted as being only partly consistent with the over-optimism explanation and the divergence of opinion hypothesis.

5. Robustness Checks

We next check the robustness of empirical results. We expand the measures of financial health by relating accounting performance to an item reported in balance sheets, namely pre-issue assets. We maintain three groups of the reported accounting effect: net income, operating income, and cash flow. Taken together, it gives us three additional measures of pre-issue accounting performance: net profitability of assets (ROA), operating profitability of assets (OROA), and operating cash flow to assets (OCFA).

Initial public offerings are partitioned into quantiles using the median value of each of the mentioned additional performance measures in a similar way to Sections 4.2 and 4.3. Following this, we get IPOs with a weaker pre-issue performance (L) and those with a better performance (H). We repeat the calendar-time portfolio estimation based on the CAPM model, the Fama-French 3-factor model, the Carhart 4-factor model, and the Fama-French 5-factor model (CAPM, 3FF, 4C, and 5FF, respectively) and re-estimate factor regressions in quantiles for each of the additional measures. Additionally, factor regressions are run for IPOs that have gone public within the previous 36 or 24 months (Panel A and Panel B, respectively, of Table 5). The intercept is interpreted as the IPO portfolio monthly return. The results (only intercepts and statistical significance, for brevity) are detailed in Table 5. To make it more informative, both basic and additional measures are presented.

Table 5. Intercepts in calendar-time portfolio regressions for IPO quantiles (robustness check for different ratios as a base of quantile grouping).

	CAPM (L)	CAPM (H)	3FF (L)	3FF (H)	4C (L)	4C (H)	5FF (L)	5FF (H)
				Panel A: 36-month portoflio				
α (ROS)	−0.012 ***	−0.005	−0.014 ***	−0.006 *	−0.011 ***	−0.006 *	−0.015 ***	−0.008 ***
	(−2.793)	(−1.593)	(−3.675)	(−1.961)	(−2.643)	(−1.856)	(−3.906)	(−2.748)
α(H)−α(L)		0.086 **		0.099 **		0.058		0.081 **
α (OROS)	−0.012 ***	−0.006 *	−0.014 ***	−0.007 **	−0.011 ***	−0.006 *	−0.014 ***	−0.009 ***
	(−2.790)	(−1.668)	(−3.676)	(−2.091)	(−2.811)	(−1.700)	(−3.923)	(−2.791)
α(H)−α(L)		0.073 **		0.084 **		0.065 *		0.068 *
α (OCFS)	−0.011 ***	−0.006 *	−0.013 ***	−0.007 **	−0.012 ***	−0.005	−0.014 ***	−0.009 ***
	(−2.641)	(−1.741)	(−3.222)	(−2.436)	(−2.700)	(−1.597)	(−3.795)	(−2.898)
α(H)−α(L)		0.067 *		0.065 *		0.080 *		0.066 *
α (ROA)	−0.014 ***	−0.003	−0.016 ***	−0.004	−0.012 ***	−0.005	−0.017 ***	−0.006 **
	(−3.099)	(−0.970)	(−4.094)	(−1.298)	(−2.880)	(−1.465)	(−4.384)	(−2.001)
α(H)−α(L)		0.126 ***		0.146 ***		0.084 **		0.129 ***
α (OROA)	−0.013 ***	−0.004	−0.015 ***	−0.005	−0.013 ***	−0.005	−0.016 ***	−0.008 **
	(−3.032)	(−1.275)	(−4.092)	(−1.624)	(−3.152)	(−1.343)	(−4.361)	(−2.389)
		0.104 **		0.118 ***		0.094 **		0.098 **
α (OCFA)	−0.011 ***	−0.006 *	−0.013 ***	−0.007 **	−0.012 ***	−0.005	−0.014 ***	−0.009 ***
	(−2.654)	(−1.782)	(−3.279)	(−2.448)	(−2.799)	(−1.569)	(−3.777)	(−2.927)
α(H)−α(L)		0.067 *		0.066 *		0.084 **		0.067*
				Panel B: 24-month portfolio				
α (ROS)	−0.010 **	−0.006 *	−0.013 ***	−0.007 **	−0.011 **	−0.007 *	−0.012 ***	−0.008 **
	(−2.221)	(−1.818)	(−2.846)	(−2.102)	(−2.204)	(−1.887)	(−2.864)	(−2.237)
α(H)−α(L)		0.045		0.062		0.039		0.057
α (OROS)	−0.010 **	−0.007 *	−0.012 ***	−0.008 **	−0.011 **	−0.007 *	−0.012 ***	−0.009 **
	(−2.247)	(−1.972)	(−2.787)	(−2.244)	(−2.262)	(−1.669)	(−2.697)	(−2.348)
α(H)−α(L)		0.034		0.050		0.051		0.038
α (OCFS)	−0.009 **	−0.007 **	−0.011 **	−0.009 ***	−0.011 **	−0.006 *	−0.011 ***	−0.008 **
	(−2.182)	(−2.043)	(−2.490)	(−2.656)	(−2.345)	(−1.689)	(−2.753)	(−2.415)
α(H)−α(L)		0.024		0.016		0.055		0.033
α (ROA)	−0.014 ***	−0.003	−0.017 ***	−0.003	−0.013 ***	−0.004	−0.016 ***	−0.004
	(−3.015)	(−0.744)	(−3.853)	(−0.844)	(−2.787)	(−0.924)	(−3.743)	(−0.984)
α(H)−α(L)		0.132 ***		0.163 ***		0.111 ***		0.146 ***
α (OROA)	−0.015 ***	−0.001	−0.018 ***	−0.002	−0.015 ***	−0.001	−0.017 ***	−0.002
	(−3.285)	(−0.258)	(−4.040)	(−0.428)	(−3.102)	(−0.369)	(−3.916)	(−0.676)
α(H)−α(L)		0.173 ***		0.198 ***		0.162 ***		0.171 ***
α (OCFA)	−0.009 **	−0.008 **	−0.011 **	−0.010 ***	−0.010 **	−0.008 **	−0.011 ***	−0.010 ***
	(−2.046)	(−2.260)	(−2.457)	(−2.813)	(−2.175)	(−2.006)	(−2.777)	(−2.663)
α(H)−α(L)		0.007		0.005		0.029		0.016

Note: The difference α(H)−α(L) is annualized. The t-statistic is in parentheses. *, **, and *** indicate significance at the 10, 5, and 1 percent levels, respectively.

The underperformance of initial public offerings in Poland was mainly driven by IPOs with a high level of divergence of opinion proxied with low pre-issue accounting profitability. Alphas reported for IPOs with a lower performance range from −10.8% to −21.6% annually. The statistically significant long-term returns of IPOs with a low pre-issue accounting performance were negative in all of the specifications. A high level of divergence of opinion about the future prospects of companies approximated with a worse pre-issue performance resulted in a severe underperformance measured with alpha. The differences between quantiles based on profitability were economically important and statistically significant in most of the specifications. The underperformance of the high-profitable IPOs is not too strong and it is not statistically significant in some specifications. Such results may be interpreted as being only partly consistent with the over-optimism explanation and with the divergence of opinion hypothesis. In some specifications, the intercepts for high-performance IPOs were not statistically significant. The group of less profitable companies could consist of companies with a lower level of divergence of opinion because of really good financial health, as well as IPO companies that artificially managed earnings for the moment of going public. This could influence the mixed results of the robustness check.

The robustness check of the differences between quantiles based on cash flows reveals that the differences were statistically significant in half of specifications and were much lower than differences based on profitability. Cash flows are usually perceived as being not so easily managed as earnings.

If we take the cash flow ratios as a proxy for the divergence of opinion level, then the results are not so undisputable. The results of the robustness check are an argument for setting a question in further research: are cash flows less important than earnings in the process of assessment of the financial health of the IPO company by investors, even if earnings seem to be managed more easily? Finally, investors seem to be more worried.

6. Conclusions

This research has aimed to discuss the sources of long-term underperformance of initial public offerings of equities (IPO). We have explored the relationship between pre-issue financial health and subsequent long-term relative equity returns in Poland. This paper provides some international evidence on the long-term performance after going public for the Warsaw Stock Exchange. Poland was an example of an emerging market during the sample period, but its continuous improvements in capital market infrastructure and steady economic progress have led to its recent reclassification as a developed country by FTSE Russell. Poland is also an important European player in terms of capital market development. Providing empirical conclusions in the area of long-term underperformance explanation is important for both investors and academics.

This paper contributes to the existing research as it tests the long-term returns of IPOs with the calendar-time portfolio approach. Starting with January 2002, calendar month rolling portfolios of firms that had gone public in the previous 36 or 24 months were constructed with monthly rebalancing as some IPO companies exited and entered. Monthly excess returns were regressed on factor models. We started with the CAPM model that includes the market risk factor. Then, we tested with the Fama-French 3-factor model that expands on the CAPM by adding two more factors to the model: size risk and value risk factors. The Carhart 4-factor model is an expansion of the FF3 as it adds the momentum factor. Finally, the Fama-French 5-factor model that describes risk along with investment and profitability represents the latest innovation in asset pricing models. We reported evidence on strong underperformance following the initial public offering for different specifications of the calendar-time portfolio methodology. The level of abnormal returns is slightly different in the alternative specifications. It ranges from −9.6% to −13.2% annually. The change of the methods of alpha's calculation does not influence the general conclusion about the economically and statistically significant negative long-term returns after the first public equity offerings in Poland. The findings about the long-term IPO underperformance using the calendar-time portfolio approach seem to be similar to the conclusions of previous studies for Poland that have revealed significant long-term IPO underperformance with the buy-and-hold approach.

The research provides evidence of the explanatory power of pre-issue accounting performance for the long-term risk-adjusted market returns. The study has used several approaches to test the robustness of results. We have applied six different measures of the pre-issue IPO financial health, namely three dimensions of the reported accounting effect (net income, operating income, and operating cash flow) and two bases of performance: one from the income statement (sales) and the second from the balance sheet (assets). Each of the six measures allowed us to divide the sample into two quantiles. Regressions were run under four factor models for 24- and 36-month portfolios in quantiles. Taken together, we repeated the calendar-time portfolio procedure in 96 research specifications. By comparing alternative estimation approaches, we reported that weak pre-issue financial profitability resulted in experiencing strong underperformance in the long-run by IPO firms in Poland, no matter the regression specification. The difference in annual returns between quantiles based on profits was quite substantial. For more profitable companies, either less severe underperformance is observed or the underperformance is even absent as the intercepts are not significant under some settings. The differences between quantiles based on cash flows were much lower and statistically significant in half of the specifications.

Theoretical explanations of IPO underperformance include the divergence of opinion together with optimistic investor theory, as well as theories relating to investor sentiment, the fads phenomenon, and market timing. Our results do not seem to support the window of opportunity hypothesis. If firms were to go public at the height of their accounting performance, thus seizing their window of opportunity, it would result in worse long-term returns for firms in good financial health. This was neither observed for quantiles based on profitability nor cash flow. Our results may be interpreted as being only partly consistent with the over-optimism explanation and divergence of opinion hypothesis (Miller 1977). Companies with a higher level of divergence of opinion proxied with lower pre-issue profitability suffered from weak market pricing in the long-term. It also seems to suggest that around-the-issue profitability influences the long-term perception of the IPO company. The results may also be, to some extent, in line with the psychological background (Kahneman and Tversky 1982) suggesting that investors may overweigh recent information and believe that a poor pre-issue performance will continue after going public. The results of the robustness check also lead us to suspect that some of the highly profitable IPO companies could manage earnings for the moment of going public as the results for highly profitable IPO firms are mixed.

Such results also provide opportunities for future research. A possible research direction may be to give additional insights into earnings manipulation around going public with the calendar-time approach. If earnings are artificially boosted around going public by accrual adjustments, a challenging direction of future research could be focused on combining the calendar-time portfolio approach together with accrual estimation. Such an approach should employ models to derive normal levels of accruals in order to observe discretionary accruals. Non-discretionary accruals may be estimated with methods such as the Jones model (Jones 1991); the Dechow, Sloan, and Sweeney model (Dechow et al. 1995); the Kothari, Leone, and Wasley model (Kothari et al. 2005); the Dechow-Dichev model in the version modified by McNichols (Dechow and Dichev 2002; McNichols 2002, 2000); and the Ball-Shivakumar model (Ball and Shivakumar 2006). Explaining the long-term IPO performance measured with the calendar-time portfolio approach combined with accruals estimation would expand the conclusions of this research and enrich the evidence on the implications of financial health together with earnings management around going public.

Author Contributions: The authors contributed equally to the research and writing of the manuscript.

Funding: Financial support for this paper from the National Science Centre, Poland, is gratefully acknowledged (the number of the research project 2015/19/D/HS4/01950).

Conflicts of Interest: The authors declare no conflict of interest. The funders had no role in the design of the study; in the collection, analyses, or interpretation of data; in the writing of the manuscript, or in the decision to publish the results.

References

Ali, Fahad, RongRong He, and Yue Xiang Jiang. 2018. Size, Value and Business Cycle Variables. The Three-Factor Model and Future Economic Growth: Evidence from an Emerging Market. *Economies* 6: 14. [CrossRef]

Alvarez, Susana, and Victor M. González. 2001. Long-Run Performance of Initial Public Offerings (IPOs) in the Spanish Capital Market. *SSRN Electronic Journal*. [CrossRef]

Aussenegg, Wolfgang. 2000. Privatization versus Private Sector Initial Public Offerings in Poland. *Multinational Finance Journal* 4: 69–99. Available online: https://ssrn.com/abstract=2627710 (accessed on 4 January 2019). [CrossRef]

Ball, Ray, and Lakshmanan Shivakumar. 2006. The Role of Accruals in Asymmetrically Timely Gain and Loss Recognition. *Journal of Accounting Research* 44: 207–42. [CrossRef]

Barber, Brad M., and John D. Lyon. 1997. Detecting long-run abnormal stock returns: The empirical power and specification of test statistics. *Journal of Financial Economics* 43: 341–72. [CrossRef]

Brav, Alon, Christopher Geczy, and Paul A. Gompers. 2000. Is the abnormal return following equity issuances anomalous? *Journal of Financial Economics* 56: 209–49. [CrossRef]

Brav, Alon, and Paul A. Gompers. 1997. Myth or Reality? The Long-Run Underperformance of Initial Public Offerings: Evidence from Venture and Nonventure Capital-Backed Companies. *Journal of Finance* 52: 1791–1821. [CrossRef]

Brycz, Bogumiła, Tadeusz Dudycz, and Michał J. Kowalski. 2017. Is the success of an issuer an investor success? Evidence from Polish IPOs. *Baltic Journal of Economics* 17: 57–77. [CrossRef]

Carhart, Mark M. 1997. On Persistence in Mutual Fund Performance. *Journal of Finance* 52: 57–82. [CrossRef]

Dechow, Patricia M., and Ilia D. Dichev. 2002. The Quality of Accruals and Earnings: The Role of Accrual Estimation Errors. *Accounting Review* 77: 35–59. [CrossRef]

Dechow, Patricia M., Richard G. Sloan, and Amy P. Sweeney. 1995. Detecting Earnings Management. *Accounting Review* 70: 193–225. Available online: http://www.jstor.org/stable/248303 (accessed on 4 January 2019).

Diether, Karl B., Christopher J. Malloy, and Anna Scherbina. 2002. Differences of Opinion and the Cross Section of Stock Returns. *Journal of Finance* 57: 2113–41. [CrossRef]

Eckbo, B. Espen, Ronald W. Masulis, and Øyvind Norli. 2000. Seasoned public offerings: resolution of the 'new issues puzzle'. *Journal of Financial Economics* 56: 251–91. [CrossRef]

Ewen, Martin. 2018. Where is the Risk Reward? The Impact of Volatility-Based Fund Classification on Performance. *Risks* 6: 80. [CrossRef]

Fama, Eugene F. 1998. Market efficiency, long-term returns, and behavioral finance. *Journal of Financial Economics* 49: 283–306. [CrossRef]

Fama, Eugene F., Lawrence Fisher, Michael C. Jensen, and Richard Roll. 1969. The Adjustment of Stock Prices to New Information. *International Economic Review* 10: 1–21. [CrossRef]

Fama, Eugene F., and Kenneth R. French. 1993. Common risk factors in the returns on stocks and bonds. *Journal of Financial Economics* 33: 3–56. [CrossRef]

Fama, Eugene F., and Kenneth R. French. 2015. A five-factor asset pricing model. *Journal of Financial Economics* 116: 1–22. [CrossRef]

Fama, Eugene F., and Kenneth R. French. 2016. Dissecting Anomalies with a Five-Factor Model. *Review of Financial Studies* 29: 69–103. [CrossRef]

Fu, Chengbo. 2018. Alpha Beta Risk and Stock Returns—A Decomposition Analysis of Idiosyncratic Volatility with Conditional Models. *Risks* 6: 124. [CrossRef]

Gao, Yan, Connie X. Mao, and Rui Zhong. 2006. Divergence of opinion and long-term performance of initial public offerings. *Journal of Financial Research* 29: 113–29. [CrossRef]

Ibbotson, Roger G. 1975. Price performance of common stock new issues. *Journal of Financial Economics* 2: 235–72. [CrossRef]

Jegadeesh, Narasimhan, and Jason Karceski. 2009. Long-run performance evaluation: Correlation and heteroskedasticity-consistent tests. *Journal of Empirical Finance* 16: 101–11. [CrossRef]

Jegadeesh, Narasimhan, and Sheridan Titman. 1993. Returns to Buying Winners and Selling Losers: Implications for Stock Market Efficiency. *Journal of Finance* 48: 65–91. [CrossRef]

Jelic, Ranko, and Richard Briston. 2003. Privatisation Initial Public Offerings: the Polish Experience. *European Financial Management* 9: 457–84. [CrossRef]

Jewartowski, Tomasz, and Joanna Lizińska. 2012. Short- and Long-Term Performance of Polish IPOs. *Emerging Markets Finance and Trade* 48: 59–75. [CrossRef]

Jones, Jennifer J. 1991. Earnings Management During Import Relief Investigations. *Journal of Accounting Research* 29: 193–228. [CrossRef]

Kahneman, Daniel, and Amos Tversky. 1982. The psychology of preferences. *Scientific American* 246: 160–73. [CrossRef]

Kooli, Maher, Jean-François L'Her, and Jean-Marc Suret. 2006. Do IPOs really underperform in the long-run? New evidence from the Canadian market. *Journal of Private Equity* 9: 48–58. [CrossRef]

Kothari, Sagar P., Andrew J. Leone, and Charles E. Wasley. 2005. Performance matched discretionary accrual measures. *Journal of Accounting and Economics* 39: 163–97. [CrossRef]

Kothari, Sagar P., and Jerold B. Warner. 2007. Econometrics of event studies. *Handbook of Empirical Corporate Finance* 1: 3–36. [CrossRef]

Levis, Mario. 1993. The Long-Run Performance of Initial Public Offerings: The UK Experience 1980–1988. *Financial Management* 22: 28–41. [CrossRef]

Lintner, John. 1969. The Valuation of Risk Assets and the Selection of Risky Investments in Stock Portfolios and Capital Budgets: A Reply. *The Review of Economics and Statistics* 51: 222–24. [CrossRef]

Lizińska, Joanna, and Leszek Czapiewski. 2014. Performance of Polish IPO firms: size and profitability effect. *Gospodarka Narodowa* 1: 53–71. [CrossRef]

Lizińska, Joanna, and Leszek Czapiewski. 2016. Is the IPO Anomaly in Poland Only Apparent or Real? In *The Essence and Measurement of Organizational Efficiency*. Edited by Tadeusz Dudycz, Grażyna Osbert-Pociecha and Bogumiła Brycz. Springer Proceedings in Business and Economics. Cham: Springer, pp. 175–94.

Loughran, Tim, and Jay R. Ritter. 1995. The New Issues Puzzle. *Journal of Finance* 50: 23–51. [CrossRef]

Lyn, Esmeralda O., and Edward J. Zychowicz. 2003. The performance of new equity offerings in Hungary and Poland. *Global Finance Journal* 14: 181–95. [CrossRef]

Lyon, John D., Brad M. Barber, and Chih-Ling Tsai. 1999. Improved Methods for Tests of Long-Run Abnormal Stock Returns. *Journal of Finance* 54: 165–201. [CrossRef]

McNichols, Maureen F. 2000. Research design issues in earnings management studies. *Journal of Accounting and Public Policy* 19: 313–45. [CrossRef]

McNichols, Maureen F. 2002. Discussion of the quality of accruals and earnings: Multiples. *Journal of Accounting Research* 40: 135–72.

Miller, Edward M. 1977. Risk, uncertainty, and divergence of opinion. *Journal of Finance* 32: 1151–68. [CrossRef]

Mitchell, Mark L., and Erik Stafford. 2000. Managerial Decisions and Long-Term Stock Price Performance. *The Journal of Business* 73: 287–329. [CrossRef]

Rajan, Rabhuram, and Henri Servaes. 1997. Analyst Following of Initial Public Offerings. *Journal of Finance* 52: 507–29. [CrossRef]

Ritter, Jay R. 1991. The Long-Run Performance of initial Public Offerings. *Journal of Finance* 46: 3–27. [CrossRef]

Sharpe, William F. 1964. Capital asset prices: A theory of market equilibrium under conditions of risk. *Journal of Finance* 19: 425–42. [CrossRef]

Shen, Zhe, Limin Chen, and Qian Sun. 2015. Do Chinese IPOs really underperform in the long run? *Journal of Portfolio Management* 41: 84–91. [CrossRef]

Teoh, Siew Hong, Ivo Welch, and Tak J. Wong. 1998. Earnings Management and the Long-Run Market Performance of Initial Public Offerings. *Journal of Finance* 53: 1935–74. [CrossRef]

11

To What Extent do Regional Effects Influence Firms' Capital Structure? The Case of Southern Italian SMEs'

Olivier Butzbach and Domenico Sarno *

Department of Political Science, University of Campania "L. Vanvitelli", 81100 Caserta, Italy; olivierkarl.butzbach@unicampania.it

* Correspondence: domenico.sarno@unicampania.it

Abstract: There is tremendous interest, in the economic literature, for the determinants of firms' capital structure decisions. A rich body of empirical works now exists that purports to identify firm- and country-level factors affecting firms' financing patterns. In addition, more recently, a new stream of studies has emerged that investigates cross-regional variation in small firms' capital structure. While small firms' leverage does seem to vary across regions, at least in countries where significant regional differences in economic and financial development and in the quality of institutions exist, not much yet is known about variation in debt maturity, in debt in relation to equity, and between different types of small firms. The present paper aims to fill this gap through an empirical analysis of cross-regional variation in the capital structure of a sample of about 30,000 Italian small firms over a 13-year period, including the aftermath of the credit crunch that followed the 2007–2008 global financial crisis. The findings confirm the view that small firms in underdeveloped regions are more financially constrained, but also amend some of the results shown in the literature, in particular by showing how small firms in Italy's Southern regions have higher levels of equity and fixed assets than small firms in other regions.

Keywords: capital structure; leverage; SMEs; cross-regional variation

JEL Classification: G32; G30; L60

---

1. Introduction

The determinants of firms' capital structure is the object of a large component of economic literature, both empirical and theoretical. Theory-wise, various arguments have been put forward concerning a firm's decision to use more debt, equity, internal funding sources, or alternative funding sources. The "pecking order" theory, first formulated by Myers (1984), is well known—but alternative theories exist, such as the "trade-off" hypothesis (See Fama and French 2002) or the financial life cycle approach (Berger and Udell 1998). Each theory generates its own set of hypotheses regarding (i) the potential preferences of firms in terms of the source of funding they wish to use to finance their investment; and (ii) the factors constraining such preferences. While hypotheses concerning preferences vary, there is a broad consensus in the literature around the likely firm-level determinants of firms' capital structure choice, i.e., firms' size, profitability, asset structure, age, and growth.

The empirical literature has largely confirmed the second set of hypotheses, e.g., those regarding the determinants of firms' capital structure choices. A firm's size is seen, in particular, as a very significant factor determining, for instance, a firm's ability to access external finance—bank debt or marketable securities. This has to do, mainly, with the greater information asymmetries presented by small and medium-sized firms (SMEs). Also, the literature widely confirms the hypothesis that profitable firms exhibit lower leverage; or that the greater a firm's fixed assets, the greater its long-term debts (Rajan and Zingales 1995; Wald 1999; Booth et al. 2001). Regarding the first set of hypotheses, the jury is still out: Several studies find evidence in favour of the pecking order theory (REF); others do not (see, for instance, Fama and French 2002); others yet find evidence compatible with both the pecking order theory and alternative theories (La Rocca et al. 2011).

While early empirical work was mostly based on one-country analyses, a rich stream of studies has emerged since the late 1990s to investigate cross-country variation in capital structure decisions. Indeed, such cross-country differences have now been amply documented (for instance, in works, such as Booth et al. 2001; Beck et al. 2008; Fan et al. 2012; Mateev et al. 2013). These studies have made an important contribution to the literature on capital structure decisions of large and small firms by highlighting the significance of country-effects, on top of firm and industry-effects. These country effects have been generally identified as either related to the structure and development of a country's financial system (Levine 1997, 2004) or to the quality and development of a country's institutions, especially legal institutions (Beck et al. 2003, 2005), or to both (La Porta et al. 1997, 1998). An ongoing debate in the literature regards the relative importance of country- and firm-effects (and industry effects) in determining firms' capital structure (Daskalakis and Psillaki 2008; De Jong et al. 2008; Fan et al. 2012).

However, firms' capital structure choices may also vary within countries. Indeed, many countries are characterized by significant cross-regional variation in terms of economic growth and legal and financial characteristics—the latter being often correlated with the former (see Guiso et al. 2004). In addition, small firms are likely to be more dependent upon local sources of funding, as they have a lower capacity than large firms to tap into national financial markets; small firms' access to finance is made harder by the significant information asymmetries that may characterize their relationships with potential investors. These characteristics make studies of cross-regional variation in small firms' capital structure particularly relevant to the broader academic discussion about capital structure decisions, explaining the emergence of a stream of empirical studies focusing on cross-regional variation in firms' capital structure (see La Rocca et al. 2010; Palacín-Sánchez et al. 2013; Serrasqueiro and Caetano 2015; Palacín-Sánchez and Pietro 2016; Matias and Serrasqueiro 2017).

This paper aims to contribute to this emerging literature on cross-regional-variation in the capital structure of small firms in three ways: First, by using a very large sample of SMEs during a relatively long period of time (longer than the typical time-frame used in the capital structure literature). In particular, the period under study encompasses the years following the 2007–2008 global financial crisis, which helps us measure the impact of the credit crunch on Italian SMEs' capital structure. Secondly, this paper contributes to the literature by highlighting variation in equity as well as debt; and by analyzing differences in debt maturity as well as total leverage (not systematically done in the literature). Third, our empirical strategy allows us to distinguish between different types of SMEs, given the heterogeneity of this group of firms, both in terms of characteristics and financial needs.

The Italian context is especially interesting for assessing cross-regional variation in the capital structure of small firms. First, SMEs are extremely numerous in Italy—as of 2015, Italy had 4,687,891 firms, of which only 3153 had more than 250 employees. Italian SMEs are present in all economic activities. Secondly, Italy has a historical record of significant and persistent cross-regional gaps in output growth, employment, and productivity: In 2017, GDP per capita was 18,200 Euro in Southern regions, 44.2% below that of Northern regions. This socio-economic development gap translates in the peculiar industrial structure of Southern Italy, characterized by more traditional activities, a lower average size of firms, and younger firms due to the higher turnover of firms' population. These characteristics have persisted until today.

Third, Italy has a long experience in policies (called *"intervento straordinario"*) adopted in the 1950s and 1960s to reduce this regional gap in socio-economic development through, in particular, a dedicated funding agency—policies that have had, historically, an impact on Sothern firms' financial constraints and strategy. However, these policies and the dedicated agency were set aside in the early 1990s.[1] At the same time, the Italian banking industry started to undergo a deep re-organization through bank privatization, banking markets de-segmentation and liberalization, and bank restructuring on a national scale. In this process, the large Southern banks, which had, in the past, played an important role in promoting and sustaining local growth, disappeared.

Finally, another set of macroeconomic factors that may have affected the capital structure of small firms in Southern Italy (especially in the latter years covered in our sample) relate to the 2007–2008 financial crisis and its consequences. In the aftermath of a credit shock, firms' financial constraints increase: Firms need to find new sources of funding for their financial needs. While large firms can easily find alternative funding sources, smaller firms have a harder time doing so, because of their opacity and riskiness; thus, they face decreasing leverage. It is likely to believe, furthermore, that these deleveraging effects are likely to be greater in less-developed areas (Beattie et al. 2006).

The analysis presented here uses data on a large panel of Italian SMEs observed over a 13-year period (from 2001 to 2013), for a total of 427,468 observations (an average of 32,882 small firms observed per year) for Italy as a whole; of which 53,971 observations (an average of 4151 small firm-observations per year) for Southern Italy only. The study compares SMEs' capital structure across Italian administrative regions, clustered in two macro-areas widely used in the literature: The less developed Mezzogiorno, composed of the eight Southern Italian regions (Abruzzo, Molise, Campania, Puglia, Basilicata, and Calabria), in addition to the two islands (Sicily and Sardinia); and the "Center-North" macro-area, composed of the other 12 administrative regions of the central and northern areas of the country.[2]

Our analysis confirms the existence of significant regional effects in the determinants of small firms' capital structure, in line with similar studies (Palacín-Sánchez et al. 2013; Serrasqueiro and Caetano 2015; Palacín-Sánchez and Pietro 2016; Matias and Serrasqueiro 2017). However, several findings contrast with the accepted views concerning the capital structure of small firms—especially in underdeveloped regions. First, small firms in Southern Italy tend to be over-capitalized, rather than suffering from equity shortage, as predicted by the literature (see, for instance, Carter and Auken 2006). Secondly, small firms in Southern Italy show high levels of indebtedness—and lower leverage elasticity—than in other Italian regions. Again, this runs counter to the argument that smaller firms in lagging regions may have more trouble accessing bank credit. Finally, while most firm-level determinants affect capital structure along the lines predicted in the literature, there is a negative relationship between leverage and the tangibility of assets in Southern Italian SMEs.

The rest of the paper is organized as follows. The next section reviews the existing literature on capital structure determinants in small firms. Sections 3 and 4 present the data and methodology used here. Section 5 shows descriptive statistics revealing some of the distinctive features of the financial structure of SMEs in southern Italy. Section 6 presents and discusses the findings of the empirical analysis. Section 7 concludes.

2. Determinants of SMEs' Capital Structure: From Firm- to Country- and Region-Effects

2.1. Firm-Level Determinants of Capital Structure Decisions

As argued above, the question of firms' capital structure decisions has aroused tremendous interest in the economic literature in the past. The theoretical foundations of such literature rest on the seminal work by Modigliani and Miller, and on the removal of some of the conditions

1 The law supporting the so-called "extraordinary intervention" for promoting growth in Southern regions was repealed in 1992; in the same year, the government ended the operations of Agensud (ex *Cassa per il Mezzogiorno*), the public agency established in 1950 and devoted to funding infrastructure in the Mezzogiorno areas.

2 The existence of a long-term North-South economic divide in Italy is well known and has led to a rich literature on the subject. The intensive interventions designed since the fifties to promote the growth of Mezzogiorno have substantially failed to achieve the convergence of the Southern area with the other regions of the Country.

imposed by their "irrelevance theorem". In explaining firms' preference for equity, debt, or retained earnings as main sources of funding, economists alternatively stress the causal role of agency costs (Jensen and Meckling 1976; Myers 1977; Harris and Raviv 1990), information asymmetries and signalling (Ross 1977; Myers and Majluf 1984; Myers 1984), or taxation (Miller 1977; De Angelo and Masulis 1980). Particularly popular approaches to understand corporate capital structure decisions are the pecking order theory, the trade-off theory, and the financial life cycle theory. In a nutshell, the pecking order theory assumes that firms' capital structure preferences depend on financing costs; and that the latter are related to information asymmetries, so that equity financing is costlier than debt, which is costlier than internal funding; hence, corporate managers prefer internal financing over debt and debt over equity (Myers and Majluf 1984). According to the trade-off perspective, by contrast, financing decisions are based on cost-benefits' assessment balancing, in particular, the dead-weight costs of bankruptcy and the tax saving benefits of debt (Kraus and Litzenberger 1973). Finally, under the financial life cycle perspective, firms' capital structure preferences varies with their life cycle: The latter determines "the nature of [a firm's] financial needs, the availability of financial resources, and the related cost of capital" (Berger and Udell 1998, p. 108). Theoretically, the analytical strength of these various approaches is considered equally relevant for the financial strategies of the firm,[3] but none of them provides an exhaustive and definitive means of explaining the actual financial (or capital structure) choices of firms.

This is especially true in the case of SMEs, where information asymmetries are believed to be higher than in large firms. In particular, small firms are deemed more "informationally opaque" than large firms (Berger and Udell 1998). From a "financial life cycle" perspective (Berger and Udell 1998; La Rocca et al. 2011), this informational opaqueness raises the cost of debt for young (and small) firms, reversing the preferences hypothesized under the pecking order theory (Berger and Udell 1998); in addition, young firms have low or no reputation, and lack tangible assets, which contributes to raising the cost of debt (La Rocca et al. 2011).

The various hypotheses formulated within the theoretical approaches briefly sketched above have been the object of a rich stream of empirical tests, which were primarily concerned with identifying the main determinants of capital structure decisions at the firm level; as mentioned in the introduction above, there is a wide consensus in the literature that such firm-level determinants are size, age, growth, profitability, and its volatility and, finally, the tangibility of assets (for examples of such consensus, see Booth et al. 2001; Hall et al. 2004; Fan et al. 2012; Matias and Serrasqueiro 2017). The nature and effects of such firm-level determinants are briefly examined below.

The effects of firm size on capital structure are potentially numerous, but they are all consistent with the idea that when the size of a firm increases, the share of debt (leverage) also increases, given that the smaller the firm, the greater the information asymmetries; and that greater information asymmetries raise the cost of debt. In addition, the impact of liquidity constraints on firm growth are likely to increase with firm size (Donati 2016). Finally, the range of funding sources available to firms is positively correlated with firm size—which increases small firms' dependence on a narrow range of sources (Lawless et al. 2015). Most empirical studies find a positive relationship between firm size and leverage, while the relationship between size and short-term debt has sometimes been found to be negative (Chittenden et al. 1996; Michaelas et al. 1999; Noulas and Genimakis 2011; Dang et al. 2018).[4]

Similarly, information asymmetry theory predicts a positive relationship between a firm's leverage and its age. Within this framework, a firm's survival mitigates the opacity of the relationship with lenders; therefore, the provision of external resources becomes easier (La Rocca et al. 2011). In contrast,

---

[3] Although the trade-off theory has been especially criticized for overemphasizing deadweight costs associated with bankruptcy; see (Miller 1977; Myers 1984).

[4] A contrasting hypothesis is formulated by Rajan and Zingales (1995) for larger firms. As they are subject to lower information asymmetry, they are encouraged to use equity financing; therefore, a negative relationship between leverage and size is predicted (Rajan and Zingales 1995).

the theory of the financial life cycle of the firm proposes a non-linear relationship between leverage and age: In the first stage of firms' existence, the demand for external resources is greater because the surviving firms grow faster; this need for external finance decreases in the maturity stage because there are fewer investment opportunities and firms are able to accumulate greater resources to finance their activities (Berger and Udell 1998). Thus, there may be a negative relationship between leverage and age—a relationship that remains negative when one focuses on short-term debt instead of long-term debt (Hall et al. 2004). The empirical evidence is, on that front, not conclusive: Both positive and negative relationships between leverage and age have been found (see, for recent examples, Beattie et al. 2006; Daskalakis and Psillaki 2008; Noulas and Genimakis 2011; La Rocca et al. 2011).

The growth rate of a firm is usually taken as an approximation of investment opportunities; its relationship with leverage is ambiguous. On the one hand, in the trade-off approach, faster growth rates tend to increase distress costs; therefore, self-financing is preferred and the relationship between leverage and growth could consequently be negative (Kraus and Litzenberger 1973). On the other hand, pecking order theory tells us that profitable firms are able to make higher earnings and thus can sustain greater debt costs; therefore, a positive relationship is predicted between leverage and growth (Myers and Majluf 1984). The empirical evidence is compatible with both these approaches as sometimes the relationship is found to be positive and sometimes negative (Rajan and Zingales 1995; Psillaki and Daskalakis 2009; Noulas and Genimakis 2011; La Rocca et al. 2011).

More broadly, the pecking order approach is usually seen in the literature as providing a better explanation of the relationship between leverage and profitability (see Mateev et al. 2013). As external finance is more expensive than internal finance, profitable firms may exhibit a general propensity to use internal resources; consequently, a negative relationship may prevail between leverage and earnings. The relationship becomes unclear in terms of the distinction between short-term debt and long-term debt. Indeed, profitable firms need to finance their growth through external resources because they have greater opportunities and the retained profits are insufficient to finance such growth in the long-run. Consequently, a positive relationship might prevail between earnings and long-term debt, while this relationship might remain negative with regard to short-term debt. The empirical evidence is compatible with all the above arguments; empirical studies generally find that leverage is correlated negatively with the profit rate, but the relationship can be positive or negative for short-term and long-term debt depending on the prevalence of the former or latter (Rajan and Zingales 1995; Adedeji 1998; Michaelas et al. 1999; Hall et al. 2004).

Earnings' volatility is usually taken as a proxy for the riskiness of business operations and for the likelihood of financial distress. A strong relationship can be predicted between leverage and the riskiness of a firm because higher debt causes greater volatility in the firm's earnings. The explanation for this relationship proposed by the pecking order theory is as effective as that of trade-off theory; internal finance is preferred and, consequently, firms reduce their leverage to reduce their cost of capital and to contain their risk. This is because a negative relationship is predicted between leverage and riskiness. Empirical analysis generally confirms this hypothesis (Cassar and Holmes 2003; Hall et al. 2004; Psillaki and Daskalakis 2009).

Finally, among other determinants of capital structure choices, the tangibility of assets, measured by the share of fixed assets to total assets, is of importance because greater fixed assets might make it easier to gain access to external finance. There are two reasons for this: First, with a high share of fixed assets, lenders are able to minimize their loss if bankruptcy occurs; secondly, the collateral of the firm will be larger. Based on these arguments, a positive relationship between asset structure and long-term debt is expected, while the relationship with short-term debt might be negative. Although the direction of the relationship is ambiguous depending on the composition of debt maturity, the available empirical evidence suggests that a positive relationship might prevail between leverage and asset structure; this result is verified effectively with reference to large firms (Demirgüç-Kunt and Maksimovic 1999). However, such a positive relationship has never been confirmed for small firms; according to several studies, the relationship is negative, especially for short-term debt (Rajan and Zingales 1995; Chittenden et al. 1996; Jordan et al. 1998; Michaelas et al. 1999; Frank and Goyal 2003).

As mentioned in the introduction above, such firm-level determinants were first the object of empirical studies conducted at the country level (usually the United States). It is only gradually, especially after the late 1990s, that economists started empirically testing capital structure theories through cross-country studies. What such studies have found can be summarized thus: On the one hand, firm-level determinants were generally found to hold across countries—in other words, the sign of the relationship between leverage and such firm-level factors was found not to change from one country to the next (see, for instance, Booth et al. 2001); on the other hand, however, these comparative studies have generally found significant cross-country variation in the capital structure of firms. For instance, in a survey of 12,726 SMEs distributed over 28 European countries, Moritz et al. identified eight different clusters or financing patterns (Moritz et al. 2016). Cross-country variation is frequently attributed, either directly or indirectly, to a variety of country-level factors, to which we now turn.

2.2. From Country-Level Factors to Cross-Regional Variation in Small Firms' Financing Patterns

Country-level factors have been early identified in the economic literature as belonging to two broad groups: Factors related to countries' legal/institutional environment, on the one hand; and factors related to countries' financial system, on the other. Both sets of factors were first analyzed in the context of studies trying to establish country-level causes of economic growth and development (Levine 1997, 2004), and within the so-called "law and finance" literature (La Porta et al. 1997, 1998). Subsequent works within the capital structure literature have amply drawn on these earlier and more general analyses.

Institutional variables, such as the nature of the legal system (i.e., a common-law versus a civil law system) and the quality of enforcement, are especially relevant because they affect the ability of capital providers to enforce debt contracts (Fan et al. 2012). As a consequence, lower quality law enforcement, measured by some authors as the absence of sound bankruptcy procedures and the perceived existence of corruption (Fan et al. 2012), by others as creditor and shareholder rights protection (De Jong et al. 2008), should be correlated with lower leverage (and, generally, lower access to external finance by firms). On the other hand, however, lower quality institutions may encourage firms to seek alternative sources of finance; as Beck et al. (2008) put it, "in countries with weaker property rights protection, we would expect substitute forms of external finance, such as informal and supplier credit or development bank financing to be used." (Beck et al. 2008, p. 469). The level of economic development is another important country-level factor that may affect firms' capital structure. Here, the empirical findings diverge: Beck et al. (2008) did not find a significant relationship between the level of economic development and small firms' financing patterns (Beck et al. 2008); while Fan et al. (2012), who studied a sample within a narrower set of countries, but over a longer period, found that debt maturity is positively related to levels of economic development (Fan et al. 2012). Finally, the structure and the functioning of a country's financial sector is widely assumed to have consequences on firms' capital structure. The frequently tested hypothesis here is that the greater the size of the banking sector, the greater the firms' leverage; while this hypothesis is confirmed in empirical studies, an additional hypothesis negatively correlating the size of the banking sector with debt maturity has been validated (Fan et al. 2012) and invalidated (Demirgüç-Kunt and Maksimovic 1999).

However, country-level factors do not only affect firms' capital structure directly. As De Jong et al. (2008) usefully pointed out, they also exert an indirect effect by influencing the role of firm-specific determinants of leverage (De Jong et al. 2008). In particular, they argue that "the roles of bankruptcy cost variables, namely tangibility, business risk, and firm size, can be mitigated in a country with a more developed bond market as bankruptcy costs are better handled because of good protection for creditors." (De Jong et al. 2008).

Are there specific country effects regarding SMEs? While earlier studies (Rajan and Zingales 1995; Demirgüç-Kunt and Maksimovic 1999; Booth et al. 2001; De Jong et al. 2008) focused mostly on large firms, it is only recently that systematic cross-country studies of SMEs' financial patterns have been undertaken (Hall et al. 2004; Beck et al. 2008; Mateev et al. 2013). As argued above, the size of the firm is a key firm-specific determinant of capital structure. The comparative literature reviewed here has argued that country-level factors may affect small firms differently than large firms. In particular, as Beck et al. argue, "better property right protection can level the playing field between small and large firms in terms of the use of external and especially bank finance." (Beck et al. 2008, p. 482).

A more fine grained understanding of the impact of varying levels and rhythms of institutional and economic development may be gained from another shift in focus, however: Hence, the emergence, in the past decade, of a new stream of studies dedicated to cross-regional comparisons of capital structure choices among SMEs (La Rocca et al. 2010, 2011; Palacín-Sánchez et al. 2013; Serrasqueiro and Caetano 2015; Palacín-Sánchez and Pietro 2016; Di Pietro et al. 2016; Matias and Serrasqueiro 2017). All these studies focus on cross-regional variation in SME financing in three Southern European countries—Italy, Spain, and Portugal. These three countries, furthermore, are characterized by significant cross-regional differences in social and economic development.

The shift in focus accomplished in these studies presents several advantages: First, it can allow us to hold some of the institutional and financial variables identified at the country level constant, since they are not liable to vary across regions of a same country. Such constant factors are: The nature of the legal system (e.g., civil vs. common law). On the other hand, several other country-level institutional and financial variables are easily transposable at the regional level, namely: The quality of legal enforcement (see Guiso et al. 2004, for an analysis of the Italian case), the amount/degree of perceived corruption, and the size and diversity of the banking sector. The size and access of the securities' markets are less relevant at the regional level when focusing on small firms' capital structure, given those firms' assumed little access to national securities market and overall reliance on local financial markets for their funding.

The second advantage is that cross-regional comparisons may highlight within-country distortions in (i) the institutional environment faced by small firms (as seen above) and (ii) the availability and the nature of financial services. Economic geography has shown how the spatial structure of financial systems may influence the availability of funding for small and new firms. Economically lagging regions, in other words, may be less well equipped with financial intermediaries and institutions, thus accentuating the "funding gap" faced by SMEs (Klagge et al. 2017).

What are, then, the main findings of this emerging literature? According to Beck et al., small firms in countries with higher financial development and/or stronger property rights use more external finance (Beck et al. 2008). Is this finding confirmed at the regional level? It does seem so. In a study of a sample of 10,242 Italian SMEs over a 10-year period (until 2005), La Rocca et al. found that, indeed, Southern Italian firms are more constrained financially and less levered (La Rocca et al. 2011). Similar results were found, on a larger sample and over a more recent six-year period, by Di Pietro et al. (2016), who also found that banking concentration at the regional level is negatively related to small firms' leverage. A positive relationship between financial development and small firms' leverage was found by Palacin-Sánchez and Di Pietro for the Spanish case (Palacín-Sánchez and Pietro 2016). All studies concur that there exists significant cross-regional variation in the capital structure of SMEs—at least in countries, such as Italy, Spain, and Portugal.

The present analysis does not directly test the potential effects of institutional and financial variables on cross-regional differences in SME financing. Rather, as spelled out in the Introduction above, the paper aims at contributing to the empirical literature by further establishing the significance of cross-regional variation; and, in particular, by distinguishing between various types of effects the region-level factors discussed above may have on the capital structure of small firms in the Italian context.

3. Data

The data set used for the empirical analysis is composed of a large panel of Italian manufacturing firms with between 10 and 249 employees, covering the years, 2001–2013. The data comes from the Italian National Institute of Statistics (ISTAT). Sampled firms are manufacturing firms, extracted from the Italian National Business Register (ASIA) and classified according to the main sectoral activity

(Isic-Rev.4) at the two-digit level—the 10–33 codes based on the NACE classification of economic activities (which follows the latest Ateco guidelines). The original data were obtained from firms' individual statements; they were completed with additional information regarding, in particular, the date of establishment, equity ownership, the composition of employment, and exports.

The data set was an unbalanced panel because:

(a) Not all firms were present for every year of the period under study; and
(b) not all the individual data were available every year of the period under study.

The panel was initially restricted to SMEs, namely firms with fewer than 250 employees and total balance sheets of less than 43 million Euro in accordance with the EU definition.[5] This sample included potentially around 570,000 observations.

Two problems made this original panel unsuitable for further analysis. A first problem concerned the extraction of data from firms' statements. Current fiscal regulation allows smaller firms to provide an "abridged balance sheet", which is a simplified statement that enables them to omit certain information that would otherwise be compulsory. For our purposes here, abridged balance sheets only contain data on total liabilities, making it possible to distinguish between short-term and long-term liabilities, but not between types of liabilities, thus making it impossible to identify the amount of financial debt or the amount of bank debt. This limitation prevented us from using conventional leverage measures for many observations. A second issue was related to the period of observation. As is well known, 2007 and 2008 saw the breakout of the global financial and banking crisis, leading to a dramatic fall in firms' turnover. Naturally, corporate financial statements during the latter part of the period under study reflected the consequences of this exceptional event. This created a potential bias for some of the financial ratios used for the empirical analysis, especially profit ratios. To avoid these sources of possible bias, we first removed those firms employing abridged balance sheets from the original data set[6] and then, to mitigate the second source of bias, we restricted the analysis only to profitable firms.

Therefore, the final data set was based on the annual average of more than 33,000 firms; for the whole 2001–2013 period, the potential sample comprised more than 427,000 firm-year observations. The Southern SMEs comprise 12.6% of the total sampled firms, namely around 54,000 firm-year observations (see Table 1 below). In the analysis, the whole sample was broken down in two size classes: (i) Small firms with 10 to 49 employees and total balance sheets of less than 10 million Euro; and (ii) medium-sized firms with 50 to 249 employees and total balance sheets of more than 10 million Euro and less than 43 million Euro.[7] Around 86% of the sample comprised small firms. From the last column of Table 1, it appears that the Southern share of sampled firms was 12.6% of the total number of observed firms; and that the share of small firms was relatively higher compared with the share of medium-sized firms (13.3% and 9.2%, respectively).

Table 1. Sample composition for year and for sized classes.

	ITALY	SOUTH	% SOUTH
2001	36,978	5406	14.6
2002	35,388	4887	13.8
2003	33,171	4396	13.3
2004	34,227	4589	13.4
2005	34,504	4425	12.8
2006	34,000	4428	13.0
2007	33,261	4178	12.6

5 The EU recommendation 2003/3061/CE contains the criteria distinguishing micro, small, and medium-sized firms, applied from the year, 2005.
6 The removed observations cover firms with a total of around 80,000 employees; obviously, most of these are very small firms.
7 The latter being the threshold used by EU official bodies to distinguish SMEs from large firms.

Table 1. *Cont.*

	ITALY	SOUTH	% SOUTH
2008	34,081	4145	12.2
2009	32,437	3898	12.0
2010	30,990	3578	11.5
2011	30,445	3542	11.6
2012	29,379	3385	11.5
2013	28,607	3114	10.9
SMALL FIRMS	360,518	47,793	13.3
MEDIUM FIRMS	66,950	6178	9.2
TOTAL SME	427,468	53,971	12.6

4. Methodology

The analysis proposed here relied on four specifications for (measurements of) the dependent variable, i.e., leverage (*LEV*):

(1) Total financial debt/equity *(TFD/EQU)*;
(2) short-term financial debt/equity (*SFD/EQU*);
(3) long-term financial debt/equity (*LFD/EQU*); and
(4) total bank debt/equity (*TBD/EQU*).

All these dependent variables were measured based on book value.[8]

The explanatory variables were: Size, age, growth, profitability, asset structure, and riskiness. In particular:

(a) Size (*SIZE*) was approximated by the annual average number of employees (EMPLOYMENT).[9]
(b) Age (*AGE*) was measured by the number of years from the establishment of the firm to the observation year.
(c) Growth rate (*GROWTH*) was measured by the annual percentage variation in total assets.
(d) Profitability was expressed by the return on investment (ROI), measured by the gross profit on investment (equity plus total debt).[10]
(e) Asset structure (*TANGIBILITY*) was the share of fixed assets out of total assets. Fixed assets were measured by the total net fixed assets, i.e., the costs of fixed assets minus accumulated depreciation.
(f) Riskiness (*RISK*) was approximated by the standard deviation of the profit rates (ROI).

The estimations were based on the full sample (ITALY), as well as on the Mezzogiorno subsample (SOUTH). For the ITALY model, a dummy variable devoted to capturing the differences in leverage for the firms in the Mezzogiorno regions was added:

(a) The regional dummy (REGIONAL DUMMY) was a variable assuming the value 1 for the observations of Southern firms and zero otherwise.

Initially, our analysis was based on the full sample; then, we restricted the analysis to profitable firms to avoid possible biases arising from the dramatic alteration in firms' data caused by the breakout

---

8 Several studies use both market and book values for the measurement of leverage. The choice to use the book value is generally justified by the argument that the optimal level of leverage depends on the trade-off between the benefits and costs of debt financing. As benefits mostly consist in cash savings arising from the debt tax shield, they can be reliably measured by book values only.

9 Alternative specification of the "size" variable were total sales or total assets. The findings using both total sales or total assets as a proxy for size did not differ significantly from findings using employment; thus, we chose to keep only one specification for size, and decided not to show the estimations with the total sales total assets variables, for the sake of brevity.

10 Preliminary elaborations using different profitability ratios (ROA, ROE) yield findings similar to those examined in the paper; they are not shown here for the sake of brevity.

of the financial crisis (see the previous section). Therefore, all variables other than profitability were expressed in natural logarithmic form; the estimated coefficients must be interpreted as the elasticity of the variables in relation to firm leverage.

The empirical model was as follows:

$$LEV^s = \beta^1\ SIZE_{i,j,h} + \beta^2\ AGE_{i,j,h} + \beta^3\ GROW_{i,j,h} + \beta^4\ PROF^s{}_{i,j,h} + \beta^5\ TANG_{i,j,h} + \beta^6\ RISK_{i,j,h} + \beta^7\ REG_{i,j,h} + \alpha_i + \alpha_j + \alpha_h + \mu_{i,j,h} \quad (1)$$

where β coefficients refer to the i-th firm of the h-th manufacturing industry for the j-th year; the peak s indicates the different specifications of the variable and α_i, α_j and α_h are the individual, temporal and industry effects; and $\mu_{i,j,h}$ is the error term.

We estimated a previous fixed effects panel. We addressed the outlier problem by dropping the observations below the 10th percentile and above the 90th percentile for the increasing distribution of the assets.

Generally, the empirical analysis indicates that both the size and the age variables are correlated with the fixed effects. Indeed, in preliminary elaborations, the correlations between the constant term and both the size variables (assets and employment) and the age variables were not negligible. Moreover, the preliminary tests indicated that the effects on leverage of both size and age variables are widely substitutable so that while the size coefficients are highly significant, the age coefficients are not different to zero systematically. Therefore, to address this problem an interaction variable was obtained by scaling the size on age in order to substitute for both of these variables. Therefore, the previous variables *SIZE* and *AGE* were substituted by the size-age variable (*EMP-AGE INTERACTION*).

Based on preliminary estimations, it emerges that the industry effects α_h were not always significant, even when statistical acceptance was fixed at below standard levels. This confirms the lack of significant differences in terms of industry impact on firm leverage.[12] For this reason, the previous empirical model maintains only the very significant temporal effects α_j and the individual effects (α_i).

Thus, the final version of the empirical model was:

$$LEV^s = \beta^1\ (EMP\text{-}AGE\ INTERACTION)_{i,j,h} + \beta^3\ GROW_{i,j,h} + \beta^4\ ROI_{i,j,h} + \beta^5\ TANG_{i,j,h} + \beta^6\ RISK_{i,j,h} + \beta^7\ REG_{i,j,h} + \alpha_i + \alpha_j + \alpha_h + \mu_{i,j,h} \quad (1a)$$

5. Descriptive Statistics: Some Distinctive Features of the Financial Structure of Southern Italian SMEs

As pointed out in the introduction above, the present study aims to highlight the determinants of cross-regional variation in small firms' capital structure by analyzing the evolution of such a capital structure in Southern Italian SMEs over the period of 2001 to 2013. In particular, we focus on the trends regarding the leverage component of SMEs' capital structure: Equity and debt. As mentioned above, such a period is marked by the breakout of the 2007–2008 financial crisis and the ensuing credit crunch, which exacerbated the collapse in output in the following years.

Thus, we broke down the period of observation into two sub-periods: 2001 to 2007 and 2008 to 2013. Table 2 shows the median values of a few equity ratios for the two sub-periods. It can be noted that the equity ratios were generally higher for Southern SMEs than Center-North SMEs; the ratios of equity to value added (EQU/VAD) and to employment (EQU/EMP) were higher, while the equity–asset ratio (EQU/TA) was lower (except for Southern medium-sized firms in the 2008–2013 sub-period). This difference reflects both the higher level of equity in Southern SMEs, and the fact that

12 This finding reaffirms the conclusions of the previous analysis. For example, in a study based on a wide sample of US companies, MacKay and Philips (2005) found that industry effects explain far less of the variation in financial structure than do firm fixed effects. Cassar and Holmes (2003) also found that industry effects have very limited impacts on firm leverage and that they do not improve the explanatory capacity of the model.

the weight of fixed assets in relation to total assets (FIX/TA) is considerably higher for Southern SMEs than for firms located in other Italian regions. These features appear more marked particularly for medium-sized firms, but they were also notable for small firms.

Table 2. Equity and asset structure ratios for sized classes (median values).

	2001–2013		2001–2007		2008–2013	
	ITALY	SOUTH	ITALY	SOUTH	ITALY	SOUTH
			EQU_VAD			
SMALL FIRMS	337.5	483.8	300.3	437.1	409.4	586.0
MEDIUM FIRMS	434.9	529.6	388.4	490.8	525.1	613.3
TOTAL	353.1	490.1	314.8	445.8	427.5	580.6
			EQU/EMP			
SMALL FIRMS	3830.0	5139.3	3108.6	4260.3	5078.4	6765.0
MEDIUM FIRMS	5620.3	5994.6	4531.7	5018.3	7539.6	7857.3
TOTAL	4106.4	5236.6	3328.4	4651.4	5463.2	5893.6
			EQU/TA			
SMALL FIRMS	71.4	68.7	74.1	70.3	67.6	66.2
MEDIUM FIRMS	69.9	69.2	73.0	71.1	65.5	66.4
TOTAL	71.1	68.8	73.9	70.4	67.2	66.2
			FIX/TA			
SMALL FIRMS	19.1	29.7	17.4	28.6	17.4	28.6
MEDIUM FIRMS	21.8	31.2	19.6	29.1	20.2	30.6
TOTAL	19.7	29.9	20.2	28.7	18.0	29.1

Legend: EQU_VAD = Equity/Value Added; EQU_EMP = Equity/Number of Employees; EQU/TA = Equity/Total Assets; FIX/TA = Fixed Assets/Total Assets.

This situation is in stark contrast with the widespread notion that firms in less advanced regions are under-capitalized. Indeed, the findings of this study reinforce the results of previous studies concerning Southern Italian firms, whereby the latter appear oversized compared to their levels of activity, i.e., there is an excess of production capacity.[13] Whether this is due to the presence of financial incentives to undertake fixed investments or to accounting constraints related to product markets, the magnitude of this over-capacity cannot entirely be explained by the likely high significance of the informal economy within the sphere of activity of Southern SMEs.

With regard to debt, Table 3 below shows the median values of a few debt indicators. Descriptive statistics confirm the higher indebtedness of Southern Italian SMEs, in contrast with the existing literature (La Rocca et al. 2010, 2011). The total financial debt to value added ratio (TFD/VAD) was notably higher in Southern firms, while the debt–equity ratio (TFD/EQU) was lower. Although banks were the main source of debt funding, the share of bank debt to total financial debt (TBD/TFD) was not very high. It can be noted that the weight of short-term debt (SFD/TFD) was unexpectedly lower than for other firms and the fact that the share of long-term debt was consequently higher contrasts with the composition of debt shown in studies covering previous periods.[14]

It is possible to infer from Table 3 that over-indebtedness was especially significant for the smaller firms in Southern Italy; in addition, while their debt-to-value added ratio was relatively higher than

[13] On the basis of wide representative samples of manufacturing firms, previous studies have shown that the equity-to-assets ratios is systematically higher in Southern Italian firms than in other Italian regions (see, for instance, Mediocredito 1997, 2000; Capitalia 2002).

[14] The surveys cited above show that in previous periods, Southern Italian manufacturing firms exhibited a greater share of short-term debt and a lower share of long-term debt than firms in other Italian regions (Mediocredito 1997, 2000; Capitalia 2002).

other classes of firms, their debt–to-equity ratio was lower—due, as explained above, to a higher level of equity. The other measures shown in Table 3, which relate to bank debt and short-term debt, confirm that small Southern firms have especially suffered from the consequences of the post-2007 crisis credit crunch in the final years of the period under study; thus, the relative distance from firms of similar size located in other Italian regions increased.

Table 3. Debt ratios for sized classes (median values).

	2001–2013		2001–2007		2008–2013	
	ITALY	SOUTH	ITALY	SOUTH	ITALY	SOUTH
			TFD/VAD			
SMALL FIRMS	372.4	506.3	381.6	492.3	356.5	519.1
MEDIUM FIRMS	482.3	654.9	501.3	668.0	448.3	637.7
TOTAL	387.2	523.3	398.0	509.2	368.7	551.1
			TFD/EQU			
SMALL FIRMS	108.5	102.9	126.3	111.5	126.3	111.5
MEDIUM FIRMS	112.4	118.1	130.2	127.6	93.8	105.9
TOTAL	109.8	104.6	126.9	113.4	89.5	94.0
			SFD/DFT			
SMALL FIRMS	91.2	85.5	92.7	88.0	92.7	89.1
MEDIUM FIRMS	78.7	75.9	79.6	76.8	77.0	74.1
TOTAL	89.0	83.9	90.4	86.2	87.0	80.2
			TBD/TFD			
SMALL FIRMS	47.9	43.2	49.1	43.1	46.4	43.4
MEDIUM FIRMS	58.3	61.0	61.3	63.3	54.2	58.2
TOTAL	49.6	45.4	51.1	45.8	47.7	45.0

Legend: TFD/VAD = Total Financial Debts/Value Added; TFD/EQU = Total Financial debts/Equity; SFD/DFT = Short-term Financial Debts/Total Financial Debts; TBD/TFD = Total Bank Debts/Total Financial Debt.

6. Results of Empirical Analysis

Table 4 below presents the statistics of all variables.

The OLS estimates for this unbalanced fixed-effects panel based on both the ITALY and SOUTH samples are shown in Table 5 below; the table presents the outcomes of the different empirical models with both the values and natural logarithms of the ROI variables.

We can stress that although coefficient values were very different, most of the directions for the relationships remained unchanged for the ROI value regression and the ROI logarithmically transformed regression. There was a positive relationship between leverage and growth; and leverage and the size–age interaction variable. While the former confirms theoretical predictions, the latter relationship does not and probably indicate the predominance of the size effect, which was expected to be positive, over the age effect, which might be ambiguous. Moreover, the relationships between the various measures of leverage and the asset structure variable, i.e., the ratio of fixed assets to total assets, were negative, an exception being the long-term leverage, which was positively related to the asset structure. This relationship, however, concerns the whole Italian sample. In the case of Southern SMEs, by contrast, the relationship between asset structure and leverage was systematically negative. While a positive relationship between asset structure and long-term debt leverage was expected because fixed assets can be used as collateral, for short-term debt leverage, a negative relationship should prevail. Therefore, the outcomes can be interpreted as the prevalence of this latter effect over the former, associated with the uses of collateral.

Table 4. Main statistics for firm-level variables.

	ITALY						SOUTH				
	AVERAGE	ST. DEV.	MIN.	MAX.	N° OBS		AVERAGE	ST. DEV.	MIN.	MAX.	N° OBS
	SMEs						SMEs				
SIZE	29.5	36.5	0.5	249.9	427,468	SIZE	24.5	31.4	0.5	249.7	53,971
AGE	31.8	11.7	6.0	182.0	427,468	AGE	28.3	10.5	11.0	113.0	53,971
GROWTH	4.6	1.1	−6.8	7.1	218,880	GROWTH	4.6	1.1	−3.9	6.7	24,548
ROI	4.1	120.7	−65,839.9	24,814.9	427,468	ROI	0.7	95.7	−4346.7	17,919.7	53,971
TANGIBILITY	21.5	19.9	0.0	99.8	427,468	TANGIBILITY	32.5	21.9	0.0	99.6	53,971
RISK	5.3	75.8	0.0	46.5	424,680	RISK	4.8	34.4	0.0	6166.6	52,315
	SMALL FIRMS (10–49 employees)						SMALL FIRMS (10–49 employees)				
SIZE	16.8	11.8	0.5	49.9	360,518	SIZE	15.4	11.6	0.5	50.0	47,793
AGE	30.9	11.3	12.0	182.0	360,518	AGE	27.9	10.0	12.0	113.0	47,793
GROWTH	4.5	1.1	−6.8	7.1	161,557	GROWTH	4.1	1.0	−2.6	6.1	19,108
ROI	4.3	130.8	−65,839.9	24,814.9	360,518	ROI	0.5	99.8	−4346.7	17,919.7	47,793
TANGIBILITY	24.6	20.5	0.0	99.8	360,518	TANGIBILITY	32.4	22.5	0.0	99.6	47,793
RISK	5.5	85.4	0.0	46,544.9	357,883	RISK	5.0	36.4	0.0	6116.6	46,715
	MEDIUM SIZED FIRMS (50–249 employees)						MEDIUM SIZED FIRMS (50–249 employees)				
SIZE	98.8	46.7	50.0	249.9	66,950	SIZE	94.8	44.5	50.0	249.7	6178
AGE	36.7	12.5	6.0	182.0	66,950	AGE	32.1	12.9	11.0	88.0	6178
GROWTH	5.1	0.9	−3.8	7.0	57,323	GROWTH	5.2	0.9	−1.3	6.7	5440
ROI	2.6	27.8	−2426.1	3182.3	66,950	ROI	2.0	57.0	−268.1	3182.3	6178
TANGIBILITY	24.3	16.3	0.0	95.5	66,950	TANGIBILITY	32.5	16.8	0.0	95.0	6178
RISK	4.1	10.6	0.0	1718.6	66,950	RISK	3.8	9.5	0.0	458.7	6140

Relationships between leverage and the profit rate and the volatility variables have opposite signs in the different regressions. The relationship was systematically negative in the ROI logarithm regression, as expected; it was also negative for the ITALY regression using ROI values, with the exception of the relationship with long-term debt leverage. By contrast, it was unexpectedly positive or close to zero for Southern firms, with the exception of short-term debt leverage. The relationships between the various leverage measures and the risk variable showed an unexpected positive relationship for the ROI value regression and a negative relationship as expected for the ROI logarithmic regression.

Finally, when we examined the regional dummy for the ITALY model, some outcomes appeared quite clear, even though the coefficients were not always significant at the conventional level. The effect on total leverage as measured by total debts over equity (TFD/EQU) was notably lower for Southern firms compared to other Italian firms; this is explained by the reduced impact on short-term debt leverage (SFD/EQU), while the effect on long-term debt leverage (LDF/EQU) appears negligible or ambiguous. There were contrasting results for Southern firms with regard to the effect on bank debt leverage (TBD/EQU) because the ROI value regression was lower for Southern firms, but higher for the ROI transformed regression. The latter finding was as expected because Southern firms exhibit greater dependence on bank resources, being less able to resort to alternative sources of funding[15].

So far the analysis has borne on the directions or sign of the relationships between the various leverage measures and the explanatory variables. Upon analyzing the estimated coefficients, several significant differences appeared between the national and the regional model. While differences in the impact of other variables on leverage can be viewed as negligible, the main difference concerns the effect of variables measuring profitability and its volatility. The inverse relationship indicating the substitution effect of the profit variable on debt for the Southern firms was not systematically proven and the effect of the risk variable was unexpectedly smaller. Naturally, it was difficult to establish how important these differences are in the comparative analysis; the evidence suggests that individual effects were of considerable importance in the empirical models, but so were the omitted variables when the relative magnitude of the constants was considered.

Table 6 below presents the estimations for the size classes distinguishing small firms from medium-sized firms. These used the logarithmically transformed variables only. Two considerations should be made here. First, the empirical findings for small firms are perfectly consistent with those for firms in the whole sample. Relationships between the leverage ratios and explanatory variables had identical signs and the coefficients were convergent. The Southern regional model shows notable differences with respect to the national model, mirroring the picture arising previously from the comparison with the full sample findings. The dummy variable tells us that the elasticity in the leverage measures for small Southern firms is lower compared to that for small Italian firms, besides that for bank debt leverage; this confirms that small Southern firms are more dependent on bank debt than small firms in other Italian regions.

Second, the regression findings for the medium-sized firm subsample validates the view that the empirical model for small firms also holds for medium-sized firms, i.e., the determinants that explain the choices concerning capital structure for larger firms are effective in explaining the choices of small firms. This was particularly true for both the total financial debt (TFD/EQU) and short-term debt leverage (SFD/EQU) models, but not for the long-term debt level (LFD/EQU) model because of the possibility that medium firms resort to alternative sources of finance. The notable difference arising from the empirical bank debt (TBD/EQU) model does not concern the direction as much as the statistical acceptance of the relationship; in the case of the medium-sized firm model for Italy, the relationship was as expected, whereas for southern firms it was not.

---

[15] It is useful to remind ourselves that from in the studies previously cited, the ratio of total financial debt to equity for Southern firms was, in the 1990s, around 80%; and it was lower by around 10% than that for firms located in other regions. In particular, the ratio of bank debt to equity was below 65%; and the difference with firms in the other Italian regions rapidly decreased at the end of the decade to around 10% (see survey by Mediocredito 2000).

Table 5. Panel estimation for ITALY and SOUTH [2001–2013 years].

	ALL FIRMS (Absolute Values of Variable)								PROFITABLE FIRMS (Natural Logarithm Transformed Variable)							
	ITALY				SOUTH				ITALY				SOUTH			
	[1]	[2]	[3]	[4]	[1]	[2]	[3]	[4]	[1]	[2]	[3]	[4]	[1]	[2]	[3]	[4]
	DFT/EQU	SFD/EQU	LFD/EQU	DBT/EQU	DFT/EQU	SFD/EQU	LFD/EQU	DBT/EQU	DFT/EQU	SFD/EQU	LFD/EQU	DBT/EQU	DFT/EQU	SFD/EQU	LFD/EQU	DBT/EQU
SIZE-AGE INTERACTION	0.003 (0.000) ***	0.002 (0.000) ***	0.001 (0.000) ***	0.004 (0.000) ***	0.006 (0.001) ***	0.003 (0.001) ***	000 (0.000) ***	0.007 (0.001) ***	0.035 (0.002) ***	0.029 (0.003) ***	0.044 (0.005) ***	0.051 (0.005) ***	0.033 (0.005) ***	0.033 (0.006) ***	0.021 (0.011) *	0.085 (0.010) ***
GROWTH	3.258 (0.302) ***	2.478 (0.268) ***	0.881 (0.102) ***	2.762 (0.231) ***	1.945 (0.773) **	0.437 (0.679)	1.459 (0.288) ***	1.767 (0.557) ***	0.019 (0.002) ***	0.016 (0.003) ***	0.031 (0.006) ***	0.027 (0.006) ***	0.034 (0.007) ***	−0.015 (0.008) *	0.067 (0.017) ***	0.046 (0.016) ***
ROI	−0.040 (0.003) ***	−0.032 (0.003) ***	−0.008 (0.001) ***	−0.026 (0.003) ***	−0.060 (0.014) ***	−0.039 (0.012) ***	−0.021 (0.005) ***	−0.215 (0.010) ***	−0.017 (0.002) ***	−0.035 (0.002) ***	0.029 (0.004) ***	−0.065 (0.004) ***	0.007 (0.005)	−0.016 (0.006) ***	0.062 (0.011) ***	0.001 (0.011)
ASSET TANGIBILITY	−1.055 (0.024) ***	−1.138 (0.021) ***	0.084 (0.008) ***	−0.643 (0.019) ***	−1.074 (0.058) ***	−1.062 (0.051) ***	−0.205 (0.021)	−0.536 (0.042) ***	−0.007 (0.000) ***	−0.012 (0.000) ***	0.002 (0.000) **	−0.004 (0.000) ***	−0.009 (0.001) ***	−0.014 (0.001) ***	−0.005 (0.001) ***	−0.003 (0.001) **
RISK	0.101 (0.021) ***	0.101 (0.019) ***	0.000 (0.000)	0.044 (0.016) ***	0.052 (0.037)	0.031 (0.032)	0.021 (0.014)	0.014 (0.027)	−0.020 (0.002) ***	−0.015 (0.002) ***	−0.026 (0.004) ***	−0.039 (0.004) ***	−0.014 (0.005) **	−0.006 (0.006)	−0.020 (0.012) *	−0.029 (0.011) **
REGIONAL DUMMY	−15.230 (6.367) **	−14.996 (8.635) **	0.005 (2.138)	−2.851 (3.855)					−0.060 (.057)	−0.102 (0.052) *	0.120 (0.132)	0.023 (0.124)				
R^2 within	0.040	0.038	0.0165	0.048	0.029	0.027	0.012	0.049	0.113	0.117	0.028	0.056	0.058	0.063	0.022	0.040
between	0.018	0.038	0.011	0.008	0.026	0.045	0.001	0.013	0.003	0.015	0.006	0.000	0.008	0.030	0.004	0.001
overall	0.015	0.029	0.014	0.011	0.026	0.044	0.002	0.025	0.008	0.019	0.009	0.006	0.010	0.032	0.005	0.008
F	466.6	457.6	180.5	570.5	43.4	41.3	19.3	75.3	854.1	893.9	130.7	333.1	46.3	50.3	13.0	27.5
F(for all u_i)	16.6	15.8	11.7	16.1	14.3	13.9	10.8	13.0	23.2	19.4	10.6	12.3	19.2	15.3	10.1	10.2
OBS	217,895	217,895	217,895	217,895	27,412	27,412	27,412	27,412	140,281	141,236	98,936	118,920	15,398	15,339	11,966	13,881
GROUPS	38,663	38,663	38,663	38,663	5275	5275	5275	5275	32,784	33,114	26,306	29,786	4065	4055	3356	3745

t-Student in parentheses; significance indicated as follows: *** 0.01, ** 0.05, * 0.1.

Table 6. Panel estimation (2001–2013 years) for small and medium sized firms (all variables expressed as natural logarithm).

	SMALL FIRMS (10–49 Employees)								MEDIUM SIZED FIRMS (50–249 Employees)							
	ITALY				SOUTH				ITALY				SOUTH			
	[1]	[2]	[3]	[4]	[1]	[2]	[3]	[4]	[1]	[2]	[3]	[4]	[1]	[2]	[3]	[4]
	DFT/EQU	SFD/EQU	LFD/EQU	DBT/EQU	DFT/EQU	SFD/EQU	LFD/EQU	DBT/EQU	DFT/EQU	SFD/EQU	LFD/EQU	DBT/EQU	DFT/EQU	SFD/EQU	LFD/EQU	DBT/EQU
SIZE.-AGE INTERACTION	0.035 (0.002) ***	0.027 (0.003) ***	0.055 (0.007) ***	0.050 (0.009) ***	0.026 (0.006) ***	0.028 (0.007) ***	0.038 (0.013) ***	0.085 (0.011) ***	0.026 (0.006) ***	0.027 (0.003) ***	0.003 (0.014)	0.061 (0.018) ***	0.041 (0.017) **	0.049 (0.018) ***	−0.048 (0.048)	0.162 (0.049) ***
GROWTH	0.019 (0.002) ***	0.015 (0.003) ***	0.035 (0.007) ***	0.025 (0.006) ***	0.034 (0.008) ***	0.013 (0.091)	0.069 (0.017) ***	0.041 (0.016) ***	0.019 (0.006) ***	0.022 (0.007) ***	0.022 (0.013) *	0.033 (0.016) **	0.026 (0.019)	0.027 (0.019)	0.071 (0.051)	0.051 (0.053)
ROI	−0.069 (0.002) ***	−0.024 (0.002) ***	0.038 (0.005) ***	−0.049 (0.004) ***	0.012 (0.006)	−0.014 (0.007) **	0.077 (0.013) ***	0.013 (0.011)	−0.044 (0.003) ***	−0.058 (0.004) ***	0.004 (0.007)	−0.103 (0.009) ***	−0.021 (0.010) **	−0.028 (0.011) ***	0.027 (0.028)	−0.041 (0.029)
ASSET TANGIBILITY	−0.007 (0.000) ***	−0.012 (0.000) ***	0.002 (0.000) **	−0.004 (0.000) ***	−0.008 (0.001) ***	−0.014 (0.001) ***	−0.006 (0.001) ***	−0.003 (0.001) **	−0.008 (0.000) ***	−0.012 (0.000) ***	0.001 (0.001)	−0.027 (0.001) **	−0.015 (0.001) ***	−0.018 (0.001) ***	−0.001 (0.004)	0.000 (0.004)
RISK	−0.022 (0.002) ***	−0.017 (0.002) ***	−0.024 (0.006) ***	−0.043 (0.005) ***	−0.011 (0.006) *	−0.003 (0.007)	−0.005 (0.013)	−0.024 (0.012) **	−0.014 (0.004) ***	−0.009 (0.004) **	−0.031 (0.008) ***	−0.023 (0.010) **	−0.033 (0.011) **	−0.017 (0.012)	−0.092 (0.030)	−0.059 (0.092) *
REGIONAL DUMMY	−0.186 (0.083) **	−0.201 (0.092) **	−0.190 (0.209)	0.187 (0.165)					0.101 (0.078)	0.089 (0.087)	0.198 (0.180)	−0.215 (0.223)				
R^2 within	0.114	0.115	0.029	0.054	0.048	0.055	0.027	0.035	0.125	0.135	0.026	0.072	0.123	0.117	0.031	0.067
R^2between	0.006	0.013	0.004	0.000	0.008	0.030	0.002	0.003	0.004	0.014	0.008	0.001	0.011	0.025	0.007	0.002
R^2overall	0.002	0.021	0.006	0.008	0.007	0.029	0.005	0.008	0.014	0.028	0.012	0.014	0.022	0.038	0.017	0.018
F	640.3	643.7	93.6	231.5	29.3	33.8	12.2	18.5	234.9	257.4	33.0	109.7	21.4	20.3	4.1	10.1
F(for all u_i)	21.9	18.4	9.8	12.4	18.1	14.1	10.7	10.2	23.1	19.3	11.0	11.1	21.7	19.1	6.9	8.6
OBS	106,896	106,438	71,587	89,749	12,235	12,181	9269	10,935	34,208	34,166	26,673	29,749	3102	3098	2638	2887
GROUPS	27,335	27,294	21,143	24,559	3519	3509	2858	3213	7849	7842	6747	7355	809	806	722	776

t-Student in parentheses; significance indicated as follows: *** 0.01, ** 0.05, * 0.1

7. Concluding Remarks

The financial strategies of a firm arise from a very complex process and neither the theories related to capital structure nor the existing empirical models appear to be completely effective in exhaustively explaining such strategies. Most findings of previous empirical studies on firms' capital structure are significantly affected or limited by the samples on which they are based. Nevertheless, in our opinion, the findings of the analysis presented here allow us to expand what we know about the capital structure of firms in less advanced areas, especially smaller firms.

First, the findings reported above mostly confirm the direction of the relationships between firm-level determinants, on the one hand, and small firms' capital structure, on the other hand. However, through our investigation of a large sample of SMEs in the Italian *Mezzogiorno*, which is a perfectly integrated, but slowly growing macro-area in the South of the country, we have verified that there are several significant differences in the regional leverage model when it is compared to the model for Italian firms as a whole. Some of these differences confirm what we already knew, for example, that firms in less advanced areas have a lower propensity to use financial leverage and a significantly higher propensity to use bank leverage. This phenomenon can be explained by the fact that it is more difficult for those firms to resort to alternative sources of finance, at the same time as there are pressures on their capacity to draw on internal finance, which means that the latter is insufficient to finance current activities, let alone the growth of the firm. Thus, the dependence on bank funding further increases. The other findings are equally notable, but it seems to us that these are affected by the dramatic events that occurred in the final years of the previous decade. They tell us that consequent to both the shock to credit supply and the dramatic fall in production, there was a reorganization of debt, specifically showing a prevalence of the replacement of short-term debt with long-term debt.

Nevertheless, from the estimation of the fixed-effects panel, other findings seem to emerge, suggesting more important structural differences in the binding of the regional leverage models. This is where our study contributes to the empirical literature on small firms' capital structure in underdeveloped areas. Although the impact of the size and age variables on the leverage of Southern firms was not significantly different from that in the rest of Italy, the elasticity of both the profit rate and the riskiness variables were unexpectedly lower than for the firms located in other regions. We may try explaining these surprising findings in the following way. First, one should note that the standard leverage model is unable to entirely capture these differences because of the importance attached to fixed effects; this is coherent with the information asymmetry approach; and the estimated fixed effects (as mainly measured by the constant) suggest that the weight of the omitted variables is great. On the basis of such evidence, we suggest that there is a need to deepen the analysis in the direction of testing how much of the fixed effects can be explained by the efficiency of local institutions or regional financial and legal systems, as well as the extent to which unexplored individual effects seem to arise. To some extent, this is the direction taken by the literature in recent years (see Section 2.2 above). In this regard, the findings presented here may be understood as a partial confirmation of the arguments put forward by, in particular, La Rocca et al. (2010, 2011).

Secondly, the empirical evidence presented here emphasizes the distinctive features of the financial structure of Southern Italian SMEs. Our findings show that Southern Italian firms are unexpectedly over-capitalized, as the share of equity is considerably higher; and, correspondingly, Southern SMEs exhibit an excess of productive capacity revealed by a higher ratio of fixed to total assets. Thus, cross-regional differences in the impact of both the profit ratio and firms' asset structure variables on leverage in the regional models may confirm the hypothesis that over-capitalization or over-capacity cannot be entirely explained by the presence of a larger informal environment or by very likely accounting constraints imposed by the incentives promoting fixed investments in less developed areas. We suspect that these conditions could actually warrant equilibrium for firms in less developed areas, which are, however, perfectly integrated in domestic and foreign financial markets. The difficulties in accessing alternative financial sources make firms more dependent on internal finance and on bank resources, and (small) firms have to choose the capital structure that eases the relationship with the banking system. In spite of the fact that appreciable gains in terms of financial management arise from such a relationship, this condition results in inefficiency for firms. It is not unlikely that there is a significant deadweight loss and that firms are hindered from exploiting growth opportunities and the propensity to innovate.

Finally, the analysis enabled us to distinguish between the model for small firms and that for medium-sized firms, reaffirming the increasingly widespread notion that the determinants explaining the capital structure choices of larger firms are equally effective in explaining the financial choices of smaller firms; naturally, the doubt that the standard empirical model is able only partially to explain firms' financial strategies remains.

The specificity of capital structure choices facing small firms in underdeveloped areas, such as Southern Italy, as shown in this study, also has policy implications. First, over-capitalization shows that industrial policy should target small firms' excessive productive capacity and find ways to reduce it while helping small firms to grow in size—an important challenge for macro-areas, such as the Mezzogiorno. Secondly, given Southern Italian small firms' persistently high levels of indebtedness, the current, ongoing transformations of the Italian banking system should be steered towards guaranteeing mechanisms to reduce the costs of excessive leverage on firms' capital structure.

Author Contributions: O.B. was mainly involved to review the economic analysis on this field examining the determinants of the capital structure choice at the firm level as much as at the country level. D.S. was principally working with the methodological approach and he was engaged with the econometric model. The empirical analysis as much as the concluding section are the result of the joint working of both the authors.

Funding: This research received no external funding.

Conflicts of Interest: The authors declare no conflicts of interest.

References

Adedeji, Abimbola. 1998. Does the Pecking Order Hypothesis Explain the Dividend Payout Ratios of Firms in the UK? *Journal of Business Finance & Accounting* 25: 1127–55.

Beattie, Vivien, Alan Goodacre, and Sarah Jane Thomson. 2006. Corporate Financing Decisions: UK Survey Evidence. *Journal of Business Finance & Accounting* 33: 1402–34.

Beck, Thorsten, Asli Demirgüç-Kunt, and Ross Levine. 2003. Law, Endowment and Finance. *Journal of Financial Economics* 70: 137–81. [CrossRef]

Beck, Thorsten, Asli Demirgüç-Kunt, and Ross Levine. 2005. Law and Firms' Access to Finance. *American Law and Economics Review* 7: 211–52.

Beck, Thorsten, Asli Demirgüç-Kunt, and Vojislav Maksimovic. 2008. Financing Patterns Around the World: Are Small Firms Different? *Journal of Financial Economics* 89: 467–87. [CrossRef]

Berger, Allen N., and Gregory F. Udell. 1998. The Economics of Small Business Finance: the Role of Private Equity and Debt Markets in the Financial Growth Cycle. *Journal of Banking and Finance* 22: 613–73. [CrossRef]

Booth, Laurence, Varouj Aivazan, Asli Demirgüç-Kunt, and Vojislav Maksimovic. 2001. Capital Structures in Developing Countries. *The Journal of Finance* 55: 87–130. [CrossRef]

Capitalia, ed. 2002. *Indagine sulle imprese manifatturiere, VIII rapport*. Milano: Il Sole-24 Ore.

Carter, Richard, and Howard Van Auken. 2006. Small Firm Bankruptcy. *Journal of Small Business Management* 44: 493–512. [CrossRef]

Cassar, Gavin, and Scott Holmes. 2003. Capital Structure and Financing of SMEs: Australian Evidence. *Accounting and Finance* 43: 123–47. [CrossRef]

Chittenden, Francis, Graham Hall, and Patrick Hutchinson. 1996. Small Firm Growth, Access to Capital Markets and Financial Structure: Review of Issue and an Empirical Investigation. *Small Business Economics* 8: 59–67. [CrossRef]

Dang, Chongyu, Zhichuan F. Li, and Chen Yang. 2018. Measuring Firm Size in Empirical Corporate Finance. *Journal of Banking & Finance January* 86: 159–76.

Daskalakis, Maria, and Nikolaos Psillaki. 2008. Do Country or Firm Factors Explain Capital Structure? Evidence from SMEs in France and Greece. *Applied Financial Economics* 18: 87–97. [CrossRef]

De Angelo, Harry, and Ronald Masulis. 1980. Optimal Capital Structure under Corporate and Personal Taxation. *Journal of Financial Economics* 8: 3–29. [CrossRef]

De Jong, Abe, Kabir Rezaul, and Thuy Nguyen. 2008. Capital Structure Around the World: the Roles of Firm-and Country-specific Determinants. *Journal of Banking & Finance* 32: 1954–69.

Demirgüç-Kunt, Asli, and Vojislav Maksimovic. 1999. Institutions, Financial Markets, and Firm Debt Maturity. *Journal of financial economics* 54: 295–336. [CrossRef]

Di Pietro, Filippo, Maria E. Bontempi, Mariaa-Jose Palacin, and Reyes Samaniego-Medina. 2016. Capital Structure across Italian Regions: The Roles of Financial and Economic Determinants. Unpublished Working Paper. Available online: https://papers.ssrn.com/sol3/papers.cfm?abstract_id=2988997 (accessed on 3 January 2019).

Donati, Cristiana. 2016. Firm Growth and Liquidity Constraints: Evidence from the Manufacturing and Service Sectors in Italy. *Applied Economics* 48: 1881–92. [CrossRef]

Fama, Eugene F., and Kenneth R. French. 2002. Testing Trade-off and Pecking Order Predictions about dividends and Debt. *The Review of Financial Studies* 15: 1–33. [CrossRef]

Fan, Joseph P., Sheridan Titman, and Garry Twite. 2012. An International Comparison of Capital Structure and Debt Maturity Choices. *Journal of Financial and Quantitative Analysis* 47: 23–56. [CrossRef]

Frank, Murray Z., and Vidhan K. Goyal. 2003. Testing the Pecking Order Theory of Capital Structure. *Journal of Financial Economics* 67: 217–48. [CrossRef]

Guiso, Luigi, Paola Sapienza, and Luigi Zingales. 2004. Does Local Financial Development Matter? *Quarterly Journal of Economics* 119: 929–69. [CrossRef]

Hall, Graham C., Patrick J. Hutchinson, and Nicos Michaelas. 2004. Determinants of the Capital Structure of European SMEs. *Journal of Business Finance and Accounting* 31: 711–28. [CrossRef]

Harris, Milton, and Artur Raviv. 1990. The Theory of Capital Structure. *Journal of Finance* 46: 297–355. [CrossRef]

Jensen, Michael C., and William H. Meckling. 1976. Theory of the Firm: Agency Costs and Ownership Structure. *Journal of Financial Economics* 3: 305–60. [CrossRef]

Jordan, Judith, Julian Lowe, and Peter Taylor. 1998. Strategy and Financial Policy in UK Small Firms. *Journal of Business Finance & Accounting* 25: 1–27.

Klagge, Britta, Ron Martin, and Peter Sunley. 2017. The Spatial Structure of the Financial System and the Funding of Regional Business: A Comparison of Britain and Germany. In *Handbook on the Geographies of Money and Finance*. Edited by Martin Ron and Jane Pollard. Cheltenham: Edward Elgar Publishing, pp. 125–55.

Kraus, Alan, and Robert H. Litzenberger. 1973. A State-Preference Model of Optimal Financial Leverage. *Journal of Finance* 28: 911–22. [CrossRef]

La Porta, Rafael, Florencio Lopez-de-Silanes, Andrei Shleifer, and Robert W. Visny. 1997. Legal Determinant of External Finance. *The Journal of Finance* 53: 1131–50. [CrossRef]

La Porta, Rafael, Florencio Lopez-de-Silanes, Andrei Shleifer, and Robert W. 1998. Law and Finance. *Journal of Political Economy* 106: 1113–55. [CrossRef]

La Rocca, Maurizio, Tiziana La Rocca, and Alfio Cariola. 2010. The Influence of Local Institutional Differences on the Capital Structure of SMEs: Evidence from Italy. *International Small Business Journal* 28: 234–57. [CrossRef]

La Rocca, Maurizio, Tiziana La Rocca, and Alfio Cariola. 2011. Capital Structure Decisions During a Firm's Life Cycle. *Small Business Economics* 37: 107–30. [CrossRef]

Lawless, Martina, Brian O'Connell, and Conor O'Toole. 2015. Financial Structure and Diversification of European Firms. *Applied Economics* 47: 2379–98. [CrossRef]

Levine, Ross. 1997. Financial Development and Economic Growth: Views and Agenda. *Journal of Economic Literature* 35: 688–726.

Levine, Ross. 2004. *Finance and Growth: Theory, Evidences and Mechanism*. NBER Working Paper n.10766. Cambridge, MA, USA: National Bureau of Economic Research.

MacKay, Peter, and Gordon M. Philips. 2005. How Does Industry Affect Firm Financial Structure? *Review of Financial Studies* 18: 1433–66. [CrossRef]

Mateev, Miroslav, Panikkos Poutziouris, and Konstantin Ivanov. 2013. On the Determinants of SME Capital Structure in Central and Eastern Europe: A Dynamic Panel Analysis. *Research in International Business and Finance* 27: 28–51. [CrossRef]

Matias, Fernanda, and Zelia Serrasqueiro. 2017. Are There Reliable Determinant Factors of Capital Structure Decisions? Empirical Study of SMEs in Different Regions of Portugal. *Research in International Business and Finance* 40: 19–33. [CrossRef]

Mediocredito, Centrale, ed. 1997. *Indagine sulle imprese manifatturiere, VI rapport*. Milano: Il Sole-24 Ore.

Mediocredito, Centrale, ed. 2000. *Indagine sulle imprese manifatturiere, VII rapport*. Milano: Il Sole-24 Ore.

Michaelas, Nicos, Francis Chittenden, and Panikkos Poutziouris. 1999. Financial Policy and Capital Structure Choice in UK SMEs: Empirical Evidence from Company Panel Data. *Small Business Economics* 12: 113–30. [CrossRef]

Miller, Merton H. 1977. Debt and Taxes. *The Journal of Finance* 32: 261–75.

Moritz, Alexandra, Joern H. Block, and Andreas Heinz. 2016. Financing Patterns of European SMEs—An Empirical Taxonomy. *Venture Capital* 18: 115–48. [CrossRef]

Myers, Stewart C. 1977. Determinants of Corporate Borrowing. *Journal of Financial Economics* 5: 147–75. [CrossRef]

Myers, Stewart C. 1984. The Capital Structure Puzzle. *The Journal of Finance* 39: 574–92. [CrossRef]

Myers, Stewart C., and Nicholas S. Majluf. 1984. Corporate Financing and Investment Decisions When Firms Have Information That Investors Do Not Have. *Journal of Financial Economics* 13: 187–221. [CrossRef]

Noulas, Anastasios, and Georgios Genimakis. 2011. The Determinants of Capital Structure Choice: Evidence from Greek Listed Companies. *Applied Financial Economics* 21: 379–87. [CrossRef]

Palacín-Sánchez, Mariaa-Jose, and Filippo Di Pietro. 2016. The Role of the Regional Financial Sector in the Capital Structure of Small and Medium-Sized Enterprises (SMEs). *Regional Studies* 50: 1232–47. [CrossRef]

Palacín-Sánchez, Mariaa-Jose, Luis M. Ramírez-Herrera, and Filippo Di Pietro. 2013. Capital Structure of SMEs in Spanish Regions. *Small Business Economics* 41: 503–19. [CrossRef]

Psillaki, Maria, and Nikolaos Daskalakis. 2009. Are the Determinants of Capital Structure Country or Firm Specific? *Small Business Economics* 33: 319–33. [CrossRef]

Rajan, Raghuram G., and Luigi Zingales. 1995. What Do We Know About Capital Structure? Some Evidence from International Data. *The Journal of Finance* 50: 1421–60. [CrossRef]

Ross, Stephen A. 1977. The Determination of Financial Structure: The Incentive-Signalling Approach. *The Bell Journal of Economics* 8: 23–40. [CrossRef]

Serrasqueiro, Zeila, and Ana Caetano. 2015. Trade-Off Theory Versus Pecking Order Theory: Capital Structure Decisions in a Peripheral Region of Portugal. *Journal of Business Economics and Management* 16: 445–66. [CrossRef]

Wald, John K. 1999. How Firm Characteristics Affect Capital Structure: An International Comparison. *Journal of Financial Research* 22: 161–87. [CrossRef]

12

Stock Price Forecast Accuracy and Recommendation Profitability of Financial Magazines

Victor Tiberius * and Laura Lisiecki

Faculty of Economics and Social Sciences, University of Potsdam, 14482 Potsdam, Germany; laura.lisiecki@gmx.de

* Correspondence: tiberius@uni-potsdam.de

Abstract: In this study, we analyze the forecast accuracy and profitability of buy recommendations published in five major German financial magazines for private households based on fundamental analysis. The results show a high average forecast accuracy but with a very high standard deviation, which indicates poor forecast accuracy with regard to individual stocks. The recommendation profitability slightly exceeds the performance of the MSCI World index. Considering the involved risk, which is represented by a high standard deviation, the excess returns appear to be insufficient.

Keywords: buy recommendations; financial magazines; forecast accuracy; MSCI World; recommendation profitability

JEL Classification: G11; G17

---

1. Introduction

Private households considering individual stocks for their personal financial investments are exposed to a plethora of possibilities. However, most of these investors lack the time, analytical skills, or even financial literacy (Gallery et al. 2011; Lusardi and Mitchell 2014) to select individual stocks professionally on their own. Financial magazines aimed at this target group regularly publish concrete buy recommendations, and by doing so, financial journalists publishing in these magazines undertake a task comparable to that of financial analysts or investment advisors.

In this paper, we analyze both the forecast accuracy and profitability of buy recommendations published in five major German financial magazines. Forecast accuracy is defined as the relative discrepancy between the published target price, interpreted as a stock price forecast, and the actual price at the end of the forecast horizon. Recommendation profitability is defined as the relative difference between the actual stock price at the date of recommendation and that at the end of the forecast horizon (Ertimur et al. 2007).

From a stockholder's perspective, forecast accuracy in and of itself is not of primary relevance, as the investor is not interested in precise forecasts but in highly profitable recommendations. A buy recommendation necessarily requires a positive difference between the current and expected future stock price. If the expected future stock price becomes a reality at the end of the forecast horizon, both the maximum forecast accuracy and the predicted recommendation profitability are achieved. If a difference between the current and the expected future stock price occurs, the actual recommendation profitability can be lower or higher than the expected one. The question of whether forecasted stock prices are accurate and whether buy recommendations are profitable is highly relevant for all private investors who base their investment decisions on buy recommendations from financial magazines.

Relatively little research has been conducted on financial forecast accuracy. The body of research focuses mainly on earnings forecasts rather than on stock price forecasts. Past earnings forecast accuracy is regarded as an important indicator for future forecast accuracy (Brown 2001), assuming that past forecast performance will continue. According to Hall and Tacon (2010), this assumption is justified because good forecasting ability appears to be persistent. Stickel (1992) found that members of the *Institutional Investor* All-America Research Team conduct more frequent forecasts and have better accuracy than other analysts. Analysts' forecasts are more accurate for companies located in industries in which they formerly worked (Bradley et al. 2017; Mikhail et al. 1999).

Several scholars have investigated analysts' recommendation profitability. For example, Bjerring et al. (1983) found that investors who followed the recommendations of a Canadian brokerage house would have gained above-market returns. Elton et al. (1986) and Desai et al. (2000) reached a similar conclusion. According to Ertimur et al. (2007), more accurate forecasts also produce higher profits than rough estimates. Other researchers suggest that there is no association between forecast accuracy and a recommendation's profitability (Hall and Tacon 2010; Mikhail et al. 1999). Positive forecasts and their resulting buy recommendations can lead to increased stock prices (Barber et al. 2006, 2010; Kerl and Walter 2007; Mathur and Wahed 1995; Womack 1996), thereby forming self-fulfilling prophecies as stock buyers increase their market demand and thereby raise stock prices. This case is especially true when herding occurs among financial analysts and buy recommendations are expressed by multiple analysts, suggesting a consensus among them (Clement and Tse 2005; Desai et al. 2000; Welch 2000). Forecast revisions lead to adjusted investment behavior by private investors, depending on prior forecast accuracy and other characteristics (Clement and Tse 2003). When the accuracy of prior forecasts is good, private investors expect the revised forecasts to be accurate and follow the new recommendations.

Even though stock prices are based on expected future earnings, other factors, such as the overall economic and sector-specific outlook, current interest rates, or disruptive threats by innovative competitors, also have an influence on stock prices. Thus, forecasting stock prices is more complex than forecasting future earnings alone because these other factors and their interdependencies must also be considered in the forecasts.

Even though relations between financial journalism and the stock market have been subject to some rare research (e.g., Ahern and Sosyura 2015; Douglas et al. 2012), only financial analysts'—not financial journalists'—forecasting accuracy and recommendation profitability have been considered by scholars so far. This salient research gap is remarkable, considering that thousands of explicit buy recommendations are published worldwide monthly and that these can have significant economic and social consequences for followers (Gallery et al. 2011).

2. Data and Methodology

The sample for this study consists of 554 buy recommendations published in the five major German financial magazines *Börse Online* (circulation: 24,540 copies in the fourth quarter 2016[1]), *Der Aktionär* (37,875), *Euro am Sonntag* (70,332), *Focus Money* (123,378), and *WirtschaftsWoche* (135,394), between 7 December 2016 and 2 February 2017. The financial magazines covered stocks of large and second-line companies that have their registered headquarters in countries all over the world, so long as they are also listed on a German stock market.

The sample included only buy recommendations based on fundamental analysis. The magazines also published another 92 buy recommendations based on technical analysis. However, because only 19 of these recommendations mentioned a concrete target price, these were not included in the sample due to their lack of representativeness.

For the analysis, the corporation's name, the stock's International Securities Identification Number (ISIN), and the target stock prices were retrieved from the magazines. Additional information published by the magazines—e.g., fundamental data, such as the current or expected price-to-earnings (P/E) ratio,

---

1 Retrieved from the quarter circulation database at https://www.ivw.eu.

the price-to-book (P/B) ratio, or dividend payout ratio and small verbal statements regarding past stock developments and its future outlook (e.g., based on its financial outlook and firm-level disclosures by the firms' Chief Financial Officers (CFO) (Hope 2003))—was not part of the analysis.

Additionally, the actual stock prices on the publication date and after the end of the forecast horizon were retrieved from the online finance portal *www.boerse.de* to facilitate comparison with the target prices given in the recommendation. The time horizon was one year after publication, as confirmed by the magazines' chief editors in personal communication with the paper's second author. For chart-based forecasts, the time horizon was only three months, providing yet another reason to exclude them from the analysis. The time horizon of one year has the additional advantage that short-term market responses to buy recommendations do not become an issue in our analysis. Several studies found that stock prices are affected by published recommendations. For example, this finding was made by Lloyd-Davies and Canes (1978), who examined recommendations published after they had previously been disseminated to analysts' clients. The effect lasted for approximately 20 trading days. A similar observation was made by Beneish (1991) and Mathur and Wahed (1995), who examined published buy recommendations based on rumors or analysts' recommendations. They found a stock price increase one day before and two days after the publication date. Kerl and Walter (2007) found that price-pressure and information effects resulted in a stock price increase within five days of publication, especially for small stocks and glamour stocks. Such effects can be ignored using a long time horizon. The magnitude of the price change depends on the strength of the recommendation, the magnitude of the change in the recommendation, the reputation of the analyst, the size of the brokerage house, the size of the recommended firm, and simultaneous earnings forecast revisions (Stickel 1995).

Based on the gathered data, the following variables were calculated: the forecast error for each recommendation to buy the stock s as

$$FE_s = \frac{tsp_{t1} - asp_{t1}}{tsp_{t1}},$$

where tsp_{t1} is the target stock price and asp_{t1} is the actual stock price, both one year after publication of the recommendation ($t1$); the average forecast error for each magazine as

$$FE_m = \frac{\sum_{n=i}^{k} FE_s}{k-i},$$

where i to k is the range of stocks recommended in magazine m; the total average forecast error as

$$FE = \frac{\sum_1^N FE_s}{N},$$

where N is the total number of all buy recommendations; the recommendation profitability for each buy recommendation as

$$RP_s = \frac{asp_{t1} - asp_{t0}}{asp_{t0}},$$

where asp_{t0} is the actual stock price at the date of the publication ($t0$); the average recommendation profitability for each magazine as

$$RP_m = \frac{\sum_i^k RP_s}{k-i},$$

and the total average recommendation profitability as

$$RP = \frac{\sum_1^n RP_s}{n}.$$

For simplicity, transaction costs were not considered. Only buy rather than sell recommendations were included in the sample because sell recommendations were rarely published by the magazines and, due to missing prior buy information (buy date $t-1$ and price sp_{t-1}), neither forecast accuracy nor recommendation profitability could have been calculated.

3. Results

For all 554 buy recommendations, the average forecast error was +0.0095, which indicates a very high overall forecast accuracy. However, the standard deviation was 0.3287, which indicates that the forecast accuracy for individual stocks was rather poor. Figure 1 shows the distribution of the forecast error around its average value (+0.0095).

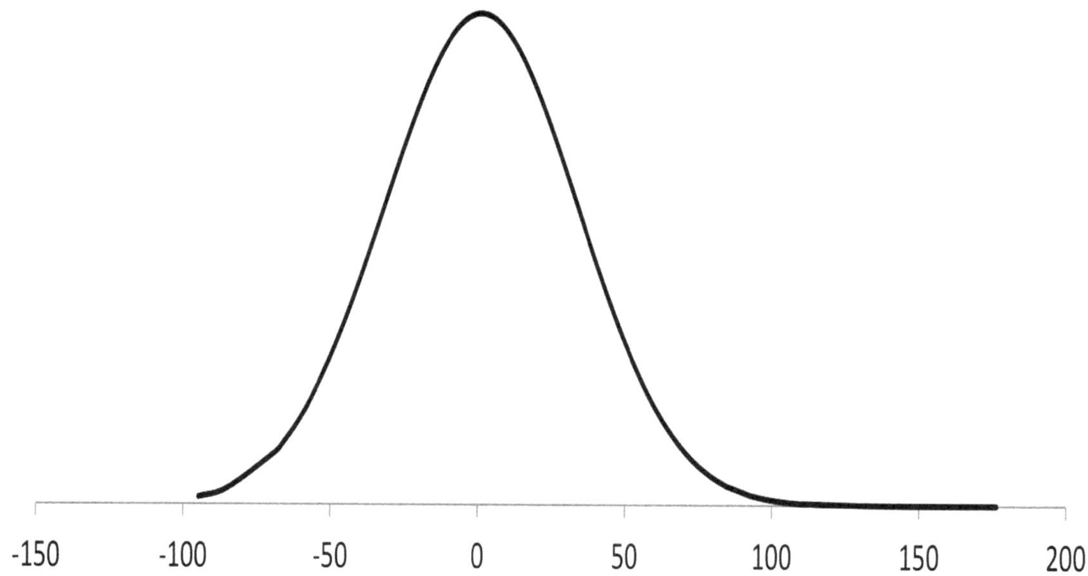

Figure 1. Distribution of the forecast error.

The most accurate forecast was for Palfinger AG, which had a discrepancy of 0.0000 for both the target and actual prices one year after publication, exactly 36.00 Euros each. The highest negative forecast discrepancy was −0.9481 for the stock of Steinhoff International Holdings NV, which crashed because of an accounting scandal that was unanticipated by the financial journalist and the market in general. The highest positive forecast discrepancy was +1.7644 for Siltronic AG.

The average recommendation profitability of all 554 buy recommendations was 0.2745 per year, which is an attractive overall return. Financial journalists generated an attractive alpha compared to the highly diversified MSCI World index, which increased from 5334.630 on 7 December 2017, to 6273.35 on 6 December 2018, an increase of 0.1820.

However, the recommendation profitabilities for individual stocks were greatly scattered again. The highest profit was +2.9563 for Aixtron SE, and the highest loss was −0.9360 for Steinhoff International Holdings NV. Of all buy recommendations, 0.2184 led to a loss, in congruence with Mathur and Wahed (1995) findings that long-term investors earn below market rates of return when following secondary information, such as buy recommendations published in financial magazines, based on rumors or financial analysts' prior buy recommendations. Similarly, Palmon et al. (2009) found that investors who followed financial magazines' columnists' recommendations would not have received abnormal returns.

The results for each magazine can be found in Table 1. The representativeness of the results of *WirtschaftsWoche* is limited, as the magazine contained only 10 forecasts. However, we included the magazine due to its high circulation.

Table 1. Results for each magazine.

Magazine	Börse Online	Der Aktionär	Euro am Sonntag	Focus Money	Wirtschafts-Woche	Overall
			Forecast error			
FE	0.0342	0.0016	−0.0136	0.0213	0.0594	0.0095
Standard deviation (SD) of FE	0.3144	0.3657	0.2179	0.2768	0.5604	0.3287
Highest negative FE_s	−0.6383	−0.8500	−0.4870	−0.5330	−0.9481	−0.9481
Highest positive FE_s	1.1100	1.7644	0.4939	0.8486	0.7569	1.7644
Smallest FE_s	0.0000	0.0054	0.0047	0.0012	0.0021	0.0000
			Recommendation profitability			
RP	0.2907	0.3022	0.1515	0.2871	0.2408	0.2745
Maximum profit	2.9563	2.2228	0.7995	2.2320	1.3276	2.9563
Maximum loss	−0.5751	−0.6727	−0.3677	−0.3655	−0.9360	−0.9360
Percentage of loss-generating recommendations	0.2229	0.3760	0.2000	0.1896	0.4000	0.2960

4. Discussion

4.1. Assumptions

The analysis is based on a number of assumptions. First, it is assumed that a virtual investor builds a portfolio that represents all given buy recommendations. Because readers of financial magazines usually do not follow all given buy recommendations, individual portfolios will be realized and will have different performances. Second, it is assumed that exactly the same amount is invested in every recommended stock because the financial magazines recommend only which stocks to buy but obviously not how much money to invest. However, an equal allocation of stocks in the portfolio is neither sensible nor possible due to different prices for different stocks. Third, it is assumed that readers buy the recommended stocks on publication day and sell them exactly one year later. Again, this assumption is unrealistic because individual readers can buy stocks later and sell them before or after the forecast horizon ends. Thus, the financial magazines' portfolios are a theoretical construct rather than a real phenomenon. However, in this restrictive way, the analysis is legitimate because these parameters are immanent to the financial magazine design: They give more buy recommendations than a usual reader can follow, they do not give concrete recommendations on the weighing of the stocks in the portfolio, they appear on a certain publishing date, and the defined time horizon for the forecasts is one year.

4.2. Risk Adjustment

Because portfolio management should always be related to both return and risk, a solely profitability-oriented view on magazines' buy recommendations would obscure equally important risk considerations. There are different measures for risk-adjusted return. For example, the prominent Sharpe (1994) ratio measures the return per unit of deviation in the portfolio, or concretely, it is the relation between the value of the excess of the asset return over the benchmark return (usually government bonds considered riskless) and the standard deviation of the asset excess return (usually the portfolio's volatility). In a loose analogy to this measure, a risk-adjusted perspective on the financial magazines' excess return can be calculated as

$$RP_{riskadj} = \frac{RP - R_{index}}{\text{SD}} = 0.2814.$$

The return of the MSCI World index (R_{index}) for the period of one year after the first buy recommendation cannot be interpreted as a risk-free rate but as a legitimate benchmark return that stockholders might have gained by investing in a highly diversified exchange-traded fund (ETF) that represents the 1649 stocks of this index worldwide. The difference between the recommendation profitability of the magazines (RD_m) and the return of the MSCI World index (R_{index}) has to be considered in relation to the standard deviation of the forecast errors (SD), analogous to the volatility of a portfolio. A ratio of 1.000 would suggest an even relation between return and risk. The actual ratio of 0.2814 suggests that the relation of excess return compared to the MSCI World index, in relation to forecast errors, is too high.

Another method to evaluate the risk-adjusted returns of the buy recommendations is to compare the magazine-specific Sharpe ratios,

$$SR_m = \frac{RP_m}{SD_m},$$

with the Sharpe ratio of the MSCI World index

$$SR_{index} = \frac{RP_{index}}{SD_{index}}.$$

In both cases, we dispense with the subtraction of the risk-free interest rate in the numerator because it is currently approximately zero (e.g., slightly negative in Europe and slightly positive in the U.S.). The Sharpe ratios are depicted in Table 2. The values show very good risk-adjusted returns for *Focus Money* and for *Börse Online*. However, the Sharpe ratio of the MSCI World index is much higher.

Table 2. Sharpe ratios of magazines and MSCI World index.

Börse Online	Der Aktionär	Euro am Sonntag	Focus Money	Wirtschafts-Woche	All Magazines	MSCI World
0.9246	0.8264	0.6953	1.037	0.4297	0.8351	4.008

5. Conclusions

From a pure forecasting perspective, finance magazines are highly accurate on average but with a high standard deviation. Thus, financial journalists' forecast accuracy for individual stocks was rather poor.

Stockholders who would have followed all buy recommendations would have generated an excess profit compared to that of the broader stock market. This outcome is consistent with findings suggesting that analysts prefer to pick high momentum and growth stocks (Jegadeesh et al. 2004), especially high-tech stocks (Kwon 2002) that have outperformed in recent years. However, considering the high error rate of buy recommendations leading to high losses, following all buy recommendations can only be suggested for investors with an above-average risk appetite. Two risk-adjusted perspectives relating the returns to the MSCI World index performance and Sharpe ratios confirm this finding.

6. Limitations and Future Research

The study has several limitations. First and foremost, the data stem from a rather short, three-month period. For a preliminary study such as this, the insights are interesting. However, future studies should include longer periods. Second, the study covered a long bull market phase. Picking stocks and forecasting rising stock prices appears to be easier during such phases rather than in bear or highly volatile markets. Future research should also examine forecast accuracies and recommendation profitabilities in bear or more volatile markets. We expect that both forecast accuracy and recommendation profitability would suffer in such markets. However, Sharpe ratio comparisons with the MSCI World index would also show completely different results. For example, its return one year later (7 December 2017, to 6 December 2018) was −0.0123, and the Sharpe ratio was only 0.4457. Third, only German financial magazines were studied. To preclude a national or cultural bias, financial magazines from other countries should also be examined. Fourth, forecasts depend not only on forecasters' characteristics (Brown 2001; Clement and Tse 2003) but also on their forecast methods. This study focused on forecasts based on fundamental analyses alone. Future studies should also consider covering other sources, such as recommendations based on technical analysis and sentiment analysis. Fifth, future studies might also cover other underlying elements besides stocks, e.g., commodity prices, bond prices, or currencies.

Author Contributions: V.T. and L.L. jointly developed the study design. L.L. conducted the study. V.T. and L.L. jointly analyzed the data. V.T. wrote the first draft and revised paper. L.L. edited the revision.

Funding: The APF was funded by the Deutsche Forschungsgemeinschaft (DFG) and the Open Access Publishing Fund of University of Potsdam. We gratefully acknowledge their support.

Conflicts of Interest: The authors declare no conflict of interest.

References

Ahern, Kenneth R., and Denis Sosyura. 2015. Rumor Has It: Sensationalism in Financial Media. *Review of Financial Studies* 28: 2050–93. [CrossRef]

Barber, Brad M., Reuven Lehavy, Maureen McNichols, and Brett Trueman. 2006. Buys, holds, & sells: The distribution of investment banks' stock ratings & the implications for the profitability of analysts' recommendations. *Journal of Accounting & Economics* 41: 87–117. [CrossRef]

Barber, Brad M., Reuven Lehavy, and Brett Trueman. 2010. Ratings Changes, Ratings Levels, & the Predictive Value of Analysts' Recommendations. *Financial Management* 39: 533–53. [CrossRef]

Beneish, Messod D. 1991. Stock Prices and the Dissemnation of Analysts' Recommendations. *Journal of Business* 64: 393–416. [CrossRef]

Bjerring, James H., Josef Lakonishok, and Theo Vermaelen. 1983. Stock prices and financial analysts' recommendations. *Journal of Finance* 38: 187–204. [CrossRef]

Bradley, Daniel, Sinan Gokkaya, and Xi Liu. 2017. Before an Analyst Becomes an Analyst: Does Industry Experience Matter? *Journal of Finance* 72: 751–91. [CrossRef]

Brown, Lawrence D. 2001. How important Is Past Analyst Forecast Accuracy? *Financial Analysts Journal* 57: 44–49. [CrossRef]

Clement, Michael B., and Senyo Y. Tse. 2003. Do Investors Respond to Analysts' Forecast Revisions as if Forecast Accuracy Is All That Matters? *Accounting Review* 78: 227–49. [CrossRef]

Clement, Michal B., and Senyo Y. Tse. 2005. Financial Analyst Characteristics & Herding Behavior in Forecasting. *Journal of Finance* 60: 307–41. [CrossRef]

Desai, Hemang, Ding Liang, and Ajai K. Singh. 2000. Do All-Stars Shine? Evaluation of Analyst Recommendations. *Financial Analysts Journal* 56: 20–49. [CrossRef]

Douglas, Casey, Joseph Engelberg, Diego García, and Christopher Alan Parsons. 2012. Journalists and the Stock Market. *Review of Financial Studies* 25: 639–79. [CrossRef]

Elton, Edwin J., Martin J. Gruber, and Seth Grossman. 1986. Discrete expectational data and portfolio performance. *Journal of Finance* 41: 699–713. [CrossRef]

Ertimur, Yonca, Jayanthi Sunder, and Shyam V. Sunder. 2007. Measure for Measure: The Relation between Forecast Accuracy and Recommendation Profitability of Analysts. *Journal of Accounting Research* 45: 567–606. [CrossRef]

Gallery, Natalie, Cameron Newton, and Chrisann Palm. 2011. Framework for assessing financial literacy and superannuation investment choice decisions. *Australasian Accounting, Business and Finance Journal* 5: 3–22.

Hall, Jason L., and Paul B. Tacon. 2010. Forecast accuracy and stock recommendations. *Journal of Contemporary Accounting & Economics* 6: 18–33. [CrossRef]

Hope, Ole-Kistian. 2003. Disclosure Practices, Enforcement of Accounting Standards, & Analysts' Forecast Accuracy: An International Study. *Journal of Accounting Research* 41: 235–72. [CrossRef]

Jegadeesh, Narasimhan, Joonghyuk Kim, Susan D. Krische, and Charles M. C. Lee. 2004. Analyzing the Analysts: When Do Recommendations Add Value? *Journal of Finance* 59: 1083–124. [CrossRef]

Kerl, Alexander G., and Andreas Walter. 2007. Market Responses to Buy Recommendations Issued by Personal Finance Magazines: Effects of Information, Price-Pressure, and Company Characteristics. *Review of Finance* 11: 117–41. [CrossRef]

Kwon, Sung S. 2002. Financial Analysts' Forecast Accuracy & Dispersion: High-Tech versus Low-Tech Stocks. *Review of Quantitative Finance & Accounting* 19: 65–91. [CrossRef]

Lloyd-Davies, Peter, and Michael Canes. 1978. Stock prices and the publication of second-hand information. *The Journal of Business* 51: 43–56. [CrossRef]

Lusardi, Annamaria, and Olivia S. Mitchell. 2014. The Economic Importance of Financial Literacy: Theory and Evidence. *Journal of Economic Literature* 52: 5–44. [CrossRef] [PubMed]

Mathur, Ike, and Amjad Wahed. 1995. Stock price reactions to securities recommended in business week's "Inside Wall Street". *Financial Review* 30: 583–604. [CrossRef]

Mikhail, Michael B., Beverly R. Walther, and Richard H. Willis. 1999. Does Forecast Accuracy Matter to Security Analysts? *Accounting Review* 74: 185–200. [CrossRef]

Palmon, Dan, Ephraim F. Sudit, and Ari Yezegel. 2009. The value of columnists' stock recommendations: An event study approach. *Review of Quantitative Finance and Accounting* 33: 209–32. [CrossRef]

Sharpe, William F. 1994. The Sharpe Ratio. *Journal of Portfolio Management* 21: 49–58. [CrossRef]

Stickel, Scott E. 1992. Reputation & Performance Among Security Analysts. *Journal of Finance* 47: 1811–36. [CrossRef]

Stickel, Scott E. 1995. The Anatomy of the Performance of Buy and Sell Recommendations. *Financial Analysts Journal* 51: 25–39. [CrossRef]

Welch, Ivo. 2000. Herding among security analysts. *Journal of Financial Economics* 58: 369–96. [CrossRef]

Womack, Kent L. 1996. Do brokerage analysts' recommendations have investment value? *Journal of Finance* 51: 137–67. [CrossRef]

13

The Impact of College Athletic Success on Donations and Applicant Quality

Benjamin Baumer [1] and Andrew Zimbalist [2,*]

1 Program in Statistical and Data Sciences, Smith College, Northampton, MA 01063, USA; bbaumer@smith.edu
2 Department of Economics, Smith College, Northampton, MA 01063, USA
* Correspondence: azimbali@smith.edu

Abstract: For the 65 colleges and universities that participate in the Power Five athletic conferences (Pac 12, Big 10, SEC, ACC, and Big 12), the football and men's basketball teams are highly visible. While these programs generate tens of millions of dollars in revenue annually, very few of them turn an operating "profit." Their existence is thus justified by the claim that athletic success leads to ancillary benefits for the academic institution, in terms of both quantity (e.g., more applications, donations, and state funding) and quality (e.g., stronger applicants, lower acceptance rates, higher yields). Previous studies provide only weak support for some of these claims. Using data from 2006–2016 and a multiple regression model with corrections for multiple testing, we find that while a successful football program is associated with more applicants, there is no effect on the composition of the student body or (with a few caveats) funding for the school through donations or state appropriations.

Keywords: college sports; finances; economics

JEL Classification: C4; I2; H7; Z2

---

1. Introduction

Intercollegiate athletics is in a turbulent period. Recruiting and academic scandals along with antitrust litigations are erupting with unprecedented frequency. The Rice Commission on reforming college basketball called for a panoply of structural reforms.

Meanwhile, the financial outcomes of college athletic departments remain bleak for the vast majority of institutions. NCAA reports consistently show that in recent years only about 20 out of roughly 130 athletic departments in FBS (the Football Bowl Subdivision of Division I, the most commercial subdivision in the NCAA) run an operating surplus. FBS itself is subdivided into the Power Five or Autonomous Conferences (Pac 12, Big 10, SEC, ACC and Big 12) with 65 schools and the five Non-Autonomous Conferences with 64 schools. The Power Five command the large television contracts, control the football championship playoff and enjoy much larger attendance at their games.

During the 2015–2016 school year, the median reported operating deficit at all FBS athletic programs was $14.4 million. At the Power Five schools, the median reported operating deficit was $3.6 million. There were 24 Power Five schools during 2015–2016 that experienced an operating surplus—the median surplus for these schools was $10 million (NCAA 2017).

Because of accounting irregularities, however, it appears that most FBS athletic departments do not include significant shares of their capital costs in their reports to the NCAA. According to one NCAA study, capital costs, properly reckoned, exceed $20 million annually at the average FBS school (Orszag and Orszag 2005). If these and other indirect costs were included, most estimates suggest that no more than a half dozen programs would have a true surplus.

To be sure, there is an active debate about the underlying economic reality of intercollegiate athletic programs. For instance, many economists assert that it is improper to include the cost of athletic scholarships in the financial reports because they do not represent the actual marginal costs to the school. That is, even though the school may charge $50,000 tuition, the incremental cost of educating an additional student is close to zero. Put differently, an economics professor will get paid, say, $150,000, whether she has 120 or 121 students in her introductory macroeconomics class and there are no additional facility costs incurred by the extra student.

While this is a fair point, it is also reasonable to note that fielding an FBS football team requires 85 scholarships. If the relevant alternative is having no football team, then it is no longer true that the incremental cost of educating 85 students is zero. Indeed, it is misleading to think that the marginal cost of educating a single football player is zero. The school expends considerable resources on tutoring centers and academic support to keep players eligible.

It might also be relevant to consider the opportunity cost of a football scholarship. If low income and highly qualified students do not get scholarships, and thus do not attend the school, then the school may suffer from lower graduation rates, fewer serious students in the classroom and a lower profile for its student body in terms of standardized test scores and school rank.

Further, even if all athletic aid were eliminated from the financials, it would only amount to a median savings of $4.6 million—well below the median operating deficit of $14.4 million in FBS. Moreover, standard athletic accounting does not include a host of indirect expenses, such as a share of the school president's time, travel, office, and administrative assistants' salaries.

The reality is that intercollegiate athletic departments are not profit maximizers. They do not have shareholders who demand quarterly profits to boost stock prices or corporate dividends. Instead, they have stakeholders who want victories. Subject to some constraints, athletic directors are win maximizers. The conventional method for maximizing wins is to hire well-known coaches at multi-million dollar salaries, invest lavishly in athletic and tutoring facilities and spend freely on recruitment. Thus, when revenues rise, the athletic director finds more than enough ways to spend the bounty. And even if the football or men's basketball team yields a surplus, much of it is drained by the deficits experienced by the 15 or more "non-revenue" men's and women's sports. The consequence is that the vast majority of programs run in deficit.

How, then, can these hyper-commercialized, massive athletic programs be justified? One line of defense holds that while the programs might run financial deficits, they provide invaluable exposure and advertising for the university. This branding value, in turn, produces an increase in applications. These applications fill empty beds in the dormitories and enable the college to be more selective in its admissions policies, yielding an improvement in the quality of the student body (usually measured in standardized test scores). Additionally, alumni and athletic boosters become excited by team success or media prominence and open up their wallets, leading to increased donations and endowment growth. And, in some cases, this line of reasoning goes, state legislators also become enthused and allocate more budgetary assistance to the university.

Of course, even if it could be verified that athletic success leads to these salutary outcomes, it would not justify the tens of millions of dollars of investment that most FBS universities make annually. This is because only roughly half of all teams have a winning record and only a handful of teams achieve top ranking. If regression analysis shows that winning is positively correlated with applications, this implies both that applications tend to go up when wins increase and that applications tend to go down when wins decrease. Further, many, if not most, FBS universities bend the rules or cheat in order to promote athletic success. Some of these schools get caught and scandals ensue. The resulting ignominy may have negative enduring effects on applications, donations and legislative appropriations. The lowering of admissions' standards for athletes and the creation of sham courses also serve to dilute the educational experience and intellectual spirit on the campus.

In this paper we endeavor to expand upon, clarify, and update the existing scholarly literature on whether athletic success in football and men's basketball leads to increased applications, enhanced quality of the student body, more donations and greater state support. This updating is important because the organization and rules affecting college sports have been in flux in the 21st century. We consider evidence from 2005–2006 through 2015–2016 for the 65 Power Five schools in the FBS. These schools are athletically the most successful and best known by a considerable margin and, therefore, the most likely to garner the positive publicity effects from athletic success.

In what follows we review the existing scholarship, describe our data sources and our data profile, discuss our models and results and draw conclusions. The evolution of the literature is not linear and the current state of knowledge remains ambiguous.

2. Review of the Literature

2.1. Athletic Success and the Quantity and Quality of Applications

One of the first and most frequently cited studies on the impact of athletic success on admissions is McCormick and Tinsley (1987). They gather data on 150 schools for 1971. On the basis of a multiple regression test with several control variables, they estimate that a school with a "big-time" athletics program had 3% higher SAT scores than schools without such a program. They identified 63 of the schools in their sample to have a big-time program. A difficulty with this cross-sectional analysis is that characteristics not identified by the control variables of a school lead to an incomplete model specification. In an attempt to rectify this deficiency, McCormick and Tinsley test a second model with data from 1981 to 1984, focusing exclusively on schools with big-time programs. They explore the link between changes in SAT scores and changes in athletic performance over this period. None of the estimated coefficients are statistically different than zero at standard confidence levels.

Bremmer and Kesselring (1993) essayed a retest of the McCormick and Tinsley hypotheses, using data from 1989 for 132 schools and from 1981–1989 for 53 schools. They find no evidence that basketball or football success led to increased SAT scores of matriculated students.

Tucker and Amato (1993) adapt the McCormick and Tinsley model by using a new metric of athletic success—whether the school was in the Associated Press top twenty ranking in football or basketball. They find no relationship between basketball success and SAT scores, but that a football program ranked in the top twenty for ten consecutive years (1980–1989) would attract a freshman class with 3% higher average SAT scores than a program which never ranked in the top twenty.

Murphy and Trandel (1994) construct a ten-year panel, 1978–1987, and use team win percentage as the measure of athletic success. They use school fixed effects and, thereby, control more effectively for unobserved differences among institutions. Murphy and Trandel find that a 50% increase in a team's win percentage results in a rather small increase of only 1.3% in the number of its applicants.

Mixon (1995) employs a different measure of basketball success—the number of rounds through which the school's team advanced in March Madness in the spring before the applications were filed the next fall[1]. Mixon's estimate was positive and statistically significant, suggesting that the average SAT score in the entering class increased by 1.7 points for each additional round the school's team was in the tournament.

Toma and Cross (1998) examine the records for the thirteen different universities that won the FBS football championship between 1979 and 1992 and the eleven different universities that won the NCAA men's basketball tournament over the same period. They track the quantity and quality of undergraduate applications for five years preceding and succeeding their championship for each of these schools. They find a clear correlation between winning a championship and the number of applicants, but are unable to identify any measurable impact of a championship on the quality of admitted or entering students.

---

1 Mixon also co-authored two cross-sectional studies based on data from 1990 and 1993 that found a relationship between athletic success or prominence and the attraction of a school to out-of-state residents (Mixon and Hsing 1994; Mixon and Ressler 1995).

Zimbalist (2001) uses data from 86 FBS colleges from 1980 through 1995 and performs a variety of fixed effect multiple regressions, using different measures of athletic success. The tests reveal that, while there is some tendency for athletic success to increase applications, there is no significant relationship between athletic success and average SAT scores.

In a study under commission from the NCAA, Litan, Orszag, and Orszag (Litan et al. 2003) use a fixed-effects model for 1993–2001 and are unable to find a statistically significant relationship between football winning percentage and SAT scores of the incoming class.[2]

Tucker (2005) considers evidence from 1990, 1996, 2000, 2001 and 2002 from 78 Division I schools. He finds that after 1996 football success has a positive impact on the average SAT scores of the incoming class. He argues that the perfection of the Bowl Championship Series played a central role in bringing increased attention and, hence, advertising exposure to the top football programs.

Smith (2008), in contrast, considers data from Division I schools during 1994–2005 and finds little evidence to support a link between different measures of men's basketball success and four measurements of student quality. The one exception was that schools that had a "breakout" year (lagged two years) experienced an 8.86 point average increase in the SAT scores of the 75th percentile of the entering class. Breakout was defined in various ways, but basically denoted that a school went from a perennial losing record to a strong winning record.

Pope and Pope (2009), using a data set from 330 Division I schools during 1983–2002, find that certain types of athletic success appear to increase interest in a school from applicants with high, medium and low SAT scores, but that the increase in enrollments from the students with SAT scores above 600 in English and in Math is weaker and less reliable. Indeed, for some of the athletic performance variables the relationship between athletic success and the log of enrollment is significantly negative. Further, any impact tends to be in the next year with no significant effect after two or three years. In the end, Pope and Pope conclude that "the summary data ... would suggest that athletically successful schools actually saw slightly lower long-run growth in applications and enrollments." One important caveat in interpreting these results is that Pope and Pope test fixed effect multiple regressions with control variables and thirty-two athletic performance variables. At a 0.10 level of significance, one would anticipate that 3.2 variables would achieve statistical significance randomly. The authors should have, but did not, control for the multiplicity problem.[3] Multicollinearity among the performance variables presents another challenge in interpreting the coefficients.[4]

Pope and Pope (2014) use a Division I data set of 332 schools during 1994–2001 to test the impact of men's basketball and football on the propensity of high school applicants to send their SAT scores to a school. They find that a school with stellar results in either sport receives on average up to 10% more SAT scores. They also find that the relationship is stronger for some demographic subgroups, such as males, people of color, out-of-state students and high school athletes. They do not test for actual applications to the school or for eventual enrollments. Pope and Pope model one to three year lags and find that the statistical significance of sports success "decays very quickly across time."

In sum, the various studies lend some support to the notion that robust athletic success can lead to an increase in applications to a school. The correlate of this proposition is that poor athletic performance can lead to falling applications. There is only weak support, if any, for the claim that sport success leads to an increase in the quality of students. The increase in applications in some cases, however, may assist a school in filling empty beds in its dormitories. These conclusions are supported

---

2 For a summary of the literature through 2004, see Frank (2004).

3 See, for instance, Benjamini and Hochberg (1995).

4 Castle and Kostelnik (2011) examine 14 Division II schools in Pennsylvania during 1995–2004 and find weak evidence that some measures of athletic success were correlated with an increase in applications and the SAT scores of the entering class. Three studies found that football success was associated with lower student grades; see Clotfelter (2011); Lindo, Swensen, and Waddell (Lindo et al. 2012); and Hernández-Julián and Rotthoff (2014).

anecdotally by a self study done at the University of Massachusetts following its ascent to basketball fame in the mid-1990s under John Calipari.

> The period from fall 1988 to fall 1990 did not include outstanding basketball years. In 1991, UMass was a semi-finalist in the NIT and in the four years since has been featured consistently on national television, has been ranked consistently in the top twenty and has gone to the NCAA tournament . . . It is clear that after double digit declines in out-of-state applications from fall 1988 to fall 1991, we experienced two years of double digit increases in fall 1993 and 1994. It has been suggested that this bump in applications might be related to, among other things, the greater awareness of the university beyond Massachusetts, at least partially as a result of the success in basketball.
>
> It has been reported that the University of Connecticut experienced a similar application increase after their very successful Elite Eight season in 1991, with a 26% increase in out-of-state and 6% increase of in-state applications. Despite the growth of applications correlated with UConn basketball success, the conclusion was that there was no impact on yield (enrollment divided by admittances). With the numbers of applications up, it would also be expected that the quality of students enrolled might increase because of a larger pool on which to draw. The Connecticut experience indicates no changes in the quality of students. In the UMass figures there was a decrease in the SAT scores of applicants and enrolled students for both in- and out-of-state students. In fact, this [1995–1996] was the first year that the SAT scores of out-of-state students fell below in-state. None of this suggests that team success carries beyond the application stage. In fact, in the year following the "Dream Season," UConn applications dropped back to earlier numbers. Their conclusion was that there was no lasting impact on the admission numbers. (Massachusetts Football Task Force 1996)

2.2. *Athletic Success and Alumni Giving*

Studies on alumni or other giving are less numerous and less complete. The primary reason for this is that the availability of data on alumni giving is spotty. Sigelman and Carter (1979) assemble data from the Council for Financial Aid to Education (CFAE) from 1966–1967 to 1975–1976 and test the relationship between the yearly change in total giving to the annual fund and athletic success, measured by win percentages in football and men's basketball and a dummy variable indicating whether the team participated in the post-season. Sigelman and Carter do not find any statistically significant relationships between giving and athletic success, and even note that some of the coefficients were negative.

Brooker and Klastorin (1981) critique the Sigelman and Carter study on the grounds that it does not control for institutional heterogeneity. They adjust for this by using institutional fixed effects and find some positive and some negative relationships between athletic success and giving. Together, they run tests on 1740 coefficients and find only 1.7% of them to be significant at the 0.10 level, which is fewer than the number that would be expected by chance. The authors do not report the magnitude of the effects.

Sigelman and Bookheimer (1983) introduce a fixed effects model and break down alumni contributions into two components, restricted gifts to the athletics department and unrestricted gifts to the annual fund. They find that the two types of giving are uncorrelated with each other and that only gifts to the athletics department are correlated with sport success (football, not basketball). More precisely, they estimate that a 10% increase in football win percentage over the previous four years leads to a $125,000 increase in donations to the athletics department (measured in 1983 dollars).

Grimes and Chressanthis (1994) focus on one school, Mississippi State, over a 30-year period between 1962 and 1991. They considered success of the football, basketball and baseball teams. Winning success in football had a negative coefficient that was not statistically significant. Basketball's coefficient was significant at the 0.05 level and positive, but extremely small.

Baade and Sundberg (1996) construct a data set from Division I schools during 1973–1979. They employ both winning percentage and bowl or March Madness appearances as measures of sport success. They find no impact on giving from increased winning percentages, but a modest effect for postseason appearances. They do not distinguish between athletic and academic giving.

Rhoads and Gerking (2000) follow the modelling of Baade and Sundberg with data for 1986–1987 to 1995–1996.[5] They run their tests first without institutional fixed effects and find impact very similar to those of Baade and Sundberg. They run the tests again with fixed effects and none of the athletic success variables are statistically significant predictors of giving. Rhoads and Gerking also estimate that being placed on NCAA probation for a basketball violation reduces total giving by $1.6 million (measured in 1987 dollars).

Turner, Meserve, and Bowen (Turner et al. 2001) consider a data set of 15 private schools during 1988–1989 to 1997–1998. Using a fixed effects model, they find that football win percentage has no significant effect on the *rate* of giving among alumni in FBS programs, but that it has a highly significant (at 0.01) and negative effect on the giving *amount* among alumni. Specifically, an increase of 12 wins is associated with a *decrease* in giving by $270 for an average person.

Humphreys and Mondello (2007), based on 320 Division I schools from 1976 to 1996 find that postseason play was positively correlated with giving to athletics, but not to giving to academics. Stinson and Howard (2008) investigated 208 institutions from Divisions I-AA and I-AAA and found no correlation between giving to athletics and giving to academics.[6]

2.3. *Athletic Success and State Budgetary Support*

Three scholarly articles have explored the impact of university athletic success on legislative appropriations. Humphreys (2006) estimates a reduced form model with data from 1975 to 1996 that controls for state and institution specific characteristics.[7] He finds that state appropriations are 8% higher for institutions in FBS (formerly Division IA), other things equal. The presence of an increase in state support for having an FBS football team of $2.6 million on average (in 1982 dollars) may do little more than offset the additional net costs of fielding the team. Humphreys, however, does not find that either appearance in a bowl game or achieving a national ranking in the top 25 had a statistically significant impact on state appropriations.

Alexander and Kern (2010) consider 117 schools from FBS, FCS and Division II for the period 1983–1984 to 2006–2007. They do not explain why their sample is more heavily weighted to FBS or why certain schools were omitted. They find that increases in basketball and football win percentage for schools in FBS do produce a statistically significant increase in state appropriations, but appearances in major bowl games or in the NCAA Final Four does not. The three models that they test yield R-squares of 0.05, 0.05 and 0.08, suggesting that they are underspecified and calling into question the reliability of their coefficient estimates.

---

5 Goff (2000) also considers the impact of sport success on the endowment. Goff, however, only looks at endowment data only for two schools, Georgia Tech and Northwestern. While he finds no statistically significant relationship between sport success and donations at Georgia Tech, Goff does find one at Northwestern. However, Goff notes that the finding for Northwestern may have been affected by an accounting change at the school (moving a substantial amount of cash into long-term equity during the period studied.) In any event, the data base is much too thin to assign much importance to these results.

6 Koo and Dittmore (2014), based on an unexplained sample of 155 schools from Divisions I, II and III during 2002–2003 to 2011–2012, purport to find a positive correlation between athletic giving lagged one year and current academic giving. They conclude that athletic giving does not crowd out academic giving. They do not offer an explanation of why they lag athletic giving; any crowding out would presumably happen in the same year. It is also not clear what their full model is and whether, for instance, they detrended their data or used time fixed effects. Walker (2015) uses a sample of between 954 and 1052 schools during 2002–2011 and finds that appearances in the Final Four are significantly associated with increases in private donations, but, again, he does not break out athletic and academic donations and does not provide a full description of his model.

7 There was a prior study to Humphreys, but is was based on only one year (1980–1981) and 52 DIA schools (Coughlin and Erekson 1986).

Jones (2015) uses a difference-in-difference model that focused on six universities that transitioned from FCS to FBS between 2000 and 2010. Jones finds that when the six schools were compared to all other FCS schools, there is no significant correlation between FBS affiliation and state appropriations. When the six schools are compared only to other FCS schools in the same region, there is still no significant correlation. Only when the comparison is made between FCS schools in the same region and within the same propensity score range[8] did the move to FBS yield a significant relationship with state appropriations. Jones concludes that this result provides some support for the hypothesis of a positive effect between NCAA subdivision and state support.

2.4. Anderson on Athletic Benefits

Anderson (2017) deploys the most sophisticated econometric treatment of the relationships between athletic success and various school outcome variables in the extant literature, uses the most recent data, and has been cited numerous times as representing the state of current knowledge on these matters; hence, this paper warrants a separate and more detailed discussion. He considers a data set for FBS schools from 1986 to 2009 and employs a propensity score model to estimate these relationships. Anderson's motivation for adopting this framework is the difficulty of unraveling causality from observational data, especially given that selection bias (e.g., recruiting skill of coaches and administrators), reverse causality (e.g., athletic success begets donations, which are in turn spent to achieve greater athletic success), and confounding variables are likely present.[9]

Anderson's basic approach is to use bookmaker spreads for individual football games to establish (via a fifth order polynomial logistic model) a probability of winning (the propensity score). Actual wins are then conditioned on the propensity score and used as the independent variable (or treatment). This method depends on the assumption that gambling is efficient (the bookmaker spread represents full and rationally-processed information to determine the likelihood of contest outcome; put differently, all the relevant variables that impact a game's result are subsumed into the point spread.[10]) Anderson then essentially runs school applications, SAT scores and donations on the difference between the actual and the expected wins during a season. Thus, Anderson is estimating the effect of unexpected wins (losses) on his school outcome variables.

While it is interesting to know what the effect of unexpected wins is, it is likely a different effect than wins or general athletic success. Few would question, for instance, that a football or men's basketball team that rises from sport oblivion to prominence in one year will experience an uptick in applications, donations or state appropriations (see previous discussion of UMass/UConn.)[11] This is a different matter than a team perennially appearing in March's Elite Eight or Final Four or in the Football Championship Playoff.

Anderson does indeed find that unexpected wins are associated with increased applications, higher SAT scores and increased donations to the athletics department (but not to the general fund).

---

8 Jones' propensity score includes a number of school characteristics, including size, percentage of full-time students, percent of graduate students, degree of institutional urbanization, freshmen retention rate, and total education expenditures.

9 Reverse causality would not appear to a significant issue when considering applications or SAT scores and athletic success. That is, while it may be logical to expect athletic success to increase applications or SAT scores, it does not seem plausible that more applications or higher SAT scores would engender greater athletic success. Top football and basketball players in FBS are recruited and, by all accounts, base their decisions on factors related to the athletics program. The effects of confounding variables, such as the managerial talent of a school president or provost, along with other unquantifiable attributes, could be accounted for by team fixed effects. Reverse causality may be an issue with athletic success and donations. In such a case, however, one would expect that the presence of reverse causality would strengthen the estimated correlation between the variables. Since Anderson's use of a propensity score is intended to mitigate the impact of reverse causality, other things equal, one would expect his model to imply a weaker correlation between athletic success and donations, contrary to his findings.

10 For this crucial assumption to be statistically valid, the R_2 from this equation must be very high, approaching 1. Anderson, however, does not mention what the R_2 is in this test. It is nonetheless true that the literature on sports betting markets indicates that they operate efficiently. See, for example, the discussion in Lopez, Matthews, and Baumer (Lopez et al. 2018).

11 Such a finding would be consistent with the empirical work of Smith (2008), op. cit., and his "breakout" variable.

Notably, Anderson's strongest result is for donations to the athletics department, but this finding relies on a very incomplete data set on donations (495 observations for BCS[12] athletic donations versus 1560 observations possible for 65 schools over 24 years). He also runs tests separately for the Power Five conferences within FBS and for the remaining FBS (or "Group of Five") conferences and finds that his relationships only hold for the Power Five schools.

Three other points from Anderson are worth noting. First, he finds little evidence that the positive effect of unexpected wins lasts more than one year. Second, his positive results appear to be considerably weaker than he claims. Thus, after correcting for multiple testing, none of his treatment variables are significant at the 0.05 level. His Alumni Athletic Operating Donations variable comes closest with significance at the 0.053 level, but this variable is missing more than two-thirds of its possible observations, creating a possible selection bias.[13] Third, in his conclusion, Anderson misrepresents his own results when he states: "Consider a school that improves its season wins by three games . . . . This school may expect alumni athletic donations to increase by $409,000 (17%), applications to increase by 406 (3%) . . . ." But Anderson is not looking at the net benefit of three wins; he is looking the net benefit of three wins over expectation. That is, if a team wins three more games but the betting markets expected the team would win three more games, there would be no net benefit.

2.5. Summary of the Existing Literature

Overall, the literature on the impact of college sport success on the quantity and quality of applications and enrollments, donations to the athletics department and general fund, and state appropriations is mixed and somewhat inconclusive. When significant results have been found, they have tended to be small in practical magnitude. Much of the existing scholarship is limited by methodological issues and data availability and most studies have not considered evidence from the 2000s. Each new study appears to use a new set of schools, conferences or divisions, a different set of athletic success variables, distinct issues with missing data, and different modelling of the relationship between the treatment and outcome variable. Given the restructuring of the NCAA subdivisions and conferences, the emergence of conference-owned RSNs and attendant spurt in television revenues, the increased autonomy of the Power Five conferences and the enhanced role of athletics in university finances and governance since 2000, it makes sense to examine the stability of the relationships between success in sports and possible indirect benefits for the school with more recent data. In what follows, we attempt to overcome some of the methodological issues of previous work and to construct a more up-to-date data set.

3. Our Data

Anderson (2017) found that for 1986–2009, the Power Five conferences are the most athletically prominent and the most likely to experience benefits from athletic success. As an update, our data covers the eleven academic years from 2005–2006 through 2015–2016 (plus the three preceding years for lagged variables) for the 65 schools that were members of Power Five conferences in 2015–2016[14]. Our data sources are the Council for Advancement and Support of Education annual Voluntary Support of Education (VSE) surveys, Integrated Postsecondary Education Data System (IPEDs) surveys, the National Center for Education Statistics for high school graduates, the US Census Bureau for

---

12 BCS stands for Bowl Championship Series and refers to universities prior to 2014 in today's Power Five conferences plus the former Big East conference. The BCS conferences were sometimes referred to as the AQ or Automatic Qualifying conferences.

13 Anderson, Table 3, p. 127. In his conclusion (p. 132), Anderson suggests that school investments in athletics may have net revenue payoffs, but to conclude this he misleads because the NCAA definition of revenue includes athletic donations, and, indeed, is a major share of athletic department revenues for FBS schools.

14 Conference alignment was retroactively fixed to the 2015–2016 alignment. A school like the University of Utah, which moved from the Mountain West Conference to the Pac-12 in 2012, is considered to have always belonged to the Pac-12 for the purposes of this study.

demographic information, and Sports-Reference.com. The data are available through the colleges package for R, available on GitHub (Baumer 2018).

Our school benefit response variables—summarized in Table 1—include the number of applications (*Applied*, measured in thousands), the average 75th percentile SAT score across three portions of the exam (*SAT75p*), the admissions rate (*Admit*) and yield (*Yield*), donations to athletics by alumni (*Athletics*, in millions of dollars), total donations by alumni (*Alumni*, in millions of dollars), total non-athletic donations by alumni (*NonAthletics*) and total state appropriations to the school (*State*, in millions of dollars), also computed per student (*StatePC*, in thousands).

Table 1. Data profile, response variables.

Statistic	N	Mean	St. Dev.	Pctl (25)	Pctl (75)
Applied	711	21.786	11.470	13.058	28.030
SAT75p	675	661.211	50.828	630.000	696.667
Donations	605	178.522	152.569	85.672	230.596
Athletics	356	20.128	14.453	11.939	26.523
NonAthletics	356	154.485	159.349	66.488	197.043
State	558	279.541	137.115	174.574	371.532
StatePC	557	58.073	26.899	39.911	71.806
Yield	711	0.408	0.111	0.338	0.459
Admit	711	0.591	0.214	0.453	0.762

We note that for variables derived from IPEDS (acceptance rate, number of applicants, yield, and 75th percentile SAT score), we have nearly complete coverage with only one school (Maryland) failing to report in multiple years. Notably, as is the case with Anderson's data set, the extent of the missing data for donations is much larger. We have athletic donations data for only 356 school-years and total donations data for 605 school years out of a total possible 715 observations. The pattern of missing data in donations suggests a possible bias, as certain schools (mostly private, notably Notre Dame, Boston College, Miami (FL), Syracuse, Wake Forest) simply did not report donation data (the data is certainly not missing at random). Hence, our findings for the athletic donations response variable should be interpreted with caution. Of course, private schools do not receive state funding, but this does not fully account for the missing data for that variable—state-related schools like Penn State and Pittsburgh also did not report state funding. Many of these variables are strongly right-skewed, and in these cases we have fit the model to their logarithm.

Our athletic success treatment variables—summarized in Table 1—include measures of being good, great, and the best at both basketball and football. Specifically, for both sports we record the cumulative winning percentage over the previous three seasons (*BBWpct*, *FBWpct*), as well as any Final Four appearances[15] and national championships in any of the three preceding seasons. Thus, we consider one, two, and three year lags on the Final Four (*BBFF*1, *BBFF*2, *BBFF*3, and *FBFF*1, *FBFF*2, *FBFF*3, respectively) and championship variables (*BBChamps*1, *BBChamps*2, *BBChamps*3, and *FBChamps*1, *FBChamps*2, *FBChamps*3, respectively). The choice to include cumulative winning percentage over three years—as opposed to say, winning percentage in each of the previous three years—was designed to smooth out year-to-year noise in winning percentage, while still reflecting relevant recent history.

Our control variables include median income per capita in the state (*Income*, in thousands of dollars), number of high school diplomas issued in the state in the previous year (*HSDiplomas*, in thousands), and state funding, both overall and per student (*State* and *StatePC*, respectively). These variables help account for variation in the income and population of each state, in addition to

15 Final Four appearances in basketball are measured by performance in the NCAA Tournament. Final Four appearances in football are measured by end-of-season national ranking by the Associated Press.

the support from state government (only relevant for public schools). While it may be the case that state household income is less relevant for private schools, such schools often draw regional interest and represent only about one-fifth of the schools considered. Further, to control for the unobserved heterogeneity of the 65 institutions we tested both school (*School*) and year (*Year*) fixed effects, with both variables treated as categorical.[16] The fixed effect for *School* should capture the effect of the long-term branding value of the school's athletic program (i.e., Duke basketball), as well as many other attributes. The fixed effect for *Year* should capture changes due to inflation and other economic conditions.

The data in Table 2 come exclusively from Sports-Reference and the US Census Bureau, and there is no missing data. As the number of high school diplomas awarded is right-skewed, we use the logarithm of this variable in our models.

Table 2. Data profile, explanatory variables.

Statistic	N	Mean	St. Dev.	Pctl (25)	Pctl (75)
HSDiplomas	715	106.500	100.914	39.227	127.515
Income	715	26.349	3.709	23.797	28.351
BBFF1	715	0.046	0.210	0	0
BBFF2	715	0.045	0.207	0	0
BBFF3	715	0.045	0.207	0	0
BBWpct	715	0.599	0.124	0.514	0.694
BBChamps1	715	0.013	0.112	0	0
BBChamps2	715	0.011	0.105	0	0
BBChamps3	715	0.013	0.112	0	0
FBFF1	715	0.060	0.238	0	0
FBFF2	715	0.060	0.238	0	0
FBFF3	715	0.060	0.238	0	0
FBWpct	715	0.570	0.175	0.444	0.700
FBChamps1	715	0.015	0.123	0	0
FBChamps2	715	0.015	0.123	0	0
FBChamps3	715	0.015	0.123	0	0

4. Our Models

We tested a wide variety of models, including semi-logs, different lag patterns and interactive effects, and focus here on the most important results (please see our data Appendix A for additional information).[17] Unless otherwise indicated, our standard errors are robust (using the HC1 sandwich variance-covariance matrix (Zeileis and Hothorn 2002)) and our p-values are corrected for multiplicity via the Benjamini-Hochberg method (Benjamini and Hochberg 1995)[18], which controls the false discovery rate. All computations were performed in R version 3.4 (R Core Team 2018).

---

[16] We also collected many variables that were not included in our regression models. For example, cost of attendance, state population, etc. These variables are included in the colleges package (Baumer 2018), but are often incomplete and/or strongly correlated with our other explanatory variables.

[17] None of the models we explored but are not reporting offered substantially different or contradictory results to the ones offered here.

[18] All reported p-values were adjusted using the p.adjust() function in the stats package.

Our general regression model for each response variable y_j is:

$$\begin{aligned} y_i &= \beta \cdot X + \varepsilon_j \\ &= \beta_{j0} + \alpha_j \cdot Year + \gamma_j \cdot School + \beta_{j1} \cdot \log(HSDiplomas) + \beta_{j2} \cdot Income \\ &+ \theta_{j1} \cdot BBWpct + \theta_{j2} \cdot BBChamps1 + \theta_{j3} \cdot BBChamps2 + \theta_{j4} \cdot BBChamps3 \\ &+ \theta_{j5} \cdot BBFF1 + \theta_{j6} \cdot BBFF2 + \theta_{j7} \cdot BBFF3 \\ &+ \lambda_{j1} \cdot FBWpct + \lambda_{j2} \cdot FBChamps1 + \lambda_{j3} \cdot FBChamps2 + \lambda_{j4} \cdot FBChamps3 \\ &+ \lambda_{j5} \cdot FBFF1 + \lambda_{j6} \cdot FBFF2 + \lambda_{j7} \cdot FBFF3 \\ &+ \varepsilon_j \end{aligned}$$

where each α_j is a vector of length 10 containing the fixed effects associated with each academic year (relative to 2005–2006), each γ_j is a vector of length 64 containing the fixed effects associated with each school (relative to the University of Alabama, which comes first alphabetically[19]), β_{j1} and β_{j2} are control variables associated with the number of high school diplomas granted in the previous year and the per capita income in the corresponding state, the θ's are associated with the school's recent success in basketball, the λ's are associated with the school's recent success in football, and the error terms $\epsilon_j \sim N(0, \sigma_{\epsilon_j})$, for some fixed value of σ_{ϵ_j}.[20] For readability we omit the $j$subscripts in what follows.

5. Our Results

In each of the models we fit, *School* and *Year* (which is treated as a categorical variable) were statistically significant. For clarity of presentation we relegate these results to our data Appendix A, but these effects capture much of the variability in the data. There are obvious broad trends, such as a general increase in the number of applications over time, and obvious school-specific effects for which these variables control. Multicollinearity among the explanatory variables of interest—as measured by generalized variance inflation factors (Fox and Monette 1992)—does not appear to be problematic in these models.[21]

5.1. *Athletic Success and the Quantity and Quality of Applications*

Our first model, shown below, tests the effect of athletic success on school applications,

$$y_1 = log(Applied) = \beta_1 \cdot X + \epsilon_1.$$

Results from this model are shown in Table 3.

19 The success of the University of Alabama's football team impacts our interpretation of the football-related variables. However, using Alabama as the reference group has no impact on any term's statistically significance, since we consider only the significance of the *School* variable as a whole.

20 Note that our models do not directly account for the possibility that a school is not simultaneously investing in competitive athletics and other areas of school achievement or marketing. That is, if a school hired a new football coach for \$10 million, leading to an appearance in the national football playoffs, at the same time that it hired two nobel prize winning professors and began a multimillion dollar marketing campaign, then attributing an increase in applications, in entering students SAT scores or in alumni donations to football success would be spurious. There are two caveats to such an endogeneity concern. First, we do employ institutional fixed effects that may attenuate or eliminate such a problem. Second, we do not know of any evidence that such behavior occurred. In any event, we are not attributing causality to the treatment variables in our models; rather, we are noting the presence or absence of statistically significant relationships and the magnitude of such relationships.

21 We computed generalized variance inflation factors raised to the $1/(2 \cdot df)$ power, as recommend by Fox and Monette (1992) for all explanatory variables in all models. Those factors were only above 2 for the control variables number of high school diplomas (ranging from 20.8 to 23.9) and per capita income (8.9 to 10.0).

Table 3. Models for Applicants.

	Dependent Variable	
	Log(Applied) (1)	**Admit** (2)
log(HSDiplomas)	0.127 (0.124) $p = 0.440$	−0.086 (0.075) $p = 0.399$
Income	0.012 (0.011) $p = 0.424$	0.003 (0.006) $p = 0.763$
BBFF1	−0.014 (0.022) $p = 0.676$	−0.002 (0.013) $p = 0.954$
BBFF2	−0.030 (0.019) $p = 0.209$	−0.001 (0.020) $p = 0.990$
BBFF3	0.018 (0.024) $p = 0.593$	−0.008 (0.017) $p = 0.826$
BBWpct	0.067 (0.059) $p = 0.412$	−0.009 (0.036) $p = 0.919$
BBChamps1	0.059 (0.033) $p = 0.145$	−0.008 (0.020) $p = 0.857$
BBChamps2	0.095 (0.035) $p = 0.016$ **	−0.003 (0.023) $p = 0.094$
BBChamps3	−0.010 (0.046) $p = 0.855$	0.018 (0.022) $p = 0.605$
FBFF1	0.031 (0.022) $p = 0.270$	−0.008 (0.009) $p = 0.596$
FBFF2	0.010 (0.021) $p = 0.778$	0.004 (0.008) $p = 0.810$
FBFF3	0.023 (0.020) $p = 0.412$	−0.005 (0.008) $p = 0.713$
FBWpct	0.144 (0.044) $p = 0.004$ ***	−0.053 (0.024) $p = 0.077$ *
FBChamps1	0.013 (0.042) $p = 0.832$	−0.021 (0.015) $p = 0.322$
FBChamps2	0.045 (0.042) $p = 0.424$	−0.009 (0.017) $p = 0.763$
FBChamps3	0.042 (0.043) $p = 0.459$	0.004 (0.018) $p = 0.919$
Constant	1.810 (0.571) $p = 0.005$ ***	0.930 (0.336) $p = 0.020$ **
Observations	711	711
R^2	0.955	0.920
Adjusted R^2	0.949	0.909
Residual Std. Error (df = 620)	0.115	0.065
F Statistic (df = 90; 620)	147.817 ***	79.434 ***

Note: * $p < 0.1$; ** $p < 0.05$; *** $p < 0.01$.

Out of the 14 athletic performance variables, only two are statistically significant at the 0.10 level: *BBChamps*2 and *FBWpct*. *BBChamps*2 is significant at the 0.05 level and its coefficient (θ_3) indicates a national championship two years earlier is associated with a 10% increase in applications.[22] *FBWpct* is significant at the 0.001 level and its coefficient (λ_1) indicates an additional win per year on average over the previous three seasons is associated with a 1.1% increase in applications.[23]

These results are consistent with the bulk of previous literature that big-time football and men's basketball success does provide an advertising (and/or anticipated quality of life) effect which boosts applications to a university. Two additional observations are in order. First, the effect for increasing win percentage in the regular season does not apply to basketball (after controlling for football) and for football the magnitude of the effect is rather modest. Thus, direct advertising of a school's academic programs and campus life might be more effective in generating applications than investing in its basketball or football success. Second, the other observed impact occurs only for the rarest of accomplishments (1 out of 65 in each year): a national championship. Investing in creating a national championship basketball or football team entails very high risk for rather ordinary returns. Further, the returns in the form of increased applications appear to delay for one year and then dissipate by year three.

Table 3 also shows the results for a model for the rate of admissions. These results are highly consistent with the previous ones, due to the obvious functional dependence between the rate of admission and the number of applicants (the number of students is largely fixed at most schools). The negative coefficient for football winning percentage—the only variable to achieve statistical significance at the 0.10 level—implies that greater success in football is associated with higher selectivity.

Albeit tenuous, the existence of a statistically significant link between athletic success and applications leads to the next question: whether athletic success improves a school's admission yield (the percent of admitted students who enroll.) We ran the following equation to test this relationship.

$$y_3 = Yield = \beta_3 \cdot X + \epsilon_3$$

Results for this model as shown in Table 4. Of the 14 athletic performance variables, only one is statistically significant at the 0.10 level. *FBWpct* is significant at the 0.05 level with an association between an extra regular season win on average over the previous three years and an increased yield of 0.476 percentage points; that is, a yield of 30% would increase to 30.476%. While football's impact appears to be statistically significant but small, performance of the men's basketball team does not have a statistically significant impact on yield.

If athletic success may lead to an uptick in applications, even with a steady yield, the school may become more selective. Greater selectivity, in turn, may lead to an improvement on the quality of the student body, often represented by a school's SAT scores.

In the following equation we test what impact athletic success has on the 75th percentile of SAT scores across the three sections of the exam (Math, English, Writing) for the 65 Power Five schools in our sample.

$$y_4 = SAT75p = \beta_4 \cdot X + \epsilon_4$$

The results from this model are also shown in Table 4. Only one of the 14 athletic performance variables achieve statistical significance at the 0.10 level: *BBWpct*. The coefficient of *BBWpct* (θ_1) implies that every regular season win on average over three years is associated with a 0.6 point increase in the average across the English, Writing and Math portions of the SAT for the 75th percentile of the school's student body—a statistically significant effect with no practical impact.

---

22 The coefficient was 0.095 and *exp*(0.095) = 1.1.

23 The coefficient was 0.144 and *exp*(0.144/13) = 1.011 (divided by an average of 13 regular season games).

Table 4. Models for Admissions.

	Dependent Variable	
	SAT75p (1)	**Yield** (2)
log(HSDiplomas)	17.070 (14.516) $p = 0.397$	0.082 (0.059) $p = 0.255$
Income	−1.457 (1.033) $p = 0.286$	0.001 (0.005) $p = 0.880$
BBFF1	0.108 (3.459) $p = 0.980$	0.003 (0.012) $p = 0.902$
BBFF2	−0.100 (3.914) $p = 0.980$	0.015 (0.022) $p = 0.627$
BBFF3	1.963 (3.631) $p = 0.741$	0.0002 (0.013) $p = 0.887$
BBWpct	17.937 (7.451) $p = 0.041$ **	−0.002 (0.013) $p = 0.987$
BBChamps1	−7.067 (6.423) $p = 0.418$	0.0003 (0.017) $p = 0.987$
BBChamps2	−0.140 (5.528) $p = 0.980$	−0.019 (0.022) $p = 0.512$
BBChamps3	−2.869 (6.094) $p = 0.787$	−0.001 (0.015) $p = 0.980$
FBFF1	−9.598 (7.237) $p = 0.327$	−0.001 (0.009) $p = 0.944$
FBFF2	1.231 (3.781) $p = 0.874$	−0.005 (0.007) $p = 0.573$
FBFF3	−7.317 (6.818) $p = 0.426$	−0.011 (0.008) $p = 0.241$
FBWpct	−4.963 (6.418) $p = 0.600$	0.062 (0.023) $p = 0.019$**
FBChamps1	7.934 (9.794) $p = 0.589$	−0.002 (0.014) $p = 0.944$
FBChamps2	−1.843 (4.135) $p = 0.798$	−0.012 (0.016) $p = 0.586$
FBChamps3	−0.445 (9.155) $p = 0.980$	−0.020 (0.011) $p = 0.139$
Constant	580.580 (55.642) $p = 0.000$ ***	0.152 (0.265) $p = 0.698$
Observations	675	711
R^2	0.925	0.803
Adjusted R^2	0.914	0.775
Residual Std. Error (df = 620)	14.941 (df = 585)	0.053 (df = 620)
F Statistic (df = 90; 620)	81.070 *** (df = 89; 585)	28.153 *** (df = 90; 620)

Note: * $p < 0.1$; ** $p < 0.05$; *** $p < 0.01$.

5.2. Athletic Success and Alumni Giving

Our next test explores the relationship between alumni donations and athletic success. As was the case with Anderson (2017), who also relied on data from the annual survey of the Council for Aid to Education, there is a substantial problem with missing data. Many of the respondent schools simply do not answer the survey questions on alumni donations or do not do so completely or on a regular annual basis. In Anderson's data set, approximately two-thirds of donation data is missing, in ours approximately 15% of overall donations and about half of athletics donations are missing (359 out of 715). Accordingly, although there is no obvious pattern to which schools did not report, our results must be interpreted with caution. The following equation examines the relationship between alumni donations to athletics and athletic performance, with the standard control variables. Its results are shown in Table 5.

$$y_5 = log(Athletics) = \beta_5 \cdot X + \epsilon_5$$

Table 5. Models for Donations.

	Dependent Variable	
	log(Athletics) **(1)**	**log(NonAthletics)** **(2)**
log(HSDiplomas)	−0.453 (1.144) $p = 0.932$	0.508 (0.331) $p = 0.269$
Income	0.040 (0.090) $p = 0.919$	0.068 (0.029) $p = 0.058$ *
BBFF1	−0.118 (0.307) $p = 0.932$	0.123 (0.085) $p = 0.292$
BBFF2	0.014 (0.151) $p = 0.978$	−0.027 (0.068) $p = 0.887$
BBFF3	0.113 (0.137) $p = 0.919$	0.010 (0.058) $p = 0.929$
BBWpct	0.331 (0.510) $p = 0.919$	−0.020 (0.183) $p = 0.952$
BBChamps1	−0.092 (0.290) $p = 0.932$	−0.052 (0.171) $p = 0.893$
BBChamps2	−0.153 (0.254) $p = 0.919$	0.036 (0.080) $p = 0.876$
BBChamps3	−0.349 (0.194) $p = 0.629$	0.020 (0.075) $p = 0.893$
FBFF1	0.027 (0.328) $p = 0.978$	−0.087 (0.086) $p = 0.584$
FBFF2	0.349 (0.333) $p = 0.919$	−0.046 (0.067) $p = 0.759$
FBFF3	0.203 (0.269) $p = 0.919$	−0.120 (0.071) $p = 0.201$
FBWpct	0.321 (0.273) $p = 0.919$	0.250 (0.111) $p = 0.071$ *

Table 5. *Cont.*

	Dependent Variable	
	log(Athletics) **(1)**	**log(NonAthletics)** **(2)**
FBChamps1	−0.310 (0.589) $p = 0.919$	−0.053 (0.103) $p = 0.838$
FBChamps2	0.045 (0.408) $p = 0.978$	−0.141 (0.094) $p = 0.274$
FBChamps3	0.365 (0.382) $p = 0.919$	−0.027 (0.123) $p = 0.917$
Constant	3.079 (5.783) $p = 0.919$	1.039 (1.559) $p = 0.759$
Observations	356	356
R^2	0.709	0.939
Adjusted R^2	0.636	0.924
Residual Std. Error (df = 284)	0.589	0.213
F Statistic (df = 71; 284)	9.725 ***	61.789 ***

Note: * $p < 0.1$; ** $p < 0.05$; *** $p < 0.01$.

None of the 14 athletic performance variables is statistically significant at the 0.10 level.[24]

$$y_6 = log(NonAthletics) = \beta_6 \cdot X + \epsilon_6$$

This equation examines the relationship between donations to the school's general fund minus athletic donations (Non-Athletic Donations) and athletic performance.

Only one of the 14 athletic performance variables is statistically significant at the 0.10 level: *FBWpct*. However, the effect size—an expected increase of 1.94% for each additional victory per year—is small. Nine of the 14 coefficients had negative signs.

5.3. Athletic Success and State Budgetary Support

Our final model was on the relationship between academic performance and state funding for public universities. The results are shown in Table 6.

$$y_7 = State = \beta_7 \cdot X + \epsilon_7$$

Three of the 14 athletic performance variables were significant at the 0.10 level: *BBFF*1, *FBFF*1, and *FBFF*2.

The nominal interpretation of the first coefficient (θ_5) is that a Final Four appearance in the previous basketball season is associated with a 5.3% increase in state funding. However, this is nearly offset by a −3.9 decrease associated with actually winning the championship, although this effect is not statistically significant. It is hard to square the idea that teams that reach the Final Four tend to receive greater increases in state funding than teams that win the championship.

24 The high adjusted p-values for the coefficients in the *Athletics* regression are a result of the unadjusted p-values being relatively uniformly distributed with a large mean (0.48).

Table 6. Models for Funding.

	Dependent Variable	
	log(State) **(1)**	**log(StatePC)** **(2)**
log(HSDiplomas)	−0.103 (0.198) $p = 0.705$	−0.024 (0.177) $p = 0.905$
Income	−0.028 (0.031) $p = 0.471$	−0.032 (0.023) $p = 0.214$
BBFF1	0.052 (0.023) $p = 0.044$ **	0.049 (0.030) $p = 0.154$
BBFF2	0.032 (0.029) $p = 0.377$	0.037 (0.034) $p = 0.338$
BBFF3	−0.005 (0.041) $p = 0.937$	−0.011 (0.050) $p = 0.870$
BBWpct	0.042 (0.117) $p = 0.800$	0.059 (0.095) $p = 0.623$
BBChamps1	−0.040 (0.043) $p = 0.471$	−0.071 (0.058) $p = 0.296$
BBChamps2	−2.869 (6.094) $p = 0.787$	−0.058 (0.052) $p = 0.334$
BBChamps3	−0.016 (0.052) $p = 0.823$	−0.017 (0.069) $p = 0.867$
FBFF1	−0.064 (0.031) $p = 0.073$ *	−0.079 (0.031) $p = 0.019$ **
FBFF2	−0.059 (0.029) $p = 0.079$ *	−0.039 (0.031) $p = 0.276$
FBFF3	−0.035 (0.027) $p = 0.286$	−0.028 (0.025) $p = 0.338$
FBWpct	−0.159 (0.155) $p = 0.411$	−0.023 (0.109) $p = 0.870$
FBChamps1	0.073 (0.041) $p = 0.129$	0.094 (0.056) $p = 0.151$
FBChamps2	0.057 (0.052) $p = 0.387$	0.041 (0.067) $p = 0.623$
FBChamps3	0.011 (0.034) $p = 0.823$	0.006 (0.045) $p = 0.905$
Constant	5.863 (1.225) $p = 0.00001$ ***	4.190 (0.966) $p = 0.00005$ ***
Observations	558	557
R^2	0.949	0.942
Adjusted R^2	0.941	0.933
Residual Std. Error (df = 481)	0.216	0.177
F Statistic (df = 76; 481)	117.728 ***	103.449 ***

Note: * $p < 0.1$; ** $p < 0.05$; *** $p < 0.01$.

Further muddying the waters is the fact that the effects on the football side show the same offsetting pattern, but in the opposite direction (negative for reaching the Final Four, positive for winning the championship).

When we consider the state funding per capita (as in Table 6), the statistical significance of all variables save for *FBFF*1 disappears, and the direction of the effect remains negative.

6. Conclusions

Previous literature on the effect of athletic success on applications, quality of the student body, donations and state funding has been inconclusive. Researchers have employed different methodologies and models and most have been limited by incomplete data. We develop a recent data set for the Power Five conferences during the eleven years from 2006 through 2016 and use fixed effects linear regression models to retest these relationships. We report robust standard errors and control for multiple testing. We find that certain measures of football success have a modest positive and short-lived impact on student applications, but no clear impact on admission yield or on the quality of the student body. Although hampered by incomplete data, we also found that athletic success did not have a statistically significant effect on donations. Final Four appearances in both basketball and football showed some statistical significance associated with state funding, but the direction and robustness of these findings is unclear.

Author Contributions: The authors contributed equally to this article.

Acknowledgments: The authors would like to thank Junzhou Liu, our data collection assistant, as well as Michael Lopez, Roger Noll, Brad Humphreys, Ann Kaplan, Nick Horton, Dennis Coates, the reviewers and the associate editor for helpful comments and suggestions.

Conflicts of Interest: The authors declare no conflict of interest

Appendix A

ANOVA tables

Below we present the ANOVA tables for all models discussed in the paper. Note the persistent statistical significance of the Year and School terms.

Table A1. ANOVA table for log(Applied).

	Df	Sum Sq	Mean Sq	F Value	Pr(>F)
Year	10	26.197	2.620	198.729	0.000
school_name	64	148.990	2.328	176.601	0.000
log(hs_diplomas_lag1)	1	0.008	0.008	0.578	0.447
per_capita_income	1	0.008	0.008	0.602	0.438
bball_avg_wpct_lag3	1	0.020	0.020	1.5474	0.214
bb_champs_lag1	1	0.011	0.011	0.867	0.352
bb_champs_lag2	1	0.056	0.056	4.278	0.039
bb_champs_lag3	1	0.008	0.008	0.613	0.434
fball_avg_wpct_lag3	1	0.288	0.288	21.859	0.000
fb_champs_lag1	1	0.016	0.016	1.241	0.266
fb_champs_lag2	1	0.023	0.023	1.777	0.183
fb_champs_lag3	1	0.036	0.036	2.749	0.098
Residuals	626	8.252	0.013		

Table A2. ANOVA table for SAT75p.

	Df	Sum Sq	Mean Sq	F Value	Pr(>F)
Year	10	12,802.322	12,802.322	5.654	0.000
school_name	63	1,591,052.696	25,254.805	111.543	0.000
log(hs_diplomas_lag1)	1	417.541	417.541	1.844	0.175
per_capita_income	1	400.511	400.511	1.769	0.184
bball_avg_wpct_lag3	1	1199.903	1199.903	5.300	0.022
bb_champs_lag1	1	278.781	278.781	1.231	0.268
bb_champs_lag2	1	8.558	8.558	0.038	0.846
bb_champs_lag3	1	20.627	20.627	0.091	0.763
fball_avg_wpct_lag3	1	865.252	865.252	3.822	0.051
fb_champs_lag1	1	0.010	0.010	0.000	0.995
fb_champs_lag2	1	7.444	7.444	0.033	0.856
fb_champs_lag3	1	394.777	394.777	1.744	0.187
Residuals	591	133,810.192	226.413		

Table A3. ANOVA table for log(Donations).

	Df	Sum Sq	Mean Sq	F Value	Pr(>F)
Year	10	9.510	9.510	33.107	0.000
school_name	59	241.490	4.093	142.499	0.000
log(hs_diplomas_lag1)	1	0.176	0.176	6.141	0.014
per_capita_income	1	0.302	0.302	10.500	0.001
bball_avg_wpct_lag3	1	0.000	0.000	0.011	0.918
bb_champs_lag1	1	0.005	0.005	0.180	0.671
bb_champs_lag2	1	0.015	0.015	0.510	0.476
bb_champs_lag3	1	0.028	0.028	0.988	0.321
fball_avg_wpct_lag3	1	0.204	0.204	7.100	0.008
fb_champs_lag1	1	0.016	0.016	0.573	0.450
fb_champs_lag2	1	0.001	0.001	0.027	0.870
fb_champs_lag3	1	0.030	0.030	1.033	0.310
Residuals	525	15.080	0.029		

Table A4. ANOVA table for log(Athletics).

	Df	Sum Sq	Mean Sq	F Value	Pr(>F)
Year	10	10.467	1.047	3.028	0.001
school_name	45	225.721	5.016	14.513	0.000
log(hs_diplomas_lag1)	1	0.051	0.051	0.147	0.702
per_capita_income	1	0.071	0.071	0.204	0.652
bball_avg_wpct_lag3	1	0.125	0.125	0.362	0.548
bb_champs_lag1	1	0.045	0.045	0.129	0.720
bb_champs_lag2	1	0.002	0.002	0.005	0.941
bb_champs_lag3	1	0.078	0.078	0.226	0.635
fball_avg_wpct_lag3	1	0.647	0.647	1.8722	0.172
fb_champs_lag1	1	0.446	0.446	1.289	0.257
fb_champs_lag2	1	0.150	0.150	0.433	0.511
fb_champs_lag3	1	0.4360.	0.436	1.263	0.262
Residuals	290	100.232	0.346		

Table A5. ANOVA table for log(NonAthletics).

	Df	Sum Sq	Mean Sq	F Value	Pr(>F)
Year	10	8.851	0.885	19.548	0.000
school_name	45	188.907	4.198	92.717	0.000
log(hs_diplomas_lag1)	1	0.066	0.066	1.457	0.228
per_capita_income	1	0.316	0.316	6.979	0.009
bball_avg_wpct_lag3	1	0.000	0.000	0.001	0.977
bb_champs_lag1	1	0.006	0.006	0.140	0.708
bb_champs_lag2	1	0.001	0.001	0.016	0.898
bb_champs_lag3	1	0.010	0.010	0.226	0.635
fball_avg_wpct_lag3	1	0.157	0.157	3.462	0.064
fb_champs_lag1	1	0.024	0.024	0.523	0.470
fb_champs_lag2	1	0.066	0.066	1.459	0.228
fb_champs_lag3	1	0.023	0.023	0.517	0.473
Residuals	290	13.130	0.045		

Table A6. ANOVA table for log(State).

	Df	Sum Sq	Mean Sq	F Value	Pr(>F)
Year	10	1.997	0.200	4.294	0.000
school_name	50	414.854	8.297	178.446	0.000
log(hs_diplomas_lag1)	1	0.003	0.003	0.066	0.798
per_capita_income	1	0.094	0.094	2.013	0.157
bball_avg_wpct_lag3	1	0.006	0.006	0.125	0.724
bb_champs_lag1	1	0.004	0.004	0.096	0.756
bb_champs_lag2	1	0.003	0.003	0.067	0.796
bb_champs_lag3	1	0.000	0.000	0.004	0.950
fball_avg_wpct_lag3	1	0.075	0.075	1.607	0.205
fb_champs_lag1	1	0.003	0.003	0.063	0.801
fb_champs_lag2	1	0.001	0.001	0.019	0.891
fb_champs_lag3	1	0.004	0.004	0.086	0.770
Residuals	487	22.644	0.046		

Table A7. ANOVA table for log(StatePC).

	Df	Sum Sq	Mean Sq	F Value	Pr(>F)
Year	10	5.056	5.056	16.124	0.000
school_name	50	240.754	4.815	153.543	0.000
log(hs_diplomas_lag1)	1	0.002	0.002	0.061	0.804
per_capita_income	1	0.106	0.106	3.387	0.066
bball_avg_wpct_lag3	1	0.022	0.022	0.690	0.407
bb_champs_lag1	1	0.000	0.000	0.004	0.953
bb_champs_lag2	1	0.006	0.006	0.202	0.653
bb_champs_lag3	1	0.004	0.004	0.139	0.710
fball_avg_wpct_lag3	1	0.027	0.027	0.861	0.354
fb_champs_lag1	1	0.005	0.005	0.167	0.683
fb_champs_lag2	1	0.001	0.001	0.042	0.838
fb_champs_lag3	1	0.003	0.003	0.083	0.774
Residuals	486	15.241	0.031		

Table A8. ANOVA table for Yield.

	Df	Sum Sq	Mean Sq	F Value	Pr(>F)
Year	10	0.823	0.082	29.646	0.000
school_name	64	6.200	6.200	34.880	0.000
log(hs_diplomas_lag1)	1	0.007	0.007	2.608	0.107
per_capita_income	1	0.000	0.000	0.151	0.698
bball_avg_wpct_lag3	1	0.000	0.000	0.117	0.732
bb_champs_lag1	1	0.001	0.001	0.395	0.530
bb_champs_lag2	1	0.000	0.000	0.021	0.884
bb_champs_lag3	1	0.000	0.000	0.001	0.976
fball_avg_wpct_lag3	1	0.022	0.022	7.883	0.005
fb_champs_lag1	1	0.000	0.000	0.057	0.812
fb_champs_lag2	1	0.002	0.002	0.825	0.364
fb_champs_lag3	1	0.008	0.008	2.791	0.095
Residuals	626	1.739	0.003		

Table A9. ANOVA table for Admit.

	Df	Sum Sq	Mean Sq	F Value	Pr(>F)
Year	10	0.364	0.036	8.796	0.000
school_name	64	29.422	0.460	111.044	0.000
log(hs_diplomas_lag1)	1	0.009	0.009	2.088	0.149
per_capita_income	1	0.002	0.002	0.494	0.482
bball_avg_wpct_lag3	1	0.001	0.001	0.257	0.612
bb_champs_lag1	1	0.002	0.002	0.367	0.545
bb_champs_lag2	1	0.001	0.001	0.256	0.613
bb_champs_lag3	1	0.000	0.000	0.017	0.896
fball_avg_wpct_lag3	1	0.034	0.034	8.164	0.004
fb_champs_lag1	1	0.007	0.007	1.604	0.206
fb_champs_lag2	1	0.001	0.001	0.321	0.571
fb_champs_lag3	1	0.000	0.000	0.000	0.990
Residuals	626	2.592	0.004		

References

Alexander, Donald L., and William Kern. 2010. Does Athletic Success Generate Legislative Largess from Sports-Crazed Representatives? The Impact of Athletic Success on State Appropriations to Colleges and Universities. *International Journal of Sport Finance* 5: 253–67.

Anderson, Michael L. 2017. The Benefits of College Athletic Success: An Application of the Propensity Score Design. *Review of Economics and Statistics* 99: 119–34. [CrossRef]

Baade, Robert A., and Jeffrey O. Sundberg. 1996. What Determines Alumni Generosity? *Economics of Education Review* 15: 75–82. [CrossRef]

Baumer, Benjamin S. 2018. Colleges: Data About College Enrollments, Donations, and Athletics. Available online: http://github.com/beanumber/colleges (accessed on 1 November 2018).

Benjamini, Yoav, and Yosef Hochberg. 1995. Controlling the False Discovery Rate: A Practical and Powerful Approach to Multiple Testing. *Journal of the Royal Statistical Society. Series B (Methodological)* 57: 289–300. [CrossRef]

Bremmer, Dale S., and Randall G. Kesselring. 1993. The Advertising Effect of University Athletic Success: A Reappraisal of the Evidence. *The Quarterly Review of Economics and Finance* 33: 409–21. [CrossRef]

Brooker, George W., and Theodore D. Klastorin. 1981. To the Victors Belong the Spoils? College Athletics and Alumni Giving. *Social Science Quarterly* 62: 744–50.

Castle, Joshua, and Robert Kostelnik. 2011. The Effects of an Institution's Athletic Success on the Future Freshmen Application Pool at Ncaa Division Ii Universities. *Journal of Issues in Intercollegiate Athletics* 4: 411–27.

Clotfelter, Charles T. 2011. *Big-Time Sports in American Universities*. New York: Cambridge University Press.

Coughlin, Cletus C., and O. Homer Erekson. 1986. Determinants of State Aid and Voluntary Support of Higher Education. *Economics of Education Review* 5: 179–90. [CrossRef]

Fox, John, and Georges Monette. 1992. Generalized collinearity diagnostics. *Journal of the American Statistical Association* 87: 178–83. [CrossRef]

Frank, Robert H. 2004. *Challenging the Myth: A Review of the Links among College Athletic Success, Student Quality, and Donations*. Miami: Knight Foundation Commission on Intercollegiate Athletics.

Goff, Brian. 2000. Effects of University Athletics on the University: A Review and Extension of Empirical Assessment. *Journal of Sport Management* 14: 85–104. [CrossRef]

Grimes, Paul W., and George A. Chressanthis. 1994. Alumni Contributions to Academics: The Role of Intercollegiate Sports and Ncaa Sanctions. *American Journal of Economics and Sociology* 53: 27–40. [CrossRef]

Hernández-Julián, Rey, and Kurt W. Rotthoff. 2014. The Impact of College Football on Academic Achievement. *Economics of Education Review* 43: 141–47. [CrossRef]

Humphreys, Brad R. 2006. The Relationship Between Big-Time College Football and State Appropriations for Higher Education. *International Journal of Sport Finance* 1: 119–28.

Humphreys, Brad R., and Michael Mondello. 2007. Intercollegiate Athletic Success and Donations at Ncaa Division I Institutions. *Journal of Sport Management* 21: 265–80. [CrossRef]

Jones, Willis A. 2015. High-Level Football and Appropriations to Universities: Are Sports-Crazed Representatives Responsive to Ncaa Divisional Affiliation? *Journal of Education Finance* 40: 438–55.

Koo, Gi-Yong, and Stephen W. Dittmore. 2014. Effects of Intercollegiate Athletics on Private Giving in Higher Education. *Journal of Issues in Intercollegiate Athletics* 7: 1–16.

Lindo, Jason M., Isaac D. Swensen, and Glen R. Waddell. 2012. Are Big-Time Sports a Threat to Student Achievement? *American Economic Journal: Applied Economics* 4: 254–74. [CrossRef]

Litan, Robert E., Jonathan M. Orszag, and Peter R. Orszag. 2003. *The Empirical Effects of Collegiate Athletics: An Interim Report*. Washington, DC, USA: Sebago Associates.

Lopez, Michael, Gregory J. Matthews, and Benjamin S. Baumer. 2018. How Often Does the Best Team Win? A Unified Approach to Understanding Randomness in North American Sport. *Annals of Applied Statistics* 12: 2483–516. [CrossRef]

Massachusetts Football Task Force. 1996. *Final Report of the I-a Football Task Force*. Boston: University of Massachusetts.

McCormick, Robert E., and Maurice Tinsley. 1987. Athletics Versus Academics? Evidence from Sat Scores. *Journal of Political Economy* 95: 1103–16. [CrossRef]

Mixon, Franklin G., Jr. 1995. Athletics Versus Academics? Rejoining the Evidence from Sat Scores. *Education Economics* 3: 277–83. [CrossRef]

Mixon, Franklin G., Jr., and Yu Hsing. 1994. The Determinants of Out-of-State Enrollments in Higher Education: A Tobit Analysis. *Economics of Education Review* 13: 329–35. [CrossRef]

Mixon, Franklin G., Jr., and Rand W. Ressler. 1995. An Empirical Note on the Impact of College Athletics on Tuition Revenues. *Applied Economics Letters* 2: 383–87. [CrossRef]

Murphy, Robert G., and Gregory A. Trandel. 1994. The Relation between a University's Football Record and the Size of Its Applicant Pool. *Economics of Education Review* 13: 265–70. [CrossRef]

NCAA. 2017. *Revenues and Expenses of Division I Intercollegiate Athletics Program, 2004–2016*. Indianapolis: NCAA.

Orszag, Jonathan M., and Peter R. Orszag. 2005. *The Physical Capital Stock Used in Collegiate Athletics*. Indianapolis: NCAA.

Pope, Devin G., and Jaren C. Pope. 2009. The Impact of College Sports Success on the Quantity and Quality of Student Applications. *Southern Economic Journal* 75: 750–80.

Pope, Devin G., and Jaren C. Pope. 2014. Understanding College Application Decisions: Why College Sports Success Matters. *Journal of Sports Economics* 15: 107–31. [CrossRef]

R Core Team. 2018. *R: A Language and Environment for Statistical Computing*. Vienna: R Foundation for Statistical Computing.

Rhoads, Thomas A., and Shelby Gerking. 2000. Educational Contributions, Academic Quality, and Athletic Success. *Contemporary Economic Policy* 18: 248–58. [CrossRef]

Sigelman, Lee, and Samuel Bookheimer. 1983. Is It Whether You Win or Lose? Monetary Contributions to Big-Time College Athletic Programs. *Social Science Quarterly* 64: 347–59.

Sigelman, Lee, and Robert Carter. 1979. Win One for the Giver? Alumni Giving and Big-Time College Sports. *Social Science Quarterly* 60: 284–94.

Smith, D. Randall. 2008. Big-Time College Basketball and the Advertising Effect: Does Success Really Matter? *Journal of Sports Economics* 9: 387–406. [CrossRef]

Stinson, Jeffrey L., and Dennis R. Howard. 2008. Winning Does Matter: Patterns in Private Giving to Athletic and Academic Programs at NCAA Division I-AA and I-AAA Institutions. *Sport Management Review* 11: 1–20. [CrossRef]

Toma, J. Douglas, and Michael E. Cross. 1998. Intercollegiate Athletics and Student College Choice: Exploring the Impact of Championship Seasons on Undergraduate Applications. *Research in Higher Education* 39: 633–61. [CrossRef]

Tucker, Irvin B. 2005. Big-Time Pigskin Success: Is There an Advertising Effect? *Journal of Sports Economics* 6: 222–29. [CrossRef]

Tucker, Irvin B., and Louis Amato. 1993. Does Big-Time Success in Football or Basketball Affect Sat Scores? *Economics of Education Review* 12: 177–81. [CrossRef]

Turner, Sarah E., Lauren A. Meserve, and William G. Bowen. 2001. Winning and Giving a Study of the Responsiveness of Giving to Performance on the Field. *Social Science Quarterly* 82: 812–26. [CrossRef]

Walker, Adam G. 2015. Division I Intercollegiate Athletics Success and the Financial Impact on Universities. *SAGE Open* 5: 1–13. [CrossRef]

Zeileis, Achim, and Torsten Hothorn. 2002. Diagnostic Checking in Regression Relationships. *R News* 2: 7–10.

Zimbalist, Andrew. 2001. *Unpaid Professionals: Commercialism and Conflict in Big-Time College Sports*. Princeton: Princeton University Press.

Permissions

All chapters in this book were first published in IJFS, by MDPI; hereby published with permission under the Creative Commons Attribution License or equivalent. Every chapter published in this book has been scrutinized by our experts. Their significance has been extensively debated. The topics covered herein carry significant findings which will fuel the growth of the discipline. They may even be implemented as practical applications or may be referred to as a beginning point for another development.

The contributors of this book come from diverse backgrounds, making this book a truly international effort. This book will bring forth new frontiers with its revolutionizing research information and detailed analysis of the nascent developments around the world.

We would like to thank all the contributing authors for lending their expertise to make the book truly unique. They have played a crucial role in the development of this book. Without their invaluable contributions this book wouldn't have been possible. They have made vital efforts to compile up to date information on the varied aspects of this subject to make this book a valuable addition to the collection of many professionals and students.

This book was conceptualized with the vision of imparting up-to-date information and advanced data in this field. To ensure the same, a matchless editorial board was set up. Every individual on the board went through rigorous rounds of assessment to prove their worth. After which they invested a large part of their time researching and compiling the most relevant data for our readers.

The editorial board has been involved in producing this book since its inception. They have spent rigorous hours researching and exploring the diverse topics which have resulted in the successful publishing of this book. They have passed on their knowledge of decades through this book. To expedite this challenging task, the publisher supported the team at every step. A small team of assistant editors was also appointed to further simplify the editing procedure and attain best results for the readers.

Apart from the editorial board, the designing team has also invested a significant amount of their time in understanding the subject and creating the most relevant covers. They scrutinized every image to scout for the most suitable representation of the subject and create an appropriate cover for the book.

The publishing team has been an ardent support to the editorial, designing and production team. Their endless efforts to recruit the best for this project, has resulted in the accomplishment of this book. They are a veteran in the field of academics and their pool of knowledge is as vast as their experience in printing. Their expertise and guidance has proved useful at every step. Their uncompromising quality standards have made this book an exceptional effort. Their encouragement from time to time has been an inspiration for everyone.

The publisher and the editorial board hope that this book will prove to be a valuable piece of knowledge for researchers, students, practitioners and scholars across the globe.

List of Contributors

Tihana Škrinjarić and Boško Šego
Faculty of Economics and Business, University of Zagreb, 10000 Zagreb, Croatia

Dev Shah, Haruna Isah and Farhana Zulkernine
School of Computing, Queen's University, Kingston, ON K7L 2N8, Canada

Jaehwan Park
Commodity Research Center, Public Procurement Service, Daejeon 35208, Korea

Nora Muñoz-Izquierdo
CUNEF—Colegio Universitario de Estudios Financieros, Leonardo Prieto Castro, 2, Ciudad Universitaria, 28040 Madrid, Spain

María-del-Mar Camacho-Miñano, María-Jesús Segovia-Vargas and David Pascual-Ezama
Facultad de Ciencias Económicas y Empresariales, Complutense University of Madrid, Campus de Somosaguas, Pozuelo de Alarcón, 28223 Madrid, Spain

Nikolay Khabarov, Andrey Krasovskii and Michael Obersteiner
Ecosystems Services and Management Program (ESM), International Institute for Applied Systems Analysis (IIASA), Schlossplatz 1, A-2361 Laxenburg, Austria

Ruben Lubowski
Environmental Defense Fund, 1875 Connecticut Ave NW #600, Washington, DC 20009, USA

Gang Wang
Department of Economics, The College of Wooster, 206 Morgan Hall, Wooster, OH 44691, USA

Jaehwan Park
Commodity Research Center, Public Procurement Service, Daejeon 35208, Korea

Jyh-Horng Lin
Department of International Business, Tamkang University, New Taipei City 25137, Taiwan

Pei-Chi Lii and Fu-Wei Huang
Department of Management Sciences, Tamkang University, New Taipei City 25137, Taiwan

Shi Chen
School of Economics, Southwestern University of Finance and Economics, Chengdu 611130, China

Marwa Zouaoui
Department of Finance, Northern Border University, Arar 91431, Saudi Arabia
Department of Finance, ISG Tunisia, University of Tunis, Tunis 20000, Tunisia

Leszek Czapiewski and Joanna Lizińska
Department of Corporate Finance, Poznań University of Economics and Business, 61-875 Pozna´ n, Poland

Olivier Butzbach and Domenico Sarno
Department of Political Science, University of Campania "L. Vanvitelli", 81100 Caserta, Italy

Victor Tiberius and Laura Lisiecki
Faculty of Economics and Social Sciences, University of Potsdam, 14482 Potsdam, Germany

Benjamin Baumer
Program in Statistical and Data Sciences, Smith College, Northampton, MA 01063, USA

Andrew Zimbalist
Department of Economics, Smith College, Northampton, MA 01063, USA

Index

www.ingramcontent.com/pod-product-compliance
Lightning Source LLC
LaVergne TN
LVHW060530210926
848485LV00005B/1177
* 9 7 8 1 6 3 9 8 7 2 2 4 4 *